Francis Andrew March

Introduction to Anglo-Saxon

An Anglo-Saxon reader, with philological notes, a brief grammar, and a vocabulary

Francis Andrew March

Introduction to Anglo-Saxon
An Anglo-Saxon reader, with philological notes, a brief grammar, and a vocabulary

ISBN/EAN: 9783337075439

Printed in Europe, USA, Canada, Australia, Japan

Cover: Foto ©Paul-Georg Meister /pixelio.de

More available books at **www.hansebooks.com**

Introduction to Anglo-Saxon.

AN

ANGLO-SAXON READER,

WITH

PHILOLOGICAL NOTES, A BRIEF GRAMMAR,

AND A VOCABULARY.

By FRANCIS A. MARCH, LL.D.,

PROFESSOR OF THE ENGLISH LANGUAGE AND COMPARATIVE PHILOLOGY IN LAFAYETTE COLLEGE, AUTHOR OF "A COMPARATIVE GRAMMAR OF THE ANGLO-SAXON LANGUAGE," "METHOD OF PHILOLOGICAL STUDY OF THE ENGLISH LANGUAGE," ETC.

NEW YORK:
HARPER & BROTHERS, PUBLISHERS,
FRANKLIN SQUARE.
1879.

Entered, according to Act of Congress, in the year 1870, by
FRANCIS A. MARCH,
In the Clerk's Office of the District Court of the United States for the Eastern District of Pennsylvania.

PREFACE.

It seems to be agreed that every English scholar ought to have some scholarly knowledge of the English language. Then every English scholar ought to study Anglo-Saxon. He ought to read representative passages in representative books of the literature thoroughly, dwelling on them line by line, and word by word, and making the text the foundation of general philological study. At least a daily lesson for one term ought to be given to this study in each of our colleges.

Enough such extracts for two terms' work are here given in a critical text. The notes contain, besides explanatory matter, outlines of the literature, biographical sketches of the authors, and bibliographical notices of manuscripts and editions. The author's Comparative Grammar opens with a history of the language, and illustrates the grammatical forms by those of the Sanskrit, Greek, Latin, Gothic, Old Saxon, Old Friesic, Old Norse, and Old-High German. It is part of the plan to give a full etymological vocabulary. Thus it is supposed that apparatus is provided for as thorough study of a portion of this tongue as can be given to Greek or Latin with our college text-books.

In this edition a brief grammar has been introduced, that it may be fitted for general use as an introduction to the study of Anglo-Saxon in High Schools and Academies where they might fear the Comparative Grammar. The etymological part of the Vocabulary is reserved for a future edition. It was thought best to make sure of the completeness of the list of words by working it over in class before giving it its final shape.

The selections were stereotyped, and the book and its plan announced in 1865.

F. A. M.

Easton, Pa., June, 1870.

CONTENTS.

I. READER.

PROSE.

From the Gospels:

	PAGE
The Sower	1
The Lord's Prayer	2
The Good Samaritan	3
The Lord's Day	4
The Sower	5
Trust in God	6
The Prodigal Son	7
Love your Enemies	9
Extract in Gothic	9

Dialogues of Callings:

The Scholar	13
The Ploughman	13
The Shepherd	14
The Oxherd	14
The Hunter	14
The Fisher	15
The Fowler	16
The Merchant	17
The Shoemaker	18
The Salter	18
The Baker	18
The Cook	18
The Scholar	19
The Counsellor, Smith	19
The Scholar	20

From the Anglo-Saxon Chronicle ... 23

Conversion of the Anglo-Saxons:

Gregory	35
Paulinus	38

Anglo-Saxon Laws:

Æthelbirht	41
Hlothhere and Eadric	42
Ine	42

	PAGE
Alfred	43
Ecgbyrht	44
Cnut	45

Poets:

Orpheus	46
Cædmon	47

POETRY.

The Traveler	51
Beowulf	51

Cædmon:

The First Day	52
Satan's Speech	52
The Exodus	54

Beowulf:

A Good King	56
Obsequies of Scyld	56
Hrothgar and Heorot	57
Grendel	57
Beowulf sails for Heorot	58
The Warden of the Shore	59
A Feast of Welcome	61
Good-night	62
Hrunting, the Good Sword	62
It fails at Need	63
The Right Weapon	63

Alfred's Meters of Boethius:

Introduction	64
Meter VI	64
Meter X	65

Saws	66
Threnes	68
Deor's Complaint	69
Rhyming Poem	70

NOTES,

CRITICAL, HISTORICAL, AND BIBLIOGRAPHICAL, pp. 71-93.

	PAGE		PAGE
Outline of Anglo-Saxon Prose	83	Outlines of Anglo-Saxon Poetry	83
Theological Writings:		Ballad Epic:	
Bible Translations	71	Beowulf	87
Homilies of Ælfric	75	Bible Epic:	
Philosophy:—Boethius	81	Cædmon	84, 85
History:		Ecclesiastical Narrative	84
The Chronicle	73	Secular Lyrics:	
Beda	75, 81	The Traveler	84
Orosius	83	The Wanderer	92
St. Guthlâc	83	Deor's Complaint	92
Law	76-81	Gnomic Verses	91
Alfred	77	Didactic:	
Natural Science	83	Alfred's Boethius	90
Grammar:—Ælfric	72	Task Poem	93

II. GRAMMAR.

	PAGE		PAGE
Historical Introduction	95	Participle	121
PHONOLOGY:		Potential	122
Alphabet	98	Other periphrastic	122
Punctuation	99	Passive Voice	123
Sounds	99	*Weak Verb.*	
Accent	100	Active Voice	125
Vowel Variation	100	Passive Voice	127
ETYMOLOGY:		Varying Presents	127
Nouns—Declension 1	102	Syncopated Imperfects	128
" 2	105	*Weak and Strong.*	
" 3	106	Umlaut in Present	129
" 4	106	Assimilation in Present	129
Proper Names	107	Varying Imperfects	130
Adjectives—Declension	108	*Irregular Verbs.*	
Comparison	110	Preteritives	130
Pronouns	112	No connecting Vowel, *eom,*	
Numerals	114	*dón, gán,* etc.	113
Verb	116	SYNTAX	133-141
Conjugations	117	PROSODY:	
Paradigms.		Rhythm, Feet, Verse	142
Strong Verb.		Cæsura, Rime, Alliteration	143
Indicative	118	Common Narrative Verse	145
Subjunctive	120	Rhyming Verses	146
Imperative	121	Long Narrative Verse	147
Infinitive	121		

III. VOCABULARY ... 149

Appendix ... 165

ANGLO-SAXON READER.

[In pages 1–12, accent the first syllable of every word, unless an acute accent is printed over some other syllable. Words not in the Vocabulary are in the notes. §§ refer to the Author's Grammar.]

1. THE SOWER.

Luke, viii., 5–8.—Sum man his sǽd seóþ: þá hé þæt seóp, sum feól pið þone peg, and peard fortred'en, and heofenes fugelâs hit frǽton. And sum feól ofer þone stân, and hit forscranc', forþam'-þe hit pǽtan nǽfde. And sum feól on þá þornâs, and þá þornâs hit forþrys'môdon. And sum feól on gôde eorðan, and porhte hundfealdne pæstm.

Mark iv., 3–9.—Út côde se sǽdere his sǽd tô sâpenne, and þá hé seóp, sum feól pið þone peg, and fugelâs cômon, and hit frǽton. Sum feól ofer stân'-scyl'ian, þǽr hit nǽfde mycele eorðan, and sóna up eôde, forþam' hit nǽfde eorðan þicnesse. Þá hit up eôde, seó sunne hit forspǽl'de, and hit for-scranc', forþam' hit pyrtruman nǽfde.

---

1. *Sum*, a, § 136, 3, so English *some* in the plural; *man*, man, § 84; *his*, from *hé*, § 130; *sǽd*, *es*, n., seed, acc. sing.; *seóp*, sowed, imp. ind., from *sápan*, imp. *seóp, seópon*, p. p. *sápen*, conj. 5, § 208; *þá*, when; *þæt*, that, from *se*, § 133; *feól*, fell, imp. ind. sing., 3d, from *feallan*, imp. *feól, feóllon*, p. p. *feallen*, conj. 5, § 208; *pið þone weg*, along the way, § 359; *peard fortred'en*, was trodden out, passive, imp. ind., sing., 3d., from *for-tredan*, imp. *-træd, -trǽdon*, p. p. *-treden*, conj. 1, § 199, *for-*, Ger. *ver-*, § 254; *heofenes*, heaven's, from *heofon*, § 79; *fugelâs*, fowls, from *fugol*, § 79; *hit*, it, from *hé*, § 130; *fr-ǽton*, ate up, imp. ind. pl., 3d, from *fr-etan*, imp. *-ǽt, -ǽton*, p. p. *-eten*, conj. 1, § 199, *fr-*<*for-*, § 254; *ofer þone stán*, over the stone, on the rock; *for-scranc'*, shrank away, imp. ind. sing., 3d, from *for-scrincan*, imp. *-scranc, -scruncon*, p. p. *scruncen*, conj. 1, § 201; *for-þam'-þe*, for this that, because; *pǽtan*, wet, moisture, from *pǽta*, n, m., § 95; *nǽfde*, had not, *ne+hæfde*, imp. of *habban*, §§ 45, 222; *on þá þornâs*, among the thorns, *þorn*, *es*, m., § 341; *for-þrys'môdon*, choked out, from *forþrysmian*, imp. *-þrysmôde*, p. p., *þrysmôd*, conj. 6; *gôde eorðan*, good earth, sing. acc.; *porhte*, worked, produced, imp. sing., 3d, from *pyrcan*, imp. *porhte, porhton*, p. p. *geporht*, conj. 6, § 211; *hundfealdne pæstm*, hundred-fold fruit, *hundfeald*, adj., strong form, § 103.

Út côde, out yode, went forth, irreg. imp. of *gán*, § 208; *se sǽdere*, the sower, *sǽdere*, *s*, m.; *sǽd, es*, n.; *tô sápenne*, to sow, gerund, §§ 173, 175, from *sápan*, conj. 5, § 208, 2, to denote purpose, § 454; *cômon*, came, *cuman*, imp. *com, cômon*, p. p. *cumen*, conj. 1, § 200; *fugelâs, frǽton*, see above; *stán-scylian*, stone-shelly place, *stán-scyli-e*, -an, f.; *mycele*, much, f. sing. acc. from *mycel*, § 104; *sôna up eôde*, soon up yode (sprang); *þicnesse*, sing. acc. from *þicnes*, *se*, f., thickness; *seó sunne*, *seó*, fem., from *se*; *hit for-spǽlde*, swealed it away, parched it, *spǽlan*, imp. *spǽlde*, conj. 6; *for-scranc*, see above; *pyrtruman*, root, *pyrt, wort*,

And sum feól on þornâs; þâ stigon þâ þornâs, and forþrys'-môdon þæt, and hit pæstm ne bær.

And sum feól on gôd land, and hit sealde, up stígende and pex-ende, pæstm; and ân brohte þrŷtigfealdne, sum syxtigfealdne, sum hundfealdne.

Gehŷr'e, se þe eâran hæbbe tô gehŷr'anne.

---

2. Lord's Prayer.

Matthew, vi., 9–13.—Fæder ûre, þû þe eart on heofenum, si þîn nama gehâl'gôd. Tô be-cum'e þîn rîce. Gepeorð'e þîn pilla on eorðan spâ spâ on heofenum. Ûrne dæg'hpamlîc'an hlâf syle ûs tô dæg. And forgyf' ûs ûre gyltâs, spâ spâ þê forgyf'að ûrum gyltendum. And ne gelæd' þû ûs on costnunge, ac âlŷs' ûs of yfle. Sôðlîce.

Luke xi., 2-4.—Ûre Fæder, þû þe on heofene eart, si þîn nama gehâl'gôd. Tô cume þîn rîce. Gepeorð'e þîn pylla on heofene and on eorðan. Syle ûs tô dæg ûrne dæg'hpamlîc'an hlâf. And forgyf' ûs ûre gyltâs, spâ þê forgyf'að ælcum þêrâ þe pið ûs âgylt'. And ne læd þû ûs on costnunge; ac âlŷs' ûs fram yfele.

plant, *truma*, n, m., trimmer, strengthener; *stigon*, stied, ascended, *stigan*, imp. *stâh*, *stigon*, p. p. *stigen*, conj. 2, § 205; *þornâs*, *forþrysmôdon*, *pæstm*, see above; *bær*, bore, *beran*, imp. *bær*, *bæron*, p. p. *beren*, conj. 1, § 199; *sealde* (sold), gave, *sellan*, imp. *sealde*, conj. 6, § 209, *b*; *stígende* (stying), springing, p. pr., neut. sing., nom., from *stigan*, conj. 2, § 119, *a*; *pex-ende*, from *pexan* = *peaxan*, wax, grow, imp. *p(e)ôx*, *p(e)ôxon*, p. p. *pexen*, conj. 4; *ân*, one, some; *brohte*, brought, bore, *brengan*, imp. *brohte*, p. p. *broht*, conj. 6, § 209, *e*; *prŷtigfealdne*, thirty-fold, from *prŷtigfeald*, adj., m. sing. acc., with *pæstm*. *Ge-hŷr'e*, let him hear, subjunctive for imperat., § 421, 3, *ge-hŷr'an*, imp. *ge-hŷrde*, p. p. *ge-hŷred*, conj. 6; *se þe*, who, demon. *se* with relative sign *þe*, § 380, 3; *hæbbe*, subj. pres. of *habban*, §§ 160, 427; *tô ge-hŷr'anne*, to hear, gerund, § 452.

2. *Fæder*, father, sing. voc., §§ 67, 100; *ûre*, of us, our, plur. gen. of *íc*, § 130; *þû þe*, who, *þû*, thou, sing. nom., § 130, *þe* relative sign changing *þû* to a relative, §§ 134, 381, 2; *eart*, from *eom*, § 213; *heofenum*, heavens, pl. dat. of *heofon*; *si gehâl'gôd*, be hallowed, passive, subj. pres. sing., 3d, from *hâlgian*, conj. 6, §§ 179, 187, subj. for imperative, § 421, 3; *Tô be-cume*, let come to us, subj., 3d, for imperative, *cuman*, imp. *com*, *cômon*, p. p. *cumen*, conj. 1, § 200; *þîn rîce*, thy reign, compare *-ric* in *biskoprîc*; *gepeorð'e*, subj. for imperative from *ge-peordan*, imp. *-peard*, *-purdon*, p. p. *porden*, Ger. *werden*, Old Engl. *worth*, be, be done; *eorðan*, sing. dat., from *eorde*; *spâ spâ*, so so, as; *ûrne*, pron., poss. sing., acc. masc., from *ûre*, § 132; *dæg'hpam-lîc'-an*, weak, sing. acc. masc., from *dæghpamlîc*, daily, §§ 105, 108; *hlâf*, loaf, bread; *syle* > sell, give, imperat., from *syllan* = *sellan*, conj. 6, § 188, *b*; *ûs*, pl. dat., from *íc*, § 297; *tô dæg*, to day, *tô*, prep., at, on, *dæg*, day, sing. acc. after *tô*, *tô þissum dæge* (on this day) has the same sense, § 352; *and*, general sign of connected discourse, § 463; *for-gyf'*, imperat., from *for-gifan*, conj. 1, § 199, *for-*, § 254; *gyltâs*, debts, guilt, pl. acc., from *gylt*; *þê*, we, from *íc*, § 130; *ûrum gyltendum*, our debtors, pl. dat. after *forgifað*, § 297, *gyltend*, *es*, m.; *gelæd'*, pres. imperative, from *gelædan*, § 185; *costnunge*, sing. acc., from *costnung*, *e*, f., temptation; *â-lŷs'*, imperat., from *â-lŷsan*, loose, release; *of*, from; *yfle*, sing. dat., from *yfel*, §§ 79, 301, 305, 348; *sôðlîce*, soothly, amen, interj.; *þêrâ*, of those, pl. gen. of *se*, § 133; *âgylt*, is indebted, ind. sing., from *â-gyltan*, imp. *-gylte*, p. p. *-gylt*, § 192.

3. THE GOOD SAMARITAN.

Luke, x, 25-37.—Pâ ârâs' sum êgleâp man, and fandôde his, and cpæđ: Lâreôp, hpæt dô ic þæt ic êce lîf hæbbe? Pâ cpæđ hê tô him: Hpæt ys geprit'en on þêre æ? hû rætst þû? Pâ and'sparô'de hê: Lufâ Dryhten þînne God of ealre þînre heortan, and of ealre þînre sâple, and of eallum þînum mihtum, and of eallum þînum mægene; and þînne nêhstan spâ þê sylfne. Pâ cpæđ hê: Ryhte þû and'sparô'dest: dô þæt, þonne lyfâst þû. Pâ cpæđ hê tô þam Hælende, and polde hine sylfne geriht'pîsian: And hpylc ys mîn nêhsta? Pâ cpæđ se Hælend, hine up beseônd'e: Sum man fêrde fram Hier'usal'em tô Hiericho, and becom' on þâ sceađan, þâ hine bereâf'edon, and tintregôdon hine, and forlêt'on hine sâm'-cuc'ene. Pâ gebyr'ede hyt þæt sum sacerd fêrde on þam ylcan pege; and þâ hê þæt geseah', hê hine forbeâh'. And ealspâ se diâcon, þâ hê pæs piđ þû stôpe, and þæt geseah', hê hyne eâc forbeâh'. Pâ fêrde sum Samar'itân'isc man piđ hine: þâ hê hine geseah', þâ peard hê mid mild'-heort'nysse ofer hine âstyr'ed. Pâ geneá'læhte hê, and prâd his pundâ, and

---

3. *Â-râs'*, arose, *â-ris'an*, imperf. -*râs'*, -*ris'on*, p. p. -*ris'en*, conj. 2, *æ-gleâp*, law-clever; *fandôde*, tried, examined, *fandian*, imperf. *fandôde*, p. p. *fandôd*, akin to *findan*, find; *his*, genitive after *fandôde*, § 315, III.; *cpæđ*, quoth, *cpedan*, imperf. *cpæđ*, *cpædon*, p. p. *cpeden*, conj. 1, § 197; *lâreôp*, teacher, from *lâr*, lore; *dô*, shall do, subj. pres. sing., 1st, from *dôn*, imperf. *dide*, p. p. *dôn*, irreg., § 213; *ê-ce* (for *aye*), everlasting; *hæbbe*, subj. pres.; *ys* = *is*; *ge-prit'an*, imperf. *ge-prât'*, *ge-prit'on*, p. p. *ge-prit'en*, conj. 2; *æ*, law, f. ind., § 100; *rætst*, readest, *rædan*, imperf. *rædde*, p. p. *ræded*, *ræd*, conj. 6, *rædest* > *rætst*, irreg. like *bintst*, § 192; *lufâ*, impera. of *lufian*; *of*, out of, from, with dative of source; *nêhsta*, n, m., superlative of *neâh*, nighest one, neighbor; *þê*, acc. of *þû*; *sylf*, self, declined like an adjective, § 131; *ryhte*, adv., = *rihte*; *dô*, imperat.; *þonne*, then; *lyfâst*, pres. for fut., from *lîfian*, conj. 6, §§ 222, 413, 4. *Hælende*, Savior, healing one; *polde*, would, *pillan*; *ge-riht'-pîs-ian*, justify, conj. 6; *riht-pîs*, wise in right, Engl. righteous; *hpylc*, which, who = *hpâ-lîc*, Latin *qua-lis*; *hine up beseônd'e*, looking up at him, a translation of Latin *suspiciens*, which some copies have for *suscipiens*; *seônde*, p. pr., from *seôn*, imperf. *seah*, *sægon*, p. p. *ge-sep'en*, conj., §§ 197, 190; *fêrde*>*fêran*, fare, go; *Hier'usal'em*, es, m., but bere dative undeclined; *Hiericho*, acc., undeclined; *be-com'*, came, *becum'an*; *on þâ sceađan*, among the thieves (those who *scathe*), § 341, II.; *be-reâf'edon*, bereft, stript, *be-reâf'ian*, imperf. -*reâf'ede*, p. p. -*reâf'ed*, conj. 6; *tintregôdon*, tormented, *tintreg-ian*, imperf. -*ôde*, p. p. -*ôd*, conj. 6; *for-lêt'on*, left, *for-lêt'an*, imperf. -*lêt'*, -*lêt'on*, p. p. -*læt'en*, conj. 5, *for-*, Ger. *ver-*, as in *for-sake*, *for-bid*, § 254; *sâm-cucene* (semi-quick), *cucene* for *eucenne*, acc. of *eucen* = *cpicen*, §§ *id*, 119, *c*; *ge-byr'ede hyt*, it was brought about, *ge-byr'ian*, imperf. -*byr'ede*, p. p. *byr'ed*, conj. 6, akin to *beran*, bear, *hyt*, bad spelling for *hit*; *sacerd*, *es*, m., priest, from Latin *sacerdos*, akin to *sacred*, *sacerdotal*; *fêrde*, *fêran*, conj. 6; *ylcan*, same, weak decl., § 133, 3; *ge-seah'*, saw, *ge-seôn'*, imperf. -*seah'*, -*sægon*, p. p. -*sep'en*, conj. 1, § 199; *hine for-beâh'*, turned away from him, *for-bûg'an*, imperf. -*beâh'*, -*bug'on*, p. p. -*bug'en*, conj. 3, Engl. bow; *eal-spâ*, all so, also; *diâcon*, *es*, m., deacon, Levite; *hê*, repeated subject, § 287; *hyne*=*hine*, bad spelling; *eâc*, Ger. *auch*, Engl. *eke*, also; *piđ* (with), beside; *þâ . . . þâ*, when . . . then; *peard â-styr'ed*, imperf. passive *â-styr'ian*, imperf. -*styr'ede*, p. p. -*styr'ed*, stir, conj. 6; *mild-heortnys*, se, f. (mild-heartedness), compassion; *geneá'læhte*, drew nigh, *ge-neâ'-læcan*, imperf. -*læhte*, p. p. *læht*, conj. 6; *prâd*, bound up, *prîdan*, wreathe, imperf. *prâd*, *prîdon*, p. p. *priden*,

on-âgeât' ele and pîn, and hine on his nŷten âset'te, and gelǽd'de on his lǽce-hûs, and hine gelâc'nôde, and brohte ôðrum dæge tpegen penegâs, and sealde þam lǽce, and þus cpæð: Begŷm' hys; and spâ-hpæt'-spâ þû mâre tô ge-dôst', þonne ic cume, ic hit forgyld'e þê. Hpylc þǽrâ þreôrâ þyncð þê þæt sig þæs mǽg þe on þâ sceaðan befeôl'? Pâ cpæð hê: Se þe hym mild'-heort'nysse on dyde. Pâ cpæð se Hǽlend: Gâ, and dô calspâ.

4. THE LORD'S DAY.

Matthew, xii., 1–13.—Se Hǽlend fôr on reste-dæg ofer æcerâs; sôðlîce his leorning-cnihtâs hingrede, and hig ongun'non pluccian þâ ear and etan. Sôðlîce þâ þâ sundor-hâlgan þæt ge-sâp'on, hî cpǽdon tô him: Nû þîne leorning-cnihtâs dôð þæt him âlŷf'ed nis reste-dagum tô dônne. And hê cpæð tô him: Ne rǽdde gê hpæt Dauid dyde þâ hine hingrede, and þâ þe mid him pǽron, hû hê in-eô'de on Godes hûs, and æt þâ offring-hlâfâs þe nǽron him âlŷf'ede tô etanne, ne þâm þe mid him pǽron, bûton þâm sacerdum ânum? Oððe ne rǽdde gê on þǽre ǽ, þæt þâ sacerdâs on reste-dagum on þam temple gepem'mað þone reste-dæg, and

conj. 6, § 205; *pund*, *e*, f., wound; *on âgeât'*, poured in, *â-geôt'an*, imperf. -*geât'*, -*gut'on*, p. p. -*gut'en*, conj. 3, akin to *gush*, *guzzle*; *nŷten*, beast, akin to *neat*; *â-set'te*, set, *âsett'an*, conj. 6; *lǽce-hûs*, *es*, n., leech house, hospital, hotel; *ge-lâc'nôde* (leeched), doctored, *ge-lâc'nian*, imperf. -*lâc'nôde*, p. p. *lâc'nôd*; *brohte* < *brengan*, conj. 6, § 209; *ôðrum* < *ôðer*, other, second, next, dative of time, § 304; *penegâs*, *peneg*, *es*, m., penny, stamped money, akin to *pawn*, Latin *pannus*; *sealde* < *sellan*, conj. 6, § 209; *lǽce*, *s*, m., leech; *cpæð*, quoth, < *cpaðan*, conj. 1; *begŷm'*, imperat. *be-gŷm'an*, imperf. -*gŷm'de*, p. p. -*gŷm'ed*, conj. 6; *hys*, bad spelling for *his*, genitive after *begŷm*, § 315; *mâre*, neuter acc. with *spâ-hpæt'-spâ*; *tô ge-dôst'*, doest to him, *ge-dôn'*, irreg. § 213; *cume*, *forgyld'e*, pres. for future, § 413; *þyncð*, seemeth, *þyncan*, imperf. *puhte*, p. p. *gepuht'*, conj. 6, § 211; *þæt*, that, conjunction; *sig* for *si*, may be < *eom*; *þæs mǽg*, the kinsman of him; *þe*, that, who; *mild-heortnysse*, acc., see above; *on dyde*, did, showed, from *dôn*. *Gâ*, go, *gân*, irreg., imperf. *eôde*, p. p. *gân*, § 213; *dô* < *dôn*, § 213; *eal-spâ*, all so, likewise.

4. *Fôr* < *faran*, imperf. *fôr*, *fôron*, p. p. *faren*, conj. 4, fare, go, in fare-well; *reste-dæg*, *es*, m., rest-day, dative irreg., § 71; *æcerâs* < *æcer*, acre, Lat. *ager*, Gr. ὑγρός, Ger. *acker*, field; *leorning-cnihtâs*, learning knights, disciples, Ger. *knecht'*, servant, -*cniht*, *es*, m.; *hingrede*, it hungered, impersonal imperf. of *hingrian* (*y* > *i*), conj. 6, governing the acc. of the persons hungering, § 290, c; *on-gun'non*, imperf. of *on-ginn'an*, conj. 1; *pluccian*, pluck, imperf. *pluccôde*, p. p. *pluccôd*, from Romanic *piluccare*, Lat. *pilus*, hair; *ear*, *es*, n., ear; *þâ þâ*, when the; *sundor-hâlga*, n, m. (sundered holy), Pharisees; *ge-sâp'on* < *ge-seôn'*, -*seah'*, -*sâp'on*, p. p. *sep'en*, conj. 1; *cpǽdon* < *cpedan*, § 197; *dôð* < *dôn*, irreg., § 213; *þæt*, what; *nis* = *ne* + *is*, § 213; *tô dônne*, gerund < *dôn*; *Ne rǽd'de gê*, read ye not, *rǽdan*, read, imperf. *rǽd'de*, conj. 6, *rǽdde* before the subject, § 170; *pǽron*, § 213; *in-eô'de*, in yode, entered, irreg., from *in-gân'*, § 213; *æt* < *etan*; *offring-hlâf*, *es*, m., offering-loaves, show-bread; *nǽron* = *ne* + *pǽron*, were not, § 213; *sacerdum*, plur. dat. *sacerd*, *es*, m. < Lat. *sacerdos*, priest, akin to sacred, sacerdotal; *ânum* < *ân*, alone; *ǽ*, f. indec., law; *ge-pem'man*, pro-

synd bûton leahtre? Ic secge sôðlîce eôp þæt þes is mǽrra
þonne þæt templ. Gif gê sôðlîce þiston hpæt is, Ic pille mild-
heortnesse and nâ on-sægd'nesse, ne geniđ'ráde gê ǽfre un'scyldig'e. Sôðlîce mannes sunu is eâc reste-dæges hláford.

9. Pâ se Hǽlend þanon fôr, hê com in tô heorâ gesom'nunge;
þâ pæs þǽr ân man se hæfde for-scrunc'ene hand. And hig
âcsôdon hine, þus cpeðende: Is hit âlŷf'ed tô hǽlanne on reste-
dagum? þæt hig prehton hine.

Hê sǽde him sôðlîce: Hpylc man is of eôp, þe hæbbe ân sceâp,
and gif þæt âfylđ' reste-dagum on pyt, hû ne nimđ hê þæt, and
hefđ hit up? Þitodlîce miclô mâ man is sceâpe betera; þitodlîce
hit is âlŷf'ed on reste-dagum pel tô dônne. Pâ cpæð hê tô þam
men: Áþen'e þîne hand. And hê hî âþen'ede; and heô pæs hâl
gepord'en spâ seô ôðer.

---

5. The Sower.

Matthew, xiii., 4–8.—Sôðlîce, ût eôde se sǽdere his sǽd tô
sâpenne: and þâ-þâ hê seôp, sume hig feôllon pið peg, and fuglás
cômon and ǽton þâ.

Sôðlîce sume feôllon on stǽnihte, þǽr hit næfde mycle eorđan,
and hrædlîce up sprungon, for-þam'-þe hig næfdon þǽre eorđan

fane, imperf. -pem'đe, p. p. -pemm'ed, conj. 6; synd<com, § 213; leahtre, dative from leahtor,
es, m., blame, crime; þes, this man; mǽrra, adj. comp. nusc.=mára (more), greater; templ
= tempel, § 73, 6; þiston, irreg. <pitan, know, Engl. wit, wist, § 212; mild-heortnes, se, f.,
mercy; on-sægd'nes, se, f., sacrifice, akin to say, as that which is vowed, dedicated; ge-
niđ'ráde, imperf. subj. plur. -de for -don before gê, § 170, ge-niđ'rian, imperf. -niđ'ráde, p. p.
niđ'rád, conj. 6, humiliate, condemn, from niðer, nether, beneath; un'-scyldige, adj. plur.,
the guiltless, scyldig, Ger. schuldig, akin to shall, owe, § 212; hláf-ord, es, m., lord, loaf-mas-
ter, -ord akin to Ger. wirth, Fries. werda, host, housekeeper; com<cuman; ge-som'nung=
ge-sam'nung, assembly, akin to sam, same; for-scrinc'an, imperf. -scranc, -scrunc'on, p. p.
-scrunc'en, shrunken away; hig < hí, they; tô hǽlanne, gerund from hǽlan, imperf. hǽlde,
p. p. hǽled, heal, akin to hál, hale, whole; prehton, subj. imperf., from preccan, attack,
conj. 6, § 209, akin to wreak; sǽde<secgan, imperf. sægde>sǽde, p. p. sægd, sǽd, conj. 6,
§ 209; áfylđ', falleth, pres., á-feall'an, imperf. -feól', -feóll'on, p. p. -feall'en, conj. 5, § 209; pyt,
es, m., pit, from Lat. put-eus; hú, inter. sign, § 397, b; nimđ<níman, take; hefđ, heaveth,
hebban, § 207; pitodlîce, verily, so then; miclô mâ, more by much, § 302, d; sceâpe, dat. after
comp. betera, § 303; men, dat. of man, § 84; á-þen'e, stretch forth, á-þen'ian, imperf. -þen'ede,
conj. 6, akin to Lat. tendo; hí, acc. sing. fem. of hê, § 130; ge-pord'en, p. p. from gepeord'an.

5. For unexplained words, see pp. 1-2.—Sôðlîce (soothly), truly, lo! interj.; þá-þá (then
when), when; hig=hí, g, dissimilated, § 27; sume hig, some they fell=some of them fell,
appositive for partitive, § 287, c; þâ, them, plur. acc. from se; sôðlîce, and, but, general
connective, § 463, 8; stǽniht, acc. sing. stǽniht, e, f., stony ground; þǽr hit næfde, where
it had not, careless for hig næfdon, sǽd might be either sing. or plur.; hrædlîce, quickly,
akin to Engl. rath, rather; sprungon, sprang, springan, imperf. sprang, sprungon, p. p.

dýpan: sôðlíce, up âsprung'enre sunnan, hig âdrup'edon and forscrunc'on, for-þam'-þe hig næfdon pyrtrum:

Sôðlíce sume feóllon on þornâs, and þâ þornâs peôxon and forþrys'môdon þâ:

Sume sôðlíce feóllon on gôde eorðan, and sealdon pæstm, sum hundfealdne, sum syxtigfealdne, sum þrittigfealdne.

6. Trust in God.

Matthew, vi., 26-33.—Beheald'að heofenan fuglâs: forþam'þe hig ne sâpað, ne hig ne rîpað, ne hig ne gaderiað on berne; and eôper heofonlîca Fæder hig fêt. Hû ne synd gê sêlran þonne hig? Hpylc eôper mæg sôðlíce geþenc'an þæt hê ge-eâc'nige âne elne tô his anlîcnesse?

And tô hpî synd gê ymb'-hýd'ige be reâfê? Besceâp'iað æceres lilian, hû hig peaxað; ne spincað hig, ne hig ne spinnað: ic secge eôp sôðlíce, Þæt furðon Salomon on eallum hys puldre næs oferprig'en spâ spâ ân of þysum.

Sôðlíce, gif æceres peôd, þæt þe tô dæg ys, and byð tô morgen on ofen âsend', God spâ scrýt, eâlâ gê gehpæd'es geleâf'an, þam myclê mâ hê scrýt eôp.

Nellen gê eornostlîce beôn ymb'-hýd'ige, þus cpeðende, Hpæt ete pê? oððe hpæt drince pê? oððe mid hpam beô pê oferprig'ene? Sôðlíce ealle þâs þing þeôðâ sêcað: pitodlíce, eôper Fæder pât þæt gê ealrâ þyssâ þingâ beþurf'on.

Eornostlîce sêcað ærest Godes rîce and his riht'pîs'nesse, and ealle þâs þing eôp beôð þærtô ge-eâc'nôde.

---

sprungen, conj. 1; *dýpa,* n. m. acc., depth; *â-sprung'enre,* p. p. sing., f., dat. absolute from *âsprinᵍ'an,* conj. 1, the sun having (sprung up) risen, § 304, d; *âdrúp'edon,* dried, *â-drup'-ian,* imp. *-ede, -edon,* p. p. *-ed,* conj. 6; *pyrtrum, es,* m.=*pyrtruma,* see page 1.

6. *for-þam'-þe,* for this that, for ∷ *sâpan,* sow, imp. *sôp, seôpon,* p. p. *sâpen,* conj. 5; *ne ne,* emphatic, § 400; *rîpan,* reap, imp. *râp, ripon,* p. p. *ripen,* conj. 2; *bern, es,* n., barn, <*ber-ern,* barley house, § 229: some texts read *ber-ern,* acc. plur. like the Greek; *fêt*<*fêded,* § 194, 36, 5; *synd*=*sind,* from *eom,* § 213; *sêlran*<*sêl,* §§ 123, 128; *eôper,* §§ 130, 312; *mæg geþenc'an,* § 176, *ge-eâc'n-ian,* imp. *-ôde,* p. p. *-ôd,* conj. 6, add, *ehe, -ige,* subj., (§ 184, 425; *eln, e,* f., Lat. *ulna,* ell; *anlîcnes, se,* f., likeness, stature; *tô hpî,* to what end, wherefore, § 352, IV., 135; *ymb'-hýd'ig,* adj., anxious about, worried; *be-sceâp'ian,* imp. *-ôde,* p. p. *-ôd,* behold (*sceâp*>*show*), conj. 6; *lilie, -an,* f., lily; *spincan,* imp. *spanc, spuncon,* p. p. *spuncen,* conj. 1, Old Engl. swink, toil; *spinnan,* spin, imp. *span, spunnon,* p. p. *spunnen,* conj. 1, § 201; *ofer-prîh'an,* imp. *-prâh', -prig'on,* p. p. *-prig'en,* conj. 2, § 205, cover over, dress (rig); *peôd, es,* n., weed; *þæt þe,* that that, which, § 380; *âsend',* p. p., § 190; *scrýt*<*scrýdan,* §§ 192, 36, 5, akin to shroud; *gehpæd'e,* adj., little; *þam myclê mâ,* more by much than that, (§ 303, 302, *d; ete*<*etad,* § 165; *þingâ,* gen., § 317, *b; riht'pîs'nes, se,* f., righteousness; *ge-eâc'nian,* conj. 6, add, see over.

7. THE PRODIGAL SON.

Luke, xv., 11–32.—11. Sôðlíce sum man hæfde tpegen sunâ.

12. Pâ cpæð se gingra tô his fæder, Fæder, syle mê mînne dǽl mînre ǽhte þe mê tô gebyr'eð. Pâ dǽlde hê hym hys ǽhte.

13. Pâ, æfter feâpa dagum, ealle his þing gegad'eró'de se gingra sunu, and férde præclíce on feorlen ríce, and forspil'de þâr his ǽhtâ, lybbende on his gǽlsan.

14. Pâ hê hig hæfde ealle âmyrr'ede, þâ pearð mycel hunger on þam ríce; and hê pearð pædla.

15. Pâ férde hê and folgôde ânum burh'-sitt'endum men þæs ríces: þâ sende hê hine tô his túne, þæt hê heólde hys spýn.

16. Pâ gepil'nôde hê his pambe gefyll'an of þâm beân'-codd'um þe þâ spýn ǽton; and him man ne scalde.

17. Pâ beþoh'te hê hine, and cpæð, Eâlâ hû fela yrðlingâ on mînes fæder hûse hlâf genôh'ne habbað, and ic hêr on hungre forpeorð'e!

18. Ic arîs'e, and ic fare tô mînum fæder, and ic secge him,

19. Eâlâ fæder, ic syngôde on heofenâs, and befor'an þê, nú ic neom pyrðe þæt ic beó þîn sunu nemned: dô mê spâ ǽnne of þínum yrðlingum.

20. And hê arâs' þâ, and com tô his fæder. And þâ gyt, þâ hê pæs feor, his fæder hê hyne geseah', and pearð mid mild'-heort'nesse âstyr'ed, and âgén'

---

12. *gingra*, comparative of *geong*, young, § 124; *ǽhte*, akin to *âgan*>Engl. *owe, own; gebyr'ed*, from *ge-byr'ian*, imp. *ge-byr'ede*, p. p. *ge-byr'ed*, conj. 6, be-falleth, akin to *bear, is borne; dǽlde*, dealt; *hym, hys*, bad spelling for *him, his*.

13. —*feâpa*, few, here undeclined, dat. plur., *feâpum, feâum, feâm*, are the common forms; *gegad'erian*, imp. *gegad'eróde*, p. p. *gegad'eróð*, conj. 6, gather; *præ-líce*, adv., exile-like, abroad, akin to *wretch; feor-len*, adj., far; *ríce*, Engl. *-ric*, Ger. *reich; for-spill'-ed*, spill away, destroy, imp. *spil'de*, p. p. *-spill'ed*, conj. 6; *lybbende*, bad spelling for *libbende*, living; *gǽlsan*, riotousness, luxury, Ger. *geil - heit*, akin to Engl. *gala, gǽlsa*, n, m.

14. —*hig*<*hî*, plur. of *hê*, them; *â-myrr'an*, imp. *-myrr'ede*, p. p. *-myrr'ed*, destroy, dissipate, akin to Engl. *mar; pearð*<*peordan; hunger, es*, m.; *pædla*, n, m., pauper, vagabond, akin to *padan*, go about > *wade*, waddle.

15. —*burh'-sitt'endum*, borough-sitting, dat. sing. from *burh'-sitt'ende*, adj.; *men*, dat. sing. of *man*, § 84; *túne*, dat., § 352 (town), inclosure; *healdan*, imp. *heóld, heóldon*, p. p. *healden*, conj. 5, *heólde*, subj. imp., might (hold) keep; *hys spýn (y, ȝ* for *i, î*).

16. —*pamb, e*, f., Engl. *womb*, belly; *beân'-cod, des*, m., bean cod, husk; *man*, (indefinite) one, § 136, 2; *scalde*<*sellan*.

17. —*beþoh'te*, bethought, *be-þenc'an*, imp. *-þoh'te*, p. p. *-þoht'*, conj. 6, § 209; *hine*, himself, § 131; *fela*, many, indecl., Ger. *viel*, Gr. πολύς, akin to *full; yrðlingâ*, gen. plur. partitive, Engl. *earthling; hlâf*>*loaf; genôh'ne*, acc. sing. of *ge-nôh'*, adj., enough; *hungre*, see over; *forpeorð'an*, be away, perish, imp. *-peard', -purð'on*, p. p. *-pord'en*, conj. 1, Ger. *werden*, O. E. *worth, for-*, Ger. *ver.*, as in *forsake*, § 254.

18. —*arîs'e*, pres. for future, § 413.

19. —*syng-ian*, sin, imp. *-óde*, p. p. *-óð*, conj. 6, imp. for perf., § 414; *neom*=*ne+com*, am not, § 213; *pyrðe*, worthy; *dô*, imperat. of *dón*, do, make; *mê*, acc.

20. —*arâs', arîs'an; þâ*, then; *com*, from *cuman*; and then yet, when; *feor*, prep., far from, § 336; *hê*, § 288, *b; hyne*, bad spelling for *hine; geseah'*<*gescôn'; pearð*<*peordan; â-styr'-ian*, imp. *-ede*, p. p. *-ed*, conj. 6, stirred; *mild'-heort'nes, se*, f., mild heart, compassion;

hine arn, and hine beclyp'te, and cyste hine.

21. Þâ cpæd his sunu, Fæder, ic syngôde on heofen, and be-for'an þê, nû ic ne com pyrðe þæt ic þîn sunu beô genem'ned.

22. Þâ cpæd se fæder tô his þeôpum, Bringað raðe þone sê-lestan gegyr'elan, and scrŷdað hine; and syllað him hring on his hand, and gescŷ' tô his fôtum;

23. And bringað ân fæt styric, and ofslead'; and uton etan, and gepist'full'ian:

24. forþam' þes mîn sunu pæs deâd, and hê ge-cd'cucôde; he forpeard', and hê ys gemêt'. Þâ ongun'non hig gepist'lâc'an.

25. Sôðlîce his yldra sunu pæs on æcere; and hê com: and þâ hê þam hûse geneâ'læh'te, hê gehŷr'de þone spêg and þæt pered.

26. Þâ clypôde hê ænne þeôp, and âcsôde hine hpæt þæt pêre.

27. Þâ cpæd hê, Þîn brôðer com, and þîn fæder ofslôh' ân fæt cealf; forþam' þe hê hine hâlne onfêng'.

28. Þâ gebealh' hê hine, and nolde in gân': þâ côde his fæder ût, and ongan' hine biddan.

29. Þâ cpæd hê, his fæder and'spariend'e, Efne, spâ fela geârâ ic þê þeôpôde, and ic næfre þîn gebod' ne forgŷm'de,

---

âgên'=ongeân', against, towards; *irnan*, imp. *arn, urnon*, p. p. *urnen*, metathesis for *rin-nan*, run, conj. 1, § 204; *be-clypp'an*, imp. *be-clyp'te*, p. p. *be-clypt'*, conj. 6, § 189; *be-clip*, embrace; *cyssan*, imp. *cyste*, p. p. *cyst*, conj. 6.

21. —See verse 19.

22. —*þeôp*, O. Engl. *thew*, servant, akin to Ger. *dienst, dirne*, O. Engl. *therne*; *bringan*, imp. *brang, brungon*, p. p. *brungen*, conj. 1; bring; *raðe*>*rathe*, Bring the *rathe* primrose, Milton, Lycidas, 142, comp. *rather*, sooner; *sêlestan*, superl. of *sêl*, good, akin to Ger. *see-lig*, O. Engl. *seely*, Engl. *silly*; *ge-gyr'ela, n, m.*, robe, akin to *gear*, *garb*; *scrŷdan*, akin to shroud; *hring*, *es*, m., ring, Ger. *ring*, Lat. *circus*, Gr. κιρκος; *fôt*, Ger. *fusz*, Lat. *pes*, Gr. πούς, declension, § 84.

23. —*fæt*, *te*, adj., fat; *styric*, *es*, m., stark, calf, Ger. *sterke*, akin to *steer*, Ger. *stier*, Lat. *taur-us*, Gr. ταύρος, Sansk. *sthûra-s*; *of-slead'*<*of-sleân'*; *uton*, subj. of *pîtan*, go, §§ 176, 224, 443, like Lat. *eamus*, Fr. *allons*, let us (go to) eat; *ge-pist'-full'ian*, imp. *-ôde*, p. p. *-ôd*, conj. 6, *pist*, existence, victuals, from *pesan*, be, *pist'-fullo*, fulness of victuals, a feast, *gepist'full'ian*, to feast, be merry.

24. —*ge-cd'-cuc'-ian*, imp. *-ôde*, p. p. *ôd*, conj. 6, *ed'-*, §§ 15, *a*, 254, back, again, *cuc*<*cpic*, quick, alive, Lat. *vîv-us*, Gr. βίος, Sansk. *g'îv-a-s*; *for-pcard'*, see verse 17; *ys*, bad for *is*; *ge-mêt'-an*, imp. *-mêtt'e*, *-mêt'ed*, p. p. *-mêt'*, met, found; *on-ginn'an*, begin; *gepist'-lâc'an, -læh'te, -læht'*, conj. 6, see verse 23, *lâc, lâcan*, akin to *-lock, wed-lock*, §§ 229, 233, 250.

25. —*yldra*, comp. of *eald*, old, § 124; *æcere*, see over; *geneâ'læh'te, geneâ'lâc'an*, come near; *spêg*, akin to *sough*, and to Ger. *schwegel-pfeife*; *pered*, company, akin to *per*, man, Goth. *vair*, Lat. *vir*, Sansk. *vîra*.

26. —*clyp-ian*, imp. *-ôde*, p. p. *-ôd*, conj. 6, O. Engl. *clepe, yclept*, in heaven *yclept* Euphrosyne, Milton, L'Al., 12; *âcsôde*>asked, metathesis; *pêre*, subj., <*pesan*, §§ 423, 425.

27. —*of-sleân'*, imp. *-slôh', -slôg'on*, p. p. *-slag'en*, conj. 4, § 207; *hâlne*, acc. of *hâl*, (w)hole, hale, Ger. *heil*, Gr. καλός; *on-fôn'*, imp. *-fêng', -fêng'on*, p. p. *-fang'en*, conj. 5, §§ 208, 216, Ger. *fangen*, fang, catch, receive.

28. —*gebealh' hine*, swelled himself, was angry, § 290, *d*, *ge-belg'an*, imp. *-bealh', -bulg'on*, p. p. *-bulg'en*, conj. 1, akin to bulge, belly, bellows; *nolde*=*ne pûlde*<*pillan*, § 212; *gân*, imp. *côde*, p. p. *gân*, irreg. go, (yode) went, gone, § 213; *biddan*, Ger. *bitten*, bid, ask.

29. —*and'spariend'e*, answering, *and'-*, § 15, *a*, Lat. *ante-*, Gr. ἀντί, in return, § 254, *sparian*, swear, speak emphatically; *efne*, akin to *efen*, even, § 263; *fela*, so many of years, see verse 17; *þeôpôde*<*þeôpian*, see *þeôp*, verse 22, *ge-bcôd'*, from *beôdan*, Ger. *bicten*, bid, order, *beôdan* and *biddan* (see verse 28) unite in Engl. *bid*, akin to *bead*; *for-gŷm'-an*, imp. *-gŷm'de*, p. p. *-gŷm'ed*, Goth. *gáumjan*, Ger. *gaumen*, O. Engl. Scot. *yeme*, *goam*, to see,

and ne sealdest þû mê nǣfre ân ticcen, þæt ic mid mînum freôndum gepist'fullôde;

30. ac syððan þes þîn sunu com, þe his spêde mid mylt'-ystrum âmyr'de, þû ofslôg'e him fæt cealf.

31. Þâ cpæð hê, Sunu, þû eart symle mid mê, and ealle mîne þing synd þîne: þû gebyr'ede gepist'full'ian and gebliss'ian: forþam' þes þîn brôðer þæs deâd, and hê ge-ed'eucôde; hê forpearð', and hê ys gemêt'.

---

8. LOVE YOUR ENEMIES.—*Matthew*, v., 38–48.

ANGLO-SAXON.

38. Gê gehŷr'don þæt ge-cped'en pæs, Eâge for eâge and tôð for tôð,

39. Sôðlîce ic secge côp, Ne pinne gê ongên' þâ þe côp yfel

GOTHIC OF ULPHILAS.

38. Hâusi'dêd'uþ þatei kviþan ist, Âugô und âugin, jah tunþu und tunþâu.

39. Iþ ik kviþa izvis ni and'-stand'an allis þamma un'sêl'jin;

---

8. This extract is prepared to give definite knowledge of the relation between the Gothic of Ulfilas and the Anglo-Saxon, and for introduction to Comparative Grammar, especially to etymology and phonology. Each Gothic word is first turned into an English word of the same root, so far as may be. These are helped out by other words in italics, so as to form a sort of translation to one who knows the meaning of the passage. The words are then explained, and laws of change referred to as given in the Grammar. Grimm's law applies to almost every word, and is here referred to once for all, §§ 18, 41.

care for; *ticcen*, *es*, n., kid, Ger. *zicke*, kid, *ziege*, goat; *freônd*, Ger. *freund* < *freôn*, to love; *gepist'fullôde*, see verse 23.

30. —*ac*, but, § 262; *siððan* (since), as soon as; *spêd* > Engl. *speed*, haste, success, wealth; *myltystr-e*, *an*, f., harlot, from *myltan*, melt, yield (in virtue), *-estre*, §§ 228, 232; *âmyr'de* = *âmyrr'ede*, see verse 14; *ofslôg'e*, verse 27.

31. —*symle*, always, akin to *same*, Lat. *simul*, *semper*; *mid*, Ger. *mît*, Gr. μετά, § 254; *þâ gebyr'ede*, it became thee, see verse 12; *gepist'full'ian*, see verse 23; *ge-bliss'-ian*, imp. *-ôde*, p. p. *-ôl*, conj. 6, be blissful, akin to *bless*; *ge-ed'eucôde*, see verse 24; *forpearð'*, *gemêt'*, verse 24.

8.—38. Hear-did-ye that-*which* queth-en is, Eye *for* eye, *and* tooth *for* tooth. *Hâusi-dêdup* = *hŷr-don*, *hâusjan*, A.-S. *hŷran* > hear, Ger. *hören*, *âu* > *eâ* > *ê*, §§ 18, 38, *s* > *r*, § 41, 3, *b*, *-dêdup*, A.-S. *-don*, did, Ger. *-te*, weak inflection, § 168; *þat-ei*, A.-S. *þæt* > that, Ger. *das*, *-ei*, § 468; *kviþan*, A.S. *cpeðen* > O. E. quethe, he-queath, quoth, O. H. G. *chedan*; § 197; *ist*, A.-S. *is* > is, Ger. *ist*, Lat. *est*, Gr. ἐστι,

Sansk. *ásti*, § 213; *pæs* > was, Goth. *vas*, Ger. *war*, § 213, 41, 3, *b*; *âugô*, A.-S. *eâge* > eye, Ger. *auge*, vowel change, §§ 18, 38, declension, § 95; *und*, A.-S. *ôð*, Ger. *unt*, § 254; *for*, Goth. *faur*, Ger. *für*, § 254; *ja-h*, and, A.-S. *ge*, O. H. Ger. *jo-h*, Lat. *ja-m*, § 262; *tunþu*, A.-S. *tôð* > tooth, Ger. *zahn*, Lat. *dent-is*, Gr. ὁ-δόντ-ος, Sansk. *dant-as*, § 37, declension, §§ 86, 93.

39. But I queth *to*-you not *to*-stand-*against at*-all the unseely; *but* if *any*-one-*who*-*ever* thee *strike* by dexter thine chin, wind *to*-him also the other. *Iþ*, but, A.-S. *ed-*, *oð-ðe*, O. H. G. *ed-*, Lat. *at*, § 262; *ik*, A.-S. *ic* > I, Ger. *ich*, Lat. *ego*, Gr. ἐγώ, Sansk. *aha'm*, § 130; *kviþa*, verse 38, inflection, § 165; *secge* > say, Ger. *sagen*; *izvis*, *côp* > you, § 130; *ni*, A.-S. *ne*, n-ot, O. H. G. *ni*, *ne*, Lat. *ne*, Gr. νη-, Sansk. *na*, § 254; *and'-stand'an*, *and-*, A.-S. *and-* > an, in an-swer, Ger. *ant-*, Lat. *ante*, Gr. ἀντί, Sansk. *ánti*, § 254, *standan*, A.-S. *standan* > stand, Ger. *stehen*, Lat. *sta-re*, Gr. ἵστη-μι, Sansk. *sthâ*, § 216; *pinne* < *pinnað* before *ge*, § 165; *ongên'* for *ongeðn'*, Ger. *ent-gegen*, § 251; *allis*, A.-S. *ealles*, Ger. *alles*, § 251:

dóð; ac gyf hpâ þê sleâ on þîn spŷðre penge, gegear'pâ him þæt ôðer.

40. And þam þe pylle on dôme pið þê flîtan, and niman þîne tunecan, læt him tô þînne pæfels.

41. And spâ-hpâ'-spâ þê genŷt' þûsend stapâ, gâ mid him ôðre tpâ þûsend.

42. Syle þam þe þê bidde, and þam þe æt þê pille borgian ne pyrn þû him.

43. Gê gehŷr'don þæt ge-

ak jabâi hvas þuk stâutái bi taihsvôn þeina kinnu, vandei imma jah þô anþara.

40. Jah þamma viljandin miþ þus stâua jah pâida þeina niman, aflêt' imma jah vastja.

41. Jah jabâi hvas þuk ananâuþ'jái rasta áina, gaggáis miþ imma tvôs.

42. Pamma bidjandin þuk gibáis, jah þamma viljandin af þus leihvan sis ni us'vand'jáis.

43. Háus'idêd'uþ þatei kviþan

þamma, A.-S. *þam*, him, Ger. *dem*, Gr. τῳ, Sansk. *tá-smái*, § 104; *þá þe*, § 104; *ȝfel*, verse 45; *un'sêljin*, *un-*, § 254, *sêls*, A.-S. *sêl*, *sælig*>seely, silly, Ger. *selig*, akin to Lat. *salvus*, Gr. ὅλοός, declension weak, § 107; *ak*, A.-S. *ac*, O. H. G. *oh*, but, § 262; *jabai*, A.-S. *gif*>if, O. H. G. *ibu*, § 262; *hvas*, A.-S. *hpá*>who, Ger. *wer*, Lat. *qui-s*, Sansk. *kas*, § 135; *þuk*, A.-S. *þec*>thee, Ger. *dich*, Lat. *té*, Gr. τέ, Sansk. *trá*, § 130; *stáut-ai*, Ger. *stossen*, Lat. *tund-o*, Gr. Τυδ-εύς, Sansk. *tud*; *sleâ*<*slean*>slay, Ger. *schlagen*, Goth. *slahan*; *bi*, A.-S. *bi*>by, Ger. *bei*, § 254; *taihsvôn*, Lat. *dexter*; *spŷdre*, right, comp. of *spid*, strong; *þeina*, A.-S. *þin*>thine, Ger. *dein*, Lat. *tuus*, § 132; *kinnu*, A.-S. *cinne*>chin, Ger. *kinne*, Lat. *gena*, Gr. γένυ-ς, declension, § 93; *penge*, s, n., wang, cheek, Ger. *wange*; *vandei*, *vandjan*, A.-S. *pendan*>wend, Ger. *wenden*; *imma*, A.-S. *him*>him, Ger. *ihm*, § 130; *þá anþara*, A.-S. *þæt óðer*>that other, Ger. *die andere*, Gr. ἕτερος, Sansk. *antará*, § 126.

40. *And the-*one willing *with* thee *a-law-suit* and *tunic* thine *to-*him, let off *to-*him *also* vest. *Jah*, verse 38; *þamma*, verse 39; *viljandin*, p. pr. *viljan*, A.-S. *pillan*>will, Ger. *wollen*, Lat. *volo*, Gr. βούλομαι, Sansk. *var*, *val*, § 212; *miþ*, A.-S. *mid*, Ger. *mit*, Gr. μετά, Sansk. *mi-thás*, § 254; *pið*>with, Goth. *viþra*, Ger. *wider*, § 254; *þus*, see *þuk*, verse 39; *stáua*, judge, judgment, Grimm says from *stabs*, A.-S. *stæf*>staff, Ger. *stab*, and so *staff-bearer*; *jah*, verse 38; *páide*, A.-S. *pád*, Ger. *pfeit*, Gr. βαίτη, a borrowed word, akin to *pæd*>weeds, O. H. G. *wát*; *tunec-e*, *-an*, f., from Lat. *tunica*; *þeina*, verse 39; *niman*, A.-S. *niman*>nim, Ger. *nehmen*, take, § 165;

af-, A.-S. *of-*>off, of, Ger. *ab-*; *lêtan*, A.-S. *lætan*>let, Ger. *lassen*; *imma*, verse 39; *jah*, verse 38; *vastja*, Lat. *vest-is*, vest, Gr. ἐσθής, A.-S. verb *perian*>wear (s>r, § 41); *pæfels*, better *pefels*<*pefan*, weave.

41. And if *any-one-*who-*ever* thee need rest one, go *with* him two. *ana-náuþjái*, *ana*, verse 45, *náuþjan*, A.-S. *nŷdan*>need, Ger. *noth*; *ge-nŷt'*<*ge-nŷdan*, compel, inflection, §§ 170, 192; *rasta*, A.-S. *reste*>rest, Ger. *rast*, resting-place, mile; *þûsend*>thousand, Ger. *tausend*, Goth. *þusundi*, § 139; *stæpe*, s, m.>step; *áina*, A.-S. *án*>one, an, a, Ger. *ein*, Gr. ἕν-ος, Lat. *un-us*, § 139; *gaggáis*, A.-S. *gá*>go, Ger. *gehen*, § 213; *tvôs*, A.-S. *tpá*>two, Ger. *zwei*, § 139.

42. *To-*the-*one* bidding thee give, *and from-*the-*one* willing of thee *to-*take-*a-*loan *self* not wend. *Bid-jandin*, p. pr. *bidjan*, A.-S. *biddan*>bid (ask), Ger. *bitten*; *gib-áis*, A.-S. *gifan*>give, Ger. *geben*; *syle*>sell; *leihvan*, A.-S. *lihan*, Ger. *leihen*>*lân*>loan; *borgian*>borrow, Ger. *borgen*, to give on borowe, security<*beorgan*>bury, secure; *sis*, dative of *seina*, A.-S. *sin*, Ger. *sich*, self, § 131; *us'vand'jáis*, Ger. *abwenden*, *us-*, A.-S. *or-*, Ger. *ur-*, away, *vandjan*, verse 39; *pyrnan*, imp. *pyrnde*, p. p. *pyrned*, conj. 6, warn off, repel, deny, akin to *parnian*, Ger. *warnen*, warn.

43. Hear-did-ye that-*which* queth-en is, be-Friend nighest thine, *and be-*foe fiend thine. *Háus'idêd'up* —*ist*, verse 38; *fri-jos*, A.-S. *freôgan*, Ger. *freien*, love, kiss, woo, Sansk. *pri*, Gr. πρῷ-ος, hence *freónd*>friend, Ger. *freund*, p. pr.; *lufan*, Goth. *liuban*, Ger. *lieben*, Lat. *lubet*, *libet*, Gr. λίπ-τομαι, Sansk. *lubh*; *nêh-*, A.-S. *nêh-stan*, *nêxtan*, Ger. *náhst*,

cpcd'en pæs, Lufâ þînne nêxtan, and hatâ þînne feônd :

44. Sôðlîce ic secge eôp, Lufiað eôpre fŷnd, and dôð pel þâm þe eôp yfel dôð, and gebidd'að [for eôpre êhterâs and] tælendum eôp ;

45. þæt gê sîn eôpres Fæder bearn þe on heofonum ys, se þe dêð þæt hys sunne up âspringð' ofer þâ gôdan and ofer þâ yfelan, and hê læt rînan ofer þâ riht'- pîs'an and ofer þâ un'rihtpîsan.

ist, Frijôs nêhvundjan þeinana, jah fiâis fiand þeinana :

44. aþþan ik kviþa izvis, Frijôþ fijands izvarans [þiuþjâiþ þans vrikandans izvis] vâila tâujâiþ þâim hatjandam izvis, jah bidjâiþ bi þans us'þriut'audans izvis ;

45. ei vairþâiþ sunjus attins izvaris þis in himinam, untê sunnôn seina ur'rann'eiþ ana ubilans jah gôdans, jah rigneiþ ana garaiht'ans jah ana in'vind'ans.

---

nearest ; *fiáis,* hate, *fijan,* A.-S. *fian,* O. H. G. *fién* > *fiand,* A.-S. *feônd* > fiend, Ger. *feiad,* p. pr., hating, used as a substantive ; *hat-ian,* imp. *-ôde,* p. p. *-ôd,* conj. 6, hate, Goth. *hatan,* Ger. *hassen,* perhaps akin to Lat. *odi.*

44. *But*-then I queth *to*-you, be-Friend fiends yours, bless those wreaking *on*-you, well do to-them hating you, and bid by those out-*thrusting* you.   *ap-þan,* Lat. *at,* but, see verse 39 and § 262, *-þan,* demons. particle, § 262 ; *þiuþjáiþ—izvis,* εὐλογεῖτε τοὺς καταρωμένους ὑμᾶς, is omitted in the Latin, and so in the Anglo-Saxon ; *þiuþjan,* do good, bless < *þiuþ,* good, not in other tongues, root *þiv,* grow, akin to A.-S. *peóp, þipe,* boy, servant ; *þans,* acc. plur. of demons., §§ 104, 107 ; *vrikandans,* cursing, *vrikan,* A.-S. *precan* > wreak, Ger. *rächen ; váila,* A.-S. *pel* > well, Ger. *wohl ; táu-jáiþ,* A.-S. *tapian* > taw, Ger. *zauen,* make, equip, do, a kindred stem to *dôn* > do, Ger. *thun,* Gr. θε-, τί-θη-μι, Sansk. *dhâ ; þâim,* dat. plur., A.-S. *þâm* > them, Ger. *dem ; hatjandam,* verse 43 ; *biddan,* verse 42 ; *us'þriut'-audans,* p. pr., *us*-, verse 42, *þriutan,* A.-S. *preótan,* Ger. *ver-driessen,* Lat. *trudo,* extrude ; *êhtere, s,* m., persecutor ; *tælendum,* p. pr., *tæl-an,* imp. *-de,* p. p. *-ed,* conj. 6, speak evil, akin to Gothic *taljan,* A.-S. *tellan* > tell, Ger. *zählen,* tale, tally.

45. That *you*-may-worth sons *of*-Father your the-*one* in *heavens, since* sun *his* up-runneth on evil *and* good, and *he*-raineth on righteous *and* on in-wound.   *Ei,* that, if, pronominal, probably from relative *ja,* and so akin to Gr. *εἰ,* Lat. *s-i,* § 262 ; *vaírþ-áiþ,* A.-S. *peordan* > O. E. worth, be, Ger. *werden ; sunus,* A.-S. *sunu* > son, Ger. *sohn,* Gr. *ὐ-ιός,* Sansk. *sû-nus* < *su,* bear ; *bearn* > bairn, Goth.

barn < Goth. *bairan,* A.-S. *beran* > bear, Ger. *ge-bähren,* Lat. *fero,* Gr. φέρω, Sansk. *bi-bhár-mi ; attins,* father, O. H. G. *atto,* Ger. child-speech *ette,* Sansk., Gr., Lat. *atta,* similar words far and wide beyond the Indo-European tongues, so as to suggest that they are interjectional. The linguals in this use are as common as the labials *pá-pá, ab-bá, má-má ; dá-dá* > Engl. dad, is widespread ; *þis,* genitive of article, verse 39, § 104 ; *in,* A.-S. *in* > in, Ger. *ein,* Lat. *in,* Gr. *ἐν,* Sansk. *and,* § 254 ; *himinam,* plur. dat. of *himins,* declined as in § 70, Ger. *himmel,* and in the other Teutonic tongues except A.-S., from root *him,* cover, and so analogous to Low Ger., O. Sax., A.-S., *heafon* > heaven, root *hib* > heave ; *untê,* O. H. G. *unza,* unto, until, since, compare *und,* verse 38 ; *sunnôn* < *sunnô,* f., § 95, c, A.-S. *sunne* > sun, Ger. *sonne ; sein,* A.-S. *sin,* Ger. *sein,* his, § 132 ; *ur'-rann'eiþ, ur-* = *us-,* verse 42, *rannjan,* cause to rain, *rann-eiþ* = -*jiþ,* 3d sing., § 165, *d,* < *rinnan,* imp. *ran,* A.-S. *rinnan* > run, Ger. *rinnen ; â-spring'an,* conj. 1 : *ana,* A.-S. *an, on* > on, Ger. *an,* Gr. *ἀνά,* Lat. *an-,* Sansk. *and,* § 254 ; *ubilans,* declension, § 107, A.-S. *yfelan* > evil, Ger. *übel ; gôd,* A.-S. *gôd* > good, Ger. *gut ; rigneiþ* < *rignjan,* inflect., § 165, *a,* A.-S. *rínan* > rain, Ger. *regen,* Lat. *rigo,* Gr. βρέχ-ειν, root *vragh,* Sansk. ; *ga-raiht'-ans,* declension, § 107, A.-S. *riht-pís* > righteous, Ger. *recht,* Lat. *rect-us,* root *rg',* Gr. ὀρέχ-ειν, Lat. *reg-o,* Goth. *rakjan,* A.-S. *ræan* > reach, Ger. *reichen ; in'-vínd'-ans,* § 107, in-, see over ; *vindan,* A.-S. *pindan* > wind, Ger. *winden,* twisted, perverted, wrong ; *un'-riht-pís,* adj., unrighteous.

46. Gyf gê sôdlîce þâ lufiađ þe eôp lufiađ, hpylce mêde habbađ gê: hû ne dôđ mânfulle spâ?

47. And gyf gê þæt ân dôđ þæt gê eôpre gebrôđ'ra pylcumiađ, hpæt dô gê mâre? hû ne dôđ hæđene spâ?

48. Eornostlîce beôđ fulfrem'ede, spâ eôper heofonlîca Fæder is fulfrem'ed.

46. Jabâi âuk frijôþ þans frijôndans izvis âinans, hvô mizdônô habâiþ? niu jah þâi þiudô þata samô tâujand?

47. Jah jabâi gôleiþ þans frijônds izvarans þatâinei, hvê managizô tâujiþ? niu jah môtarjôs þata samô tâujand?

48. Sijâiþ nu jus fullatôjâi, svasvê atta izvar sa in himinam fullatôjis ist.

46. If eke *you-be-friend* those *be-friending you al-one*, what mede have-*you*? Do-not they *also* of-the-dutch that same do? *âuk*, A.-S. *eâc* > eke, Ger. *auch*, § 254; *frijôþ*, verse 43, inflect., § 165, *d*; *âinans*, acc. pl., verse 41; *hvô*, verse 39; *hpyle* < *hpâ-lîc*, Ger. *welch*, which, § 135; *mizd-ônô*, gen. pl. of *mizdô*, decline, § 95, A.-S. *meord*, Gr, μισθ-ός, akin to A.-S. *mêd*, *e*, f. > meed, Ger. *miethe*; *habâiþ*, inflect., § 170, A.-S. *habbađ*, have, Ger. *haben*, akin to Lat. *habeo*; *ni-u*, A.-S. *ne*, not, verse 39, *hû ne*, emphatic interrog., §§ 252, 397; *þâi*, they, § 104; *þiudô*, gen. plur. < *þiuda*, declens., § 88, A.-S. *þeôd* > O. Engl. thede, people, O. H. G. *diota*, akin to A.-S. *þeodisc*, people, Ger. *deutsch* > Dutch; *mânful*, adj., sinful, *mân*, sin, akin to *mæne* > mean, Goth. *ga-mâins*, Ger. *ge-mein*, common, *ful* > full, Goth. *fulls*, Ger. *voll*, Gr. πλέος, Lat. *ple-nus*, Sansk. *pûr*, § 229; *samô*, A.-S. *same* > same, O. H. G. *samo*, Lat. *sim-ilis*, Gr. ὁμ-ός, Sansk. *sam-as*, see *sam-*, § 254; *spđ*, § 252; *tâujand*, 3d plur., inflect., § 165, verse 44.

47. And if *you-greet* those friends yours that-*al-one*, what more do-*ye*? Do-not *also* meters that same do? *gôleiþ*, *gôljan*, greet, akin to A.-S. *gâl* > O. Engl. gole, glad, Ger.

geil, Goth. *gâiljan*, rejoice, and perhaps to A.-S. *galan* > -*gale*, nightin-gale, Ger. *gellen*, yell, cry; *pyl-cumian*, imp. -*ôde*, p. p. -*ôd*, conj. 6, Ger. *willkommen*, welcome < *pil-cuma*, a wished-for comer, *pillan*, verse 40, *cuman* > come, Goth. *kviman*, Ger. *kommen*, Sansk. *gâ* > *grâ* > *ra*, Lat. ve-*nio*, βα, Gr. ἔ-βη-ν, parasitic *v* and Grimm's law, § 33; *managizô*, comp. of *managg*, much, many, A.-S. *maneg* > many, Ger. *manch*, comparative endings, § 123, *a*; *mâre* > more, Goth. *mâiza*, Ger. *mehr*, Lat. *major*, Gr. μείζων. Sansk. *mâhi-jâs* (§ 123, *a*); *môtarjôs* < *môta*, Ger. *maut*, tax, Grimm says akin to *mêde*, verse 46; *hæđen* > heathen, Goth. *hâiþnô*, Ger. *heiden* < A.-S. *hæđ* > heath, Goth. *hâiþi*, Ger. *heide*, dwellers on the heath, compare *pagan* < *paganus*.

48. *Be* now you full-done, so-so *Father* your the in *heavens* full-done is. *sijâiþ*, 2d plur., pres. subj. of the verb to be, A.-S. *sîn*, §§ 213, 170; *nu*, A.-S. *nû* > now, Ger. *nu-n*, Gr. *vῦ*, Lat. *nunc*, Sansk. *nu*, § 252; *jus*, § 130; *fulla-tôjâi*, *fulls*, verse 46, *tôjâi*, do, akin to *tâu-jan*, verse 44; *svasvê*, A.-S. *spâ* > so, Ger. *so*, § 252; *sa*, A.-S. *se*, Sansk. *sa*, Gr. ὁ, article, § 104.

---

9. The Lord's Prayer in Gothic.

Matthew, vi., 9–13.—*Atta unsar þu in himinam, Veihnâi namô þein. Kvimâi þiudinassus þeins. Vairþâi vilja þeins, svê in himina jah ana airþâi. Hlâif unsarana þana sinteinan gif uns himma daga. Jah aflêt' uns þatei skulans sijáima, svasvê jah veis aflêt'am þâim skulam unsarâim. Jah ni briggâis uns in frâistubnjâi, ak lâusei uns af þamma ubilin; untê þeina ist þiudangardi jah mahts jah vulþus in âivins. Amén.*

The next part of the Reader is prepared on a plan somewhat like that proposed by Thomas Jefferson to the University of Virginia. Facing each page of Anglo-Saxon will be found its counterpart in a sort of English. Each word is changed into the form which it took when the inflections weakened and it became English. Many are long since obsolete. Such are explained in the foot-notes. A good deal of knowledge of Anglo-Saxon and of the growth of English may be gained very fast and very easily by such apparatus.

In the translation, words in italics are not of the same root as the Anglo-Saxon which they represent, or are added.

In the foot-notes—

(Ch.) means that the word before it is in Chaucer.

(H.) Halliwell's Dictionary of Archaic and Provincial Words.

(P. P.) Piers Ploughman.

(S.) Stratmann, Dictionary of the English of the 13th, 14th, and 15th Centuries.

(Wycl.) Wycliffe.

(?) not found by me as yet.

When there is no sign of this sort the word is in Webster's Dictionary. Look for parts of compounds; especially drop *i-*, *be-*, and the like. If the proper meaning is not seen in Webster, look at what he says in the etymology, or look at the Vocabulary of this Reader.

Two pages of poetry (p. 52*, 53*) are prepared in the same way.

DIALOGUES OF CALLINGS.

1. Teacher and Scholar.

The learner saith:

We childer[1] bid[2] thee, O lo lore-*master*, that thou teach us to-speak in Latin i-rerd[3] rightly, forthat[4] un-i-lered[5] we are, and i-wemmedly[6] we speak.

The lore-*master* answereth:

What will ye speak?

S. What reck we what we speak, but[7] it right speech *be*, and behoove-*full*, not idle or frakel[8]?

T. Will ye be (be-)swinged on learning?

S. Liefer[9] is to-us to-be (be-)swinged for lore, than it ne[10] to-ken; ac[11] we wit thee bile-whit[12] *to-be*, and to-nill[13] (on-bi-)lead[14] swingels[15] on-us, but[16] thou be to-i-needed[17] from us.

T. I ax[18] thee, what speakest thou? What hast thou of work?

S. I am monk, and I sing each day seven tides[19] mid[20] i-brothers, and I am busied in reading and in song, ac[11] though-whether[21] I would between learn to-speak in Latin i-rerd[3].

T. What ken these thy i-feres[22]?

S. Some are earthlings[23], some shepherds, some oxherds, some eke[24] so-like[25] hunters, some fishers, some fowlers, some chapmen[26], some shoe-wrights, some salters, some bakers.

2. Teacher and Ploughman.

T. What sayest thou, earthling[23], how bi-goest[27] thou work thine?

Pl. O lo, lief[28] lord, thraly[29] I derve[30]; I go out on day-red[31], thewing[32] oxen to field, and yoke hem[33] to sull[34]; nis[35] it so stark[36] winter that I dare lout[37] at home for awe of lord mine; ac[11] yoked[39] oxen[39], and i-fastened[39] share[39] and coulter mid[20] the sull[34], each day I shall car[38] full acre or more.

---

[1] children (Ch.). [2] pray. [3] language (Π.). [4] because. [5] unlearned (S.). [6] corruptly; *teem*, a spot. [7] if only. [8] vile (S.). [9] pleasanter. [10] not. [11] but (S.). [12] gentle (S.). [13] not wish. [14] inflict (?). [15] blows. [16] unless. [17] compelled (S.). [18] ask. [19] times. [20] with (P. P.). [21] whether or no, notwithstanding. [22] comrades (S.). [23] ploughmen. [24] also. [25] likewise. [26] merchants. [27] practisest (Π.). [28] dear. [29] hard (Π.). [30] toil (S.). [31] dawn (S.). [32] driving (S.). [33] 'em, them (Ch.). [34] plow. [35] is not. [36] severe. [37] loiter, lurk (Ch., P. P.). [38] plough. [39] dative absolute, § 304, *d*.

DIALOGUES OF CALLINGS.

1. Teacher and Scholar.

Se leornere segeð:

Ƿé cildru biddað þé, eálá láreóƿ, þæt þú tǽce ús sprecan on Ledenê gereordê rihte, forþam ungelǽrede pé sindon, and gepemmedlíce pé sprecað.

Se láreóƿ andsperáð:

Hƿæt ƿille gé sprecan?

Le. Hƿæt rêce pé hƿæt pé sprecân, bûtan hit riht sprǽc sí, and behêfe, næs ídel oððe fracod?

Lƿ. Ƿille gé beón bespungen on leornunge?

Le. Leófre is ús beón bespungen for láre, þænne hit ne cunnan; ac pé piton þé bilepitne pesan and nellan onbelǽdan spinglá ús, bútan þú beó tô-genýded fram ús.

Lƿ. Ic áxie þé, hƿæt spricst þú? Hƿæt hæfst þú peorces?

Le. Ic com munuc, and ic singe ǽlcê dæg seofon tídá mid gebróðrum, and ic com bysgód on rǽdinge and on sangê; ac þeáhhƿæðere ic polde betpeónan leornian sprecan on Ledenê gereordê.

Lƿ. Hƿæt cunnon þás þíne geféran?

Le. Sume sind yrðlingás, sume sceáphirdás, sume oxanhirdás, sume cắc spylce huntan, sume fisceras, sume fugeleras, sume cýpmen, sume sceó-ƿyrhtan, sume sealteras, sume bæceras.

---

2. Teacher and Ploughman.

Lƿ. Hƿæt segst þú, yrðling, hú begést þú peorc þín?

Y. Eálá, leóf hláford, þearle ic deorfe; ic gá út on dægrêd, þýpende oxan tô feldá, and geocie hí tô sulh; nis hit spá stearc pinter, þæt ic durre lutian æt hám for egé hláfordes mínes; ac geocódum oxum, and gefæstnódum sceare and cultre mid þǽre sulh, ǽlcê dæg ic sceal erian fulne æcer oððe máre.

Lþ. Hæfst þû ænigne geféran?

Y. Ic hæbbe sumne cnapan þýpendne oxan mid gadîsenê, þe eâc spylce nû hâs is for cýle and hreâmê.

Lþ. Hpæt mâre dêst þû on dæg?

Y. Gepislîce þænne mâre ic dô. Ic sceal fyllan binnan oxenà mid hîgê, and pæterian hî, and scearn heorâ beran ût.

Lþ. Hîg! hîg! Micel gedeorf is hit!

Y. Gea, leôf, micel gedeorf hit is, forþam ic neom freô.

---

3. Teacher and Shepherd.

Lþ. Hpæt segst þû, sceâphirde? Hæfst þû ænig gedeorf?

S. Gea, leôf, ic hæbbe; on forepeardne morgen ic drîfe sceâp mîne tô heorâ læse, and stande ofer hî on hæte and on cýle mid hundum, þý læs pulfas forspelgen hî, and ic ongeân læde hî tô heorâ loca, and melce hî tpeôpa on dæg, and loca heorâ ic hebbe þærtô, and cêse and buteran ic dô, and ic com getrýpe hlâforde mînum.

---

4. Teacher and Oxherd.

Lþ. Eâlâ, oxanhirde, hpæt pyrcst þû?

O. Eâlâ, hlâford mîn, micel ic gedeorfe: þænne se yrðling unscenð þâ oxan, ic læde hî tô læse, and ealle niht ic stande ofer hî paciende for þeôfum, and eft on ærmergen ic betæce hî þam yrðlinge pel gefylde and gepæterôde.

Lþ. Is þes of þînum geférum?

O. Gea, hê is.

---

5. Teacher and Hunter.

Lþ. Canst þû ænig þing?

H. Ânne cræft ic can.

Lþ. Hpilcne?

H. Hunta ic com.

Lþ. Hpæs?

H. Cyninges.

Lþ. Hû begæst þû cræft þînne?

H. Ic brede mê max, and sette hî on stôpe gehæpre, and ge-

T. Hast thou any i-fere¹?

Pl. I have some² knave³ thewing⁴ oxen with gad-iron, that eke⁵ so-like⁶ now hoarse is for chill and ream⁷.

T. What more doest thou a⁸ day?

Pl. I-wis⁹ then more I do. I shall fill bins of oxen mid¹⁰ hay, and water hem¹¹, and shern here¹² bear out.

T. Hi! hi! Much derf¹³ is it!

Pl. Yea, lief¹⁴, much derf¹³ it is, forthat¹⁵ I nam¹⁶ free.

---

3. TEACHER AND SHEPHERD.

T. What sayest thou, shepherd? Hast thou any derf¹³?

S. Yea, lief¹⁴, I have; on forward¹⁷ morning I drive sheep mine to here¹² lease¹⁸, and stand over hem¹¹ on heat and on chill mid¹⁰ hounds, the less¹⁹ wolves for-swallow²⁰ hem¹¹, and I again lead hem¹¹ to here¹² locks, and milk hem¹¹ twice a⁸ day, and locks here¹² I heave thereto²¹, and cheese and butter I do²², and I am true to-lord mine.

---

4. TEACHER AND OXHERD.

T. Oh, lo, oxherd, what workest thou?

O. Oh, lo, lord mine, much I derve¹³: then²³ the earthling²⁴ unsheneth²⁵ the oxen, I lead hem¹¹ to lease¹⁸, and all night I stand over hem¹¹ watching for thieves, and after on ere-morning¹⁷ I beteach²⁶ hem¹¹ to-the earthling²⁴ well i-filled and i-watered.

T. Is this of thy i-feres¹?

O. Yea, he is.

---

5. TEACHER AND HUNTER.

T. Kenst thou any thing?

H. One craft I ken.

T. Which?

H. Hunter I am.

T. Whose?

H. King's.

T. How bi-goest²⁷ thou craft thine?

H. I braid me meshes, and set hem¹¹ on a stow²⁸ i-happy²⁹, and

---

¹ fere, comrade. ² a. ³ boy. ⁴ driving (S.). ⁵ also. ⁶ likewise. ⁷ shouting (S.). ⁸ on. ⁹ certainly, I wis. ¹⁰ with (Ch.). ¹¹ them (Ch.). ¹² their (Ch.). ¹³ toil (S.). ¹⁴ dear, sir. ¹⁵ because. ¹⁶ am not (Ch.). ¹⁷ early. ¹⁸ leasow, pasture. ¹⁹ less for that, lest. ²⁰ for-, Germ. ver-, § 254, 2 (S.). ²¹ also I move their folds. ²² make. ²³ when. ²⁴ ploughman. ²⁵ unyokes (?). ²⁶ assign (Ch.). ²⁷ practice (Ch.). ²⁸ place (S.). ²⁹ fit.

i-tyht¹ hounds mine, that wild-deer² hi³ egg⁴, till-that-that hi³ come to the nets un-fore-show-edly⁵, that hi³ so be be-grined⁶, and I off-slay hem⁷ on⁸ the meshes.

T. Ne⁹ canst thou hunt but mid¹⁰ nets?

H. Yea, but¹¹ nets hunt I may.

T. How?

H. Mid¹⁰ swift hounds I be-take¹² wild-deer.²

T. Which wild-deer² swithest¹³ i-fangest¹⁴ thou?

H. I i-fang¹⁴ harts, and boars, and roebucks, and roes, and whilom hares.

T. Wert thou to day on hunting?

H. I nas¹⁵, forthat¹⁶ Sunday is, ac¹⁷ yester day I was on hunting.

T. What i-latchedst¹⁸ thou?

H. Twain harts and one boar.

T. How i-fangest¹⁴ thou hem⁷?

H. Harts I i-fang¹⁴ on⁸ nets, and boar I off-slew.

T. How wert thou dursty¹⁹ to-off-stick boar?

H. Hounds (be-)drove him to me, and I there, to-gainst²⁰ standing, ferly²¹ off-stuck him.

T. Swithy²² thristy²³ thou wert then?

H. Ne⁹ shall hunter fright-full be, forthat¹⁶ mis-like²⁴ wild-deer² won²⁵ in woods.

T. What dost thou by²⁶ thy hunting?

H. I sell²⁷ to-king so-what-so²⁸ I i-fo¹⁴, forthat¹⁶ I am hunter his.

T. What selleth²⁷ he thee?

H. He shrouds²⁹ me well and feeds, and whilom he selleth²⁷ me horse or badge³⁰, that the more lustily craft mine I be-go³¹.

---

6. Teacher and Fisher.

T. Which craft kenst thou?

F. I am fisher.

T. What (be-)gettest thou of thy craft?

F. Bi-live³², and shroud²⁹, and fee³³.

T. How i-fangst¹⁴ thou fishes?

F. I a-sty³⁴ my ship, and werp³⁵ meshes mine on⁸ ac³⁶, and angle I werp³⁵ and spirt-net³⁷, and so-what-so²⁸ hi³ i-haft³⁸, I nim³⁹.

T. What if it unclean fishes be?

---

¹ educate, train (S.). ² beasts. ³ they (P. P.). ⁴ pursue. ⁵ unexpectedly. ⁶ taken in a grin, or snare. ⁷ them (Ch.). ⁸ in. ⁹ not. ¹⁰ with (Ch.). ¹¹ without. ¹² catch. ¹³ most (Ch.). ¹⁴ take (S.). ¹⁵ was not (Ch.). ¹⁶ because. ¹⁷ but (P. P.). ¹⁸ took. ¹⁹ daring (S.). ²⁰ against (?). ²¹ suddenly (S.). ²² very (Ch.). ²³ bold (Orm.). ²⁴ unlike, various. ²⁵ live. ²⁶ with. ²⁷ give. ²⁸ whatsoever. ²⁹ clothes. ³⁰ ring, bracelet. ³¹ practice (Ch.). ³² victuals (P. P.). ³³ money. ³⁴ mount. ³⁵ throw (S.). ³⁶ water, river (S.). ³⁷ fishing-net (H.). ³⁸ catch (?). ³⁹ take.

tyhte hundâs mîne, þæt pildeôr hî êhtàn, ôđ-þæt-þe hî cumân tô þâm nettum unforesceâpôdlîce, þæt hî spâ beôn begrinôde, and ic ofsleâ hî on þâm maxum.

Lp. Ne canst þû huntian bûtan mid nettum?

H. Gea, bûtan nettum huntian ic mæg.

Lp. Hû?

H. Mid spiftum hundum ic betæce pildeôr.

Lp. Hpilce pildeôr spiđôst gefêhst þû?

H. Ic gefô heortâs, and bârâs, and rân, and râgan, and hpîlon haran.

Lp. Þære þû tô dæg on huntnôđe?

H. Ic næs, forþam sunnan dæg is, ac gystran dæg ic pæs on huntunge.

Lp. Hpæt gelæhtest þû?

H. Tpegen heortâs and ânne bâr.

Lp. Hû gefênge þû hî?

H. Heortâs ic gefêng on nettum, and bâr ic ofslôh.

Lp. Hû pære þû dyrstig ofstician bâr?

H. Hundâs bedrifon hine tô mê, and ic þær, tôgeânes standende, færlîce ofsticôde hine.

Lp. Spîđe þrîste þû pære þâ.

H. Ne sceal hunta forhtful pesan, forþam mislîce pildeôr puniađ on pudum.

Lp. Hpæt dêst þû be þînre huntunge?

H. Ic sylle cyninge spâ-hpæt-spâ ic gefô, forþam ic eom hunta his.

Lp. Hpæt sylđ hê þê?

H. Hû scrŷt mê pel and fêt, and hpîlum hê sylđ mê hors ođđe beâh, þæt þŷ lustlîcôr cræft mînne ic begange.

6. Teacher and Fisher.

Lp. Hpilcne cræft canst þû?

F. Ic eom fiscere.

Lp. Hpæt begytst þû of þînum cræfte?

F. Bigleofan, and scrûd, and feoh.

Lp. Hû gefêhst þû fiscâs?

F. Ic âstîge mîn scip, and peorpe max mîne on eâ, and angel ic peorpe and spyrtan, and spâ-hpæt-spâ hî gehæftađ, ic genime.

Lp. Hpæt gif hit unclêne fiscâs beôđ?

F. Ic þeorpe þá unclǽnan út, and genime mé clǽne tó mete.
Lp. Hpǽr cýpst þú fiscás þíne?
F. On ceastre.
Lp. Hpá bygð hí?
F. Ceasterpare. Ic ne mæg spá fela gefón spá-fela-spá ic mæg gesyllan.
Lp. Hpilce fiscás geféhst þú?
F. Ælás and hacodás, mynás and ælepútan, sceótan and lampredan, and spá-hpylce-spá on pætere spimmað.
Lp. For hpý ne fiscást þú on sǽ?
F. Hpílum ic dó, ac seldon, forþam micel répet mé is tó sǽ.
Lp. Hpæt féhst þú on sǽ?
F. Hǽringás and leaxás, merespín and styrian, ostran and crabban, musclan, pinepinclan, sǽcoccás, fage, and flóc, and lopystran, and fela spilces.
Lp. Pilt þú fón sumne hpæl?
F. Nic.
Lp. For hpý?
F. Forþam plihtlíc þing hit is gefón hpæl. Gebeorhlícre is mé faran tó eá mid scipe mínum, þænne faran mid manigum scipum on huntunge hranes.
Lp. For hpý spá?
F. Forþam leófre is mé gefón fisc þæne ic mæg ofsleán, þænne þe ná þæt án mé, ac eác spilce míne geféran mid áne slege hé mæg besencan odðe gecpylman.
Lp. And þeáh, manige gefóð hpælás, and ætberstað fréenessá, and micelne sceat þanon begitað.
F. Sóð þú segst, ac ic ne geþristige for módes mínes nýtenysse.

7. Teacher, Fowler, and Hunter.

Lp. Hpæt segst þú, fugelere? Hú bespíest þú fugelás?
Fug. On fela pisená ic bespíce fugelás; hpílum mid nettum, hpílum mid grinum, hpílum mid líme, hpílum mid hpistlunge, hpílum mid hafoce, hpílum mid treppan.
Lp. Hæfst þú hafoc?
Fug. Ic hæbbe.
Lp. Canst þú temian hí?
Fug. Geá, ic can. Hpæt sceoldon hí mé, bútan ic cúðe temian hí?

F. I werp¹ the unclean out, and i-nim² me clean to³ meat.
T. Where chopst⁴ thou fishes thine?
F. On Chester⁵.
T. Who buyeth hem⁶?
F. Chester-were⁷. I ne⁸ may so fele⁹ i-fon¹⁰ so-fele-so⁹ I may i-sell.
T. Which fishes i-fangst¹⁰ thou?
F. Eels and haked¹¹, minnows and eel-pouts, shot¹² and lampreys, and so-which-so¹³ on water swimmeth.
T. For why ne⁸ fishest thou on sea?
F. Whilom I do, ac¹⁴ seldom, forthat¹⁵ much rowing to-me is to sea.
T. What fangst¹⁰ thou on sea?
F. Herrings and laxes¹⁶, mere-swine¹⁷ and sturgeons, oysters and crabs, muscles, pinewincles, sea-cockles, fadge, and flowks, and lobsters, and fele⁹ of such.
T. Wilt thou fon¹⁰ some whale?
F. Not I.
T. For why?
F. Forthat plightly¹⁸ thing it is to-ifon¹⁰ whale. I-burg-lier¹⁹ is to-me to-fare²⁰ to ac²¹ mid²² ship mine, than to-fare²⁰ mid²² many ships a hunting of grampus.
T. For why so?
F. Forthat¹⁵ liefer²³ is to-me to-ifon¹⁰ fish that I may off-slay, than that no²⁴ that one²⁴ me, ac¹⁴ eke²⁵ such²⁵ my i-feres²⁶ mid²² one sley²⁷ he may (be-)sink *or* i-quell²⁸.
T. And though²⁹ many i-fo¹⁰ whales, and at-burst³⁰ freeness³¹ and much scot³² thence (be-)get.
F. Sooth thou sayest, ac¹⁴ I ne thristy³³ for mood's mine ne-wit-iness³⁴.

---

7. TEACHER, FOWLER, AND HUNTER.

T. What sayest thou, fowler? How be-swikest³⁵ thou fowls?
F. On fele⁹ wise³⁶ I be-swike³⁵ fowls; whilom with nets, whilom with grins, whilom with lime, whilom with whistling, whilom with hawk, whilom with trap.
T. Hast thou hawk?
F. I have.
T. Canst thou tame hem⁶?
F. Yea, I can. What should hi³⁷ me, but³⁸ I could tame hem⁶?

¹ throw (S.). ² take. ³ as, for. ⁴ sell. ⁵ city; compare *West-chester*. ⁶ them (Ch.). ⁷ Citizens; compare *were-wolf*. ⁸ not. ⁹ so many as. ¹⁰ take. ¹¹ pike. ¹² trout. ¹³ such as. ¹⁴ but (P. P.). ¹⁵ because. ¹⁶ salmon. ¹⁷ porpoise. ¹⁸ perilous (?). ¹⁹ safer, *iboruwen*, safe (S.). ²⁰ go. ²¹ river (S.). ²² with (Ch.). ²³ preferable. ²⁴ not only. ²⁵ likewise, also. ²⁶ comrades. ²⁷ blow (S.). ²⁸ kill. ²⁹ yet. ³⁰ escape (S.). ³¹ danger (?). ³² money. ³³ dare (compare adj., S.). ³⁴ dullness (?). ³⁵ catch. ³⁶ ways. ³⁷ they (profit) (P. P.). ³⁸ unless.

H. Sell[1] me a hawk.

F. I sell[1] lustliche[2] if thou sellest[1] me a swift hound. Which hawk wilt thou have, the more[3], whether-the[4] the less?

H. Sell[1] me the more[3].

T. How (a-)feedest thou hawks thine?

F. Hi[5] feed hem[6]-selves and me on winter, and on lent[7] I let hem[6] (at-)wind[8] to wood, and i-nim[9] me birds[10] on harvest, and tame hem[6].

T. And for why (for-)lettest thou the i-tamed (at-)wind[8] from thee?

F. For-that[11] I nill[12] feed hem[6] on summer, for-that[11] that hi[5] thraly[13] eat.

T. And many feed the i-tamed over summer, that eft[14] hi[5] *may*-have yare[15].

F. Yea, so hi[5] do, ac[16] I nill[12] oth[17] that one[18] derve[19] over hem[6], for-that[11] I can others, no[20] that one[18], ac[16] eke so-like many, i-fon[21].

---

8. Teacher and Merchant.

T. What sayest thou, monger[22]?

M. I say that behoove*full* I am ye[23] to-king, and aldermen, and wealthy, and all folks.

T. And how?

M. I (a-)sty[24] my ship mid[25] lasts[26] mine, and row over sea-like deals[27], and chop[28] my things, and buy things dear-worth[29], that on this land ne[30] be a-kenned[31], and I it to i-lead[32] you hither mid[25] mickle[33] plight[34] over sea, and whilom[35] forlideness[36] I thole[37] mid[25] loss of-all things mine, uneath[38] quick[39] at-bursting[40].

T. Which things (i-)leadest[32] thou to-us?

M. Palls[41] and silks, dear-worth[29] gems, and gold, selcouth[42] reef[43] and wort-i-mang[44], wine, and oil, elephant's bone, and maslin[45], *bronze*, and tin, sulphur, and glass, and of-the-like fele[46].

T. Wilt thou sell things thine here, all so[47] thou hem[6] i-broughtest there?

M. I nill[12]. What then me framed[48] i-derf[49] mine? Ac[16] I will hem[6] chop[28] here lovelier[50] than I buy there, that some i-strain[51] me I may-(be-)get, thence[52] I me (a-)feed, and my wife, and my son.

---

[1] give. [2] with pleasure (S.). [3] larger. [4] or (S.). [5] they (P. P.). [6] 'em, them (Ch.). [7] spring. [8] fly off (S.). [9] take. [10] young. [11] because. [12] will not. [13] very much (H.). [14] after. [15] ready, trained. [16] but (P. P.). [17] for (?). [18] alone. [19] toil (S.). [20] not that only, but likewise also many. [21] catch (S.). [22] merchant. [23] both (?). [24] ascend. [25] with (P. P.). [26] loads (Ch.). [27] parts, regions. [28] sell. [29] of great worth (S.). [30] not. [31] produced, kinded (S.). [32] bring to (S.). [33] much. [34] danger. [35] sometimes. [36] wreck (?). [37] suffer. [38] not easily. [39] alive. [40] escaping (S.). [41] purple cloth. [42] seldom seen, rare. [43] robes. [44] spices (?). [45] brass. [46] many (P.P.). [47] at the same price. [48] profited (S.). [49] toil (S.). [50] dearer (?). [51] gain (S.). [52] whence.

H. Syle mê ânne hafoc.

Fug. Ic sylle lustlîce, gif þû sylst mê ânne spiftne hund. Hpilcne hafoc pilt þû habban, þone mâran, hpæðer þe þone læssan?

H. Syle mê þone mâran.

Lp. Hû âfêst þû hafocâs þîne?

Fug. Hî fêdað hî selfe and mê on pintrâ, and on lencten ic læte hî ætpindan tô pudâ, and genime mê briddâs on hærfeste, and temige hî.

Lp. And for hpŷ forlætst þû þâ getemedan ætpindan fram þê?

Fug. Forþam ic nelle fêdan hî on sumerâ, forþam þe hî þearle etað.

Lp. And manige fêdað þû getemedan ofer sumor, þæt eft hî habban gearpe.

Fug. Gea, spâ hî dôð, ac ic nelle oð þæt ân deorfan ofer hî, forþam ic can ôðre, nâ þæt ânne, ac eâc spilce manige, gefôn.

---

8. Teacher and Merchant.

Lp. Hpæt segst þû, mangere?

M. Ic secge þæt behêfe ic eom ge cyninge, and ealdormannum and peligum, and eallum folce.

Lp. And hû?

M. Ic âstîge mîn scip mid hlæstum mînum, and rôpe ofer sælîce dælâs, and cŷpe mîne þing, and bycge þing deôrpyrðe, þâ on þissum lande ne beôð âcennede, and ic hit tôgelæde côp hider mid miclum plihte ofer sæ, and hpilum forlidenesse ic þolie mid lyrô ealrâ þingâ mînrâ, uneâðe epic ætberstende.

Lp. Hpilce þing gelædst þû ûs?

M. Pællâs and sîdan, deôrpyrðe gimmâs, and gold, seleûðe reâf, and pyrtgemang, pîn, and ele, ylpes bân, and mæsling, ær, and tin, spefel, and glæs, and þylces fela.

Lp. Pilt þû syllan þing þîne hêr, eal spâ þû hî gebohtest þær?

M. Ic nelle. Hpæt þænne mê fremôde gedeorf mîn? Ac ic pille hî cŷpan hêr luflîcôr þænne ic gebycge þær, þæt sum gestreôn mê ic begite, þanon ic mê âfêde, and mîn pîf, and mînne sunu.

9. Teacher and Shoemaker.

Lp. Þû, sceô-pyrhta, hpæt pyrcest þû ûs nytpyrðnesse?
S. Is pitodlîce cræft mîn behêfe þearle eôp, and neôdþearf.
Lp. Hû?
S. Ic bycge hŷdâ, and fel, and gearcie hî mid cræfte mînum, and pyrce of him gescŷ mislîces cynnes; spiftlerâs, and sceôs, leðer-hosan, and butericâs, bridel-þpangâs, and gerêdu, and flaxan, and higdifatu, spurleðeru, and hælftrâ, pusan, and fætelsâs, and nân côper nele oferpintran bûtan mînum cræfte.

10. Teacher and Salter.

Lp. Eâlâ, sealtere, hpæt ûs fremâð cræft þîn?
Sealt. Pearle fremâð cræft mîn eôp eallum: nân côper blisse brŷcð on gereordunge, oððe metê, bûtan cræft mîn gistlîðe him beô.
Lp. Hû?
Sealt. Hpilc mannâ peredum þurhbrŷcð mettum bûtan spæcce sealtes? Hpâ gefylð cleôfan his, oððe hêdernu, bûtan cræfte mînum? Efne, butergeþpeor ælc and cŷsgerun losað eôp, bûton ic hyrde ætpese eôp, þe ne furðon pyrtum côprum, bûtan mê, brûcað.

11. Teacher and Baker.

Lp. Hpæt segst þû, bæcere? Hpam fremâð cræft þîn, oððe hpæðer bûtan þê pê mâgon lif âdreôgan?
B. Gê mâgon pitodlîce þurh sum fæc bûtan mînum cræfte lif âdreôgan, ac nâ lange, ne tô pel; sôðlîce bûtan cræfte mînum ælc beôd æmtig bið gesepen, and bûtan hlâfe ælc mete tô plættan bið gehpyrfed. Ic heortan mannes gestrangie; ic mægen perâ com; and furðon lytlingâs nellað forbŷgean mê.

12. Teacher and Cook.

Lp. Hpæt seegað pê be coce? hpæðer pê beþurfon on ænigum cræfte his?
C. Gif gê mê ût-âdrîfað fram côprum gefêrscipe, gê etað pyrtâ

9. Teacher and Shoemaker.

T. Thou, shoe-wright, what workest thou us of nut-worth-ness[1]?

S. Is witterly[2] craft mine behoove*full* thraly[3] to-you, and need-tharf[4].

T. How?

S. I buy hides and fells, and yark[5] hem[6] mid[7] craft mine, and work of hem[6] (i-)shoes of mis-like[8] kind; swiftlers[9], and shoes, leather-hose, and bottles, bridle-thongs, and i-readies[10], and flasks, and *heedy*-fats[11], spur-leathers, and halters, purses and pouches, and none of you nill[12] over-winter but[13] my craft.

---

10. Teacher and Salter.

T. O lo, salter, what us frameth[14] craft thine?

S. Thraly[3] frameth[14] craft mine you all: none of-you bliss brooketh[15] on i-rerding[16], or meat[17], but[13] craft mine guestly[19] to-him be.

T. How?

S. Which of men wered[20] through-brooketh meats but[13] swack[21] of-salt? Who i-filleth cleve[22] his, or heed-erne[23], but[13] craft mine? Even[24], butter-thwer[25] each and cheese-i-runnet loseth to-you, but[13] I herd[26] at-be to-you, that[27] ne[28] forthen[29] worts[30] your, but[13] me, brook[15].

---

11. Teacher and Baker.

T. What sayest thou, baker? Whom frameth[14] craft thine, or whether but[13] thee we may life (a-)dree[31]?

B. Ye may witterly[2] through some fac[22] but[13] my craft life (a-)dree[31], ac[33] no[34] long ne[35] too[36] well; soothly[37] but[13] craft mine each bode[38] empty beeth[39] seen[35], and but[13] loaf each meat to wlating[40] beeth i-warped. I heart of-man i-strengthen; I main[41] of-were[42] am; and forthen[29] littlings[43] nill[44] for-bug[45] me.

---

12. Teacher and Cook.

T. What say we by[46] cook? Whether we be-tharf[47] in any *respect* craft his?

C. If ye me out-a-drive from your i-fere-ship[48], ye eat worts[30]

---

[1] usefulness (see *nut*, use, S.). [2] certainly (P.P.). [3] very much (H.). [4] needful (tharf=need, Ch.). [5] prepare (H.). [6] 'em, them (Ch.). [7] with (P.P.). [8] unlike, various (S.). [9] slippers. [10] trappings. [11] bath-buckets (?). [12] wish not to pass the winter. [13] without (S.). [14] profiteth (H.). [15] enjoyeth. [16] luncheon (?). [17] dinner. [18] unless. [19] hospitable. [20] sweet, fresh meats thoroughly enjoys (S.). [21] taste (?). [22] cellar (S.). [23] pantry. [24] aye. [25] churning (?). [26] keeper, preserver. [27] who, *i. e.*, you. [28] not. [29] furthermore (S.). [30] vegetables. [31] endure. [32] time (?). [33] but (P.P.). [34] not. [35] nor. [36] so. [37] in truth. [38] table (H.). [39] seems. [40] loathing (S.). [41] strength. [42] men; compare *were*-wolf. [43] children. [44] will not. [45] shun (S.). [46] about. [47] need (tharf=need, Ch.). [48] company (see i-fere, S.).

your green, and flesh-meats your raw, and ne[1] forthen[2] fat broth ye may but[3] craft mine have.

T. We ne[1] reck by[4] craft thine, ne[5] he[6] to-us need-tharf[7] is, for-that[8] we-selves may seethe the things that to seethe are, and brede[9] the things that to brede[9] are.

C. If ye for that me from-a-drive[10], that ye thus do, then be ye all thralls, and none of-you ne[1] beeth lord; and, though-whether[11] but[3] craft mine ye ne[1] eat.

13. TEACHER AND SCHOLAR.

T. O lo! thou monk, that me to speakest, even[12] I have a-found thee to-have good i-feres[13], and thraly[14] need-tharf[7]; and I ask[15] them.

S. I have smiths, iron-smiths, gold-smith, silver-smith, ore[16]-smith, tree-wright[17], and many other of-mis-like[18] crafts be-gangers[19].

T. Hast thou any wise i-thought-*full*[20] *one?*

S. I-wisly[21] I have. How may our gathering but[3] i-thinking[20] *one* be wissed[22]?

14. TEACHER, COUNSELOR, SMITH, AND OTHERS.

T. What sayest thou, Wise? Which craft to-thee is[23] i-thought[23] be-twixt[26] those further[24] *to be?*

C. I say to thee, to-me is i-thought[23] God's thewdom[25] between[26] those crafts eldership to-hold, so so it is (i-)read on gospel, Foremost seek riche[27] God's, and righteousness his, and those things all be to-i-eked[28] to-you.

T. And which to-thee is[23] i-thought[23] betwixt[26] world-crafts to-hold elderdom[29]?

C. Earth-tilth[30], forthat[8] the earthling[31] us all feeds.

The Smith sayeth:

Whence to-the earthling[31] sull-share[32] or coulter, that no gad hath but of craft mine? Whence fisher angle, or shoe-wright awl, or seamer needle? Nis[33] it of my (i-)work?

The I-thinking-*one* answereth:

Sooth, witterly[34], sayst thou; ac[35] to-all us liefer[36] is to-wick[37] mid[38] the earthling[31] than mid[38] thee; forthat[8] the earthling[31] selleth[39] us loaf and

---

[1] not. [2] furthermore (S.). [3] without (?). [4] care for. [5] nor. [6] it. [7] needful (tharf=need, Ch.). [8] because. [9] roast (S.). [10] drive from you. [11] whether or no, notwithstanding. [12] truly (?). [13] comrades (S.). [14] very (H.). [15] ask about them=who are they? [16] copper-smith. [17] carpenter. [18] unlike, various (S.). [19] practisers (?). [20] counselor (?) [21] certainly (Ch.). [22] guided (Ch.). [23] seems. [24] foremost. [25] service (S.). [26] betwixt, amongst. [27] kingdom (bishop-*ric*, H.). [28] added (?). [29] supremacy. [30] farming (Wycl.). [31] farmer. [32] plow-share. [33] is not (Ch.). [34] certainly (P. P.). [35] but (S.). [36] pleasanter, better. [37] reside, have a *wick* or house. [38] with (P. P.). [39] giveth, supplieth.

eôpre grêne, and flǽsc-mettâs côpre hreâpe, and ne furđon fæt broď gê mâgon bûtan cræfte mînum habban.

Lp. Đê ne rêcađ be cræfte þînum, ne hû ûs neôdþearf is, forþam þê selfe mâgon seôđan þâ þing þe tô sceôđenne sind, and brǽdan þâ þing þe tô brǽdenne sind.

C. Gif gê for þý mê fram-âdrîfađ, þæt gê þus dôn, þonne beô gê ealle þrǽlâs, and nân côper ne biđ hlâford; and, þeâh-hpæđere bûtan cræfte mînum gê ne etađ.

---

13. Teacher and Scholar.

Lp. Eâlâ, þû munuc, þe mê tô spricst, efne ic hæbbe âfandôd þê habban gôde geferan, and þearle neôdþearfe; and ic âhsie þâ.

Le. Ic hæbbe smiđâs, îsene-smiđâs, gold-smiđ, seolfor-smiđ, ârsmiđ, treôp-pyrhtan, and manige ôđre mislierâ cræftâ bîgengerâs.

Lp. Hæfst þû ænigne pîsne geþeahtan?

Le. Gepislîce ic hæbbe. Hû mæg ûre gegaderung bûtan geþeahtende beôn pîsôd?

---

14. Teacher, Counselor, Smith, and others.

Lp. Hpæt segst þû, Ƿîsa? Hpilc cræft þê is geþuht betpux þǽs furđra þesan?

G. Ic secge þê, mê is geþuht Godes þeôpdôm betpeoh þâs cræftâs ealdorscipe healdan, spâ spâ hit is gerǽd on godspelle, Fyrmest sêcead rîce Godes, and rihtpisnesse his, and þâs þing ealle beôđ tôgeýhte côp.

Lp. And hpilc þê is geþuht betpux porold-cræftâs healdan ealdordôm?

G. Eorđ-tilđ, forþam se yrđling ûs ealle fêt.

Se Smiđ segeđ:

Hpanon þam yrđlinge sulh-scear ođđe culter, þe nâ gade hæfđ, bûton of cræfte mînum? Hpanon fiscere angel, ođđe sceô-pyrhtan æl, ođđe seâmere nǽdl? Nis hit of mînum gepeorce?

Se Geþeahtend andsperâđ:

Sôđ pitodlîce segst þû; ac eallum ûs leôfre is pîcian mid þam yrđlinge þænne mid þê; forþam se yrđling sylđ ûs hlâf and drenc: þû, hƿæt sylst þû ûs on smiððan þînre, bûtan îsene fȳr-spearcan, and spêgingâ beâtendrâ slecgeâ, and blâƿendrâ byligâ?

Se Treôp-pyrhta segeð:

Hƿilc côper ne notâð cræfte mînô; þonne hûs, and mislîce fatu, and scipu côp eallum ic ƿyrce?

Se Smið andƿyrt:

Eâlâ treôp-pyrhta, for hƿȳ spâ spricst þû, þonne ne furðon ân þyrl bûtan cræfte mînum þû ne miht dôn?

Se Geþeahtend segeð:

Eâlâ geferan and gôde ƿyrhtan! Uton tôƿeorpan hƿætlîcôr þûs geflitu, and sî sib and geþƿǣrness betƿeoh ûs, and fremige ânrâ gehƿylc ôðrum on cræfte his, and geþƿǣriân symble mid þam yrðlinge, þǣr þe bigleofan ûs, and fôdor horsum ûrum habbað; and þis geþeaht ic sylle eallum ƿyrhtum, þæt ânrâ gehƿylc cræft his geornlîce begange; forþam se þe cræft his forlǣt, hê byð forlǣten fram þam cræfte. Spâ hƿæðer þû sî, spâ mæssepreôst, spâ munuc, spâ ceorl, spâ cempa, begâ þê selfne on þisum: beô þæt þû eart, forþam micel hȳnd and sceamu hit is men, nelle ƿesan þæt þe hê is, and þæt þe hê ƿesan sceal.

---

15. Teacher and Scholar.

Lр. Eâlâ cild, hû côp lîcað þeôs sprǣc?

Lc. Ʋel heô lîcað ûs, ac þearle deôplîce þû spricst, and ofer mǣðe ûre þû forðtȳhð þâ sprǣce; ac sprec ûs æfter ûrum andgite, þæt ƿê mǣgen understandan þâ þing þe þû spricst.

Lр. Ic âhsige côp for hƿȳ spâ geornlîce leornige gê?

Lc. Forþam þê nellað ƿesan spâ stunte nȳtenu, þâ nân þing ƿitað bûtan gærs and ƿæter.

Lр. And hƿæt ƿille gê?

Lc. Ʋê ƿillað ƿesan ƿîse.

Lр. In hƿilcum ƿîsdôme? Ʋille gê ƿesan prætige, oððe þûsendhiƿe, on leâsungum lytige, on sprǣcum gleâplîce, hindergeâƿe, ƿel sprecende and yfele þencende, sƿǣsum ƿordum underþeôdde, fâcen piðinnan tȳdrende, spâ spâ byrgels, mettum oferƿepeorce, piðinnan ful stencê?

drink: thou, what sellest[1] thou us in smithy thine, but iron fire-sparks, and sweying[2] of-beating sledges, and of-blowing bellows?

The Tree-wright[3] sayeth:

Which of-you ne[4] noteth[5] craft mine; then[6] house, and mis-like[7] fats[8], and ships for-you all I work?

The Smith anwordeth[9]:

O lo, tree-wright[3], for why so speakest thou, then[6] ne[5] forthen[10] one thirl[11] but[12] craft mine thou ne[4] might do?

The I-thinking[13] sayeth:

O lo, i-feres[14] and good wrights! Wite-we[15] to-warp[16] whatliker[17] those i-flites[18], and *be* sib[19] and i-thwerness[20] betweohs[21] us, and frame[22] of-ones[23] i-which[22] to-other in craft his, and i-thwer[24] symble[25] mid[26] the earthling[27], there[28] we belive[29] for-us, and fodder for horses our have; and this i-thought I sell[1] to all wrights, that of-ones[30] i-which[30] craft his yernliche[31] be-go[32]; forthat that[33] that craft his for-letteth[34], he beeth for-let[34] from the craft. So whether[35] thou *be*, so[36] mass-priest, so monk, so churl, so kemp[37], be-go[32] thee self on this: be that thou art, forthat mickle hinth[38] and shame it is to-man, nill-he[39] *to-be* that that he is, and that that he be shall[40].

15. Teacher and Scholar.

T. O lo, child, how to-you liketh[41] this speech?

S. Well *she*[42] liketh[41] to-us, ac[43] thraly[44] deeply thou speakest, and over meeth[45] our thou forth-tuggest the speech; ac[43] speak to-us after our an-git[46], that we may understand the things that thou speakest.

T. I ask you for why so yernliche[31] learn ye?

S. Forthat we nill[47] *to-be* so-as stunt[48] neat[49], that none thing wit[50] but grass and water.

T. And what will ye?

S. We will *to-be* wise.

T. In which wisdom? Will ye be pretty[51], or thousand-hued, in leasings[52] litty[53], in speeches gleve[54], hinder-yeepe[55], well speaking and evil thinking, to-sweet words under-theed[56], faken[57] within tudring[58], so so[36] buryel[59], with meted[60] over-i-work, within full with-stench?

---

[1] give. [2] sounding (P. P.). [3] carpenter. [4] not. [5] useth (S.). [6] since. [7] unlike, various. [8] vessels, utensils. [9] answers (H.). [10] furthermore (S.). [11] hole; compare nos-*tril*. [12] without. [13] counselor (?). [14] comrades (S.). [15] go we=let us (S.). [16] throw away (S.). [17] very promptly (S.). [18] strifes (S.). [19] peace. [20] concord (?). [21] among (Ch.). [22] aid (H.). [23] each one the other. [24] agree (?). [25] always (?). [26] with (P. P.). [27] farmer. [28] with whom. [29] victuals (P. P.). [30] each one. [31] earnestly (S.). [32] practice (S.). [33] he. [34] let go, abandon (Ch.). [35] whatever. [36] as, for example. [37] champion. [38] loss (S.). [39] if he will not. [40] ought. [41] pleaseth (Ch.). [42] the speech. [43] but (S.). [44] very (H.). [45] age (S.). [46] understanding (?). [47] will not. [48] stupid. [49] cattle. [50] know. [51] crafty. [52] lies. [53] cunning, nimble (H.). [54] clever (S.). [55] sly (yeepe, cunning, P. P.). [56] addicted (?). [57] deceit (S.). [58] begetting (S.). [59] sepulchre (S.). [60] painted (S.).

S. We nill[1] so *to-be* wise, forthat he nis[2] wise that mid[3] dydring[4] him self biswiketh[5].

T. Ac[6] how will ye?

S. We will to-be bilewit[7], but[8] likening[9], and wise, that we bow from evil, and do good; yet though-whether[10] deeplier mid[3] us thou smeest[11] than eld[12] our anfon[13] may; ac[6] speak to-us after our i-wonts not so deeply.

T. I do all-so[14] ye bid. Thou, knave[15], what didst thou to day?

S. Many things I did. On this night, then-then[16] knell[17] I i-heard, I arose off my bed, and yode[18] to church, and sang uht-song[19] mid[3] i-brothers; after that we sang by all-hallows, and day-red-ly[20] love-songs[21], after these, prime, and seven psalms mid[3] litanies, and capital mass; sithen[22] undern-tide, and did mass by day; after these we sung midday, and ate, and drunk, and slept, and eft we arose, and sung nones, and now we are here afore thee, yare[23] to-i-hear what thou to us may say.

T. When will ye sing even, or night-song?

S. Then[16] it time be.

T. Wert thou to day (be-)swinged[24]?

S. I nas[25], forthat warily I me held.

T. And how thine i-feres[26]?

S. What me askest thou by that? I ne[27] dare ope to-thee digels[28] our. Of-ones[29] i-which[29] wots if he swinged[24] was or no.

T. What eatest thou a day?

S. Yet flesh-meats I brook[30], forthat child I am under yerde[31] *living*[32].

T. What more eatest thou?

S. Worts, and eggs, fish, and cheese, butter, and beans, and all clean things I eat mid mickle thanking.

T. Swithy[33] wax-yerne[34] art thou, then thou all things eatest that thee to-forn i-set *are*.

S. I ne[27] am so mickle swallower, that I all kinds of meats on one i-rerding[34] eat may.

T. Ac[6] how.

S. I brook[30] whilom these meats, and whilom others mid[3] soberness, so so is-deft for-a-monk, not with over-*eating*, forthat I am none glutton.

T. And what drinkest thou?

S. Ale, if I have, or water, if I have-not ale.

---

[1] will not. [2] is not (Ch.). [3] with (P. P.). [4] illusion, diddling (?). [5] deceiveth (P. P.). [6] but (S.). [7] gentle (S.). [8] without. [9] hypocrisy (?). [10] whether or no. [11] scrutinizest (?). [12] age. [13] receive (S.). [14] just as. [15] boy. [16] when. [17] bell. [18] went. [19] early morning (S.). [20] dawn (S.). [21] *lof*, praise, lauds (S.). [22] since. [23] ready. [24] whipped. [25] was not. [26] comrades (S.). [27] not. [28] secrets (S.). [29] each one. [30] use. [31] rod, yard. [32] perhaps akin to *drudging*. [33] very (Ch.). [34] greedy (?). [35] repast (?).

Le. Dû nellað spâ pesan pîse, forþam hê nis pîs, þe mid dy-drunge hine selfne bespîcð.

Lp. Ac hû pille gê?

Le. Dê pillað beôn hilepite, bûtan lîcetunge, and pîse, þæt pê bûgen fram yfele, and dôn gôd; git þeâh-hpæðere deôplîcôr mid ûs þû smeâgest þænne yld ûre anfôn mæge; ac sprec ûs æfter ûrum gepunum næs spâ deôplîce.

Lp. Ic dô ealspâ gê biddað. Þû, cnapa, hpæt dydest þû tô dæg?

Le. Manige þing ic dyde. On þisse nihte, þâþâ cnyl ic gehŷrde, ic ârâs of mînum bedde, and côde tô cyricean, and sang uht-sang mid gebrôðrum; æfter þâ pê sungon be callum hâlgum, and dægrêdlîce lofsangâs; æfter þissum, prîm, and seofon scalmâs mid letanium, and capitol-mæssan; siððan underntîde, and dydon mæssan be dæge; æfter þissum pê sungon middæg, and æton, and druncon, and slêpon, and eft pê ârison, and sungon nôn, and nû pê sind hêr ætforan þê, gearpe gehŷran hpæt þû ûs secge.

Lp. Hpænne pille gê singan æfen, oððe niht-sang?

Le. Þonne hit tîma bið.

Lp. Þære þû tô dæg bespungen?

Le. Ic næs, forþam pærlîce ic mê heôld.

Lp. And hû þîne geferan?

Le. Hpæt mê âhsâst þû be þam? Ic ne dear yppan þê dêglu ûre. Ânrâ gehpilc pât gif hê bespungen pæs oððe nâ.

Lp. Hpæt itst þû on dæg?

Le. Git flæsc-mettum ic brûce, forþam cild ic com under gyrde drohtniende.

Lp. Hpæt mâre itst þû?

Le. Dyrtâ, and ægru, fisc, and cêse, buteran, and beânâ, and ealle clæne þing ic ete mid micelre þancunge.

Lp. Spîðe paxgeorn eart þû, þonne þû ealle þing itst þe þê tôforan gesette sind.

Le. Ic ne com spâ micel spelgere, þæt ic ealle cyn mettâ on ânre gercordunge etan mæge.

Lp. Ac hû?

Le. Ic brûce hpîlum þissum mettum, and hpîlum ôðrum mid sŷfernesse, spâ spâ dafenâð munuce, næs mid oferhropse, forþam ic com nân glûto.

Lp. And hpæt drincst þû?

Le. Ealu, gif ic hæbbe, oððe pæter, gif ic næbbe ealu.

Lp. Ne drincst þû pîn?

Le. Ic ne eom spâ spêdig þæt ic mæge bycgan mê pîn; and pîn nis drenc cildâ, ne dysigrâ, ac ealdrâ and pîsrâ.

Lp. Hpær slæpst þû?

Le. On slæp-erne mid gebrôðrum.

Lp. Hpâ âpecð þê tô uht-sange?

Le. Hpîlum ic gehŷre cnyl, and ic ârîse; hpîlum lâreôp mîn âpecð mê stîðlîce mid gyrde.

Lp. Eâlâ gê gôde cildru, and pynsume leorneras, eôp manað eôper lâreôp þæt gê hŷrsumiän godcundum lârum, and þæt gê healdân eôp selfe ænlîce on ælcere stôpe. Gâð þeâplîce, þonne gê gehŷrân cyricean bellan, and gâð intô cyricean, and âbûgað eâdmôdlîce tô hâlgum pefodum, and standað þeâplîce, and singað ânmôdlîce, and gebiddað for eôprum synnum, and gâð ût bûtan hygeleâste tô clûstre, oððe tô leornunge.

T. Ne[1] drinkest thou wine?

S. I ne[1] am so speedy[2] that I may buy me wine; and wine nis[3] drink of-children, ne[4] dizzy[5], ac[6] of-old and wise.

T. Where sleepest thou?

S. On sleep-erne[7] mid i-brothers.

T. Who awaketh thee to uht-song[8]?

S. Whilom I hear knell[9], and I arise; whilom lore*master* mine awakes me stithly[10] mid[11] yerde[12].

T. O lo, ye good childer[13], and winsome learners, you moneth[14] your lore*master* that ye hersumen[15] godcund[16] lores[17], and that ye hold you selves anlike[18] in each stow[19]. Go thewly[20], then[21] ye i-hear church's bells, and go into church, and (a-)bow edmodly[22] to holy *altars*, and stand thewly[20], and sing one-mood-ly[23], and i-bid[24] for your sins, and go out but[25] heedlessness to cloister or to learning[26].

---

[1] not. [2] rich. [3] is not (Ch.). [4] nor. [5] foolish. [6] but (S.). [7] *erne*, room. [8] early morning service (S.). [9] bell. [10] harshly (S.). [11] with (P. P.). [12] rod, yard. [13] (Ch.). [14] admonisheth (S.). [15] obey (S.). [16] divine (S.). [17] precepts. [18] elegantly (onlîche, S.). [19] place (S.). [20] becomingly: see *thews*, customs. [21] when. [22] humbly (S.). [23] with one mind. [24] pray. [25] without. [26] gymnasium.

ANGLO-SAXON CHRONICLE.

Brytene îgland is ehta hund mîlâ lang, and tpâ hund mîlâ brâd; and hêr sind on þam îgland fîf geþeôdu, Englisc, Bryttisc, Scottisc, Pihtisc and Bôclæden. Ǣrest pêron bûend þises landes Bryttâs; þâ cômon of Armorica, and gesǣton sûðanpearde Brytene ǣrest. Pâ gelamp hit þæt Pihtâs cômon sûðan of Sciððian, mid langum scipum, nâ manegum; and þâ cômon ǣrest on norð Ybernian up, and þâ cpǣdon þâ Scottâs, "Ðê piton ôðer îgland hêr be eâstan, þǣr gê mâgon eardian, gif gê pillað; and gif hpâ eôp piðstent, pê eôp fultumiað." Pâ fêrdon þâ Pihtâs, and geférdon þis land norðanpeard.

Pâ gelamp hit ymbe geârâ ryne þæt Scottâ sum dǣl gepât of Ybernian on Brytene, and þæs landes sumne dǣl ge-eôdon.

Sixtigum pintrum ǣr þam þe Crist pǣre âcenned, Gaius Iûlius se câsere ǣrest Rômânâ Brytenland gesôhte; and Bryttâs mid gefeohtô cnysede, and hî oferspîdde. Pâ flugon þâ Bryttâs tô þâm pudu-pêstenum, and se câsere ge-eôde pel manige heáh burh mid miclum gepinne, and eft gepât intô Galpalum.

A.D. 47. Hêr Claudius ôðer Rômânâ cyningâ Brytenland gesôhte, and þone mǣstan dǣl þæs îglandes on his gepeald onfêng. Pâ fêng Nero tô rîce æfter Claudie, se æt neâhstan forlêt Brytene îgland for his uncâfscipê.

A.D. 167. Hêr Eleutherius on Rôme onfêng bisceopdôme. Tô þam Lûcius Brytene cyning sende stafâs, and bæd fulpihtes; and hê him sôna sende; and þâ Bryttâs punôdon on rihtum geleâfan ôð Dioclitiânes rîce.

A.D. 189. Sevêrus fêrde mid herê on Brytene, and mid gefeohtê geeôde þæs îglandes micelne dǣl; and þâ hê hine forgyrde mid dîcê and mid eorðpeallê fram sǣ tô sǣ. Hê rîcsôde seofontŷne geâr, and þâ geendôde on Eoferpîc.

A.D. 381. Hêr Gotan tôbræcon Rômeburh, and næfre siððan Rômâne ne rîcsôdon on Brytene. Hî rîcsôdon on Brytene feôper hund pintrâ, and hund-seofontig pintrâ siððan Gaius Iûlius þæt land ǽrest gesôhte.

A.D. 443. Hêr sendon Brytpalâs ofer sǽ tô Rôme, and heom fultumes bǽdon pið Pihtâs; ac hî þǽr næfdon nânne, forþam þe Rômâne fyrdôdon pið Ætlan Hunâ cyninge. And þâ sendon hî tô Anglum, and Angelcynnes æðelingâs þæs ilcan bǽdon.

A.D. 449. Hêr Hengest and Horsa fram Pyrtgeorne gelaðôde, Bryttâ cyninge, gesôhton Brytene Bryttum tô fultume. Hî cômon mid þrîm langum scipum. Se cyning geaf heom land on sûðan-eâstan þissum lande, pið þam þe hî sceoldon feohtan pið Pyhtâs. Hî þâ fuhton pið Pyhtâs, and sige hæfdon spâ-hpǽr-spâ hî cômon. Hî þâ sendon to Angle, and hêton sendan heom mâre fultum; and þâ cômon þâ men of þrîm mǽgðum Germânie,—of Eald-Seaxum, of Anglum, of Iôtum.

Of Iôtum cômon Cantpare, and Pihtpare, and þæt cyn on Pest-Seaxum þe man nû git hêt Iôtenâ cyn. Of Eald-Seaxum cômon Eâst-Seaxe, Sûð-Seaxe, and Pest-Seaxe. Of Angle, se â siððan stôd pêste betpix Iôtum and Seaxum, cômon Eâst-Angle, Middel-Angle, Mearce, and calle Norðhymbre.

Heorâ heretogan pǽron tpegen gebrôðru Hengest and Horsa, Pihtgilses sunâ; Pihtgils pæs Pitting, Pitta Pecting, Pecta Pô-dening: fram þam Pôdne âpôc eal ûre cynecyn, and Sûðanhym-brâ eâc.

A.D. 455. Hêr Hengest and Horsa fuhton pið Pyrtgeorne þam cyninge. Horsan man þǽr ofslôh; and æfter þam Hengest fêng tô rîce, and Æsc his sunu. Æfter þam Hengest and Æsc fuhton pið Pealâs, and genâmon unârîmedlîcu herereâf; and þâ Pealâs flugon þâ Engle spâ fŷr.

A.D. 488. Hêr Æsc fêng tô rîce, and pæs feôper and tpêntig pintrâ Cantparâ cyning.

A.D. 495. Hêr cômon tpegen ealdormen on Brytene, Cerdîc and Cynrîc his sunu, mid fîf scipum, and on þam ilcan dæge fuhton pið Pealâs.

A.D. 519. Hêr Cerdíc and Cynríc Ƿest-Seaxená ríce onfêngon, and siððan rícsôdon Ƿest-Seaxená cynebearn of þam dæge. Æfter þam hí gefuhton pið Bryttâs, and genâmon Ƿihte îgland.

A.D. 534. Hêr Cerdíc forðfêrde, and Cynríc his sunu fêng tô ríce, and rícsôde forð six and tpêntig pintrâ.

A.D. 538. Hêr sunne âþýstrôde feôpertŷne dagum êr calende Martii fram ǽrmorgene ôð undern.

A.D. 540. Hêr sunne âþýstrôde on tpelftan calendes Iúlii, and steorran hí æteôpdon fulneâh healfe tîd ofer undern.

A.D. 560. Hêr Ceâpliu ríce onfêng on Ƿest-Seaxum.

A.D. 565. Hêr Columba mæsse-preôst côm tô Pyhtum, and hí gecyrde tô Cristes geleâfan. Hí sind pærterás be norðum môrum, and heorâ cyning him gesealde þæt îgland þe man Iî nemneð. Þǽr se Columba getimbrôde mynster. Þâ stôpe habbað nû git his yrfe-peardâs. Sûð-Pyhtâs pǽron miclê ǽr gefullôde; heom bodôde fulpiht Ninna bisceop, se pæs on Rôme gelǽred, þæs cyrice is æt Hpîterne.

A.D. 596. Hêr Grêgorius pâpa sende tô Brytene Augustînum mid pel manegum munucum, þe Godes pord Englâ þeôde godspellôdon.

A.D. 601. Hêr sende Grêgorius pel manige godcunde lâreôpâs Augustîne tô fultume, and betpeônum þâm pæs Paulînus. Paulînus bisceop gehpyrfde tô Criste Eâdpine Norðhymbrâ cyning.

A.D. 604. Hêr Eâst-Seaxe onfêngon geleâfan and fulpihtes bæd under Mellite bisceope, and Sǽbrihte cyninge, þone Æðelberht Cantparâ cyning gesette þǽr tô cyninge.

A.D. 606. Hêr forðfêrde Grêgorius pâpa, and hêr Æðelfrið lǽdde his ferde tô Legaceastre, and þǽr ofslôh unrîm Ƿalenâ; and spâ pearð gefylled Augustînes pîtegung þe hê cpæð, Gif Dealás nellað sibbe pið ûs, hí sculon æt Seaxenâ handâ forpurðan. Þǽr man slôh eâc tpâ hund preôstâ, þâ cômon þider þæt hí sceoldon gebiddan for Ƿalenâ here.

A.D. 611. Hêr Cynegils fêng tô rîce on Þest-Seaxum, and heóld ân and þrittig pintrâ, and hê ǽrest Þest-Seaxenâ cyningâ pæs gefullôd. Byrînus bodôde ǽrest Þest-Seaxum fulpiht. Hê côm þider be Honóries pordum þæs pâpan, and hê þǽr pæs bisceop ôđ his lîfes ende.

A.D. 635. Hêr Cynegils pæs gefullôd from Byrîne in Dorceceastre.

A.D. 642. Hêr Cênpealh, Cynegilses sunu, fêng tô Þest-Seaxenâ rîce, and heóld ân and þrittig pintrâ.

A.D. 645. Hêr Cênpealh cyning pæs âdrifen of his rîce fram Pendan cyninge, forþam hê his speostor forlêt; and hê pæs on Eâst-Anglum þreô geâr on prǽce.

A.D. 646. Hêr Cênpealh pæs gefullôd.

A.D. 658. Hêr Cênpealh gefeaht piđ Þealàs, and hî geflŷmde ôđ Pedridan.

A.D. 664. Hêr sunne âþŷstrôde on þam forman Prîmilces, and côm micel manepealm on Brytene îgland, and on þam epealme forđfêrde Tuda bisceop; and Earcenbriht Cantparâ cyning forđfêrde, and Colman mid his gefêrum fôr tô his cŷđđe; and se arcebisceop Deusdedit forđfêrde.

A.D. 672. Hêr forđfêrde Cênpealh, and Seaxburh his epên rîcsôde ân geâr æfter him.

A.D. 674. Hêr fêng Æscpine tô rîce on Þest-Seaxum. Hê pæs Cênfûsing; Cênfûs Cênferđing; Cênferđ Cûđgilsing; Cûđgils Ceôlpulfing; Ceôlpulf Cynrîcing.

A.D. 676. Æscpine forđfêrde and Centpine fêng tô rîce, se pæs Cynegilsing. Hê geflŷmde Brytpealàs ôđ sǽ and rîcsôde nigon geâr.

A.D. 678. Hêr ætŷpde se steorra þe man clypâđ comêtan, and scân þrî mônđâs ælcê morgenê spilce sunnebeâm.

A.D. 685. Hêr Ceadpalla ongan æfter ríce pinnan. Se Ceadpalla pæs Cênbryhting; Cênbryht Ceadding; Ceadda Cûding; Cûđa Ceâplîning; Ceâplîn Cynrícing. Mûl pæs Ceadpallan brôđer. Pŷ ilcan geârê peard on Brytene blôdig rên, and meolc and butere purdon gepended tô blôde.

A.D. 686. Hêr Mûl and Ceadpalla Cent and Piht forhergôdon.

A.D. 687. Hêr Mûl peard on Cent forbærned, and þŷ geârê Ceadpalla eft forhergôde Cent.

A.D. 688. Hêr fôr Ceadpalla tô Rôme, and fulpiht onfêng æt Sergie þam pâpan, and se pâpa hine hêt Petrus, and hê siđđan ymbe seofon niht fordfêrde under Cristes clâđum, and þŷ ilcan geârê Ine fêng tô Pest-Seaxenâ ríce.

A.D. 693. Cantpare geþingôdon pid Ine, and him gescaldon þrittig þûsend sceattâ tô cynebôte, forþam þe hí Mûl his brôđer forbærndon. Ine getimbrôde þæt mynster æt Glæstingabyrig, and hê rícsôde seofon and þrittig pintrâ, and siđđan hê fêrde tô Rôme, and þær punôde ođ his ende-dæg.

A.D. 726. Hêr Æđelheard fêng to Pest-Seaxenâ ríce, Ines mæg; and heôld feôpertŷne geâr.

A.D. 729. Hêr comêta se steorra hine ætŷpde, and se hâlga Ecgbyrht fordfêrde.

A.D. 733. Hêr sunne aþŷstrôde, and peard eall þære sunnan trendel spilce speart scild; and Acca pæs âdrifen of bisceopdôm.

A.D. 734. Hêr pæs se môna spilce hê pære mid blôđe begoten, and fordfêrde Tâtpine arcebisceop, and eâc Bêda.

A.D. 740. Hêr fordfêrde Æđelheard cyning, and fêng Cûdrêd his mæg tô Pest-Seaxenâ ríce, and heôld sixtŷne pintrâ, and heardlîce hê gepan pid Æđelbald, Mearcenâ cyning, and pid Pealâs.

A.D. 744. Hêr steorran fôron spíđe scotiende, and Pilfrid se geonga, se pæs bisceop on Eoforpíc, fordfêrde.

A.D. 754. Cūđrōd forđférde, and Sigebriht his mǣg fēng tō Ꝥest-Seaxenā ríce, and heóld ān geār; and Cynepulf and Ꝥest-Seaxenā pitan benāmon Sigebriht his mǣg his ríces for unrihtum dǣdum. And se Cynepulf oft mid miclum gefeohtum feaht pið Brytpealās.

And ymb ān and þrittig pintrā þæs þe hē ríce hǣfde, hē polde ādrǣfan ūt ānne æđeling, se pæs Cyneheard hāten, and pæs Sigebrihtes brōđer. Þā geāhsōde hē þone cyning lytle perode on píf-cȳđđe on Merantūne, and hine þǣr berād, and þone būr ūtan beeōdon, ǣr hine þā men onfundon, þe mid þam cyninge pǣron. Þā ongeat se cyning þæt, and hē on þā duru eōde, and þā unheānlíce hine perōde, ōđ hē on þone æđeling lōcōde; and þā ūtrǣsde on hine, and hine miclum gepundōde. And hí ealle on þone cyning feohtende pǣron ōđ þæt hí hine ofslægenne hǣfdon.

Þā on þæs pífes gebǣrum onfundon þæs cyninges þegnās þā unstilnesse, and þider urnon, spā-hpile-spā þonne gearo peard hrađōst. And heorā se æđeling ǣghpilcum feorh and feoh beād; and heorā nǣnig þicgan nolde, ac hí simle feohtende pǣron, ōđ hí ealle lǣgon būtan ānum Brytiscum gísle, and hē spíđe gepundōd pæs.

Þā on morgene gehȳrdon þæt þæs cyninges þegnās þe him beǣftan pǣron, þæt se cyning ofslægen pæs, þā ridon hí þider, and his caldorman Osríc and Þígferđ his þegn; and þone æđeling on þǣre byrig mētton. And beād hē heom heorā āgenne dōm feōs and landes, gif hí him þæs ríces ūđon; and heom cȳđde, þæt heorā mǣgās him mid pǣron, þā þe him fram noldon. And þā cpǣdon hí, þæt heom nǣnig mǣg leōfra nǣre þonne heorā hlāford, and hí nǣfre his banan folgian noldon.

And hí þā ymb þā geatu feohtende pǣron, ōđ þæt hí þǣr inne fulgon, and þone æđeling ofslōgon, and þā men þe mid him pǣron, ealle būtan ānum.

Se Cynepulf rícsōde ān and þrittig pintrā, and his líc liged on Ꝥintanceastre, and þæs æđelinges on Axanmiustre.

A.D. 757. Hēr Eādberht Norđhymbrā cyning fēng tō scǣre.

A.D. 761. Hēr pæs se micela pinter.

A.D. 773. Hēr ōdȳpde reād Cristes mǣl on heofenum æfter sunnan setlgange, and pundorlíce nǣdran pǣron gesepene on Sūđ-Seaxenā lande.

A.D. 784. Hêr onfêng Beorhtrîc Ƿest-Seaxenâ ríce, and hê rícsôde sixtŷne geâr: and on his dagum cômon êrest scipu Norđmannâ of Heređalande.

A.D. 785. Hêr pæs geflitfullic synođ.

A.D. 793. Hêr pêron rêđe forebêcna cumene,—þæt pêron ormete þodenâs and ligræscâs, and fŷrene dracan pêron gesepene on þam lyfte fleôgende. Pâm tâcnum sôna fyligde micel hunger, and earmlíce hêđenrâ mannâ hergung âdiligôde Godes cyrican in Lindisfarena-eâ þurh reâflâc and mansliht.

A.D. 800. Hêr pæs se môna âþŷstrôd on þêre ôđre tíde on nihte on þone scofonteôđan calendes Februâries; and Beorhtrîc cyning forđfêrde, and Ecgbryht fêng tô Ƿest-Seaxenâ ríce.
Hine hæfđe êr Offa Mearcenâ cyning and Beorhtrîc Ƿest-Seaxenâ cyning ût âflŷmed þrî geâr of Angelcynnes lande on Francland, êr hê cyning pêre; and for þŷ fultumôde Beorhtrîc Offan, þŷ þe hê hæfđe his dôhtor him tô cpêne.

A.D. 823. Hêr Ecgbryht and Beornpulf Mearcenâ cyning fuhton on Ellendûne, and Ecgbriht sige nâm. Pâ sende hê Æđelpulf his sunu of þêre fyrde and Ealbstân his bisceop and Ƿulfheard his ealdorman tô Cent miclê perodê, and hí Baldred þone cyning norđ ofer Temese âdrifon; and Cantpare heom tô cyrdon, and Sûđrige, and Sûđ-Seaxe, and Eâst-Seaxe; and þŷ ilcan geârê Eâst-Englâ cyning and seô þeôd gesôhton Ecgbriht cyning heom tô friđe and tô mundboran for Mearcenâ ege.

A.D. 827. Hêr geeôde Ecgbriht cyning Mearcenâ ríce, and eal þæt be sûđan Humbre pæs; and hê pæs se eahtođa cyning þe Brytenpealda pæs. Ærest pæs Ælle þe þus micel ríce hæfđe; se æftera pæs Ceâplîn, Ƿest-Seaxenâ cyning; se þridda pæs Æđelbriht, Cantparâ cyning; se feorđa pæs Râdpald, Eâst-Englâ cyning; se fífta pæs Eâdpine, Norđanhymbrâ cyning; sixta pæs Ospald, þe æfter him rícsôde; scofođa pæs Ospio, Ospaldes brôđer; eahtođa pæs Ecgbriht.

A.D. 837. Hêr Ecgbriht cyning forđfêrde, and fêng Æđelpulf Ecgbrihting tô Ƿest-Seaxenâ ríce. On his dagum cômon þâ Deniscan on Brytene. And se cyning and his ealdormen mid

Dorsǽtum and mid Somersǽtum gefuhton pið hǽðenne here geond stôpa; and þǽr peard manig man ofslægen on gehpæðere hand.

A.D. 853. Hêr sende Æðelpulf cyning Ælfrêd his sunu tô Rôme. Pâ pæs domne Leo pâpa on Rôme, and hê hine tô cyninge gehâlgôde, and hine him tô bisceop-sunâ genam.

A.D. 855. Hêr gebôcôde Æðelpulf cyning teôðan dǽl his landes ofer eal his rîce, Gode tô lofe and him selfum tô êcere hǽle; and þŷ ilcan geârê fêrde tô Rôme, and þǽr pæs tpelfmônað puniende; and þâ hê hâmpeard fôr: and him þâ Carl, Francenâ cyning, his dôhtor geaf him tô cpêne. Seô pæs gehâten Ieoþete. Æfter þam hê gesund hâm côm, and ymb tpâ geâr þæs þe hê of Francum côm, hê gefôr. Hê rîcsôde nigonteôðe healf geâr. Pâ fêng Æðelbald his sunu to Pest-Seaxenâ rîce, and rîcsôde fîf geâr.

A.D. 860. Hêr Æðelbald forðfêrde, and fêng Æðelbriht to eallum þam rîce, his brôðor; and hê hit heôld on gôdre geþþǽrnesse fîf geâr.

A.D. 866. Hêr fêng Æðerêd Æðelbrihtes brôðer to Pest-Seaxenâ rîce, and þŷ ilcan geârê côm micel hǽðen here on Angelcynnes land, and þæt land eal geeôdon, and fordidon ealle þâ mynstre þâ hî tô cômon. And gefeaht Æðerêd and Ælfrêd his brôðer pið þone here geond stôpa, and þǽr pæs micel pælsliht on gehpæðre hand.

A.D. 872. Hêr gefôr Æðerêd cyning. Pâ fêng Ælfrêd Æðelpulfing his brôðor to Pest-Seaxenâ rîce; and þæs ymb ânne mônað gefeaht Ælfrêd cyning pið ealne þone hǽðenne here lytle perodê æt Piltûne, and hine lange on dæg geflŷmde; and þâ Deniscan âhton pælstôpe gepeald. And þæs geâres purdon nigon folc-gefeoht gefohten pið þone here on þŷ cynerîce be sûðan Temese, bûtan þam þe heom Ælfrêd þæs cyninges brôðer, and ânlîpige ealdormen, and cyninges þegnâs oft râdâ onridon, þe man nâ ne rîmde.

A.D. 878. Hêr hine bestæl se here on midne pinter ofer tpelftan niht tô Cippanhâmme, and geridon Pest-Seaxenâ land, and þǽr gesǽton, and micel þæs folces ofer sǽ ádrǽfdon; and þæs óðres þone mǽstan dǽl hí geridon and heom gecyrdon bútan þam cyninge Ælfréde. Hé lytlé peroðó uneáðelíce æfter pudum fór, and on mórfæstenum. And þæs ilcan pintres pæs se gúðfana genumen þe hí Hræfn hóton.

And þæs on Eástran porhte Ælfréd cyning lytlé peroðó gepeorc æt Æðelingá íge, and of þam gepeorce pæs pinnende pið þone here. Þa on þǽre seofoðan pucan ofer Eástran hé geráð tó Ecgbrihtes stáne be eástan Sealpudá, and him cómon þǽr ongeán Sumorsǽte ealle and Pilsǽte and Hámtúnscír, se dǽl þe hire behconan sǽ pæs; and his gefægene pǽron.

And hé fór ymb áne niht of þám pícum to Igleá, and þæs ymb áne niht to Eðandúne, and þǽr gefeaht pið ealne þone here, and hine geflýmde, and him æfter ráð óð þæt gepeorc, and þǽr sæt feópertýne niht; and þá sealde se here him gíslás and micle áðás, þæt hí of his cyneríce poldon; and him eác gehéton þæt heorá cyning fulpihte onfón polde.

And hí þæt geléstou; and þæs ymb þrí pucan cóm se cyning Guðrum þrítigá sum þará manná þe on þam here peorðóste pǽron, æt Alre, þæt is pið Æðelingá íge. And his Ælfréd cyning onféng þǽr æt fulpihte, and his crismlýsing pæs æt Þedmór; and hé þæs tpelf niht mid þam cyninge, and hé hine miclum and his geféran mid feó peorðóde.

A.D. 885. Hér forðférde se góda pápa Marínus, se gefreóde Angelcynnes scóle be Ælfrédes béne, Pest-Seaxená cyninges, and hé sende him micle gifá, and þǽre róde dǽl þe Crist on þrópóde, and þý ilcan geáró se here bræc frið pið Ælfréd cyning.

A.D. 897. Þá hét Ælfréd cyning timbrian lange scipu ongeán þás æscás, þá pǽron fulneáh tpá spá lange spá þá óðre; sume hæfdon sixtig árá, sume má; þá pǽron ægðer ge spiftran ge unpealtran, ge eác heáhran þonne þá óðre. Nǽron hí náðor nó on Frysisc gesceapene nó on Denisc, bútan spá him selfum þuhte þæt hí nytpeorðóste beón mihton. Þý ilcan sumerá forpearð ná læs þonne tpéntig scipá mid mannum mid eallé be þam súðriman.

A.D. 901. Hér gefór Ælfréd Æðulfing six nihtum ǽr calrá háligrá mæssan. Hé pæs cyning ofer eal Angelcyn bútan þam dǽle þe under Dená anpealde pæs. And þá féng Eádpeard his

sunu tô þam ríce. On his dagum bræc se here þone frid, and forsâpon ælc riht þe Eâdþeard cyning and his þitan heom budon; and se cyning heom pið feaht, and hî geflŷmde, and heorâ fela þûsendâ ofslôh; and hê geporhte, and getimbrôde, and geniþôde
5 fela burgâ þe hî hæfdon ǽr tôbrocen.

A.D. 925. Hêr Eâdþeard cyning forðfêrde, and Ælfþeard his sunu spíðe hraðe þæs, and heorâ líc liegað on Ðintanceastre. And Æðelstân þæs of Mearcum gecoren tô cyninge, and hê fêng tô Norðanhymbrâ ríce, and ealle þâ cyningás þe on þisum íg-
10 lande pǽron hê gepylde. Hê rícsôde feôpertŷne geâr and týn pucan, and forðfêrde on Gleâpeceastre. Þâ Eâdmund his brôðer fêng tô ríce, and hê hæfde ríce seofoðe healf geâr, and Liofa hine ofstang æt Puclancyrcan. Þâ æfter him fêng Eâdrêd æðeling his brôðer tô ríce. Eâdrêd rícsôde teôðe healf geâr, and þâ fêng
15 Eâdþíg to Þest-Seaxenâ ríce, Eâdmundes sunu cyninges.

A.D. 959. Hêr forðfêrde Eâdþíg cyning, and Eâdgâr his brôðer fêng tô ríce; and hê genam Ælfþryðe him tô epêne. Heô þæs Ordgâres dôhtor ealdormannes.

A.D. 975. Hêr geendôde eorðan dreâmás
20   Eâdgâr Englâ cyning,—ceás him ôðer leôht.
And hêr Eâdþeard, Eâdgâres sunu, fêng tô ríce, and on hærfeste æteôpde comêta se steorra, and côm þâ ôn þam æftran geâre spíðe micel hunger. And þâ (A.D. 978) peard Eâdþeard cyning ofslægen on âfentîde æt Corfes-geate. Ne peard Angelcynne
25 uân pyrse dǽd gedôn þonne þeôs þæs. Æðelrêd æðeling Eâdþeardes brôðer fêng tô þam ríce.

A.D. 991. Hêr man gerǽdde þæt man geald ǽrest gafol Deniscum mannum for þam micelan brôgan þe hí þorhton be þam sǽriman; þæt þæs ǽrest týn þûsend pundâ. Þone rǽd gerǽdde
30 ǽrest Sigeríc arcebisceop.

A.D. 994. Hêr côm Anlâf and Spegen mid feôper and hundnigontigum scipum; and hî þorhton þæt mǽste yfel þe ǽfre ǽnig here dôn mihte on bærnete and hergunge, and on manslihtum, ǽgðer be þam sǽriman on Eâst-Seaxum, and on Centlande,
35 and on Sûð-Seaxum, and on Hâmtûnscîre. Þâ peard hit spâ micel ege fram þam here, þæt man ne mihte geþencan and ne âsmeâ-

gan hú man hí of earde ádrîfan sceolde, oððe þisne eard pið Lí gehealdan. Æt nýhstan næs nân heâfodman þæt fyrde gaderian polde; ac æle fleâh spâ hê mæst mihte, nê furðon nân scîr nolde ôðre gelæ̂stan. Þonne nam man frið and grið pið hí, and nâ þê
5 læs for eallum þissum griðe and gafole, hí fêrdon æ̂ghpider flocmælum, and gehergódon úre earme folc, and hí rýpton and slôgon. Ealle þâs ungesælðâ ûs gelumpon þurh unrædâs. Æðelrêd pende ofer þâ sæ̂ tô Rîcarde, his epêne brôðer.

A.D. 1014. Hêr Spegen geendôde his dagâs, and se flota þâ eal
10 gecuron Cnût tô cyninge. Þâ côm Æðelrêd cyning hâm tô his âgenre þeôde, and hê glædlîce from him eallum onfangen pæs. Þâ (A.D. 1016) gelamp hit þæt se cyning Æðelrêd forðfêrde, and ealle þâ pitan þe on Lundene pæron, and seô burhparu gecuron Eâdmund Æðelrêding tô cyninge.
15 And Eâdmund and Cnût cômon tôgædre æt Olanîge, and heorâ freôndscipe þær gefæstnôdon and purdon pedbrôðru. And þâ fêng Eâdmund cyning tô Þestsexan and Cnût tô þam norð-dǽle. Þâ forðfêrde Eâdmund cyning, and pæs byrged mid his ealdan fæder Eâdgâre on Glæstingabyrig; and Cnût fêng tô eal Angel-
20 cynnes rîce.

A.D. 1028. Hêr fôr Cnût cyning tô Norðpegum of Englâlande mid fîftigum scipum Engliscrâ þegenâ, and âdrâf Ôlâf cyning of þam lande, and geâhnôde him eal þæt land. And (A.D. 1031) Scottâ cyning him tô beâh, Mælcolm, and peard his man.

25 A.D. 1035. Hêr forðfêrde Cnût cyning æt Sceaftesbyrig, and hê is bebyrged on Þintanceastre. And Harold sæde þæt hê Cuûtes sunu pære, and man ceâs Harold ofer eal tô cyninge. Hê forðfêrde on Oxnâforde, and man sende æfter Harðacnût, and hê pæs cyning ofer eal Englâland tpâ geâr bûtan týne nihtum, and
30 æ̂r þam þe hê bebyrged pære, eal folc geceâs þâ Eâdpeard Æðelrêding tô cyninge.

A.D. 1052. Hêr âlêde Eâdpeard cyning þæt heregyld þæt Æðelrêd cyning æ̂r astealde; þæt pæs on þam nigon and þrittigôðan geare pæs þe hê hit ongunnen hæfde. Þæt gyld gedrehte
35 ealle Englâ þeôde on spâ langum fyrste spâ hit bufan âpriten is. Þæt pæs æ̂fre ætforan ôðrum gyldum þe man myslîce geald, and men mid manigfealdlîce drehte.

A.D. 1066. Hêr côm Ƿillelm eorl of Normandige intô Pefena-
seâ, and Harold cyning gaderôde þâ micelne here, and côm him
tôgeânes; and Ƿillelm him côm ongeân on unƿær ær his folc ge-
fylced ƿære. Ac se cyning þeáh him spîðe heardlíce pið feaht
5 mid þâm mannum þe him gelêstan poldon, and þær pearð micel
pæl geslægen on ægðre healfe. Þær peard ofslægen Harold cyning, and þâ Frenciscan âhton pælstôpe gepeald. Þâ Ƿillelm cyning âhte ægðer ge Engláland ge Normandige. Æfter þisum
hæfde se cyning micel geþeaht and spîðe deôpe sprǽce pið his
10 pitan ymbe þis land. Hê sende þâ ofer eal Engláland intô ælcere
scîre his men, and lêt âgan ût hû fela hundredâ hîdâ ƿǽron innan
þam lande, oððe hƿæt se cyning him sylfum hæfde landes and
yrfes innan þam lande, oððe hpilce hê âhte tô habbanne tô tpelf
môndum of þǽre scîre; and hƿæt oððe hû micel ælce man hæfde
15 þe landsittende pæs innan Engláland on lande oððe on yrfe, and
hû micel feôs hit þære peorð: næs ân ǽlpig hîd nê ân gyrd
landes, nê furðon (hit is sceamu tô tellanne, ac hit ne þuhte him
nân sceamu tô dônne) ân oxa, nê ân cû, nê ân spîn næs belifen,
þæt næs geset on his geƿrite.

20 A.D. 1087. Hêr Ƿillelm forðfêrde. Se þo pæs ǽr rîce cyning
and maniges landes hláford, hê næfde þâ ealles landes bûtan seofon fôtâ mǽl. Hê lǽfde æfter him þreô sunan. Rodbeard hêt
se yldesta, se pæs eorl on Normandige æfter him. Se ôðer hêt
Ƿillelm, þe bær æfter him on Engláland þone cynehelm. Se þrid-
25 da hêt Heânrîc. Se cyning Ƿillelm pæs spîðe pîs man, and spîðe
rîce, and peorðful and strenge; man mihte faran ofer his rîce mid
his bôsme fullum goldes, ungederod. Hê sette micel deôrfrið, and
legde lagâ þǽrpið þæt spâ-hpâ-spâ slôge heort oððe hinde, þæt
hine man sceolde blendian. Hê forbeâd þâ heortâs; spilce eâc
30 þâ bârâs; spâ spîðe hê lufôde þâ heáhdeôr, spilce hê pǽre heorâ
fæder. Eâc hê sette be þâm haran þæt hî môston freô faran.
His rîce men hit mǽndon, and þâ earme men hit beceorôdon. Ac
hê pæs spâ stîð þæt hê ne rôhte heorâ ealrâ nîð.

CONVERSION OF THE ANGLO-SAXONS.

GREGORY.

1. Grêgorius se hâlga pâpa is rihtlîce Engliscre þeôde apostol. Pes eâdiga pâpa Grêgorius pæs of æðelborenre mægðe and æpfæstre âcenned; Rômânisce pitan pêron his magâs; his fæder hâtte Gordiânus, and Fêlix, se æpfæsta pâpa, pæs his fîfta fæder.
5 Grêgorius is Grêcisc nama, se spêigð on Ledenum gereorde "Vigilantius," þæt is on Englisc, "Dacolre." Hê pæs spîðe pacol on Godes bebodum, þâþâ hê sylf herigendlîce leofôde, and hê pacollîce ymbe manegrâ þeôdâ þearfe hogôde. Hê pæs fram cildhâde on bôclîcum lârum getŷd, and hê on þære lâre spâ gesæliglîce
10 þeâh, þæt on ealre Rômânâ-byrig næs nân his gelîca geþuht. Hê gecneordlæhte æfter wîsrâ lâreôpâ gebisnungum, and næs forgytol, ac gefæstnôde his lâre on fæsthafelum gemynde. Hê hlôd þâ mid þurstigum breôste þâ flôpendan lâre, þe hê eft æfter fyrste mid hunig-spêtre þrotan þæslîce bealcette.

15 2. On geonglîcum geârum, þâþâ his geôgoð æfter gecynde poruld-þing lufian sceolde, þâ ongan hê hine sylfne tô Gode geþeôdan, and tô êðele þæs uplîcan lifes mid eallum gepilnungum orðian. Pitôdlîce æfter his fæder forðsîðe seofon mynstru hê gelênde mid his âgenum. Þone ofer-câcan his æhtâ hê âspende on
20 Godes þearfum. Hê eôde ær his gecyrrednysse geond Rômânâburh mid pællenum gyrlum, and scînendum gymmum, and reâdum golde gefrætepôd; ac æfter his gecyrrednysse hê þênôde Godes þearfum, hê sylf þearfa, mid pâcum pæfelse befangen. Hê lufôde forhæfednysse on mettum, and on drence, and pæccan on syndri-
25 gum gebedum; þær-tô-câcan he þrôpôde singallîce untrumnyssâ.

3. Þâ gelamp hit æt sumum sæle, spâ spâ gŷt for oft dêð, þæt Englisce cŷpmen brohton heorâ pare tô Rômânâ-byrig, and Grêgorius eôde be þære stræt tô þâm Engliscum, heorâ þing sceâpigende. Þâ gesceah hê betpux þâm parum cŷpecnihtâs gesette,
30 þâ pæron hpîtes lîchaman and fægeres andplitan men, and æðellîce gefexôde. Grêgorius þâ beheôld þærâ cnapenâ plite, and be-

fran of hpilcere þeôde hî gebrohte pǣron. Þâ sǣde him man
þæt hî of Englâ-lande pǣron, and þæt þǣre þeôde mennisc spâ
plitig pǣre. Eft þâ Grêgorius befran hpæðer þæs landes folc
Cristen pǣre þe hǣðen. Him man sǣde þæt hî hǣðene pǣron.
5 Grêgorius þâ of inpeardre heortan langsume siccetunge teâh, and
cpæð, "Þâlâpâ, þæt spâ fægeres hipes men sindon þam speartan
deôfle underþeôdde." Eft hê âxôde, hû þǣre þeôde nama pǣre,
þe hî of-cômon. Him pæs geandpyrd, þæt hî Angle genemnôde
pǣron. Þâ cpæð hê, "Rihtlîce hî sind Angle gehâtene, forþan þe
10 hî englâ plite habbað, and spilcum gedafenað þæt hî on heofonum
englâ gefêran beôn." Gyt þâ Grêgorius befran, hû þǣre scîre
nama pǣre, þe þâ cnapan of-âlǣdde pǣron. Him man sǣde, þæt
þâ scîrmen pǣron Dêre gehâtene. Grêgorius andpyrde, "Þel hî
sind Dêre gehâtene, forþan þe hî sind fram graman generôde, and
15 tô Cristes mildheortnysse gecŷgede." Gyt þâ hê befran, "Hû is
þǣre leôde cyning gehâten?" Him pæs geandsparôd þæt se cyning Ælle gehâten pǣre. Hpæt þâ Grêgorius gamenôde mid his
pordum tô þam naman, and cpæð, "Hit gedafenað þæt Allelûia sŷ
gesungen on þam lande tô lofe þæs Ælmihtigan Scyppendes."

20 4. Grêgorius þâ sôna côde tô þam pâpan þæs apostolican setles,
and hine bæd, þæt hê Angelcynne sume lâreôpâs âsende, þe hî tô
Criste gebîgdon, and cpæð, þæt hê sylf gearo pǣre þæt peorc tô
gefremmenne mid Godes fultume, gif hit þam pâpan spâ gelîcôde.
Þâ ne mihte se pâpa þæt geþafian, þeâh þe hê eal polde; forþan
25 þe þâ Rômâniscan ceaster-geparan noldon geþafian þæt spâ ge-
togen man, and spâ geþungen lâreôp þâ burh eallunge forlête,
and spâ fyrlen præcsîð genâme.

   5. Æfter þisum gelamp þæt micel man-cpealm becom ofer
þǣre Rômâniscan leôde, and ǣrest þone pâpan Pelagium gestôd,
30 and bûton yldinge âdŷdde. Þitôdlîce æfter þæs pâpan geen-
dunge, spâ micel cpealm peard þæs folces, þæt gehpǣr stôdon
âpêste hûs geond þâ burh, bûton bûgigendum. Þâ ne mihte spâ-
þeâh seô Rômânâ-burh bûton pâpan punian, ac eal folc þone câ-
gan Grêgorium tô þǣre geþincðe ânmôdlîce geceâs, þeâh þe hê
35 mid eallum mægne piðerigende pǣre. Hpæt þâ Grêgorius, siððan hê pâpanhâd underfêng, gemunde hpæt hê gefyrn Angel-
cynne gemynte, and þǣr-rihte þæt luftŷme peorc gefremôde. Hê
nâ tô þæs hpon ne mihte þone Rômâniscan biscop-stôl eallunge
forlǣtan, ac hê âsende ôðre bydelâs, geþungene Godes þeôpan, tô
40 þisum îglande, and hê sylf miclum mid his bênum and tihtin-
gum fylste, þæt þǣrâ bydelâ bodung forðgênge, and Gode pæstm-

bǽre purde. Pǽrá bydelá naman sind þus geciᵹede, AUGUSTÍ-
NUS, MELLITUS, LAURENTIUS, PETRUS, JOHANNES, JUSTUS. Augustínus þá mid his geférum, þæt sind gerehte feôpertiᵹ perá,
férde be Grégories hǽse, ôð þæt hí to þisum íglande gesundful-
5 líce becômon.
    6. On þám daᵹum ríxôde Æðelbyrht cyning on Cantparebyrig
ríclíce, and his ríce pæs ástreht fram þǽre miclan eá Humbre
ôð súð sǽ. Augustínus hæfde ᵹenumen pealhstôdás of Francená
ríce, spá spá Grégorius him gebeád; and hé þurh þǽrá pealh-
10 stôdá múð þam cyninge and his leôde Godes pord bodôde: hú se
mildheorta Hǽlend mid his áᵹenre þrôpunge þisne scyldiᵹan
middaneard álýsde, and geleáffullum mannum heofonan ríces infær geopenôde. Pá andpyrde se cyning Æðelbriht Augustíne,
and cpæð, þæt hé fæᵹere pord and behát him cýdde; and cpæð,
15 þæt hé ne mihte spá hrædlíce þone ealdan gepunan þe hé mid
Angel-cynne heóld forlǽtan; cpæð þæt hé môste freólíce þá heofonlícan láre his leôde bodian, and þæt hé him and his geféran
bíᵹleofan þénian polde, and forᵹeaf him þá pununge on Cantparebyrig, seó pæs ealles his ríces heáfod-burh.
20   7. Ongan þá Augustínus mid his munucum tô geefenlǽcenne
þǽrá apostolá líf, mid singalum gebedum, and pæccan, and fæste-
num Gode þeópiᵹende, and lífes pord þám þe hí mihton bodi-
gende, ealle middaneardlíce þing, spá spá ælfremede, forhoᵹi-
gende, þá þing ána þe hí tô bíᵹleofan behôfedon underfônde, be
25 þám þe hí tǽhton selfe lybbende, and for þǽre sôðfæstnesse þe
hí bodôdon, ᵹearope pǽron éhtnesse tô þoliᵹenne, and deáðe
speltan, gif hí þorfton.
    8. Hpæt þá gelýfdon forpel maniᵹe, and on Godes naman ᵹe-
fullôde purdon, pundrigende þǽre bilepítnesse heorá unscǽddi-
30 gan lífes, and spétnesse heorá heofonlícan láre. Pá æt nextan,
gelustfullôde þam cyninge Æðelbrihte heorá clǽne líf and heorá
pynsume behát, þá sôðlíce purdon mid manegum tácnum gesêdde;
and hé þá gelýfende peard gefullôd, and miclum þá cristenan
geárpurðôde, and spá spá heofonlíce ceastergeparan lufôde; nolde
35 spá-þeáh nænne tô cristendôme geneádian; forþan þe hé ofáxôde
æt þám láreôpum his hǽle þæt Cristes þeópdôm ne sceal beón
geneádôd, ac selfpilles. Ongunnon þá dæghpamlíce forpel ma-
niᵹe éfstan tô gehýrenne þá hálgan bodunge, and forléton heorá
hǽðenscipe and hí selfe geþeôddon Cristes gelaðunge, on hine
40 gelýfende.
    9. Hpæt þá Grégorius miclum Gode þancôde mid blissiᵹen-

dum môde, þæt Angel-cynne spâ gelumpen pæs, spâ spâ hê self
geornlîce geþilnôde, and sende eft ongeân ærendracan tô þam ge-
leâffullan cyninge Æđelbrihte, mid gepritum and manigfealdum
lâcum, and ôđre gepritu tô Augustîne, mid andsparum ealrâ þærâ
5 þingâ þe hê hine befran, and hine eâc þisum pordum mânôde:
"Brôđer mîn se leôfôsta, ic pât þæt se Ælmihtiga God fela pundrâ
þurh þê þære þeôde þe hê geceâs gesputelađ, þæs þû miht blissigan, and eâc þê ondrædan. Pû miht blissigan geþislîce þæt
þære þeôde sâplâ þurh þâ yttran pundra beôđ getogene tô þære
10 incundan gife. Ondræd þê spâ-þeâh þæt þîn môd ne beô âhafen
mid dyrstignesse on þâm tâcnum þe God þurh þê gefremađ, and
þû þonon on îdelum puldre befealle piđinnan, þonon þe þû piđû-
tan on purđmynte âhafen bist."

10. Grêgorius âsende eâc Augustîne hâlige lâc on mæsse-reâ-
15 fum, and on bôcum, and þærâ apostolâ and martyrâ *reliquias* samod; and bebeâd þæt his æftergengan symle þone *pallium* and
þone ercehâd æt þam apostolican setle Rômâniscre gelađunge
fêccan sceoldon. Augustînus gesette æfter þisum biscopâs of his
gefêrum gehpilcum burgum on Englâ þeôde, and hî on Godes ge-
20 leâfan þeônde þurhpunôdon ôđ þisum dægđerlîcum dæge.

PAULINUS.

1. Þære tîde eâc spylce Norđanhymbrâ þeôd mid heorâ cyninge Eâdpine Cristes geleâfan onfêng, þe him Paulînus, se hâlga
bisceop, bodôde and lærde. Þâ hæfde se cyning gespræce and
geþeaht mid his pitum, and synderlîce pæs fram him callum frig-
25 nende, hpilc him þuhte and gesepen þære þeôs nipe lâr and þære
godcundnesse bîgong, þe þær læred pæs? Him þâ andsparôde
his ealdor-bisceop, Cêfî pæs hâten: "Geseoh þû, cyning, hpilc
þeôs lâr sî, þe ûs nû bodôd is. Ic þê sôđlîce andette, þæt ic cûđ-
lîce geleornôd hæbbe, þæt eallinga nâpiht mægenes nê nytnesse
30 hafađ seô æfæstnes, þe pê ôđ þis hæfdon and beeôdon, forþon nænig þînrâ þegnâ neôdlîcôr nê gelustfullîcôr hine selfne underþeôdde tô ûrâ godâ bîgange þonne ic; ac nôht þon læs manige sindon,
þâ þe mâran gife and fremsumnesse æt þê onfêngon þonne ic, and
on eallum þingum mâran gesynto hæfdon. Hpæt ic pât, gif ûre
35 godâs ænige mihte hæfdon, þonne poldon hî mê mâ fultumian,
forþon ic him geornlîcôr þeôdde and hŷrde. Forþon mê þyncec

píslíc, gif þû geseô þâ þing beteran and strengran, þe ûs nipan bodôde sindon, þæt pê þâm onfôn."

2. Pisum pordum ôðer þæs cyninges pita and ealdorman geþafunge sealde and tô þære spræce fêng and þus cpæð:

5 " Pyslíc mê is gesepen, cyning, þis andpearde lîf mannâ on eorðan tô piðmetenesse þære tîde, þe ûs uncûð is, spâ gelíc spâ þû æt spêsendum sitte mid þînum ealdormannum and þegnum on pintertîde, and sî fŷr onæled, and þîn heal gepyrmed, and hit rîne and snîpe and hægele and styrme ûte; cume þonne ân spearpa
10 and hrædlîce þæt hûs þurhfleô, þurh ôðre duru in, þurh ôðre ût gepîte: hpæt hê on þâ tîd, þâ hê inne byð, ne byð rîned mid þŷ stormê þæs pintres! ac þæt byð ân eágan bryhtm and þæt læste fæc, and hê sôna of pintrâ in pinter eft cymeð. Spâ þonne þis mannâ lîf tô medmiclum fæce ætŷpeð; hpæt þær foregênge, oððe
15 hpæt þær æfterfylige, pê ne cunnon. Forþon gif þeôs nipe lâre âpiht cûðlîcre and gerisenlîcre bringe, heô þæs pyrðe is, þæt pê þære fyligeân."

3. Pisum pordum gelîcum ôðre ealdormen and þæs cyninges þeahterâs spræcon: þâ get tô geŷhte Cêfî and cpæð, þæt hê polde
20 Paulînus þone bisceop geornlîcôr gehŷran be þam gode sprecende, þe hê bodôde; þâ hêt se cyning spâ dôn. Pâ hê þâ his pord gehŷrde, þâ clypôde hê and þus cpæð: "Geare ic þæt ongeat, þæt þæt nâpiht pæs, þæt pê beeôdon, forþon spâ miclê spâ ic geornlîcôr on þam bîgange þæt selfe sôð sôhte, spâ ic hit læs
25 mêtte. Nû þonne ic openlîce andette, þæt on þisse lâre þæt selfe sôð scîneð, þæt ûs mæg syllan þâ gife êcre eâdignesse and êces lîfes hælo. Forþon ic lære nû, cyning leôfôsta, þæt þæt tempel and þâ peofedu þâ þe pê bûtan pæstmum ænigre nytnesse hâlgôdon, þæt pê þâ hraðe forleôsân and on fŷre forbærnân."

30 4. Hpæt hê þâ se cyning openlîce andette þam bisceope and him eallum, þæt hê polde fæstlîce þâm deôfolgildum piðsacan and Cristes geleâfan onfôn! Mid þŷ hê þâ se cyning fram þam forespreecnan bisceope sôhte and âcsôde heorâ hâlignesse þe hî ær beeôdon, hpâ þâ pigbêd and þâ heargâs þârâ deôfolgildâ mid
35 heorâ hegum þe hî ymbsette pæron âîdlian sceolde and tôpeorpan; þâ andsparôde hê se bisceop: "Efne ic þâ godâs lange mid dysignesse beeôde ôð þis; hpâ mæg hî gerisenlîcôr nû tôpeorpan tô bysne ôðrâ mannâ þonne ic selfa þurh þâ snyttro þe ic fram þam sôðan Gode onfêng?" And hê þâ sôna fram him
40 âpearp þâ îdlan dysignesse þe hê ær beeôde, and þone cyning bæd, þæt hê him pæpen scalde and gestôdhors, þæt hê mihte on

D

cuman and þæt deôfolgild tôpeorpan, forþon þam bisceope ne
pæs âlýfed, þæt hê môste pæpen pegan, nê ælcôr bûtan on myran
rîdan. Pâ sealde se cyning him speord, þæt hê hine mid be-
gyrde, and nam him spere on hand, and hleôp on þæs cyninges
stêdan, and tô þâm deôfolgildum râd.

5. Pâ þæt folc hine þâ geseah spâ gescyrpedne, þâ pêndon hî,
þæt hê tela ne piste, ac þæt hê pêdde. Sôna þæs þe hê gelîhte
tô þam hearge, þâ sceât hê mid his spere, þæt hit sticôde fæste
on þam hearge, and þæs spîðe gefeônde þære ongitenesse þæs sôðan Godes bîganges, and hê þâ hêt his geferan tôpeorpan ealne
hearh and þâ getimbro, and forbærnan. Is seô stôp git ætcôped
giû þârâ deôfolgildâ nâht feor eâst fram Eoforpîc-ceastre begeondan Deorpentan þære eâ, and git tô dæg is nemned Godmund-
ingahâm, þær se bisceop þurh þæs sôðan Godes onbryrdnesse tô-
pearp and fordide þâ pigbed, þe hê self ær gehâlgôde.

Pâ onfêng Eâdpine cyning mid eallum þâm æðelingum his
þeôde and mid miclê folcê Cristes geleâfan and fulluhtes bæðe.

6. Lærde Paulînus eâc spilce Godes pord on Lindesse. Seô
mægð is seô nŷhste on sûð-healfe Humbre streâmes liged ût on
sæ. Be þisse mægðe geleâfan cpæð hê Bêda: "Mê sæde sum
ârpurðe mæsse-preôst and abbud of Peortanea þam hâm, se pæs
Dêda hâten,—cpæð þæt him sæde sum eald pita, þæt hê pære
gefullôd æt middum dæge fram Paulîne þam bisceope on Eâdpines andpeardnesse þæs cyninges, and micel menigo þæs folces
on Trentan streâme be Teôlfinga-ceastre. Sæde se ilca man hpilc
þæs bisceopes hip pære sanctes Paulînes; cpæð þæt hê pære
lang on bodige and hpon forðbeald; hê hæfde blæc feax and
blâcne andplitan and hôcihte neôsu þynne, and hê pære æghpæ-
ðer ge ârpurðlîc ge ondrysenlîc on tô seônne."

7. Is þæt sæd þæt on þâ tîd spâ micel sib pære on Brytene
æghpider ymb spâ spâ Eâdpines rîce pære, þeâh þe ân pîf polde,
mid hire nîcendum cilde heô mihte gegân bûtan ælcere sceade-
nesse fram sæ tô sæ ofer eal þis eâland. Spilce eâc se ilca cyning
tô nytnesse fand his leôdum, þæt in manigum stôpum þær þe
hlutre pyllan urnon be strætum þær mannâ færnes mæst pæs,
þæt hê þær hêt for pegfêrendrâ gecêlnesse stapulâs âsettan, and
þær ærene ceâcâs onhôn: and þâ hpæðere nænig for his ege and
for his lufan hî hrînan dorste ne nê polde bûtan tô his neôdþearf-
lîcre þênunge.

ANGLO-SAXON LAWS.

ÆÐELBIRHTES DÔMÂS.

§ 4. Gif frigman cyninge stele, nigon-gylde forgelde.

9. Gif frigman frêum stelð, þrî-gylde gebête and cyning âge þæt pîte and eal þâ æhtan.

21. Gif man mannan ofslæhð, medume leôd-geld hund scillingâ gebête.

22. Gif man mannan ofslæhð, æt openum græfe tpêntig scillingâ forgelde and in feôpertig nihtâ ealne leôd forgelde.

23. Gif bana of lande gepîteð, þâ magâs healfne leôd forgelden.

25. Gif man ceorles hlâf-ætan ofslæhð, six scillingum gebête.

39. Gif ôðer eâre nâpiht gehêreð, fîf and tpêntigum scillingum gebête.

40. Gif eâre of peorð âslagen, tpelf scillingum gebête.

41. Gif eâre þyrel peorðeð, þrîm scillingum gebête.

42. Gif eâre sceard peorðeð, six scillingum gebête.

43. Gif eâge of peorð, fîftig scillingum gebête.

50. Se þe cin-bân forslæhð, mid tpêntigum scillingum forgelde.

51. Æt þâm feôper tôðum fyrestum æt gehpilcum six scillingâs; se tôð se þanne bîstandeð, feôper scillingâs; se þe þonne bî þam standeð, þrî scillingâs, and þonne siððan gehpylc scilling.

52. Gif spræc âpyrd peorð, tpelf scillingâs; gif pido-bân gebroced peorðeð, six scillingum gebête.

53. Se þe earm þurhstingð, six scillingum gebête; gif earm forbrocen peorð, six scillingum gebête.

54. Gif man þûman of âslæhð, tpêntigum scillingum gebête; gif þûman nægl of peorðeð, þrîm scillingum gebête; gif man scyte-finger of âslæhð, eahta scillingum gebête; gif man middel-finger of âslæhð, feôper scillingum gebête; gif man gold-finger of âslæhð, six scillingum gebête; gif man þone lytlan finger of âslæhð, endleofan scillingum gebête.

55. Æt þâm næglum gehpylcum scilling.

56. Æt þam lærestan plite-þamme, þrî scillingâs, and æt þam mâran six scillingâs.

57. Gif man ôðerne mid fŷste in nâso slæhð, þrî scillingâs.

58. Gif dynt sîe, scilling. Gif hê heâhre handâ dyntes onfêhð, 5 scilling forgelde.

59. Gif dynt speart sîe bûton pâðum, þrittig scættâ gebête.

60. Gif hit sîe binnan pâðum, geƕylc XX. scættâ gebête.

HLÔÐHÆRE AND EÂDRÎC, CANTƿARÂ CYNINGÂS.

§ 11. Gif man mannan an ôðres flette mân-spara hâteð, oððe hine mid bîsmer-ƿordum scandlîce grête, scilling âgelde þam þe þæt flet âge, and six scillingâs þam þe hê þæt ƿord tô gecƕæde, and cyninge tƿelf scillingâs forgelde.

12. Gif man ôðrum steâp âsette þær men drincen bûton scylde, an eald-riht scilling âgelde þam þe þæt flet âge, and six scillingâs þam þe man þone steâp âsette, and cyninge tƿelf scillingâs.

13. Gif man ƿæpn âbregde þær men drincen and þær man nân yfel ne dêð, scilling þam þe þæt flet âge, and cyninge tƿelf scillingâs.

14. Gif þæt flet geblôdgâd ƿyrðe, forgelde þam men his mund-byrd, and cyninge fîftig scillingâs.

15. Gif man cuman feormeð þrî niht an his âgenum hâme, cêpeman oððe ôðerne, þe seð ofer mearce cumen, and hine þonne his mete fêde, and hê þonne ænigum men yfel gedô, se man þane ôðerne æt rihte gebrenge, oððe riht fore ƿyrce.

INES CYNINGES DOMÂS.

§ 6. Gif hƿâ gefeohte on cyninges hûse, sîe hê scyldig ealles his yrfes, and sîe on cyninges dôme hƿæðer hê lîf âge þe nâge.—Gif hƿâ on mynstre gefeohte, hund-tƿelftig scillingâs gebête.—Gif hƿâ on ealdormannes hûse gefeohte, oððe on ôðres geþungenes ƿitan, sixtig scillingâs gebête hê, and ôðer sixtig scillingâs geselle tô ƿîte.—Gif hê þonne on gafol-geldan hûse oððe on gebûres gefeohte, þrîtig scillingâs tô ƿîte geselle, and þam gebûre six scillingâs.—And þeâh hit sîe on middum felda gefohten, þrítig scillingâ tô pîte sîe âgifen.—Gif þonne on gebeôrscipe hîe gecîden, and ôðer heorâ mid geþylde hit forbere, geselle se ôðer þrítig scillingâs tô pîte.

7. Gif hpâ stalie spâ his pîf nyte and his bearn, geselle sixtig scillingâs to pîte.—Gif hê þonne stalie on gepitnesse ealles his hîrêdes, gangen hîe ealle on þeôpot.—Týn-pintre cniht mæg beôn þýfðe gepita.

20. Gif feorcund man oððe fremde bûtan pege geond pudu gange, and ne hrýme nê horn blâpe, for þeôf hê bið tô prôfianne oððe tô sleânne oððe tô âlýsanne.

43. Þonne man beâm on pudâ forbærne, and peorðe yppe on þone þe hit dyde, gylde hê ful pîte; geselle sixtig scillingâ forþam þe fýr bið þeôf.—Gif man âfelle on pudâ pel manege treôpâ, and pyrðe eft undyrne, forgylde þreô treôpâ, æle mid þrítig scillingum. Ne þearf hê heorâ mâ gyldan, pære heorâ spâ fela spâ heorâ pære, forþam seô æx bið melda, nalles þeôf.

ÆLFRÊDES DÔMÂS.

§ 1. Æt ærestan pê lærað, þæt mæst þearf is, þæt æghpelc mon his âð and his ped pærlîce healde.—Gif hê þonne þæs peddie þe him riht sý tô gelæstanne, and þæt âleôge, selle mid eâðmêdum his pæpn and his æhtâ his freôndum tô gehealdanne, and beô feôpertig nihtâ on carcerne on cyninges tûne, þrôpige þær spâ bisceop him scrîfe, and his mægâs hine fêden, gif hê self mete næbbe.—Gif hê mægâs næbbe, oððe þone mete næbbe, fêde cyninges gerêfa hine.—Gif hine mon tôgenêdan scyle and hê elles nylle, gif hine mon gebinde, þolige his pæpnâ and his yrfes.— Gif hine mon ofsleâ, licge hê orgylde.—Gif hê losige, sîe hê âflýmed and sîe âmænsumôd of eallum Cristes ciricum.

5. Eâc pê settað æghpelcere cirican þe bisceop gehâlgôde, þis frið: gif hîe fâh-mon geyrne oððe gewrne, þæt hine seofan nihtum nân mon ût ne teô.—Eâc cirican frið is: gif hpelc mon cirican gesêce for þârâ gyltâ hpylcum þârâ þe ær geypped nære, and hine þær on Godes naman geandette, sîe hit healf forgifen. —Se þe stalað on Sunnan niht, oððe on Geôl, oððe on Eâstran, oððe on þone Hâlgan Þunres dæg, and on Gang-dagâs, þârâ gehpelc pê pillað sîe tpý-bôte, spâ on Lencten-fæsten.

6. Gif hpâ on cirican hpæt geþeôfige, forgylde þæt ângylde,

and þæt pīte spā tô þam ángylde belimpan pille, and sleâ mon þā hand of þe hê hit mid gedyde.

23. Gif hund mon tôslīte oððe âbîte, æt forman misdǣde geselle six scillingâs gif hê him mete selle, æt æfteran cerre tpelf 5 scillingâs, æt þriddan þrittig scillingâs.—Gif æt þissâ misdǣdâ hpelcere se hund losige, gâ þeôs bôt hpæðere forð.

32. Gif mon folc-leâsunge gepyrce, and heô on hine geresp peorðe, mid nânum leôhtran þinge gebête, þonne him mon âceorfe þâ tungan of.

10 35. Gif mon cyrliscne mon gebinde unsynnigne, gebête mid týn scillingum.—Gif hine mon bespinge, mid tpêntig scillingum gebête.—Gif hê hine on hengenne âlecge, mid þrittig scillingum gebête.—Gif hê hine on bismor tô homolan bescire, mid týn scillingum gebête.—Gif hê hine tô preôste bescire unbundenne, 15 mid þrittig scillingum gebête.—Gif hê þone beard of âscire, mid tpêntig scillingum gebête.—Gif hê hine gebinde and þonne tô preôste bescire, mid sixtig scillingum gebête.

ECGBYRHT ARCEBISCEOP.

Confessionale, 32. Gif man medmycles hpæthpega deôflum onsǣgd, fæste ân geâr: gif hê mycles hpæt onsǣge, fæste týn pin-20 ter. Spâ hpylc man spâ corn bærne on þǣre stôpe þǣr man deâd pǣre, lifigendum mannum tô hǣle and on his hûse, fæste fîf pinter.

33. Ðif gif heô set hire dôhtor ofer hûs oððe on ofen forþam þe heô pille hîg fefer-âdle gebǣlan, fæste heô seofon pinter.

25 *Poenitentiale*, II., 23. Nis nâ sôðlîce âlýfed nânum Cristenum men þæt hê îdele hpatungâ begâ spâ hǣðene men dôð, þæt is þæt hîg gelýfon on sunnan and on mônan and on steorrenâ ryne, and sêcon tîdâ hpatungâ hyrâ þing tô begynnanne, nê pyrtâ gaderunge mid nânum galdre, bûtan mid pater-noster and mid crê-30 dan oððe mid sumum gebede þe tô Gode belimpe.

IV., 16. Gif ǣnig man ôðerne mid picce-cræfte fordô, fæste seofon geâr, þreô on hlâfe and on pætere, and þâ feôper þrî dagâs on pucan on hlâfe and on pætere.

17. Gif hpâ drîfe stacan on ǣnigne man, fæste þreô geâr, ân 35 geâr on hlâfe and on pætere, and þâ tpâ fæste on pucan þrî dagâs on hlâfe and on pætere. And gif se man for þǣre stacunge

deád bið, þonne fæste hé seofon geár ealspá hit hér bufon ápriten is.

18. Gif hpá piccige ymbe æniges mannes lufe and him on æte sylle oððe on drince oððe on æniges cynnes gealdor-cræftum, þæt hyrá lufu forþon þe máre beón scyle: gif hit léþede man dó, fæste healf geár Dódnes dagum and Frîge dagum on hláfe and on pætere, and þá óðre dagás brúce hé his metes bútan flæsce ánum.

19. Gif hpá hlytás oððe hpatungá begá, oððe his pæccan æt ænigum pylle hæbbe, oððe æt ænigre óðre gesceafte búton on Godes cyricean, fæste hé þreó geár, þæt án on hláfe and on pætere, and þá tpá Dódnes dagum and Frîge dagum on hláfe and on pætere and þá óðre dagás brúce his metes búton flæsce ánum.

20. Difman beó þæs ylcan pyrðe, gif heó tiláð hire cilde mid ænigum picce-cræfte oððe æt pegá geléton þurh þá corðan tîhð; ealá þæt is mycel hæðenscipe.

CNUT CYNING.

II., 5. And pé forbeódað eornostlíce ælcne hæðenscipe. Hæðenscipe býð þæt man deófol-gyld peorðige: þæt is þæt man peorðige hæðene godás and sunnan oððe mónan, fýr oððe flód, pæter-pyllás oððe stánás oððe æniges cynnes pudu-treópu, oððe picce-cræft lufige, oððe morð-peorc gefremme on ænige písan, oððe blóte oððe fyrhte oððe spylerá gedpimerá ænig þing dreóge.

73. And sitte ælc pudupe perleás tpelf-mónað, ceóse syððan þæt heó sylf pille; and gif heó binnan geáres fæce per geceóse, þonne þolige heó þære morgen-gyfe and ealrá þæra æhtá þe heó þurh ærran per hæfde, and fón þá néhstan frýnd tó þam lande and tó þam æhtan þe heó ær hæfde.—And ne bádige man æfre pudupan tó hrædlíce.

POETS.

ORPHEUS.

1. Gesǽlig byð se man, þe mæg geseôn þone hlutran ǽpelm þæs hêhstan gôdes, and of him selfum âpeorpan mæg þâ þeôstro his môdes! Dê sculon get of ealdum leâsum spellum þê sum bispell reccan: Hit gelamp giô, þætte ân hearpere pæs on þǽre
5 þeôde þe Prâcia hâtte, seô pæs on Crêcâ rîce. Se hearpere pæs spîðe ungefrǽglîce gôd, þæs nama pæs Orfeus. Hê hæfde ân spîðe ânlîc pîf, seô pæs hâten Eurydice. Þâ ongan man secgan be þam hearpere, þæt hê mihte hearpian þæt se pudu pagôde and þâ stânâs hî styredon for þý spêgê, and pildu deôr þǽr poldon
10 tô irnan and stondan spilce hî tamu pǽron, spâ stille, þeâh hî men oððe hundâs pið eôdon, þæt hî hî nâ ne onscûnedon.

2. Þâ sǽdon hî, þæt þæs hearperes pîf sceolde âcpelan, and hire sâple man sceolde lǽdan tô helle. Þâ sceolde se hearpere peorðan spâ sârig, þæt hê ne mihte on-gemong ôðrum mannum
15 beôn, ac teâh tô pudâ and sæt on þǽm muntum ǽgðer ge dæges ge nihtes, peôp and hearpôde, þæt þâ pudâs bifôdon and þâ eâ stôdon, and nân heort ne onscûnôde nǽnne leôn, nê nân hara nǽnne hund, nê nân neât nyste nǽnne andan nê nǽnne ege tô ôðrum for þǽre mergðe þæs sônes.

20 3. Þâ þǽm hearpere þâ þuhte, þæt hine nânes þinges ne lyste on þisse porulde, þâ þohte hê, þæt hê polde gesêcan helle godu, and onginnan him ôleccan mid his hearpan, and biddan þæt hî him âgêfân eft his pîf. Þâ hê þâ þider com, þâ sceolde cuman þǽre helle hund ongeân hine, þæs nama pæs Cerucrus, se
25 sceolde habban þreô heâfdu, and ongan fægenian mid his steortê, and plegian pið hine for his hearpungâ. Þâ pæs þǽr eâc spîðe egeslîc geat-peard, þæs nama sceolde beôn Caron, se hæfde eâc þreô heâfdu, and se pæs spîðe ôreald. Þâ ongan se hearpere hine biddan, þæt hê hine gemundbyrde þâ hpîle þe hê þǽr pǽre
30 and hine gesundne eft þanon brohte; þâ gehêt hê him þæt, forþam hê pæs oflyst þæs seldcûðan sônes.

4. Þâ eôde hê furðôr, ôð hê mêtte þâ graman mettenâ, þe folcisce men hâtað Parcâs, þâ hî secgað, þæt on nânum men nyton nâne âre, ac ælcum men precen be his gepyrhtum, þâ hî secgað, þæt palden ælces mannes pyrde. Þâ ongan hê biddan
5 heorâ blisse; þâ ongunnon hî pêpan mid him. Þâ eôde hê furður, and him urnon ealle helparan ongeân, and lêddon hine tô heorâ cyninge, and ongunnon ealle sprecan mid him and biddan þæs þe hê bæd. And þæt unstille hpeôl, þe Ixîon þæs tô gebunden Leuitâ cyning for his scylde, þæt ôðstôd for his hear-
10 pungâ; and Tantalus se cyning, þe on þisse porulde ungemetlîce gîfre pæs, and him þær þæt ilce yfel fylgde, þæs gîfernesse hê gestilde; and se ultor sceolde forlǽtan, þæt hê ne slât þâ lifre Tityes þæs cyninges, þe hine ǽr mid þŷ pîtnôde; and eal helparâ pîtu gestildon þâ hpîle, þe hê beforan þam cyninge
15 hearpôde.

5. Þâ hê þâ lange and lange hearpôde, þâ cleopôde se helparenâ cyning, and cpæð: "Þuton âgifan þæm esne his pîf, forþæm hê hî hæfð geearnâd mid his hearpungâ." Bebeâd him þâ, þæt hê geare pisse, þæt hê hine nǽfre underbæc ne besâpe siððan hê
20 þonan-peard pǽre, and sǽde, gif hê hine underbæc besâpe, þæt hê sceolde forlǽtan þæt pîf. Ac þâ lufe man mæg spîðe uneâðe oððe nâ forbeôdan. Þeilâ pei! hpæt Orfeus þâ lǽdde his pîf mid him, ôð þe hê com on þæt gemǽre leôhtes and þeôstro; þâ eôde þæt pîf æfter him. Þâ hê furðum on þæt leôht com, þâ beseah
25 hê hine underbæc pið þæs pîfes: þâ losâde heô him sôna.

6. Þæs spel lǽrað gehpilcne man þârâ þe pilnað helle þeôstro tô fleônne, and tô þæs sôðan Godes leôhte tô cumanne, þæt hê hine ne beseô tô his ealdum yfelum, spâ þæt hê hî eft spâ fullîce fulfremme, spâ hê hî ǽr dide; forþæm spâ-hpâ-spâ mid fulle
30 pillan his môd pent tô þâm yflum þe hê ǽr forlêt, and hî þonne fulfremeð, and hî him þonne fullîce lîciað, and hê hî nǽfre forlǽtan ne þenceð; þonne forlŷst hê eal his ǽrran gôd, bûton hê hit eft gebête.

CÆDMON.

1. On Hilde abbudissan mynstre pæs sum brôðor synderlîce
35 mid godcundre gife gemǽred and gepeorðôd, forþon hê gepunôde gerisenlîce leôð pyrcean, þâ þe tô ǽfæstnesse and tô ârfæstnesse belumpon, spâ þætte spâ-hpæt-spâ hê of godcundum stafum

þurh bóceras geleornôde, þæt hê æfter medmiclum fæce in sceôp-
gereorde mid þâ mǽstan spêtnesse and inbrydnesse geglencde
and in Englisc gereorde þelgehþǽrford brohte; and for his leôð-
songum manigrâ mannâ môd oft tô peorulde forhôhnesse and tô
5 geþeôdnêsse þæs heofonlícan lífes onbærnde pǽron.

2. And câc spilce manige ôðre æfter him on Angelþeôde on-
gúnnon ǽfæste leôð pyrcan, ac nænig hpæðre him þæt gelíce dôn
meahte, forþon hê nalæs fram mannum nê þurh man gelǽred pæs,
þæt hê þone leôðcræft geleornôde; ac hê pæs godcundlíce geful-
10 tumôd, and þurh Godes gife þone songcræft onfêng, and hê forþon næfre nôht leásungâ nê ídeles leôðes pyrcan meahte, ac efne
þâ ân þâ þe tô ǽfæstnesse belumpon and his þâ ǽfæstan tungan
gedafenôde singan. Þæs hê se man in peoruldhâde geseted ôð
þâ tîde, þe hê pæs gelýfedre yldo, and hê næfre nænig leôð ge-
15 leornôde, and hê forþon oft in gebeôrscipe, þonne þǽr pæs blisse
intingan gedêmed, þæt hí ealle sceolden þurh endebyrdnesse be
hearpan singan, þonne hê geseah þâ hearpan him neâlǽcan,
þonne ârâs hê for sceame fram þam symble and hâm côde tô his
hûse.

20 3. Þâ hê þæt þâ sumre tîde dide, þæt hê forlêt þæt hûs þæs
gebeôrscipes and ût pæs gangende tô neâtâ scypene, þârâ heord
him pæs þǽre nihte beboden; þâ hê þâ þǽr in gelimplícre tîde
his limu on reste gesette, and onslǽpte, þâ stôd him sum man æt
þurh spefn, and hine hâlette and grêtte, and hine be his naman
25 nemde, "Cædmon, sing mê hpæthpegu." Þâ andsparôde hê and
cpæð: "Ne con ic nôht singan, and ic forþon of þisum gebeôrscipe ûteôde, and hider gepât, forþon ic nôht cûðe." Eft hê
cpæð, se þe mid him spreecnde pæs, "Hpæðere þû meaht mê
singan." Cpæð hê, "Hpæt sceal ic singan?" Cpæð hê, "Sing
30 mê frumsceaft." Þâ hê þâs andspare onfêng, þâ ongan hê sôna
singan in herenesse Godes scyppendes þâ fers and þâ pord þe hê
næfre ne gehýrde; þârâ endebyrdnes þis is:

    4.   "Nû pê sceolon herian heofonríces Deard,
            Metodes mihte and his môdgeþonc,
35   perâ Duldorfæder, spâ hê pundrâ gehpæs,
            êce Dryhten, ord onstealde.
            He ǽrest gesceôp eorðan bearnum
            heofon tô hrôfe, hâlig Scyppend;
            þâ middangeard, moncynnes Deard,
40   êce Dryhten, æfter teôde
            firum foldan, Freâ ælmihtig."

5. Þá árás hé fram þam slǽpe, and eal þá þe hé slápende sang,
fæste in gemynde hæfde, and þám pordum sóna manig pord in
þæt ilce gemet Godé pyrdes songes tógeþeódde. Þá com hé on
morne tó þam tûngerêfan, se þe his caldorman pæs, and him sǽde
5 hpilce gife hé onféng, and hé hine sóna tó þǽre abbudissan ge-
lǽdde, and hire þæt cýdde and sægde. Þá hét heó gesamnian
ealle þá gelǽrdestan men, and þá leornerás, and him andpeardum
hét secgan þæt spefn and þæt leód singan, þætte ealrá heorá
dómé gecoren pǽre, hpæt oððe hponan þæt cumen pǽre. Þá
10 pæs him eallum gesepen spá spá hit pæs, þæt him pǽre fram
Dryhtne selfum heofonlíc gifu forgifen. Þá rehton hí him and
sægdon sum hálig spel and godeundre láre pord, bebudon him þá,
gif hé mihte, þæt hé him sum sunge and in spinsunge leóðsanges
þæt gehpyrfde. Þá hé þá hæfde þá písan onfangene, þá eóde hé
15 hám tó his húse, and com eft on morgen, and þý betstan leóðé geglenged him ásang and ágeaf þæt him beboden pæs.

6. Þá ongan seó abbudisse clyppan and lufian þá Godes gife in
þam men, and heó hine þá monóde and lǽrde, þæt hé peoruldhád
forléte and munuchade onfénge; and hé þæt pel þafóde; and heó
20 hine in þæt mynster onféng mid his gódum, and hine geþeódde
tó gesamnunge þárá Godes þeópá, and hét hine lǽran þæt getæl
þæs hálgan stǽres and spelles, and hé eal þá hé in gehêrnesse ge-
leornian mihte mid hine gemyngóde, and spá spá clǽne nýten
eodorcende in þæt spéteste leód gehpyrfde, and his song and his
25 leód pǽron spá pynsum tó gehýranne, þæt þá selfan his láreópás
æt his múđe priton and leornódon.

7. Sang hé ǽrest be middangeardes gesceape and be fruman
mancynnes and eal þæt stǽr Genesis, þæt is seó ǽreste Móyses
bóc, and eft be útgange Israêlá folces of Ægyptá lande, and be in-
30 gange þæs gehátlandes, and be óðrum manigum spellum þæs hálgan geprites canones bócá, and be Cristes menniscnesse, and be
his þrópunge, and be his upástígnesse on heofonás, and býg þæs
Hálgan Gástes cyme, and þárá Apostolá láre; and eft bí þam ege
þæs tópeardan dómes, and be fyrhto þæs tintreglícan píte, and
35 be spétnesse þæs heofonlícan ríces hé manig leóð geporhte; and
spile eác óðer manig be þám godcundum fremsumnessum and dó-
mum hé geporhte. On eallum þám hé geornlíce gýmde, þæt hé
men átuge fram synná lufan and mándǽdá, and tó lufan and tó
geornfulnesse ápehte gódrá dǽdá, forþon hé pæs se man spíđe
40 ǽfest, and reogollícum þeódscipum eádmódlíce underþeóded; and
pið þám þá þe on óðre písan dón poldon, hé pæs mid pylme mi

celre ellenþôdnesse onbærned, and hê forþon fægrê endê his lîf
betŷnde and geendôde.

8. Forþon þâ þære tîde neâlǽhte his gepitennesse and forðfôre, þâ þæs hê feôpertŷne dagum ǽr þæt hê þæs lîcumlîcre un-
5 trymnesse þrycced and hefigôd, hpæðere tôþon gemetlîce, þæt
hê ealle þâ tîd mihte ge sprecan ge gangan. Dæs þǽr on neâpeste untrumrâ mannâ hûs, on þam hirâ þeâp þæs þæt hî þâ untruman and þâ þe æt forðfôre pǽron in lǽdan sceoldan, and him
þǽr ætsomne þênian. Þâ bæd hê his þegn on ǽfenne þǽre nihte
10 þe hê of peorulde gangende pæs, þæt hê on þam hûse him stôpe
gegearpôde, þæt hê restan mihte. Þâ pundrôde se þegn forhpon
hê þæs bǽde, forþon him þuhte þæt his forðfôre spâ neâh ne
pǽre, dide hpæðere spâ spâ hê cpæð and bebeâd.

9. And mid þŷ hê þâ þǽr on reste eôde, and hê gefeôndê môdê
15 sumu þing ætgædere mid him sprecende and gleôpiende pæs, þe
þǽr ǽr inne pǽron, þâ pæs ofer middeniht þæt hê frægn, hpæðer
hî ǽnig hûsel þǽr inne hæfdon. Þâ andsparôdon hî and cpædon,
"Hpile þearf is þê hûsles? Ne þînre forðfôre spâ neâh is, nû
þû þus rôtlîce and þus glædlîce tô ûs sprecende eart." Cpæð hê
20 eft, "Beræð mê hpæðere hûsel tô." Þâ hê hit on handâ hæfde,
þâ frægn hê, hpæðer hî ealle smylte môd, and bûtan eallum incan
blîðe tô him hæfdon. Þâ andsparôdon hî ealle, and cpædon þæt
hî nǽnigne incan tô him piston, ac hî him ealle spîðe blîðemôde
pǽron, and hî prixendlîce hine bǽdon þæt hê him eallum blîðe
25 pǽre. Þâ andsparôde hê, and cpæð, "Mîne brôðru þâ leôfan, ic
com spîðe blîðmôd tô eôp and tô eallum Godes mannum." And
hê spâ pæs hine getrymmende mid þŷ heofonlîcan pegnestê, and
him ôðres lîfes ingang gearpôde. Þâ git hê frægn, hû neâh þǽre
tîde pǽre, þætte þâ brôðor ârîsan sceolden, and Godes lof rǽran
30 and heorâ uhtsang singan. Andsparôdon hî, "Nis hit feor tô
þon." Cpæð hê, "Tela, utan pê pel þǽre tîde bîdan!" And þâ
him gebæd, and hine gesênôde mid Cristes rôdetâcne, and his
heâfod onhylde tô þam bolstre, and medmicel fæc onslǽpte, and
spâ mid stilnesse his lîf geendôde.

35 10. And spâ pæs geporden, þætte spâ spâ hê hlutrê môdê and
bilepitê and smyltre pilsumnesse Drihtne þeôpde, þæt hê eâc
spilce spâ smyltê deâðê middangeard pæs forlǽtende and tô his
gesihðe becom, and seô tunge, þe spâ manig hâlpende pord on
þæs Scyppendes lof gesette, heô þâ spilce eâc þâ ŷtemestan pord
40 on his herenesse, hine selfne sêniende and his gâst in his handâ
bebeôdende, betŷnde.

POETRY.

DESCRIPTIONS OF GLEE-MEN AND POETS.
(*Traveler*, 135–143.)

Spâ **SC**rîđende ge**SC**eapum hpeorfađ
Gleô-men **G**umenâ geond **G**rundâ fela,
Thearfe secgađ, **Th**onc-pord sprecađ,
Simle **S**ûđ ođđe norđ **S**umne gemêtađ
Gyddâ **G**leâpne, **G**eofum unhneâpne,
5 se þe fore **D**uguđe pile **D**ôm árǽran,
EOrlscipe **Æ**fnan, ôđ þæt **EA**l scaceđ
Leôht and **L**îf somod: **L**of se gepyrceđ,
Hafađ under **H**eofonum **H**eâhfæstne dôm.

(*Beowulf*, 867–874.)

Hpîlum **C**yninges þegn,
10 **G**uma **G**ilp-blǽden, **G**iddâ gemyndig,
se þe **EA**l-fela **EA**ld-gesegenâ
VVorn gemunde, **VV**ord ôđer fand
Sôđe gebunden: **S**ecg eft ongan
Sîđ Beôpulfes **S**nyttrum styrian,
15 and on **SP**êd precan **SP**el gerâde,
VVordum **VV**rixlan.

(*Beowulf*, 89–98.)

—þǽr pæs **H**earpan spêg,
Sputol **S**ang scôpes. **S**ægde, se þe cûđe
Frumsceaft **F**irâ **F**eorran reccan,
20 cpæđ þæt se **Æ**lmihtiga **EO**rđan porhte
VVlite-beorhtne **VV**ang, spâ **VV**æter bebûgeđ,
ge**S**ette **S**ige-hrêdig **S**unnan and mônan
Leôman tô **L**eôhte **L**and-bûendum,
and ge**F**rætpâde **F**oldan sceâtâs
25 **L**eomum and **L**eâfum, **L**îf eâc gesceôp
Cynnâ geh**vv**ylcum, þârâ þe **C**pice h**vv**yrfađ.

CÆDMON'S GENESIS.
(*The First Day*, 103–134.)

Ne pæs hêr þâ giet   nymðe heolster-sceado
piht geporden,   ac þes pîda grund
stôd deôp and dim,   Drihtne fremde,
îdel and unnyt: on þone eâgum plât
5 stîð-frihð cyning,   and þâ stôpe beheôld
dreâmâ leâse,   geseah deorc gespeorc
semian sinnihte   speart under roderum,
pon and pêste,   ôð þæt þeôs poruld-gesceaft
þurh pord gepearð   puldor-cyninges.
10 Hêr ærest gesceôp   êce Drihten
helm ealpihtâ   heofon and eorðan,
rodor ârærde,   and þis rûme land
gestaðelôde   strangum mihtum,
Freâ ælmihtig.   Folde pæs þâ gyt
15 græs ungrêne: gârsecg þeahte
speart sinnihte   sîde and pîde,
ponne pægâs.   Pâ pæs puldor-torht
Heofon-peardes gâst   ofer holm boren
miclum spêdum.   Metod englâ hêht
20 lîfes Brytta   leôht forð cuman
ofer rûmne grund;   raðe pæs gefylled
Heâh-cyninges hæs: him pæs hâlig leôht
ofer pêstenne,   spâ se Dyrhta bebeâd.
Pâ gesundrôde   sigorâ Daldend
25 ofer lago-flôde   leôht pið þeôstrum,
sceade pið scîman.   Sceôp þâ bâm naman
lîfes Brytta;   leôht pæs ærest
þurh Drihtnes pord   dæg genemned,
plitebeorhte gesceaft.   Del lîcôde
30 Freân æt frymðe   forðbæro tîd:
dæg æresta geseah   deorc sceado
speart spiðrian   geond sîdne grund.

(*Satan's Speech*, 347–388.)

Satan maðelôde;   sorgiende spræc
se þe helle forð   healdan sceolde,
35 gŷman þæs grundes: pæs ær Godes engel

CÆDMON'S GENESIS.
(*The First Day*, 103–104.)

    Ne¹ was there then yet   nymthe² holster³-shadow
    wight³ i-worthen⁵,   ac⁶ this wide ground
    stood deep and dim,   to-Drihte⁷ fremde⁸,
    idle and unnut⁹: on that with-eyes wlat¹⁰
5   stith¹¹-frith¹² king,   and the stows¹³ beheld
    of-dreams¹⁴ less¹⁴,   i-saw dark i-swerk¹⁵
    seme¹⁶ sinnight¹⁷   swart under roders¹⁸,
    wan and waste,   oth¹⁹ that this world-schaft²⁰
    through word i-worth²¹   wulder²²-king's.
10   Here erst²³ i-shaped   eche²⁴ Drihte⁷,
    helm²⁵ of-all-wights²⁶,   heaven and earth,
    roder¹⁸ a-reared,   and this roomy land
    i-statheled²⁷   with strong mights,
    Frea²⁸ almighty.   Folde²⁹ was then yet
15   as-to-grass ungreen: garsedge³⁰ thatched³¹
    swart sinnight¹⁷   side³² and wide,
    wan waves.   Then was wulder²⁷-tort³³
    Heaven-ward's²⁴ ghost²⁵   over holm³⁶ borne
    with-mickle speeds.   Metod³⁷ of-angels heht³⁸,
20   life's Brytta³⁹,   light forth to-come
    over roomy ground;   rathe⁴⁰ was i-filled⁴¹
    High-king's hest: to-him was holy light
    over waste,   so the Wright⁴² (be-)bade.
    Then i-sundered   siyers'⁴³ Wielding⁴⁴
25   over leye⁴⁵-flood   light with⁴⁶ thuster⁴⁷,
    shade with⁴⁶ shimmer.   Shope⁴⁸ then for-both names
    life's Brytta³⁹;   light was erst²³
    through Drihte's⁷ word   day i-named,
    wlite⁴⁹-bright i-shaft²⁰.   Well liked⁵⁰
30   Frea²⁸ at frumthe⁵¹   forthbearing⁵² tide⁵³:
    day erst²³ i-saw   dark shadow
    swart swither⁵⁴   yond⁵⁵ side³² ground.

(*Satan's Speech*, 347–388.)

    Satan matheled⁵⁶;   sorrowing spake
    he that hell forth⁵⁷   hold should
35   to-yeme⁵⁸ the ground: was ere⁵⁹ God's angel

---

¹ not. ² except (?). ³ cave, cavernous. ⁴ aught. ⁵ existent, created. ⁶ but (P.P.) ⁷ God (P.P.). ⁸ strange (Ch.). ⁹ useless (S.). ¹⁰ looked (S.). ¹¹ strong. ¹² mind (?). ¹³ places (S.). ¹⁴ joy-less. ¹⁵ murkiness (?). ¹⁶ remain (?). ¹⁷ in sem-piternal night (?). ¹⁸ heavens (?). ¹⁹ till (?). ²⁰ creation (?). ²¹ came into being. ²² glory (S.). ²³ first. ²⁴ eternal (S.). ²⁵ protector. ²⁶ beings. ²⁷ established (S.). ²⁸ sovereign (?). ²⁹ earth (S.). ³⁰ ocean (?). ³¹ covered. ³² far, long (P.P.). ³³ bright (H.). ³⁴ warder, guardian. ³⁵ spirit. ³⁶ high sea. ³⁷ creator (?). ³⁸ ordered (P.P., Ch.). ³⁹ allotter (?). ⁴⁰ soon. ⁴¹ fulfilled. ⁴² victories' (?). ⁴³ Ruler. ⁴⁵ lake (H.). ⁴⁶ from. ⁴⁷ darkness (S.). ⁴⁸ shaped, formed (Ch., P.P.). ⁴⁹ beautiful (S.). ⁵⁰ pleased (Ch., P.P.). ⁵¹ beginning (S.). ⁵² creation's. ⁵³ time. ⁵⁴ pass away (H.). ⁵⁵ over, beyond. ⁵⁶ spoke (S.). ⁵⁷ thenceforth. ⁵⁸ keep (P.P.). ⁵⁹ once, before.

CÆDMON'S GENESIS.

      white in heaven,   oth[1] him his huie[2] forspene[3]
      and his overmet[4]   of all swithest[5],
      that he ne[6] would   wereds[17] Drihte's[8]
      word worthy[9].   Welled to-him on in[10]
5   huie[2] ymb[11] his heart;   hot was to-him out[12]
      wrothly[13] wite[14]. He then with-word quoth:
        Is this ange[15] stead[16]   unlike swithe[17]
      the other   that we ere couth[18]
      high on heaven-riche[19],   that me mine herre[20] on-loaned[21],
10   though we hine[22] for the all-wielder   owe[23] ne[6] must,
      rome[24] our riche[19]. Nafth[25] he though right i-done
      that he us hath i-felled   in-fire to bottom
      of-hell the hot,   heaven-riche[19] be-numen[26],
      hath it i-marked   mid[27] mankind
15   to i-settle. That to-me is of-sorrows most
      that Adam shall,   that was of earth i-wrought,
      mine strong   stool[28] (be-)hold,
      be to-him*self* in wynne[29],   and we this wite[14] thole[30],
      harm on this hell. Wo lo! owed[23] I my hands' i-wald[31],
20   and might one tide[32]   out worth[33],
      be one winter-stound[33],   then I mid this wered[7]—!
        Ac[34] lie me ymbe[11]   iron bonds,
      rideth[35] racket's[36] sole[37]:   I am riche[19]-less!
      have me so hard   hell clomps
25   fast befangen[38]! Here is fire mickle
      up and neath! I o[39] ne[6] i-saw
      loather[40] landscipe!   leye[41] ne[6] a-swome[42]
      hot over hell. Me have rings' i-spang[43],
      slith-hard[44] sole[37],   from-sith[45] a-merred[46],
30   a-ferred[46] me from-my feeth[47],   feet are i-bounden,
      hands i-haft[48];   are these hell-doors'
      ways forwrought[49];   so I mid[50] wight[50] ne[6] may
      off these lith[51]-bonds. Lie me about
      of-hard iron   hot i-slain[52]
35   grindels[53] great;   mid[27] that me God hath
      i-hafted[48] by the halse[54]. So I wot, he my huie[2] cuth[18]
      and that wist eke[55]   wereds[17] Drihte[8],
      that should us, *me and* Adam,   evil i-worth[56]
      ymb[11] that heaven-riche[19],   there[57] I owed[23] my hands' i-wald![31]

[1] till (?). [2] mind (S.). [3] seduced (?). [4] pride (S.). [5] mightiest (P.P., Ch.). [6] not. [7] hosts (S.). [8] Lord (P.P.). [9] honor, obey (S.). [10] within. [11] about (?). [12] without. [13] wrathful (S.). [14] punishment (Ch.). [15] narrow (S.). [16] place. [17] very (P.P., Ch.). [18] knew. [19] kingdom, -ric (S.). [20] lord (S.). [21] presented. [22] it (S.). [23] have, own. [24] use (?). [25] hath not (S.). [26] taken (Ch., P.P.). [27] with (P.P.). [28] seat. [29] joy (H.). [30] suffer. [31] power, control (S.). [32] hour. [33] be free. [34] but. [35] oppresseth. [36] bonds' (?). [37] rope (S.). [38] caught (S.). [39] ever (S.). [40] loathlier. [41] fire, low (P. P.). [42] smoulder (?). [43] fastening (H.). [44] terrible (?). [45] departure (P. P.). [46] prevented (S.). [47] path, departure (?). [48] held (?). [49] obstructed, closed (S.). [50] any way. [51] limbs. [52] forged (S.). [53] bars, clogs (S.). [54] neck. [55] also. [56] happen to. [57] if.

　　　　　hpît on heofne,　ôđ hine his hyge forspeôn
　　　　　and his ofermetto　ealrâ spîđôst,
　　　　　þæt hê ne polde　peređâ Drihtnes
　　　　　pord purđian.　Deôl him on innan
5　　　　hyge ymb his heortan;　hât pæs him ûtan
　　　　　prâdlîc pîte.　Hê þâ porđe cpæđ:
　　　　　"Is þes ænga stede　ungelîc spîđe
　　　　　þam ôđrum　þe pê ǽr cûđon
　　　　　heân on heofon-rîce,　þe mê mîn hearra onlâg,
10　　　þeâh pê hine for þam alpealdan　âgan ne môston,
　　　　　rômigan ûres rîces.　Næfđ hê þeâh riht gedôn
　　　　　þæt hê ûs hæfđ befylled　fýre tô botme
　　　　　helle þǽre hâtan,　heofon-rîce benumen,
　　　　　hafâđ hit gemearcôd　mid mon-cynne
15　　　tô gesettanne.　Pæt mê is sorgâ mǽst
　　　　　þæt Adam sceal,　þe pæs of eorđan geporht,
　　　　　mînne stronglîcan　stôl behealdan,
　　　　　pesan him on pynne,　and pê þis pîte þolien
　　　　　hearm on þisse helle.　Dâ lâ! âhte ic mînrâ handâ ge-
20　　　and môste âne tîd　ûte peorđan,　　　　　[peald
　　　　　pesan âne pinter-stunde,　þonne ic mid þýs perodê—!
　　　　　Ac liegađ mê ymbe　îren-bendâs,
　　　　rîđeđ racentan sâl:　ic eom rîces leâs!
　　　　　habbađ mê spâ hearde　helle clommâs
25　　　fæste befangen!　Hêr is fýr micel
　　　　　ufan and neođone!　ic â ne geseah
　　　　　lâđran landscipe!　lîg ne âspâmâđ
　　　　　hât ofer helle.　Mê habbađ hringâ gespong,
　　　　　slîđ-hearda sâl　sîđes âmyrred,
30　　　âfyrred mê mîn fêđe;　fêt synt gebundene,
　　　　　handâ gehæfte;　synt þissâ hel-dorâ
　　　　　pegâs forporhte:　spâ ic mid pihte ne mæg
　　　　　of þissum liođo-bendum.　Liegađ mê ymbûtan
　　　　　heardes îrenes　hâte geslægene
35　　　grindlâs greâte;　mid þý mê God hafâđ
　　　　　gehæfted be þam healse.　Spâ ic pât, hê mînne hige cûđe
　　　　　and þæt piste eâc　perodâ Drihten,
　　　　　þæt sceolde unc Adame　yfele gepurđan
　　　　　ymb þæt heofon-rîce,　þǽr ic âhte mînrâ handâ gepeald!

E

CÆDMON'S EXODUS.
(*The Flight of the Israelites*, 68–85.)

  Nearþe genýddon on norð-pegâs,
  piston him be súðan Sigelparâ land,
  forbærned burh-hleoðu, brúne leôde
  hâtum heofon-colum. Þêr hâlig God
5 pið fær-bryne folc gescylde,
  bælcê oferbrædde byrnendne heofon,
  hâlgan nettê hâtþendne lyft.
  Hæfde þeder-polcen pídum fæðmum
  eorðan and uprodor efne gedæled,
10 lædde leód-perod; líg-fýr âdranc
  hâte heofon-torht. Hæleð pâfedon,
  drihtâ gedrýmôst. Dæg-scealdes hleô
  pand ofer polcnum: hæfde pitig God
  sunnan síð-fæt seglê ofertolden,
15 spâ þâ mæst-râpâs men ne cúðon,
  nê þâ segl-rôde geseôn meahton
  eorð-búende callê cræftê,
  hú âfæstnôd pæs feld-húsâ mæst.

(106–134.)

       Folc pæs on sâlum,
20 hlúd herges cyrm. Heofon-beâcen âstâh
  æfenâ gehpam, ôðer pundor;
  syllíc æfter sunnan setl-râde beheóld
  ofer leôd-perum lígê scînan
  byrnende beâm. Blâce stôdon
25 ofer sceôtendum scîre leôman,
  scinon scyld-hreôðan, sceado spiðredon:
  neôþle niht-scúpan neah ne mihton
  heolstor âhýdan. Heofon-candel barn:
  nipe niht-peard nýde sceolde
30 pícian ofer peredum, þý læs him pêsten-gryrð
  hâr hæð holmegum pedrum
  ô fêrclammê ferhð getpæfde.
  Hæfde foregenga fýrene loccâs,
  blâce beâmâs, bæl-egsan hpeóp
35 þam here-þreâte, hâtan lígê,

CÆDMON'S EXODUS.

```
      þæt hê on pêstenne      perod forbærnde,
      nymđe hîe môd-hpate     Môyses hŷrde.
      Sceûn scîr perod,       scyldâs lixton;
      gesâpon rand-pîgan      rihtre strǣte
 5    segn ofer speotum,      ôđ þæt sǣ-fæsten
      landes æt ende          leôd-mægne forstôd,
      fûs on forđ-peg.        Fyrd-pîc ârâs,
      þyrpton hîe pêrige;     piste genôgdon
      môdige mete-þegnâs      hyrâ mægen bêtan.
10    Brǣddon æfter beorgum,  sidđan bŷme sang,
      flotan feld-hûsum:      þâ pæs feôrđe pîc,
      rand-pîgenâ ræst        be þam Reâdan sǣ.

                (154–182.)

      Þâ him eorlâ môd        ortrŷpe pearđ,
      sidđan hîe gesâpon      of sûđ-pegum
15    fyrd Faraônes           forđ ongangan,
      ofer-holt pegan,        eôred lixan,
      þûfâs þunian,           þeôd meare tredan:
      gârûs trymedon,         gûđ hpearfôde,
      blicon bord-hreôđan,    bŷman sungon.
20    On hpæl hreôpon         here-fugolâs
      hilde grǣdige;          hræfen gôl
      deâpig-feđere           ofer driht-nêum,
      þon pæl-ceûsega.        Þulfûs sungon
      atol ǣfen-leôđ          ǣtes on pênan,
25    earleâsan deôr,         epyld-rôf beôdan
      on lâđrâ lâst           leôd-mægnes fyl,
      hreôpon mearc-peardâs   middum nihtum:
      fleâh fǣge gâst,        folc pæs gehǣged.
      Hpîlum of þam perode    planee þegnâs
30    mǣton mîl-pađâs         mearâ bôgum.
      Him þǣr sige-cyning     pid þone segn foran
      mannâ þengel            mearc-þreâtê râd;
      gûđ-peard gumenâ        grîm-helm gespeôn,
      cyning cin-berge        (cumbol lixton)
35    pîges on pênum,         pæl-hlencan sceôc,
      hêht his here-ciste     healdan georne
      fæst fyrd-getrum.       Feônd onsêgon
      lâđum eâgum             land-mannâ cyme.
      Ymb hine pâgon          pîgend unforhte;
```

hâre heoro-pulfâs   hilde grêtton
þurstige þræc-pîges,   þeôden-holde.

BEOWULF.
(*A Good King*, 1–11.)

Hpæt! pê Gâr-Denâ   in geâr-dagum
þeôd-cyningâ   þrym gefrunon,
5   hû þâ æðelingâs   ellen fremedon!
Oft Scyld Scêfing   sceaðenâ þreâtum,
monegum mǽgðum   meodo-setlâ ofteâh;
egsôde eorl,   syððan ǽrest peard
feâsceaft funden;   hê þæs frôfre gebâd,
10   peôx under polcnum,   peorðmyndum þâh,
ôð þæt him ǽghpylc   þârâ ymb-sittendrâ
ofer hron-râde   hŷran scolde,
gomban gyldan: þæt pæs gôd cyning!

(*Obsequies of Scyld*, 26–52.)

Him þâ Scyld gepât   tô gescœp-hpîle
15   fela-hrôr fêran   on Freân pǽre.
Hî hyne þâ ætbǽron   tô brimes farôðe,
spǽse gesîðâs,   spâ hê selfa bæd,
þenden pordum peôld   pine Scyldingâ,
leôf land-fruma,   longe âhte.
20   Pǽr æt hŷðe stôd   hringed-stefna
îsig and ût-fûs,   æðelinges fær:
âlêdon þâ   leôfne þeôden,
beâgâ bryttan,   on bearm scipes,
mǽrne be mæste.   Pǽr pæs mâðmâ fela
25   of feor-pegum,   frætpâ, gelǽded:
ne hŷrde ic cymlîcor   ceôl gegyrpan
hilde-pǽpnum   and heaðo-pǽdum,
billum and byrnum: him on bearme læg
mâðmâ mænigo,   þâ him mid scoldon
30   on flôdes ǽht   feor gepîtan.
Nalæs hî hine læssan   lâcum teôdan,
þeôd-gestreônum,   þonne þâ dydon,
þe hine æt frumsceafte   forð onsendon

ǽnne ofer ẏđe　　umbor pesende:
þâ gyt hîe him âsetton　　segen gyldenne
heâh ofer heâfod,　　lêton holm beran,
geâfon on gâr-secg:　　him pæs geômor sefâ,
.5　murnende môd.　Men ne cunnon
secgan tô sôđe,　　sele-rǽdende,
hæleđ under heofenum,　　hpâ þæm hlæste onfêng!

(Hrothgar and Heorot, 64–83.)

Pâ pæs HRÔÐGÂRE　　here-spêd gyfen,
pîges peorđmynd,　　þæt him his pine-magâs
10　georne hýrdon,　　ôđ þæt seô geôgođ gepeôx,
mago-driht micel.　Him on môd be-arn,
þæt hê heal-reced　　hâtan polde,
medo-ærn micel　　men gepyrcean,
þone yldo bearn　　ǽfre gefrunon,
15　and þǽr on-innan　　eal gedǽlan
geongum and ealdum,　　spyle him God sealde,
bûton folc-scare　　and feorum gumenâ.
Pâ ic pîde gefrægn　　peorc gebannan
manigre mǽgđe　　geond þisne middangeard,
20　folc-stede frætpan.　Him on fyrste gelomp
ædre mid yldum,　　þæt hit peard eal gearo,
heal-ærnâ mǽst:　　scôp him HEORT naman,
se þe his pordes gepeald　　pîde hæfde.
Hê beôt ne âlêh,　　beâgâs dǽlde,
25　sinc æt symle.　Sele hlifâde
heâh and horn-geâp.

(Grendel, 99–129.)

Spâ þâ driht-guman　　dreâmum lifdon
eâdiglîce,　　ôđ þæt ân ongan
fyrene fremman,　　feônd on helle:
30　pæs se grimma gǽst　　GRENDEL hâten,
mǽre mearc-stapa,　　se þe môrâs heôld,
fen and fæsten；　　fîfel-cynnes eard
ponsǽlig per　　peardôde hpîle,
siđđan him Scyppend　　forscrifen hæfde.
35　In Caines cynne　　þone cpealm gepræc
êce Drihten,　　þæs þe hê Abel slôg:
ne gefeah hê þǽre fǽhđe,　　ac hê hine feor forpræc,

Metod for þý máné   man-cynne fram.
Þanon untýdrás   ealle onwócon,
eotenás and ylfe   and orcneás,
swylce gigantás,   þá wið Gode wunnon
lange þrage: hé him þæs leán forgeald!—
Gewát þá neósian,   syððan niht becom,
heán húses,   hú hit Hring-Dene
æfter beór-þege   gebún hæfdon;
fand þá þær inne   æðelingá gedriht
swefan æfter symble: sorge ne cúðon,
wonsceaft wera.   Wiht unhælo
grim and grædig   gearo sóna wæs,
reóc and réðe,   and on ræste genam
þrítig þegná;   þanon eft gewát
húðe hrémig   tó hám faran,
mid þære wæl-fylle   wíca neósan.
Ðá wæs on uhtan   mid ær-dæge
GRENDLES gúð-cræft   gumum undyrne:
þá wæs æfter wiste   wóp up-áhafen,
micel morgen-swég.

(144–152.)

Swá ríxode   and wið rihte wan
ána wið eallum,   óð þæt ídel stód
húsá sélest.   Wæs seó hwíl micel:
twelf wintrá tíd   torn geþolóde
wine Scyldingá,   weáná gehwelcne,
sídrá sorgá;   forþam siððan wearð
yldá bearnum   undyrne cúð,
gyddum geómore,   þætte GRENDEL wan
hwíle wið Hróðgár.

(*Beowulf sails for Heorot*, 194–228.)

Þæt fram hám gefrægn   Higeláces þegn,
gód mid Geátum,   Grendles dæda:
se wæs mon-cynnes   mægenes strengest
on þæm dæge   þysses lífes,
æðele and eácen.   Hét him ýð-lidan
gódne gegyrwan;   cwæð hé gúð-cyning
ofer swan-ráde   sécean wolde,
mærne þeóden,   þá him wæs manná þearf.

205. Hæfde se gôda   Geâtâ leôdâ
     cempan gecorone,   þârâ þe hê cênôste
     findan mihte: fîftênâ sum
     sund-pudu sôhte;   secg pîsâde,
5   lagu-cræftig mon,   land-gemyrcu.
     Fyrst forð gepât: flota pæs on ŷdum,
     bât under beorge.   Beornâs gearpe
     on stefn stigon;   streâmâs pundon
     sund pið sande.   Secgâs bæron
10   on bearm nacan   beorhte frætpe,
     gûð-searo geatolîc: guman ût scufon,
     perâs on pilsîð   pudu bundenne.
     Gepât þâ ofer pæg-holm   pindê gefŷsed
     flota fâmig-heals   fugle gelîcôst,
15   ôð þæt ymb ân-tîd   ôðres dôgores
     punden-stefna   gepaden hæfde,
     þæt þâ lîðende   land gesâpon,
     brim-clifu blîcan,   beorgâs steâpe,
     sîde sǽ-næssâs: þâ pæs sund liden
20   eoletes æt ende.   Þanon up hraðe
     Þederâ leôde   on pang stigon,
     sǽ-pudu sǽldon: syrcan hrysedon,
     gûð-gepǽdo;   Gode þancedon,
     þæs þe him ŷð-lâde   eâðe purdon.

     (*The Warden of the Shore*, 229 +.)

25   Þâ of pealle geseah   peard Scyldingâ,
     se þe holm-clifu   healdan scolde,
     beran ofer bolcan   beorhte randâs,
     fyrd-searu fûslîcu;   hine fyrpyt bræc
     môd-gehygdum,   hpæt þâ men pǽron.
30   Gepât him þâ tô paróðe   picgê rîdan
     þegn Hrôðgâres,   þrymmum cpehte
     mægen-pudu mundum,   meðel-pordum frægn:
     "Hpæt syndon gê   searo-hæbbendrâ
     byrnum perede,   þe þus brontne ceól
35   ofer lagu-strǽte   lǽdan cpômon,
     hider ofer holmâs   Hrôðgâr sêccan?
     Ic þæs ende-sǽta,   ǽg-pearde heóld,
     þæt on land Denâ   lâðrâ nǽnig
     mid scip-herge   sceððan ne meahte.

Nô hêr cûðlicôr   cuman ongunnon
lind-hæbbende!   nê gê leâfnes-pord
gûð-fremmendrâ   gearpe ne pisson,
magû gemêdu!   Næfre ic mâran geseah
eorlâ ofer eorðan,   þonne is eôper sum,
secg on searpum;   nis þæt seld-guma
pæpnum gepeorðâd,   næfne him his plite leôge,
ænlîc ansŷn.   Nû ic eôper sceal
frum-cyn pitan,   ær gê fyr heonan
leâse sceâperâs   on land Denâ
furður fêran.   Nû gê feor-bûend
mere-liðende,   mînne gehŷrað
ânfealdne geþoht;   ôfost is sêlest
tô gecŷðanne,   hpanan eôpre cyme syndon."

Him se yldesta   andsparôde,
perodes pîsa   pord-hord onleác:
"Pê synt gum-cynnes Geâtâ leôde
and Higelâces   heorð-geneâtâs.
Pæs mîn fæder   folcum gecŷðed,
æðele ord-fruma   Ecgþeôp hâten;
gebâd pintrâ porn,   ær hê on peg hpurfe
gamol of geardum;   hine gearpe geman
pitenâ pel-hpylc   pîde geond eorðan.
Pê þurh holdne hige hlâford þînne
sunu Healfdenes   sêcean epômon,
leôd-gebyrgean.   Pes þû ûs lârenâ gôd!"

286. Peard maðelôde,   þær on piege sæt
ombeht unforht: "Æghpæðres sceal
scearp scyld-pîga   gescâd pitan,
porðâ and porca,   se þe pel þenceð.
Ic þæt gehŷre,   þæt þis is hold peorod
freân Scyldingâ: gepîtað forð beran
pæpen and gepædu,   ic côp pîsige."

301. Gepiton him þâ fêran.   Flota stille bûd,
seomôde on sôle   sîd-fæðmed scip,
on ancre fæst.   Eoforlîc scionon
ofer hleôr-beran   gehroden goldê
fâh and fyr-heard;   ferh peardo heôld.
Gûð-môde grummon,   guman onetton,

```
        sigon ætsomne,    ôđ þæt hý sæl timbred
        geatolîc and gold-fåh    ongytan mihton;
        þæt pæs fore-mǽrôst    fold-bûendum
        recedâ under roderum,    on þæm se rîca bâd;
 5      lixte se leôma    ofer landâ fela.
        Him þâ hilde-deôr    hof môdigrâ
        torht getǽhte,    þæt hý him tô mihton
        gegnum gangan.    Gûđ-beornâ sum
        picg gepende,    pord æfter cpæd:
10      "Mǽl is mô tô fêran!    Fæder alpalda
        mid ûr-stafum    eôpic gehealde
        sîđâ gesunde!    ic tô sǽ pille
        piđ prâđ perod    pearde healdan."
```

A Feast of Welcome.—(*Wealhtheow, the Queen*, 612 +.)

```
        Þǽr pæs hæleđâ hleahtor;    hlyn spynsôde,
15      pord pǽron pynsume.    Eôde DEALHPEÓD forđ,
        cpên Hrôđgâres    cynnâ gemyndig,
        grêtte gold-hroden    guman on healle,
        and þâ freôlîc pîf    ful gesealde
        ǽrest Eâst-Denâ    êđel-pearde,
20      bæd hine blîđne    æt þǽre beôr-þege,
        leôdum leôfne;    hê on lust geþeah
        symbel and sele-ful,    sige-rôf cyning.
        Ymb-eôde þâ    ides Helmingâ
        duguđe and geôgođe    dǽl ǽghpylcne;
25      sinc-fato sealde,    ôđ þæt sǽl âlamp,
        þæt hiô Beôpulfe,    beâg-hroden cpên
        môđe geþungen,    medo-ful ætbær;
        grêtte Geâtâ leôd,    Gode þancôde
        pîs-fæst pordum,    þæs þe hire se pilla gelamp,
30      þæt heô on ǽnigne    eorl gelýfde
        fyrenâ frôfre.    Hê þæt ful geþeah,
        pæl-reôp pîga,    æt DEALHPEÔN,
        and þâ gyddôde    gûđe gefýsed;
        Beôpulf mađelôde,    bearn Ecgþeôpes:
35      "Ic þæt hogôde,    þâ ic on holm gestâh,
        sǽ-bât gesæt    mid minrâ secgâ gedriht,
        þæt ic ânunga    eôprâ leôdâ
        pillan geporhte,    ođđe on pæl crunge,
        feônd-grâpum fæst.    Ic gefremman sceal
```

```
            eorlîc ellen,    oððe ende-dæg
            on þisse meodu-healle    mînne gebîdan."
            Þam wîfe þâ word    wel lîcôdon,
            gilp-cwide Geâtes;    eôde gold-hroden
   5        freólîcu folc-cwên    tô hire freán sittan.
            Þâ wæs eft swâ ær    inne on healle
            þryd-word sprecen,    þeôd on sælum,
            sige-folcâ sweg,    oð þæt semninga
            sunu Healfdenes    sêccan wolde
  10        æfen-ræste.

                      (Good-Night.)
      651.            Þerod eal ârâs.
            Grêtte þâ    guma ôðerne,
            HRÔÐGÂR BEÔWULF,    and him hæl âbeâd.

     1789.            Niht-helm geswearc
  15        deorc ofer dryht-gumum.    Duguð eal ârâs;
            wolde blonden-feax    beddes neôsan,
            gamela Scylding.    Geât ungemétes wel
            rôfne rand-wîgan    restan lyste:
            sôna him sele-þegn    sîdes wêrgum,
  20        feorran-cundum    forð wîsâde,
            se for andrysnum    ealle bewcotede
            þegnes þearfe,    swylce þŷ dôgorô
            heaðo-lîðende    habban sceoldon.
            Reste hine þâ rûm-heort;    reced hlifâde
  25        geâp and gold-fâh,    gæst inne swæf,
            oð þæt hrefn blaca    heofenes wynne
            blîð-heort bodôde,    côman beorhte leôman
            ofer scadu scacan.

                (Hrunting, the Good Sword, 1455 +.)
            Næs þæt þonne mætôst    mægen-fultumâ,
  30        þæt him on þearfe lâh    þyle Hrôðgâres;
            wæs þæm hæft-mêce    HRUNTING nama,
            þæt wæs ân foran    eald-gestreônâ;
            ecg wæs îren,    âter-tânum fâh,
            âhyrded heaðo-swâtô;    næfre hit æt hilde ne swâc
  35        mannâ ængum    þârâ þe hit mid mundum bewand,
            se þe gryre-sîðâs    gegân dorste.
```

folc-stede fâra; næs þæt forma sîð,
þæt hit ellen-peorc æfnan scolde.

(It fails at Need, 1512 +.)

    Pâ se eorl ongeat,
þæt hô in nið-sele nât-hpylcum þæs,
5. þǽr him nǽnig pæter pihtê ne sceðede,
nê him for hrôf-sele hrînan ne mehte
fǽr-gripe flôdes: fŷr-leôht geseah,
blâcne leôman beorhte scînan.
Ongeat þâ se gôda grund-pyrgenne,
10 mere-pîf mihtig; mægen-rǽs forgeaf
hilde-billê, hond spenge ne oftcâh,
þæt hire on hafelan hring-mǽl âgôl
grǽdig gûð-leôð; þâ se gist onfand,
þæt se beado-leôma bîtan nolde,
15 aldre sceððan, ac seô ecg gespâc
þeôdne æt þearfe: þolôde ǽr fela
hond-gemôtâ, helm oft gescǽr,
fǽges fyrd-hrægl: þâ þæs forma sið
deôrum mâðme, þæt his dôm âlǽg.
20 Eft þæs ân-rǽd, nalas elnes læt,
mǽrðâ gemyndig mǽg Hygelâces;
pearp þâ punden-mǽl prǽttum gebunden
yrre oretta, þæt hit on eorðan læg,
stîð and stŷl-ecg; strenge getrûpôde,
25 mund-gripe mægenes. Spâ sceal man dôn
þonne hê æt gûðe gegân þenceð
longsumne lof, nâ ymb his lîf cearâð.

(The Right Weapon, 1557 +.)

   Geseah þâ on scarpum sige-eâdig bil,
eald speord eotenisc ecgum þyhtig,
30 pîgenâ peorð-mynd: þæt þæs pǽpnâ cyst,
bûton hit þæs mâre þonne ǽnig mon ôðer
tô beadu-lâce ætberan meahte,
gôd and geatolic gigantâ gepeorc.
Hê gefêng þâ fetel-hilt, freca Scyldingâ,
35 hreôh and heoro-grim hring-mǽl gebrægd.

1687. Hrôðgâr maðelôde, hilt sceâpôde,

ealde láfe,   on þæm þæs ór priten
fyrn-gepinnes: syððan flód ofslóh,
gifen geótende,   gigantâ cyn,
frêcne gefèrdon: þæt pæs fremde þeód
5 êcean Dryhtne,   him þæs ende-leán
þurh pæteres pylm   paldend sealde.
Spâ pæs on þæm scennum   scîran goldes
þurh rûn-stafâs   rihte gemearcôd,
geseted and gesæd,   hpâm þæt speord geporht,
10 írenâ cyst,   ærest pære,
preoðen-hilt and pyrm-fâh.

ALFRED'S METERS OF BOETHIUS.

Þus Ælfrêd ûs   eald-spel reahte
cyning Dest-Sexnâ,   cræft meldóde,
leóð-pyrhtâ list: him pæs lust micel,
15 þæt hê þiossum leódum   leóð spellôde,
monnum myrgen,   mislíce epidâs.

Meter VI.

Pâ se Pîsdóm eft   pord-hord onleâc,
sang sóð-epidâs,   and þus selfa cpæð:
Þonne sió sunne   speotolôst scîneð
20 hâdrôst of hefone,   hræðe bióð áþîstród
ealle ofer eorðan   óðre steorran;
forþæm hiorâ birhtu   ne bið áuht
tô gesettanne   pið þære sunnan leóht.
Þonne smolte blǽpð   sûðan and pestan
25 pind under polcnum,   þonne peaxað hraðe
feldes blôstman   fægen þæt hî môton:
ac se stearca storm,   þonne hê strong cymð
norðan and câstan,   hê genimeð hraðe
þære rôsan plite,   and eâc þâ rûman sǽ
30 norðerne ŷst   nêde gebǽdeð,
þæt hió strange geondstyred   on staðu beâteð.
Eâ lâ! þæt on eorðan   âuht fæstlíces
peorces on porulde   ne punâð ǽfre!

Meter X.

23. Hpær sind nû þæs pîsan   Dêlandes bân,
þæs gold-smiđes,   þe pæs geô mærôst?
Forþŷ ic cpæđ þæs pîsan   Dêlandes bân,
forþŷ ængum ne mæg   eorđ-bûendrâ
5   se cræft losian,   þe him Crist onlænđ.
Ne mæg mon æfre þŷ êđ   ænne præccan
his cræftes beniman,   þe mon oncerran mæg
sunnan on-spîfan   and þisne spiftan rodor
of his riht-ryne   rincâ ænig.
10 Hpâ pât nû þæs pîsan   Dêlandes bân,
on hpelcum hî hlæpâ   hrusan þeccen?
Hpær is nû se rîca   Rômânâ pita
and se ârôda,   þe pê ymb sprecađ,
hiorâ heretoga,   se gehâten pæs
15 mid þæm burhparum   Brûtus nemned?
Hpær is eâc se pîsa   and se peordgeorna
and se fæst-ræda   folces hyrde,
se pæs ûđpita   ælces þinges
cêne and cræftig,   þæm pæs Catôn nama?
20 Hî pæron gefyrn   forđ gepitene:
nât nænig mon,   hpær hî nû sindon!
Hpæt is hiorâ here   bûton se hlîsa ân?
se is eâc tô lytel   spelcrâ lâriôpâ,
forþæm þâ mago-rincâs   mâran pyrđe
25 pæron on porulde.   Ac hit is pyrse nû,
þæt geond þâs eorđan   æghpær sindon
hiorâ gelîcan   hpôn ymbspræce,
sume openlîce   ealle forgitene,
þæt hî se hlîsa   hîp-cûđe ne mæg
30 fore-mære perâs   forđ gebrengan!
Peâh gê nû pênen   and pilnigen,
þæt gê lange tîd   libban môten,
hpæt iôp æfre þŷ bet   biđ ođđe þince,
forþæm þe nâne forlêt,   þeâh hit lang þince,
35 deâđ æfter dôgorrîme,   þonne hê hæfđ Drihtnes leâfe?
Hpæt þonne hæbbe   hæleđâ ænig,
guma æt þæm gilpe,   gif hine gegrîpan môt
se êca deâđ   æfter þissum porulde?

SAWS.

Forst sceal freôsan, fŷr puðu meltan,
eorðe grôpan, îs brycgian,
pæter-helm pegan, pundrum lûcan
corðan cîðâs: ân sceal inbindan
5 forstes fetre, fela-meahtig God;
pinter sceal gepeorpan, peder eft cuman,
sumor spegle hât, sund unstille:
deôp deâda pêg dyrne bið lengest.
Holen sceal inæled, yrfe gedæled
10 deâdes monnes: dôm bið sêlâst.
Cyning sceal mid ceâpû epêne gebicgan,
buuum and beâgum: bu sceolon ærest
geofum gôd pesan. Gûð sceal in eorle
pîg gepeaxan, and pîf geþeôn
15 leôf mid hyre leôdum, leoht-môd pesan,
rûne healdan, rûm-heort beôn
mearum and mâðmum, meodo-rædenne
for gesið-mægen; simle æghpær
codor æðelingâ ærest gegrêtan,
20 forman fulle tô freân hond
ricene gerêcan and him ræd pitan,
bold-âgendum bæm ætsomne.
Scip sceal genægled, scyld gebunden,
leôht linden bord; leôf pileuma
25 frysan pîfe, þonne flota stondeð;
bið his ceôl cumen and hyre ceorl tô hâm,
âgen ætgeofa, and heô hine in laðâð,
pæsceð his pârig hrægl
and him syleð pæde nipe;
30 lið him on londe þæs his lufu Lâðeð.
Dîf sceal pið per pære gehealdan;
fela bið fæst-hydigrâ,
fela bið fyrpet-geornrâ,
freôð hŷ fremde monnan,
35 þonne se ôðer feor gepîteð.
Lida bið longe on sîðe;
â mon sceal seþeâh leôfes pênan,
gebîdan þæs hê gebædan ne mæg,
hponne him eft gebyre peorðe;

hâm cymeð, gif hê hâl leofað,
　　nefne him holm gestŷreð;
mere hafað mundum,　　mægð egsan pyn.
Ceâp-eâdig mon　　cyning píc þonne
5　　leôdon cŷpeð,　　þonne liðan cymeð:
puðâ and pætres nyttâð
　　þonne him bið píc âlŷfed;
mete bygeð, gif hê mâran þearf,
　　ærþon hê tô mêðe peorðe.
10　　Seôc se bið þe tô seldan ieteð;
　　þeâh hine mon on sunnan læ̂de,
ne mæg hê be þŷ pedrê pesan,
　　þeâh hit sŷ pearm on sumerâ;
ofercumen bið hê, ær hê âcpele,
15　　gif hê nât hpâ hine cpicne fêde.
Mægen mon sceal mid mete fêdan,
　　morðor under corðan befeolan,
hinder under hrusan,　　þe hit forhelan þenceð;
ne bið þæt geðêfe deâð,　　þonne hit gedyrned peorðeð.
20　　Heân sceal gehnîgan,　　âdl gesîgan,
ryht rogian.　　Ræ̂d bið nyttôst,
yfel unnyttôst,　　þæt unlæ̂d nimeð;
gôd bið genge　　and pið God lenge.
Hyge sceal gehealden,　　hond gepealden;
25　　seô sceal in eâgan,　　snyttro in breôstum,
þæ̂r bið þæs monnes　　môd-geþoncâs.
Mûðâ gehpylc mete þearf,　　mæl sceolon tîdum gongan.
Gold gerîseð　　on guman speorde,
sellîc sige-sceorp,　　sinc on cpêne,
30　　gôd scôp gumum,　　gûr nîð-perum
pîg tô piðre,　　píc-freoðâ healdan.
Scyld sceal cempan,　　sceaft reâfere;
sceal brŷde beâg,　　bêc leornere,
hûsl hâlgum men,　　hæ̂ðnum synne.
35　　Dôden porhte peðs,　　puldor Alpalda,
rûme roderâs;　　þæt is rîce God,
sylf sôð cyning,　　sâplâ nergend,
se ûs eal forgeaf,　　þær þe on lifgað,
and eft æt þâm ende　　eallum pealdeð
40　　monnâ cynne;　　þæt is meotud sylfa.

THRENES.

Ƿindē biƿāune   ƿeallās stondađ
hrîmē bihrorene,   hrŷđge þā ederâs.
Đôriađ þâ pîu-salo,   paldend liegađ
dreâmē bidrorene;   duguđ eal geerong
5   plone bî ƿealle: sume pîg fornom,
ferede in forđƿege;   sumne fugel ôđbær
ofer heâhne holm;   sumne se hâra pulf
deâđe gedǣlde;   sumne dreôrig-hleôr
in eorđ-seræfe   eorl gehŷdde:
10   ŷđde spâ þisne eard-geard   ældâ Scyppend,
ôđþæt burgƿarâ   breahtmâ leâse
eald enta geƿeore   îdlu stôdon.
Se þonne þisne ƿeal-steal   pîsē geþohtē
and þis deoree lif   deôpe geondþeneeđ,
15   frôd in ferđe,   feor oft gemon
pæl-sleahtâ ƿorn   and þâs ƿord âcƿiđ: [đum-gyfa?
"Hƿær eƿom mearg, hƿær eƿom mago?   hƿær eƿom mâđ-
hƿær eƿom symblâ gesetu?   hƿær sindon sele-dreâmâs?
Eâlâ beorht bune,   eâlâ byrn-ƿîga,
20   eâlâ þeôdnes þrym!   hû seô þrag geƿât,
genâp under niht-helm,   spâ heô nô ƿære!
Stondeđ nû on lâste   leôfre duguđe
ƿeal ƿundrum heâh   ƿyrmlîeum fâh:
eorlâs fornôman   aseâ þryđe,
25   ƿæpen ƿæl-gîfru,   Ƿyrd seô mǣre,
and þâs stân-hleođu   stormâs enyssađ;
hrîđ hreôsende   hruse bindeđ
pintres ƿôma: þonne ƿon cymeđ,
nîpeđ niht-seûa,   norđan onsendeđ
30   hreô hægl-fare   hæleđum on andan.
Eal is earfođlîe   corđan rîce:
onƿendeđ ƿyrdâ gesceaft   ƿeoruld under heofenum.
Hêr biđ feoh lǣne,   hêr biđ freônd lǣne,
hêr biđ mon lǣne,   hêr biđ mǣg lǣne:
35   eal þis corđan gesteal   îdel ƿeorđeđ."
Spâ eƿæđ snottor on môde,
    gesæt him sundor æt rûne.
Til biđ seþe his treôƿe gehealdeđ:
    ne sceal nǣfre his torn tô ryeene

beorn of his breôstum âcŷđan,
    nemđe hê ær þâ bôte cunne,
eorl mid elnê gefremman:
    pel biđ þam þe him âre sêceđ,
5   frôfre tô Fæder on heofonum,
    þær ûs eal seô fæstnung stondeđ.

Pêland him be purman   præces cunnâde,
ânhydig eorl,   earfôđâ dreâg;
hæfde him tô gesîđđe   sorge and longâđ,
10 pinter-cealde præce: peân oft onfond,
siđđan hine Nîđhâd   on nêde legde
sponere seono-benne,   on sŷllan mon.
    Pæs ofereôde,   þisses spâ mæg!
Beadohilde ne pæs   hyre brôđrâ deâđ
15 on sefan spâ sâr,   spâ hyre sylfre þing,
    *   *   *   *   *
    *   *   *   æfre ne meahte
þrîste geþencan,   hû ymb þæt sceolde.
    Pæs ofereôde,   þisses spâ mæg!
20 Pê geâscôdan   Eormanrîces
pylfenne geþoht;   âhte pîde folc
Gotenâ rîces;   þæt pæs grim cyning.
Sæt secg monig   sorgum gebunden,
peân on pênan,   pŷscte geneahhe,
25 þæt þæs cyne-rîces   ofercumen pære.
    Pæs ofereôde,   þisses spâ mæg!
Ic hpîle pæs   Heodeningâ scôp
dryhtne dŷre: mê pæs Deôr noma;
âhte ic fela pintrâ   folgâđ tilne,
30 holdne hlâford,   ôđ þæt Heorrenda nû
leôđ-cræftig mon   lond-ryht geþah,
þæt mê eorlâ hleô   ær gesealde.
    Pæs ofereôde,   þisses spâ mæg!

F

RHYMES.

Þer-cyn gepîteđ,   pæl-gâr slîteđ,
flâh mâh flîteđ,   flân mân hpîteđ,
borg-sorg bîteđ,   bald ald þpîteđ,
præc-fæc prîteđ,   prâđ âđ smîteđ,
5 syn-gryn sîdeđ,   searo-fearo glîdeđ.
Grorn torn græfeđ,   græft ræft hæfeđ,
searo hpît sôlâđ,   sumur-hât côlâđ,
fold-pela fealleđ,   feôndscipe pealleđ,
eorđ-mægen ealdâđ,   ellen cealdâđ.
10 Mê þæt pyrd gepæf   and gepyrht forgeaf,
þæt ic grôfe græf;   and þæt grimme geræf
fleôn flæscê ne mæg,   þonne flân-hred dæg
nŷd-grâpum nimeđ,   þonne seô neaht becymeđ,
seô mê êđles ofon   and mê hêr eardes oncon.
15 Þonne lîchoma ligeđ: limu pyrm þigeđ,
and him pynne gepigeđ   and þâ pist gebigeđ,
ôđ þæt beôđ þâ bân   gebrosnâd on ân
and æt nŷhstan nân   nefne se nêdâ tân
balapum hêr gehloten.   Ne bid se hlîsa âþroten.
20 Ǣr þæt eâdig geþenceđ;
  hê hine þû oftôr spenceđ,
byrgeđ him þâ bitran synne,
  hycgâđ tô þære betran pynne,
gemon meorđâ lisse,
25 þær sindon miltsâ blisse
hyhtlîce in heofenâ rîce.
  Uton nû hâlgum gelîce
scyldum biscerede   scyndan generede
pommum biperede,   puldrê gehêrede,
30 þær mon-cyn môt   for meotude rôt
sôđne God geseôn   and â in sibbe gefeôn!

NOTES.

PAGE 1. THE GOSPELS were read in Anglo-Saxon as part of the Church service. Several manuscripts written before the Norman Conquest are preserved. An edition was printed by Parker in 1571, by Marshall in 1665, by Thorpe in 1842. Bouterwek published the Northumbrian version of the Lindisfarne Codex (Durham Book) in 1857, and both the Lindisfarne and Rushworth for the three first Gospels have been printed for the Surtees Society, 1854–1863. Kemble at his death in 1857 was at work on an edition, of which Matthew has since been printed for the Syndics of the University Press at Cambridge. It has the Latin Vetus Italica and four Anglo-Saxon texts printed together, with the various readings of three others. Two of these are the Lindisfarne and Rushworth, the others are copies of the received version of the West-Saxon Church: the best was written about 1000. A critical edition of the Gospels is still wanting. We have a careful edition of the Psalms by Greiu. Ælfric's translation of the Heptateuch was published by Thwaites, 1698.

PAGE 2. THE LORD'S PRAYER. The end of Matthew, vi., 13, *For thine is the kingdom,* etc., is not in the Latin, and so not in the Anglo-Saxon. It is wanting in many Greek manuscripts.

PAGE 9. ULFILAS (Gothic VULFILA) was born in 311, and died in 381. He was a Goth, and for forty years bishop of the Goths in Dacia. Fragments of his translation of the Bible have been found in eight manuscripts. The extract here given is from the so-called Codex Argenteus, written on parchment in silver and gold letters, in Italy, in the fifth century, and, after various fortunes, now in the library of the University of Upsala. It had originally 330 leaves, and contained the four Gospels; of these 177 remain. The other fragments are mainly from Paul's epistles, enough to make about 145 more such pages. See further for Gothic, §§ 7–9, and the Index.

PAGE 12. THE LORD'S PRAYER. *Father* our thou in *heavens, Hallowed-be* name thine. Come *kingdom* thine. Worth will thine, so in *heaven* and on earth. Loaf our the *daily* give us *this* day. And off-let us that *in which we debtors are,* so so *also* we off-let them debtors ours. And not bring us in *temptation, but* loose us of the evil; *since* thine is *kingdom* and might and glory in ever. Amen.

Atta, v. 45; *unsar,* A.-S. *úser, úre* > our, Ger. *unser,* § 132; *þu,* v. 39, § 130, for its use as a relative, § 381; *in himinam,* v. 45; *veihnái* < *veihnan,* § 170, akin to *veihs,* holy, A.-S. *píh,* Ger. *weih-,* akin to *witch*; *namô,* declens., § 95, A.-S. *nama* > name, Ger. *name,* Lat. *nomen* > noun, Gr. ὄνομα, Sansk. *náman,* √gna, know; *þein,* v. 39; *kvimái,* v. 47; *þiudi-*

nassus, declens., § 93, from *þiuda*, v. 46; *vairþái*, v. 45; *vilja*, declens., § 95, v. 40; *spê*, v. 48; *jah*, v. 38; *ana*, v. 45; *airþ-a*, dat. *-ái*, declens., § 88, A.-S. *corde*, Ger. *erde*, √*ar*, plough, till? *Hláifs*, § 70, A.-S. *hláf* > loaf, Ger. *laib*; *þana*, § 104; *sinteins*, declens., § 107, akin to A.-S. *sin-*, O. H. G. *sin-*, Lat. *sem-*, Gr. ἕνο-ς, Sansk. *sa-ná'*, § 254; *gif*, v. 42; *uns*, *himma*, A.-S. *him*, § 130; *dags*, § 70, A.-S. *dæg*, Ger. *tag*; *aflêt'*, v. 40; *þatei*, v. 38; *skula*, declens., § 95, verb *skulan*, A.-S. *sculan* > shall, Ger. *sollen*, § 212; *sijáima*, v. 48; *veis*, § 130; *þê*, Ger. *wir*; *briggáis*, A.-S. *bringan* > bring, Ger. *bringen*; *fráistubn-i*, dat. *-jái* < *fráisan*, A.-S. *frásian* > O. Engl. *fraise*, to tempt, question, O. H. G. *freisa*; *ak*, v. 39; *láusei*, A.-S. *leôsan* > loose, Ger. *liesen*, Lat. *luo*, *so-lu-tus*, Gr. λύω, Sansk. *lú*; *ubilin*, *unté*, v. 45; *þiudan-gardi*, king-court, see *þiudinassus* above, *-gards*, A.-S. *geard* > yard, garden, Ger. *garten*, Lat. *hortus*, Gr. χόρτος, a place girt, enclosed; *máhts*, § 89, A.-S. *meahte* > might, Ger. *macht* < verb *mag*. may; *vulþus*, A.-S. *puldor*, glory, declens., § 93; *áivs*, time, declens., § 89, A.-S. *ápa* > aye, Ger. *je*; *Amén*, true, Hebrew.

PAGE 13. DIALOGUES OF CALLINGS. This was one of the standard text-books for the study of Latin in the Anglo-Saxon schools. It was prepared with interlinear Latin and Anglo-Saxon by Ælfric, the grammarian, after the Homilies (see p. 75), and enlarged by Ælfric Bata, his pupil. Manuscripts are in the British Museum and the Oxford library. It was printed by Thorpe in 1834, and has been often reprinted. It is good school-master's Anglo-Saxon, and gives a lively picture of the manners and customs of the time. It is nearly all brought in, in one place or another, in Sharon Turner's History.

1. TEACHER AND SCHOLAR.—*tǽce*, teach, subj., §§ 423, 425.—*pille* < *pillad*, *rêce* < *recad*, § 165.—*sprecân* = *sprecen*, subj., § 170.—*bútan* . . ., if only it be correct speech.—*pille gê*, Do you wish.—*hpæt spricst þú?* what will you talk about? pres. for future, § 413, 4.—*hpæt peorces*, what kind of work, § 312, *a*.—*ælcê dæg*, each day, instrumental of *dæg* without *-ê*, like the dative, § 71, *b*.—*eác spylce*, also likewise, also.

2. TEACHER AND PLOUGHMAN.—These dialogues are a continuation of the first.—*nis hit*, it is never, *nis* = *ne is*, § 213.—*gefæstnódum scearê and cultrê*, share and colter having been fastened, dative absolute, § 304, *d*.

PAGE 14. TEACHER AND OXHERD.—*betǽce*, *tǽcan*, teach, show, Lat. *ad-signo*, assign, hand over; distinguish *betǽce*, take, p. 15.

PAGE 15.—*rán*, from *rá*, *n*, m., roebucks, *rǽgan*, f., roe.

PAGE 16.—*spâ fela* . . . *spâ fela spâ*, so many . . . as.—*for hpý*, for what reason, instrumental of *hpæt*, § 135.—*mê is*, dative of possessor, § 298, *b*.—*fela spilces*, many (of) such, partitive, § 312.—*þænne þe* . . ., than one which is able to sink or kill not only me, but also my comrades: *one* understood, *þe hê*, which, § 381, *ná þæt ân*, not only, *ac eác spylce*, but also.

EXTRACT 7.—*fela þisenâ*, many (of) ways, § 312.—*sceoldon*, what should they be to me, i. e., of what use? infinitive omitted, § 435, *d*, so after *can*, I know (how to tame them).

NOTES. 73

Page 17.—*pintrâ, pudâ, sumerâ*, § 93.—*ól þæt án*, to that alone, so much.—*ná þæt*, not only. Extract 8.—*eal spâ*, all so, for the same price as.—*þanon*, whence, from which.

Page 18.—*nytpyrdnesse*, partitive genitive after *hpæt*, § 312, *a*. Extract 10.—*gereordunge*, luncheon, *metê*, dinner.—*Hpilc mannâ* . . . Which of men enjoys (sweet meats) savory dishes? *pered*, adj., sweet, dative after *purh-brýced*, § 300.—*búton ic* . . . unless I as a guard am with you, who do not even eat your vegetables without me. Extract 11.—*hpæder*, interrogative sign, need not be translated, § 397.—*tó pel*, well to that degree, so well. Extract 12.—*on ænigum*, in any way.

Page 19.—Extract 13.—*ic âhsie þâ*, I ask about those=who are those? Extract 14.—*is gepuht*, seems, Lat. *videtur*, § 408, *c*.

Page 20.—*slecgeâ*, gen. plur., § 85, *a*.—*cræftê minê*, instrumental, § 300; the text has *mínum*, dative; the schoolmaster's license has been taken to introduce the instrumental for drill.—*ne furdon*, not even.—*hpætlicór*, very quickly.—*ânrâ gehpylc*, each of ones, each one, § 386, *b*, 7.—*nelle, ne pille*, subj. pres., if he wish not to be, perhaps really a mistake for infinitive *nellan*, in analogy with Lat. *nolle.*—*pitad* rare for *piton*.

Page 21.—*be eallum hâlgum*, of all saints, all-hallows.—*be þam*, about that, dative of theme, § 334.

Page 23.—The Anglo-Saxon Chronicle. A Chronicle is known to have been kept at the monasteries as early as the time of Alfred. It has been supposed that he had it compiled, and copies made for the libraries. How the later records were kept is not known; they come down to 1154, Henry II. The Chronicle has been often printed and translated. Thorpe's edition, 1861, contains seven fully printed parallel texts, a translation, and indexes. It has been used in preparing these extracts. They are, however, much condensed and freely handled, so that the students will find it easier to read them by the aid of the vocabulary than to look up the passages in Bohn. As far as Beda's history extends, the Chronicle is, for the most part, abridged from it or drawn from a common source.

búend, inhabitants, nom. plur., § 87.—*Armorica*, Lat., undeclined, the Chr. have *Armenia*, but see Beda, 1, 1.—*ær þam þe*, before this that, before.—*ge-eóde pel manige* . . ., subdued very many (a) great town, § 395, 2. A.D. 47.—*æt neâhstan* generally means *at last*, here Beda has *pene*, almost, declension of proper names, § 101. A.D. 167—*onfêng* may take a dative, accusative, or genitive object, § 299.—*bæd* with genitive, § 315, *a*. A.D. 381.—*fcóper hund*, 400, the numerals in the Chronicle are generally denoted by the Roman letters, oftenest followed by a partitive genitive, § 393.—*hund-*, § 139. A.D. 443.—*heom*, for themselves, §§ 366, 8, 315, *a*. A.D. 449.—*Hengest* and *Horsa* are both *horses*, some suppose them mythic.—*pid þam þe*, in exchange for this, that=for which, §§ 359, 380, 3.—*Angel*, *es*, m., Angeln is now the name of a tract in Schleswig, between the Schley and Flensburg.—*nú git*, now yet.—*se â siddan* . . ., which ever since has stood waste: they are Beda's statements, 1, 15.—Woden, the god from whom

Wednesday is named, Scandinavian Odin, who is the supreme deity. A.D.
·538.—*ǽr calende: calend*, like Lat. *calendæ* in the poets, is used for *month*.
It is sometimes singular, sometimes plural. A.D. 540.—*steorran hí*, stars
they appeared; repeated subject, § 288, *b*. A.D. 565.—*se Columba*, the
Columba (above mentioned), § 368, *a*. A.D. 603.—*tó cyninge*, whom
Æthelbert, king of the men of Kent, established there *as king*: compare
English *took to wife*, § 352, factitive.—*æt handâ*, at (by) the hand. A.D.
611.—*côm, cpam > cpom > cuom > côm > com*, Orm. *comm*, is very often
marked long in the Chronicle, though the discrimination from plur. *cômon*
favors *com*. A.D. 664.—*forman*, first, Beda and the Chr. have the *5th of
the nones of May*, incorrectly. Colman was from Scotland, and had been
made bishop in Northumbria. He would not use the Roman mode of tonsure, but shaved the front hair from ear to ear in the form of a crescent; he
kept Easter at the wrong time, and had great controversies with the Roman-
ists on these matters, getting the worst of it. A.D. 687.—*eft*, again.
A.D. 688.—*Petrus*, nominative of enunciation, § 288, *e*.—*under Christes
clâdum*, in his baptismal clothes. A.D. 693.—*cynebóte*, besides the wergild
paid to the heirs of a murdered king, a *bót*, or compensation was made to
the state, generally equal to the other. The amount here paid is variously
estimated, probably £120. A.D. 754.—*pitān*, the original of Parliament.—
þæs þe, from this that, after.—*þâ on þæs pifes gebærum*, then by the woman's gestures.—*heorâ æghpilcum*, to each of them.—*lægon*, lay dead.—*þâ
on morgene . . .*, when in the morning the king's thanes, who had been left
behind him, heard that, that the king had been slain, then rode they.—
ealdorman, Lat. *dux*, was the governor of a shire. The king's *thanes* were
dignitaries like king's ministers now: they were of many kinds—*horse-thane*,
marshal; *bower-thane*, chamberlain, etc.—*þâ þe*, who, *him fram noldon*,
would not (go) from him, §§ 380, 3, 440.—*nænig mǽg nǣre*, no kinsman
could be; emphatic negation. A.D. 784.—*Heredaland*, Norway. A.D.
800.—*for þý . . . þý þe*, for this reason . . . because (that).—*tó cpêne*, as
queen, § 352. A.D. 823.—*heom tó friðe*, for themselves for peace, and as
protector. A.D. 855.—*And him þâ*, and to him then Charles, king of the
Franks, his daughter gave as a queen for him—Charles the Bald.—*þæs þe*,
from the time that, after.—*nigonteóde healf*, 18½, § 147. A.D. 872.—
and þâ Deniscan, and (=but) the Danes held possession of the slaughter-
place (battle-field).—*bûtan þam þe heom*, besides which, against them—rode.
A.D. 878.—*hine bestæl*, stole (itself), § 290, *d*.—*heom gecyrdon*, brought
into allegiance to themselves.—*æfter wudum*, among the forests, § 331.—
The Danes Ingvar and Hálfdán bore the Raven, 840 Danes died around it.
—*him ongeân*, to meet him.—*hire*, § 312.—*his*, § 315.—*him æfter*, after it,
pursued it to its intrenchment.—*poldon*, would (go), § 440.—*þritigâ sum*,
one of thirty, with twenty-nine companions, § 388.—*crismlýsing*, compare
Cristes clâdum, A.D. 688. A.D. 897.—*ongeân þâs æscâs*, against the *æscs*,
Danish long ships, like ashen spears.—*mid eallê*, and every thing. A.D.
901.—*ealrâ hâligrâ mæssan*, All-hallowmass (Oct. 26).—*forsâpon*, despised

every compact that King Edward and his Parliament offered them. A.D. 925.—*seofode healf*, 6½, § 147. A.D. 975-978.—*Corfe* was the royal residence of Elfrida, the mother-in-law of Edward. The king while hunting was allured thither alone. She received him at the gate and kissed him. The cup was offered, and as he drank, one of her attendants stabbed him in the back. He spurred away, but soon died, and the frightened horse dragged the corpse of "Edward the Martyr." Æthelred, "the Unready," was her son. A.D. 994.—*þâ peard hit*, then there was, § 397.—*frid and grid*, rhyming and alliterating emphatic tautology is a characteristic of legal and other forms in the Teutonic languages. The lawyers distinguish *frid* as general peace, *grid* a special security of particular property.—*ǽghpider*, every whither.—*flocmǽlum*, adv., in flocks or troops, § 144.—Richard II., count of Normandy. The queen's name was Emma Ælfgife, afterward wife of Cnût. A.D. 1014.—*seó burhparu*, the city, a collective singular for the body of citizens. A.D. 1028.—*peard his man*, was his man=paid him *hom*-age. A.D. 1052.—*â-léde*, abolished, § 209.—*þæs þe*, after.—*mid*, adv., also, it tormented men also manifoldly. A.D. 1066.—*Normandige*, Lat. *Normannia* (*nn* > *nd*, *î* > *ig*, dissimilation, §§ 27, 5; 175, *b*) usually is of feminine strong declension, but genitive in -*es* occurs, A.D. 1101. The *hide* is about thirty acres, the *gird* (>yard) one fourth of a hide. A.D. 1087.—*mǽl*, portion.—*þæt . . . þæt*, repeated, as in A.D. 754, and often.—*mǽndon*, bemoaned.—*nid, es*, m., opposition.

CONVERSION OF THE ANGLO-SAXONS.

PAGE 35.—GREGORY. This is taken from a homily of Ælfric, the grammarian, Hom. ii., 116. It is in Thorpe's Analecta, and elsewhere. It is here abridged. These homilies are eighty in number, and were compiled and translated from Latin works, about A.D. 990, for the unlearned, whose books, except Alfred's translations, he says were full of errors. They are, therefore, written in simple English (Anglo-Saxon), without obscure words. A careful edition, with a translation, was prepared by Thorpe for the Ælfric Society, 1844-1846.

PAGE 36, line 35.—*hpæt*, an interjection of emphasis, § 377, *b*; compare *What, Lucius! ho!* (Shakespeare, J. C., ii., 1), *What, warder! ho!* (Scott, Marmion); so Beowulf, p. 56.

PAGE 37, line 3.—*þæt*, relative, used without agreement in gender or number like English *that*, § 374, 2. 26.—*pǽron*, they were ready, *hî* understood.

PAGE 38, line 8.—*þê*, reflexive dative, § 298, *c*. 14.—*mæsse-reâfum*, robes in which to celebrate mass. 15.—*reliquias*, Latin, accusative plural of *reliquiæ*, relics. 16.—*pallium*, Latin, accusative sing. of *pallium*, pall, a consecrated scarf, embroidered with purple crosses.

PAGE 38.—PAULINUS. From Beda's Ecclesiastical History of the Angles and Saxons, book ii., chap. 13, with an introduction from chap. 9, and conclusion from chap. 16. Beda, "The Venerable Bede," was born near Wearmouth and Yarrow, A.D. 673. He went to the abbey when seven years old, and studied there till he died, May 26, 735. He was made deacon at 19, priest at 30; declined to be abbot, as bringing distraction of mind, which hinders the pursuit of learning. He was making a translation of the Gospel of John when he died. A list of 44 of his works is given by Wright. Among them are Commentaries on the Bible, Biographies, History, Treatises on Natural Science, Grammar, Versification. He was fond of his native language and poetry, and composed verses both in Anglo-Saxon and Latin. This extract may be compared with Cædmon, page 47. The liveliest parts of Gregory and the Chronicle are also in Beda. He is one of the great authors of the world. An acute observer and profound thinker, with what our critics call a poet's heart and eye, he sets forth the gentle and beautiful traits of character in the saintly heroes of his time with unmistakable relish, and in a style graceful, picturesque, at times dramatic. Some of his best scenes have often been rendered in English verse. That from Paulinus may be read in Wordsworth's Ecclesiastical Sonnets, xv.–xvii. Beda's Works have been repeatedly published both on the Continent and in England. The Ecclesiastical History was translated from the Latin by Alfred. Wheloc's edition has Latin and Anglo-Saxon in parallel columns. Folio, Cambridge, 1644. Smith's has various readings. Folio, Cambridge, 1722. A new edition is much needed.

PAGE 38, line 21.—*þǽre tíde*, A.D. 625–627. 25.—*hƿilc*, of what kind to them seemed and appeared; Beda's Latin *videtur* is tautologically rendered by *þuhte and gesepen ƿǽre*. 27.—(who) was called Cefi, § 385. 33.—*þá þe*, who, § 380, 3. 34.—*I know what*, introductory exclamation still in colloquial use: there is no Latin for it in Beda.

PAGE 39, line 4.—*tó fêng*, took up the discussion. 5.—One text has *cyning leófôsta*. 11.—*hƿæt*, lo; *rined*, wet, looks like a mistake for *hrinen*, touched, Beda's *tangitur*. 13.—*pintrâ*, § 93, i. 30.—Lo, he then, the king; repeated subject, § 288, b. 32.—*Mid þý*, When he then, the king, from the aforesaid bishop of their religion which they practised before, sought and asked who should desecrate and overthrow the idols, etc., ... then answered.

PAGE 40, line 19.—*liged*, which extends out to the sea; relative omitted, § 385. 20.—*hê Béda*, so says Alfred. 24.—*and* connects *hê* and *menigo*. 28.—*hôcihte neôsu þynne*, Bed. *nâso adunco pertenui*, his prominent feature like an eagle's beak (Wordsworth, l. c.); the texts read for *hôcihte*, *medmicle*, small, which destroys the feature; *nôsu*, f., is the more common form. 31.—*ǽghpider ymb spâ spâ*, whithersoever.—*þeáh þe*, even if. 33.—*spilce*, so much also the same king attended to utility for his people. 34–36.—*þæt ... þæt*, repeated. 37.—*þá hƿædere*, then yet, however.

ANGLO-SAXON LAWS.

A considerable body of Anglo-Saxon laws remains. Their most striking general feature is the payment of money for all sorts of offenses. Confinement was not easy or safe. The kind of offenses specified, and their comparative estimate, are fruitful in suggestions concerning the life and the character of our ancestors. The laws have been often printed. The best editions are those of Thorpe (2 vols., pp. 631, 551) and Schmid (Leipzig, 1858). The latter is in one volume, and has a critical text and translations in Latin and German in parallel columns, notes, and a glossary. The sections here selected are numbered as in Schmid.

Page 41.—Æthelbirht (-briht, i > y) was king of Kent at its conversion. See page 37. The laws were written 597–614. One manuscript copy only remains, written for Ernulf, bishop of Rochester, 1115–1125. The language used indicates that it was copied from older text, but how near the original it comes we know not.

Line 1.—*forgelde*, let him pay, subj. for imperative, § 421, 3. 2.—*gebéte*, *pite* ; besides the *bót* paid to the injured party, a penalty, *pite*, was generally paid to the crown. Compare Tacitus, Germania, c. 12. 4.—*leôd-geld=pergeld*, wergild, compensation for a man to his kin or representatives, to be distinguished from the *bót* to the lord of the slain and the *pite* to the king ; *medume*, small, half; the *bót* is to be 100 shillings, half the wergild ; *man* is freeman. 9.—*ceorl* is a freeman of low rank ; *hláf-æta*, compare *hláf-ord*. 10.—§§ 39 and 40 are perhaps transposed. *óder*, either. 16.—*cin-bân*, jawbone. Compare Goth. *kinnu*, page 10, verse 39. 17–20.—*æt . . . æt*, repeated : For the four front teeth, for each = for each of the four front teeth (pay) six shillings ; the tooth which then stands by, —(pay for it) four shillings, anacoluthon, § 288, *a*. 22.—*gebroced* is common for *gebrocen* in the laws.

Page 42, line 5.—*forgelde*, let (the striker) pay; *heâh hand*, right hand, the common Scandinavian idiom. Compare *spŷdre*, page 10, verse 39.

Hlóthhere succeeded his brother Ecgberht as king of Kent in July, 673, and reigned 11 years and 7 months. He died of wounds received in battle with his nephew *Eádric*, who then reigned one year and a half (Béd., iv., 5, 26). These laws are in the same manuscript with those of *Æthelbirht*.

Line 19.—*mund-byrd*, the fine for violating protection guaranteed by any one : a ceorl gave six shillings' worth of protection, an earl twelve, a king fifty, in Æthelbirht's time.

Ine, king of Wessex at the resignation of Ceadwalla, A.D. 688, abdicated and went to Rome in 725 (Béd., v., 7 ; and see Chronicle). His laws are found in the same manuscripts as those of Alfred, written like a continuation of Alfred's Code.

Line 27.—*geþungenes*, full grown, eminent, a member of Parliament.

Page 43, line 8.—Out of the highway through the forest, § 340. 9.—He is to be regarded as a thief, § 451, 337, II. 11.—And it is detected in the one that did it. 14.—*þritig*, undeclined, for *þritigum*. 15.—*pǽre*, subj., §§ 421, 427, let there be of them so many as there may be of them.

Alfred's Laws.—Alfred was born in 848, the youngest child of Æthelwulf and Osburga ; but he outlived his brothers, and became king of Wessex A.D. 871. He died A.D. 901. Students using this book will have read some outlines of his public life in the Chronicles; but the whole story of his brilliant youth, and his suffering and struggling manhood, with all its romantic adventures, should be made familiar. He is often called Álfred the Great; the traditions of the Saxons call him The Wise, The Truthteller, England's Shepherd, England's Darling. He was a good king, master of the arts of war and peace; a strong fighter, and an inventor of battle-ships; a statesman, a giver and codifier of laws; an educator and founder of schools; a philosopher, historian, and bard. Well he loved God's men and God's Word. He loved men of learning, and brought them about him from far countries. He loved his people, their land, and speech, and old ballads, and Bible songs; and he was the preserver of the literature and language, as well as the liberties and laws of the Anglo-Saxons.

The book of his laws begins with a history of law, gives an outline of the laws of Moses, and states the relation of them to Christ, the apostles, and Christian nations. He concludes: "I, then, Alfred, king, gathered these together, and commanded many of those to be written which our forefathers held, those which to me seemed good; and many of those which to me seemed not good, I rejected them by the counsel of my *witan*, and in other wise commanded them to be holden, for I durst not venture to set in writing much of my own, for it was unknown to me what of it would suit those who should be after us. But those which I met, either of Ine's day, my kinsman, or Æthelbirht's, who first received baptism among the English race, which seemed to me rihtest, I have here gathered, and rejected the others. I, then, Alfred, king of the West-Saxons, shewed these to all my *witan*, and they then said that it seemed good to them all to keep them." The introduction in Schmid takes up pp. 58-68, the following laws pp. 68-105. For Alfred's other works, see notes on pages 23, 38, 46, 64.

PAGE 43, line 18.—*mon=man*, §§ 23, 35, 2, *a*. 29.—*frið*, a privilege of granting protection.—*fâhmon*, one exposed to *fæhð*, the deadly feud allowed by the laws, a right of the kinsmen to whom the wergild was due to kill a murderer, adulterer, and certain other offenders, and such of their kindred as were responsible for the wergild.—*ge-ærne* and *ge-yrne* are variations of the same word; one was probably originally a gloss. 31.—For any of those offenses which was not before disclosed: *þárá þe* together is used like a nominative singular, a common idiom, the *þárá* being a repeated partitive. 33.—*Sunnan niht*, Sunday, Lat. *dies Solis*; compare fort-night, seven-night, and see note on line 34.—*Geól* (sun-wheel), Yule, was a great pagan festival at the beginning of the year, the winter solstice, afterward confounded with Christmas.—*Eástre* was a heathen goddess. April was named *Eáster-mónað*, because feasts were then celebrated in honor of her (Béd., De Temp., 13). The name is akin to *east*, Lat. *aurora*, the dawn. The festival commemorating the resurrection of Christ has in Anglo-Saxon and German received this name, but other kindred nations use *pascha*. 34.—*þunres dæg* is a translation of Latin *dies Jovis*. The astrological week was allotted to the planets by hours in the received order of their orbits; the first hour to "the widest orbit and the highest power," Saturn, the second to Jupiter, the third to Mars, the fourth to the Sun, the fifth to Venus, the sixth to Mercury, the seventh to the Moon, the eighth to Saturn again, and so on through the week. Each day was named from the planet of its first hour. Hence the order of the Latin names—*dies Saturni, dies Solis, Lunæ, Martis, Mercurii, Jovis, Veneris* (Dion Cassius, xxxvii., 18). The first use of any of these names by Roman writers is in the time of Julius Cæsar, *dies Saturni* for the Jewish Sabbath (Tibul., i., 3, 18), probably from associations with the Saturnalia as a time of rest. This first became common; the names of the other days gradually came in: all were in use at the end of the second century, and the week was finally established, in place of the old nine-day period, by Constantine. It spread from Rome over the North in advance of Christianity. The greatest of the gods of the North, the father and ruler of gods and men, is *Wóden*, Norse *Odin*, and we should have expected him to take Jupiter's day; but the early Romans did not recognize their Jupiter in any of the Germanic gods, and identified Woden with Mercury, whom indeed he does resemble in his tricks, his care of traders, and some other traits and offices (Tacitus, Germ., 9; Annal., 13, 57; compare Cæsar, 6, 17). So *dies Mercurii* was called *Wódenes dæg*, Wednesday; and Jupiter's day was given to *þuner*, Norse *Thór*. He is the son of Odin and the Earth, the strongest of the gods, the enemy of the giants, the friend of man. He has three treasures—his hammer, his belt of power, which doubles his strength, and his iron gloves. His eyes flame, his hair is red as the lightning; when he drives by with his two he-goats, the mountains tremble. He is a very fair Jupiter as thus described in Norse. The Anglo-Saxons have left no mythological matter. Holy Thursday is the day on which Christ's ascension is commemorated, ten days before Whitsuntide, which is the seventh Sunday after Easter. Three days before were procession days, *Gang-dagâs*. 35.—*Lencten* is spring, when the days *lengthen*. It began with the great festival of Odin. It has given name to the Church *Lent*.

PAGE 44, line 3.—*geselle*, let (the master) pay. 7.—*folc-leásung* Thorpe explains as a false report leading to breach of the peace, Schmid as a false accusation of crime, an offense which is visited with this penalty in Henry I., 34, 7. The tongue could be compounded for in this case as in others by a third of the wergild. 11.—*tpéntig*, undeclined, for *tpéntigum*; so *þrittig*, *sixtig*, afterwards. 13 —*homola*, see vocabulary.

EGGBYRHT was archbishop of York, 735–766. He was one of Beda's friends. He wrote much, and formed a library at York. His Confessionale and Pœnitentiale are translations from similar Latin works, in great part from the Pœnitentiale of Theodore, archbishop of Canterbury, 668–690, give rules relating to confession and penance, and were standard guides in the Church. No known manuscript has them in their original Northumbrian. They are in Thorpe's Laws, pp. 128–239. The extracts here made are in Rieger's Lesebuch.

PAGE 44, line 18.—*medmycles hpæt-hpega*, somewhat of small value, *in* minimis, Theodore. 19.—*geâr* = *pinter*. 21.—*lifigendum mannum to hǽle and on his húse*, for health to living men and (health) in his house, *pro sanitate viventium et domus*, Theodore. 23.—*pif . . . heô*, repeated subject, § 288, *b*. This fever-cure is several times mentioned in the old laws. Sometimes the child was put in the oven, sometimes over a furnace, or on the roof in the sun. The burning away of dross and disease is a natural thought, and gives rise to superstitions all over the world. So Thetis buried the infant Achilles nightly in the fire, and Demeter the child of Demophoon. Its repute for *fever* suggests homœopathy. 28.—*nê, . . .*, nor (is it permitted that he practise) the gathering of herbs. 34.—*staca*, n., commonly *stake*, is here for Latin *acus*, needle. The making of an image of a person with magic spells, and affecting the person by treating the image, drowning, hanging, melting, piercing it with a needle, etc., is an ancient and wide-spread form of magic art:

> Sagave Punicea defixit nomina cera,
> Et medium tenues in jecur egit acus?

(Ovid, Amor., iii., 7, 29. Compare Horace, Epod., 17, 76). For northern examples of needle-piercing, see Thorpe's Northern Mythology, 3, 24, 240; Grimm, Myth., 1045.

PAGE 45, line 4.—*sylle*, give (any thing) to him. 6.—*Woden's day, Frige's day*, see note on page 43, line 34. *Frige dæg*, Friday, is intended to be a translation of Latin *dies Veneris*, the day of the goddess of love. There are, however, two northern goddesses, who seem to have been confounded. Norse *Frigg* < *fria*, O. H. G. *Frija*, A.-S. *frig, fri* > free; and Norse *Freyja*, akin to Goth. *frauja*, O. H. G. *frô*, A.-S. *freâ* > frau, mistress. The former is Woden's wife, and the goddess of marriage; the latter is the wife of a man, the goddess of beauty and love, Venus, but the name of the day phonetically agrees best with *Frigg*. 10.—*gescæfte*, at any other object, *ubicunque*, Theodore. 13.—*búton*, except. 15.—*þæs ylcan*, of the same penance. 16.—The meeting of roads is a well-known place for raising the devil: there idlers congregate. Drawing through the earth, through a hole, or along in a trench scooped for the purpose, is condemned as devil's craft in Edgar's Canons, XVI. Drawing through hollow stones, trees, and bramble bushes was practised with the same thought of scraping away magical bad influences, or sometimes apparently of magnetizing with good influences (Grimm, Myth., 1118).

PAGE 45. Cnut, king of Denmark, was crowned king of England A.D. 1017. See the Chronicle, 1014-1035. He made vigorous and wise efforts to unite the Danes and Anglo-Saxons under a common government. He called assemblies of their representatives, and with their advice reissued a large body of laws, both civil and ecclesiastical. In Schmid they occupy pp. 250-321. He died A.D. 1035.

Line 27.—*morgen-gyfe*, a gift from the husband to the wife on the morning after marriage. It was hers after his death. 29.—*hâdige*, consecrate as a member of a religious order.

PAGE 46.—ORPHEUS. This is an extract from Boethius, De Consolatione Philosophiæ, chap. 35, § 6, of Alfred's translation. The life of Boethius may be read in the Classical Dictionaries. The Latin of this work is printed in Valpy's Delphin edition of the Latin Classics. It opens with the complaints of Boethius; Philosophy appears, and converses with him. She persuades him that blessedness is not in riches, power, honors, glory, or fame, but that adversity often leads to it. The Supreme Good is to be found in the Deity alone. She illustrates these views, and answers objections at length. Meter and prose alternate. This work was far more read and cherished in the Middle Ages than the classic authors of pagan times. It came home to their experiences, while Homer and Virgil, with their lying myths and barbaric tales, were as remote and unreal as the Veda and Sacu′ntala are to us. Alfred recast it, and introduced much new matter, especially Christian precepts and allusions, which are wholly absent from the original. The extract here given is written on the suggestion of Book III., Metrum 12. The story is much enlarged, and has little verbal resemblance to the Latin. Two manuscripts have been used in preparing editions, one of them thought by Wanley to be of Alfred's age. We have editions by Rawlinson, 1698; Cardale, 1829; Fox, in Bohn's library, 1864. The extract here given is in Thorpe's Analecta, Ettmüller's Scôpas and Bôceras, and elsewhere.

PAGE 46, line 1.—"The clear well-spring of the highest good" is God: this is the language of Philosophia to Boethius in Latin verse. 20.—When to the harper then it seemed, that it pleased him of nothing (=he was pleased with nothing) in this world, then thought he, *þâ þâ . . . þâ*, correlative, so line 23, page 47, 16, § 472, 3; *þuhte*, § 297; *lyste hine þinges*, §§ 290, c; 315, c. 23.—*sceold*, should (according to the story). 25.—*ongan*, he began; change of mode in lively narrative. 30.—*brohte*, subj., would bring, §§ 423, 425, c. 31.—*oflyst*, much pleased with; compare *lyste*, line 21, § 315, 1.

PAGE 47, line 2.—*þâ, who*, they say, (that *they*) know no respect for any man, but punish each man according to his works,—*who*, they say, (that *they*) control each other's fate: a repeated subject implied, § 288, b. 11.—*þæs* (*þære?*), takes the gender of *yfel?* 22.—*hpæt*, interj. 24.—*beseah he hine*, he looked around him backwards after the woman, § 359, III. 33.—*gebête*, make *bôt*, do penance for it again. Compare *gebête* in the Laws, page 41, 2, and after.

CÆDMON.—From Alfred's translation of Beda's Ecclesiastical History of the Angles and Saxons, Book IV., 24. See notes on Paulinus, page 38, and to Cædmon, page 52.

PAGE 47, line 31.—St. Hild was abbess of Whitby, and died A.D. 680. Beda was born in 673 in the same region, and must have known about Cædmon, may have seen him. 35.—*mid . . .*, by divine grace singularly magnified and dignified, since he was wont to make appropriate poems, which conduced to religion and piety.

PAGE 48.—*geglencde* agrees with *sceôpgercorde*.—*imbrydnesse* renders *compunctione*, stimulation to pious feeling, feeling; so Cuthbert speaks of Beda's repeating verses, *multum compunctus*, much touched, with deep feeling. 11.—*ac efne*, but even. 12.—*þâ ân*, those alone, *þâ þe*, which.—*his þâ ...*, which it became his (the) pious tongue to sing, § 489, *gedafenôde* governs a dative generally in West Saxon, § 299, but *mec gedæfned*, North., Luc., iv. 43. 15.—*gebeôrscipe*, by etymology, a social beer-drinking, is applied to any convivial, like Gr. συμπόσιον, *sym-posium*. Here the Latin is *convivium; symble*, line 18, is *cæna*. For German beer-drinking, see Tacitus, Germ., 22, 23.—*þonne þær þæs gedémed*, when it was decided for pleasure, § 397. 20-23.—*þâ þâ ... þâ*, when ... then.—*þæt ... þæt*, § 468.—33. Only the substance of the verses in Latin is given in Beda. It has been questioned whether Alfred rendered the Latin back or supplied the original verses. The latter is most probable. An older copy has been found added in a Latin Beda supposed to be of the 8th or 9th century. The forms resemble the earliest Anglo-Saxon Northumbrian which we have:

  Nu scylun hergan   *hefaenricaes uard,*
  metudæs maecti   *end his modgidanc,*
  uerc uuldurfadur;   *sue he uundra gihuaes,*
  eci dryctin,   *or astelidæ.*
  He aerist scop   *aelda barnum*
  heben til hrofe,   *haleg scepen:*
  þa middungeard   *moncynnæs uard,*
  eci dryctin,   *æfter tiadæ,*
  firum fold⁻,   *frea allmectig.*

  Now we-shall (should) laud   heaven-realm's Ward (guardian),
  the-Creator's might   and his thought,
  the-works of-the-glorious-Father: how he, of wonders all,
  eternal Lord,   the beginning established.
  He first shaped   for men's children
  heaven as a roof,   holy Shaper (creator),
  then mid-earth   mankind's Ward,
  eternal Lord,   afterward created,
  for men a world,   Master almighty.

This text is from Smith's Beda, p. 597; that on page 48 is from Thorpe, Analecta, p. 105, adopted on the supposition that he has corrected from some manuscript the readings given by Wheloc and Smith. 35.—*perá* is a change from *peore*, the reading of more manuscripts, *facta patris gloriæ*, Beda.—*pundrá*, partitive after *gehpæs.*—*gehpæs*, governed by *ord*. 36.—*Dryhtin*, appositive with *hê*. 38–41.—*Scyppend*, appositive with *hê*.—*Dryhten, Freâ*, appositive with *peard*. The Northumbrian variations are mostly orthographic, §§ 26, 31. The vowel quantities are like those marked in the other text.

PAGE 49, line 3.—*Godê pyrdes songes*, words of song worthy of God, *Deo digni, pyrde* usually takes a genitive, here an instrumental in analogy with the Latin ablative of price so-called, §§ 320, 302, c. 4.—*ealdorman*, governor (law term)=*qui sibi pre-erat.* 9.—*gecoren pǽre*, it might be decided. 10.—*pæs gesepen*, it appeared, *videtur, visum est.* 13.—That he would sing something for them, and would convert that, etc.—*sum sunge and* is not in some texts; Beda reads *hunc in modulationem carminis transferre.* 14.—*þâ pisan*, undertaken the matter. 15.—*geglenged* describes *þæt him beboden pæs.* 27.—*be*, of, with dative of theme, § 334.

PAGE 50, line 2.—*betýnde and geendôde*, emphatic tautology for *conclusit*; so in the next line Beda has only *discessus* for *gepitnesse and fordfôre*; and so elsewhere, repetition for emphasis and perspicuity is Anglo-Saxon. 3.—*neálǽhte*, impersonal. 4.—*ǽr*, before (his death), *þæt*, (in this condition, namely) that, etc., conjunction: then he was fourteen days before, that he was oppressed = then there were fourteen days, etc. 25.—*mine þá leófan*, § 289, *a*. 31.—*þon = þam*, § 133. 32.—*him gebæd*, prayed for himself, § 298, *c:* a frequent idiom=he offered his prayers. Alfred has added these two words. 35, 36.—*þætte . . . þæt*, repeated *that.—eâc spilce*, also. 39.—*heô þâ*, it then, repeated subject, § 288, *b*. 40.—*séniende*, he signing himself, nominative absolute, § 295; really an imitation of the Latin gerund *signando sese*, rather than a native idiom.

ANGLO-SAXON PROSE.

Specimens of Anglo-Saxon prose have now been given, arranged for ease of reading. We have remaining—

(1.) THEOLOGICAL writings.—Translations of the Bible (see pages 1-12, and notes); Homilies, page 35, and notes.

(2.) PHILOSOPHY.—Boethius, page 46, and notes.

(3.) HISTORY.—The Chronicle, page 23, and notes. Beda's Ecclesiastical History: see Paulinus, page 38, and Cædmon, page 47. Orosius, a general history of the ancient world, translated by Alfred, with additions of considerable geographical and ethnological value; repeatedly printed. Thorpe's edition, with translation and glossary, 1857, is in Bohn's Library. Many brief BIOGRAPHIES are contained in Beda and the Homilies, of which Cædmon, page 47, and Gregory, page 35, are examples: Some separate lives have been found; that of St. Guthlác has been several times printed. Goodwin, 1848.

(4.) LAW.—Pages 41-45, and notes.

(5.) NATURAL SCIENCE and MEDICINE.—Popular Treatises of Science, pp. 19, are Anglo-Saxon, Thorpe, 1841. Leechdoms, 3 vols., O. Cockayne, 1864-66.

(6.) GRAMMAR.—Ælfric, in Somner's Dictionary, 1659. Colloquy, 12-22, and notes. A few Glossaries, Wright, 1857.

ANGLO-SAXON POETRY.
[For the Anglo-Saxon versification, see §§ 496-515.]

We learn from the story of Cædmon how universal the knowledge of popular poetry was among the Anglo-Saxons. It was such a disgrace not to be able to chant in turn at feasts that Cædmon left in shame as his turn approached. Most of the poetry has perished. The early Anglo-Saxon Christians condemned whatever was mixed with idolatry, and the Normans despised or neglected all Saxon literature. But enough remains to enable us to judge pretty well of the nature of their poetry. We have—

(1.) THE BALLAD EPIC. Here, as in Greek and most other tongues, the heroic ballads of the race were brought together, exalted and beautified, and fused into long poems. Beowulf (3184 lines), and a few fragments, are left from this great world of poetry, to be compared with the Homeric poems.

(2.) THE BIBLE EPIC is a treatment of the Bible narrative, similar in exaltation and other epic traits to the ballad epic. The origin and something of the history of this style of composition has been read in this book in Cædmon, pages 47–50. We have remaining under the name of Cædmon four poems, called by Grein Genesis (2935 lines), Exodus (589 lines), Daniel (765 lines), Christ and Satan (733 lines). We have also a fragment of Judith (350 lines), Cynewulf's Christ (1694 lines), The Harrowing of Hell (137 lines), and some fragments. These poems are to be compared with the Paradise Lost and Paradise Regained of Milton, and the Christ in Hades of Lord.

(3.) ECCLESIASTICAL NARRATIVES. The lives of Saints, versified Chronicles. Of these we have Andreas (1724 lines), Juliana (731 lines), Guthlac (1353 lines), Elene (1321 lines).

(4.) PSALMS AND HYMNS. Translations of a large part of the Hebrew Psalms, and a few Christian hymns and prayers.

(5.) SECULAR LYRICS. A few from the Chronicle celebrating the heroes, and others mostly elegiac, of which those on pages 68–69 are a specimen.

(6.) ALLEGORIES, GNOMES, AND RIDDLES. The Phœnix, a translation from Lactantius, expanded (677 lines); The Panther (74 lines); The Whale (89 lines); Gnomic verses, some in dialogue between Solomon and Saturn (Grein, ii., pages 339–368); Riddles (Grein, ii., pages 369–407). Pages 66–67 are specimens.

(7.) DIDACTIC ETHICAL. Alfred's Meters of Boethius (Grein, ii., pages 295–339). Pages 64–65 are specimens. Some of the Allegories, and other pieces classed under the sixth head, have a didactic purpose in natural science.

PAGE 51. THE TRAVELER is one of the most ancient Anglo-Saxon poems. A poet tells through what countries he has traveled and whom he has seen. It is little more than a sounding roll of names, with epithets and the briefest incidents, like the catalogues in Homer and Milton. Names enough are identified to give it reality. The lines here quoted are the last.

A single copy remains in the Codex Exoniensis. This was presented by Leofric, bishop of Exeter (A.D. 1046), to the library of his cathedral. It was edited by Thorpe for the Society of Antiquaries of London (1842), with an English translation, notes, and indexes. The text and translation make 500 pages.

Line 1. So roving   in their destinies wander
        gleemen of men   through many lands,
        their need tell,   thank-words speak,
        always south or north   some one *they* meet
        in songs clever,   in gifts unsparing,
        who before man wishes   honor to rear,
(nobleness) earlship to gain,   till that all departs,
        light and life together: praise whoever winneth,
        has under heavens   high-fast (immutable) honor.

BEOWULF, see page 56.

Line 9. The hero Beowulf has slain a monster. This is part of the celebration.

                            At times *a* king's thane,
        a man glory-laden,   of songs mindfull,
        who full-many   of old sagas,
        very-many remembered,   other words found
        rightly connected.   *This* hero again began
        the feat of Beowulf   with craft to recite,
        and artfully to utter   sentences cunning,
        with words to exchange (thoughts).

10.—*gilp-hlæden*, defiance laden, having passed through many battles. 12.—*porn* adds emphasis to *eal-fela*. 13.—*sóde*, according to the laws of verse. 15.—*geráde*, exact in meter. 16.—To narrate. 16.—*þær*, in the great hall Heorot, see page 57. 18.—*sægde*, (he) said, *se þe*, who.—*cpæd*, repetition of *sægde*. 21.—*spá*, which.

PAGE 52. CÆDMON's GENESIS. For Cædmon, see page 47–51, and the notes. Only one copy of these poems has survived in old manuscript. It was apparently written in the tenth century, the last seventeen pages in a different hand from the rest (212). All that is known of it is that it belonged to Archbishop Usher, who gave it to Junius, who printed it at Amsterdam in 1655, and who bequeathed it to the Bodleian Library. It is illuminated. A careful edition, with a translation, notes, and verbal index, was edited by Thorpe for the Society of Antiquaries of London, 1832. The illuminations were published in 1833. It has since been much studied in Germany, and many valuable articles upon it have been published. Grein's critical edition and translation, Bouterwek's copious Essays in his edition (1849–1854), and Dietrich's criticisms in Haupt's Zeitschrift, deserve special attention.

There is nothing but internal evidence to show that these poems are really those described as Cædmon's by Beda, and scholars have differed about it. It seems likely that they are from his original, but changed by free rewriting in a different dialect after the lapse of three or four centuries.

Those who do not know what liberties were taken by the early copyists and bards, may compare with the four first lines of Cædmon in Beda, page 48 and note, the following opening in the manuscript of Junius.

G

> Ûs is riht micel   þæt þê roderâ peard
> peredâ puldorcining   pordum herigen,
> môdum lufien: hê is mægnâ spêd,
> heâfod ealrâ   heâhgesceaftâ,
> freâ ælmihtig.   Næs him fruma æfre
> Ôr geporden,   ne nu ende cymd
> êcean drihtnes.

For us it is a great duty   that we heavens' Ward,
men's Glory-king   with words laud,
with minds love: he is of might the fullness,
head of all   high creations,
Lord almighty.   There has not to him beginning ever,
origin been,   nor will now end come
of the eternal Lord.

Cædmon has been called the Anglo-Saxon Milton. The extracts here given will indicate on what ground.

PAGE 52. GENESIS. The opening of this book has been given above. It goes on with the story of man's first disobedience and his fall, beginning with the fallen angels. The description of Satan, *gelîc þâm leohtum steorrum*, like the bright stars; his first speech as here given; some striking expressions in the description of his fall, of hell, heaven, of Adam and Eve, strongly suggest that Milton borrowed from Cædmon; but it is most likely that these resemblances arise from their drawing from the same sources—from the Bible most; in demonology and the lore of angels from Gregory the Great. A large part of Cædmon's Genesis is occupied with the story of Abraham.

Line 1.—*pæs geporden*, had been.—*þâ giet*, as yet: there had not here as yet,   except gloom-of-shadow, aught been. 6.—*geseah*, (he) saw dark obscurity   brood in perpetual night   swart under heavens,   wan and waste,   till that this world-creation   through the word existed   of the king of glory. 11.—*helm*, (helmet) protector of all things, appositive with *Drihten*. 14.—*Freâ*, repeated subject, or appositive like *helm*. 15.—*græs*, instrumental accus., § 295, *b*. 17.—*þanne pægâs*, appositive with *gârsecg*. 20.—*lifes Brytta*, appositive with *metod*. 29.—*gesceaft*, appositive with *leôht*. 31-32.—The coming on of the first night. 34.—*ford*, henceforth. 35.—*gŷman*, (who should) govern the abyss.—*pæs*, (he) was.

PAGE 53, line 6. Compare Paradise Lost, 1, 75. 10.—*þeâh . . .*, though we it for the All-powerful   must not own,   (must not) possess our realms. 11.—*næfd*=*ne hæfd*, he has not. 13.—*benumen*, p. p. (in that he hath) deprived (us) of heaven-realm, § 301. 18.—*him*, expletive reflexive: shall be to himself in pleasure, § 298, *c*. 19.—*âhte*, subj., expressing a wish, § 421, 4. 20.—and might I one hour   out be   be one winter hour. 21.—broken sentence. 28.—*habbad âmyrred* governs accusative *mê* and genitive *sîdes*, § 317, *a*.—*sâl* appositive with *gespong*. 32.—*mid pihte*, in any way, *mæg of*, may (escape) from, § 436. 37.—and (I know) that the Lord of hosts also knew that (there) should to us, (me and) Adam, evils occur in that heaven-realm, if I had the use of my hands; *unc Adame* § 287, g, ... *þûr*, if, § 475.

PAGE 54. EXODUS has been pronounced by some a lyric in honor of Moses. It has not the rapid narrative movement of an epic, but dilates imaginatively on a few scenes. It has the usual formal opening:

*Hpæt! pê feor and neáh   gèfrigen habbađ
ofer middangeard   Moyses dómâs.*

What! we far and near   have heard
over middle-earth   Moses' laws.

It has been generally considered one of the grandest and most characteristic poems of early Teutonic literature. It is characteristic of a certain class of writing; but it should not be forgotten that if we have an Anglo-Saxon Milton we also have an Anglo-Saxon Homer.

PAGE 54, line 1.—*Nearpe...*, Straitly *they* (the Israelites marching from Egypt) struggled-forward   on the northways,   they knew to them on the south   the Sunfolks' (Ethiopian) land. 2.—*piston land*, knew the land; knew that the land lay. 4.—*heofon-colum*, instrumental after *brûne*. 5.—*fûr-bryne*, fearful burning (of the sun). 5.—*bælcê*, Ger. *gebälk*, canopy, the so-called "pillar of cloud." 7.—*nettê*, repetition of *bælce*. 8.—*peder-polcen*, Ger. *wetterwolke* (weather-welkin), storm-cloud, is the "pillar of cloud." 10.—*lig-fŷr*, *háte heofontorht*, describes the sun; *háte*, definite form, epic epithet, § 362, 1; others read it as an instrumental of *hát*, heat. 12.—*drihtá gedrýmóst*, gladdest of throngs, appositive with *Hæleđ*. 13.—*Dæg-scealdes*, trope for *sun*, *hleó dæg-scealdes*, the "pillar of cloud." 15.—*spá*, although. 18.—*mæst*, the greatest of tents. 19.—*on sálum*, in safe places, in safety. 20.—*Heofon-beácen*, the "pillar of fire." 22.—*syllic* agrees with *beam*; Strange after sun's   set took care   over the people   with flame to shine   a burning pillar. 27.—*neóple...*, deepest night-shadows   not enough might   lurking-places hide; *i. e.*, Midnight was not dark enough to hide them, the pillar was so bright. 30.—*þŷ læs...*, lest to them by the horrors-of-the-waste   the hoar heath   with raging storms   ever with sudden peril   their minds might distract. 35.—*hátan*, weak instrumental, epic epithet, § 362, 1.

PAGE 55, line 2.—*hŷrde*, subj. imperf. for *hŷrden*, § 170. 5.—*segn*, the pillar of fire. 10-11.—*flotan bræddon*, the sailors spread (with) tents over the mountains. 13.—Then to them (=the warriors) the warriors' mind became despondent. 20.—*on hpæl*, in circuit, round them; Grein suggests another *hpæl*, akin to *hpelan*, to clang, Dan. *hvael*, a shriek; *on hpæl*, with clangor 25.—*deór*, appositive with *pulfás*; *cpyldróf...*, ravenous to demand on enemies' track   the host's slaughter. 27.—*marc-peardás* are the wolves. 32.—*þengel*, appositive with *sige-cyning*, the king of Egypt. 38.—*land-mannâ*, the Egyptians.

BEOWULF has been found in only one manuscript, thought to be of the tenth century. Its existence is mentioned first in Wanley's Catalogue, 1705;

but little notice of it was taken till 1786, when two copies were made for Thorkelin, a Dane, by whom an edition was published in 1815. The manuscript had been badly injured by fire in 1731, and has had hard usage since. Since the revival of Anglo-Saxon scholarship under the impulse of Grimm, the interest in Beowulf has risen to a great heighth, and many editions, translations, and essays of elucidation and interpretation have appeared in England, Germany, and Denmark. Among others, Kemble, 1833–1837; Ettmüller, translation, 1840; Thorpe, 1855; Grein, two editions, 1857, 1867; Gruntvig, 1861; Heyne, two editions, 1863, 1868. The poem celebrates the exploits of Beowulf. We learn from it that he was the son of a sister of Hygelác, king of the Geáts (Goths), and Ecgtheów, one of the royal family of the Danes, and that after the death of Hygelác and his son he succeeded to the throne of the Goths. The exploits here celebrated are combats with monsters, after the manner of Hercules. The tendency at first was to regard Beowulf as one of the gods, and the whole poem as mythology; but it now seems clear that Beowulf was a real prince, and that a body of fact lies under the fables. The time is the beginning of the sixth century. See the note on Hygelác, page 58, line 30. The place is the island of Seeland (Zealand, the seat of Copenhagen) and the opposite Gothland. An attempt has, however, been made to locate it in England by Haigh, and very remarkable coincidences of names and distances are pointed out in favor of that theory.

PAGE 56, line 3.—*Gâr-Denâ*, the *Dene* (Danes) appear in Beowulf as the subjects of Scyld and his descendants, as living "*in Scedelandum*," "*on Scedenigge*," "*by two seas*," as we suppose, in Denmark. Their epithets are *Gâr-Dene*, Spear-Danes, *Hring-Dene*, Mailed-Danes, *Beorht-Dene*, Bright-Danes. They are divided into East, West, North, and South Danes. 6.—*Scyld*, the son of *Scéf*, was drifted to Denmark, an infant alone in a boat; he there established a royal family; at his death was again committed to the sea in a boat, and departed, as he came, into the unknown. Such was the founding of the royal line of *Hrothgar*. *Scéf* is referred to in Anglo-Saxon poetry only in line 4 of Beowulf. He is identified by Grein with *Sceáfa*, mentioned in the *Traveler* (see note on page 51) as king of the Longo-bards. He is probably also the *Sceáf* in the pedigree of Æthelwulf, Alfred's father, inaccurately described as the son of Noah, born in the ark, Chr., 855. 7.—*mágdum*, appositive, *ofteáh*, elsewhere, as here, sometimes governs the dative of the person and genitive of the object of separation, §§ 298, 317. 8.—The earl inspired terror, after he first had been found deserted. Kings are called earls as being of the same noble stock. 9.—He experienced solace for *that*, *i. e.* his desertion, § 315. 14.—*Him*, reflexive expletive, § 298, c.—*gepât féran*, § 448, 4. 18.—*pordum peóld*, ruled with words; perhaps should read *pord-onpeald âhte*, had word-sway.—*Scyldingá*, the descendants of Scyld; (2) the people ruled by them. 26.—*gegyrpan*, infinitive, to equip a ship, *i. e.* of equipping, § 449, a. 31.—*læss-an = -um*.

PAGE 57, line 6.—*sele-rædende*, hall possessors, appositive with *men*; so *hæled*. 7.—*onfèng*, with dative, § 299. 8.—*Hróthgâr*, son of *Healfdene*,

NOTES. 89

is the king of the Danes for whose relief occurred the exploits of Beowulf here sung. His wife is *Wealhtheow*. See *Scyld*, page 56, line 6. 11.—*mago-driht*, appositive with *geógod*, the band of youth, the squires. 13.—*medo-ærn*, repetition of *heal-reced*; *men*, accusative, subject of *gepyrcean*. 14.—*þone* for *þonne*, (greater) than the children of the age (men) ever heard of. 15.—(*polde*) *gedǽlan*. 17.—All, except the public lands and the lives of the people. 20.—*gelomp*, it happened. 22.—*Heort, Heorot*, i. e. hart, is found by Grein in the Danish *Hjort-holm*, a town in Zealand, about two miles from the sea. Near by is *Siæl* lake, answering to Grendel's lake. At the right distance on the opposite coast of the main-land for Beowulf's grave, he finds the ruined castle of *Bó-hús*. See note on Hygelác, page 58, line 30. 24.—*beót ne áléh*, did not belie his promise, *áléh*<*áleógan*. Here follows the passage quoted on page 51. 30.—*Grendel* was a monster of the moors, of the race of Cain. He broke into Heorot every night and carried off thirty warriors. This lasted twelve years. Then came Beowulf, fought him, wrenched his arm off. He escaped to his lair, and died. Beowulf pursued his mother to the place, killed her; found his body, cut off his head, and bore it to Hrothgar.

PAGE 58, line 1.—*Metod*, repeated subject of *forpræc*. 5.—*him*, plur. dat., indirect object. § 297; *þæs*, genitive of crime, § 320, d. 6.—*neosian húses*, examine the house, § 315, III. 7.—How the Mailed-Danes had inhabited it (the house)=how they had disposed themselves to sleep. 21.—So (Grendel) ruled. 26.—*forþam* . . ., therefore afterward was it to the children of men plainly known, by songs sadly (known), that Grendel warred long against Hrothgar. 30.—*þæt*, it, Grendel's deeds, *dǽdá* appositive with *þæt*, § 374, 2. Higelac's thane is Beowulf. Higelac (*Hygelác*) appears in Beowulf as reigning king of the Geáten (Goths). The seat of his kingdom was in the Swedish Gothland, near the River Gotha, and nearly opposite the Danish *Hjort-holm*. Several of his kindred, and two successive wives, are mentioned in Beowulf, and that he fell in an expedition against the Franks, Friesians, and *Húgen*. This seems to identify him with a Gothic king, Chocilagus, mentioned by Gregory of Tours, and the Gesta Regum Francorum, as having so adventured and died, A.D. 511; and in a tenth century tradition of the same event described as *Huiclaucus*, king of the Geti. 33.—In the day of this life=at that time, then.

PAGE 59, line 1.—*se góda*, used substantively. 3.=*fiftêná sum*, one of fifteen, with a party of fifteen, § 388. 12.—*pudu bundenne*, perhaps originally a raft, a ship. 17.—*þæt*, so far that. 20.—*eoletes* (bay<*eolh?* sea?) has not been clearly made out, *eá-láda*, watery way, Thorpe; *eá-let*, waterstay, time on the voyage, Leo, Heyne; *eolet*, hastening, rapid voyage, Ett., Grein. Compare the puzzling *sioleda*, found once only (Beowulf, 2367), meaning *bay*, *cove*, or *sea*. 25.—*geseah beran*, saw (persons) bear, § 449, a. 29.—*hpæt*, § 377. 30.—*gepât rîdan*, § 448, 4; *gepât him*, § 298, c. 35.—*lǽdan cpómon*, § 448, 4. 36.—The second section of the line is gone in the manuscript: *helmás bǽron*, Ett., Heyne; *hýde sécean*, Grein. Compare the answer to this question, page 60, line 25, We *through kind feeling come* to seek thy lord.

PAGE 60, line 1.—*cúdlicór*, more openly, with franker courtesy. 2.—Nor have ye words-of-permission of warriors completely known, the assent of men=but yet ye do not know surely whether ye can obtain permission from us warriors. 26.—*lárená gód*, good in respect of instructions, *i. e.* kindly direct us.

PAGE 61, line 4.—*se ríca*, Hrothgar. 16.—*cynná*, fitting things, manners, courtesies. 17.—*gold-hroden*, Wealhtheow. 20.—*bæd hine blidne* bade him blithe, ellipsis of *pesan*, to be, making a factitive like *wish him well*. Compare *bade him hail*, page 62, line 13. 21.—*leófne*, appositive with *hine*. 23.—*Helmingás*, the race of Helm. He is mentioned in the Traveler as ruling the Wulfings. Wealh-theow was of this race. 28.—*þancóde*, with dative *Gode* and genitive *þæs*, § 297, *d*.

PAGE 62, line 17.—*gamela*, weak form, epic epithet, § 362, 1. 18.—*rand-pigan*, appositive with *Geát*, Beowulf. 27.—*cóman . . . scacan:* for this text of Grein's first edition his last has *þá com beorht leóma   scacan ofer scadu.*—The manuscript is illegible: *þá com beorht scacan*, is one of the early copies; then came the bright light to beam over the shadows. 30.—*þyle Hródgáres*, the court officer who directed the conversation, the orator. His name was *Húnferd*. He had boasted much over the wine, but did not venture to meet Grendel. He lent Beowulf his famous sword *Hrunting* for the conflict with Grendel's mother.

PAGE 63, line 3.—*se eorl*, Beowulf. He has followed the mother of Grendel deep into the water, and comes up in a cave, her hall. Then the earl found   that he in hostile hall,   he knew not what, was. 36.—The blood of the monster melts the blade, Beowulf presents the hilt to *Hródgár*.

PAGE 64, line 5.—*him*, to them the lord paid; *þæs*, therefore.

ALFRED'S METERS are versifications of parts of Boethius. They were found in one manuscript, transcribed by Junius, but since lost. Editions are by Rawlinson, 1698; Fox, 1835; Grein, 1858. See farther in the notes to Orpheus, page 46.

Line 12.—This introduction is not by Alfred. Thus Alfred to us old-lore rehearsed   king of the West Saxons, skill displayed,   the poets' art.

Line 17.—Meter VI. is from Book II., Metrum III., of Boethius, which is given for comparison. The two first lines are Alfred's introduction.

            Cum polo Phœbus roseis quadrigis
                Lucem spargere cœperit,
            Pallet albentes hebetata vultus
                Flammis stella prementibus.
            Cum nemus flatu Zephyri tepentis
                Vernis irrubuit rosis,
            Spiret insanum nebulosus Auster,
                Jam spinis abeat decus.

Sæpe tranquillo radiat sereno
　　Immotis mare fluctibus :
Sæpe ferventes Aquilo procellas
　　Verso concitat æquore.
Rara si constat sua forma mundo
　　Si tantas variat vices,
Crede fortunis hominum caducis,
　　Bonis crede fugacibus.
Constat, æterna positumque lege est,
　　Ut constet genitum nihil.

PAGE 65. METER X. is founded on the 7th meter of Book II. The first 25 lines are expanded from two:

　　Ubi nunc fidelis ossa Fabricii jacent?
　　Quid Brutus, aut rigidus Cato?

Line 1.—*Wéland* is the hero-smith of the North. Stories of him were among the most popular of the Middle Ages. They are mostly such as the Greeks told of Hephaistos, Erichthonios, and Daidalos. He made rings, and set them with precious stones. Nídhád, a king in Sweden, had him bound in his sleep with heavy chains, and took from him a famous sword, and a ring which he gave to his daughter Beadohild. He afterward had him hamstringed, and confined to work for him. Wéland killed the sons of Nídhád. Beadohild, who had come to him to get her ring mended, he first stupefied with beer, and then ravished. He made himself wings and flew away, boasting of his revenge. He made Beowulf's famous coat of mail. The story of shooting the apple from his son's head, and the arrow "to kill thee, tyrant, had I slain my boy," familiar in connection with William Tell and William of Cloudesle, is a Wéland story, told of his brother Egil. Scott's Wayland Smith, in Kenilworth, has his name, though little else, from this source. Alfred substitutes *Wéland* for *Fabricius*, as though *Fabricius* were from *faber*, artificer.

Line 4.—*ǽngum* . . ., to any one may not the skill escape=no one may attain the skill. 6.—*þý éd* . . . *þe*, easier than; *beniman præccan cræftes*, deprive a wretch (even) of his skill, § 317;—than one may turn the sun to swerve, and this swift heaven (to swerve) from his orbit, any of heroes; *ǽnig*, appositive with *mon*. 30.—*perás*, accusative, appositive with *hi;* bring them forth well known=make them familiar. 37.—*guma*, repeated subject; What then may have　　any of heroes,　　a man, from fame . . . ?

PAGE 66. SAWS. These are often called Gnomic verses. They are from pages 338+ of the Codex Exoniensis, already described in a note on the Traveler, page 51.

Line 3.—*pundrum*, wondrously. The ice, the water-helmet, locks up the plants. 14.—*pig*, repetition of *gúd*. 22.—*bold-ágendum*, appositive with *him*, the wife should know wise counsels for them (herself and husband), the house holders both together. 25.—*frisan*, frizzled, ringleted, with a wealth of tresses, Ett., Grein; other editors "Frisian." 30.—Waiteth for him on the land   that his love demandeth. 31.—*pêre* . . ., keep faith.

PAGE 67, line 3.—*mægd egsan pyn*, the chief of terrors, *i. e.* the sea, (holdeth) a family (many sailors). Thorpe reads *mægd eágnâ pyn*, a maid is the delight of the eyes. 4.—A rich man, a king, a settlement then for his people buys, when he comes to sail, *i. e.* sailing, § 448, 4. 32.—*sceal*, ought to belong to, becomes; infinitive omitted, § 435, *d.*—*Alpalda*, The All-ruling, *i. e.* the true God, (made) the glorious (world).

PAGE 68. THRENES. This extract is from a poem in the Codex Exoniensis, pages 286+, called by Thorpe The Wanderer. The ruined castle strikes the imagination powerfully in all ages, and in the decline of the Roman Empire men thought of themselves as living in a decaying world. The Anglo-Saxon poets seem to have been especially affected by this mode of thought.

Line 6.—*sumne* . . ., one a bird bore away over the high sea: *bird* trope for *ship*, Thorpe. Grein refers it to the bird *Greif*, O. H. G. *Grif, Grifo*, which figures in Germanic story, a counterpart to Gr. *Gryps*, griffon. 11.—*burgparâ* . . ., till free from sounds of citizens old works of giants empty stood. Cities, stone figures, roads, stone swords, caves of dragons, are spoken of in Anglo-Saxon poems as *entâ gepeorc*, and that is the only way in which *ent* occurs in them. 17.—Where has come horse = what has become of horse? 21.—*genáp*, has vanished, *spâ*, as if. 22.—*on láste*, in the place of, forsaken by. 39.—*tó rycene*, too quickly.

PAGE 69, line 2.—*eorl*, appositive with *hê*, unless he first the remedy know how, the earl, with might to obtain. 4.—*him*, for himself.

The SECOND THRENE is from page 377 of the Codex Exoniensis, printed as "Deor the Scald's Complaint." See note on The Traveler, page 41.

Line 7.—*Wêland*, see page 65, 1, and note. Wêland for himself among dragons   exile experienced. No dragon story is known of Wêland. Grein proposes *pimman*, by means of woman. Rieger reads *be pornum*, manifoldly. 11.—*Nidhâd*, see note on page 65. 12.—*sýllan=séllan<sêl*, weak form, as epic epithet, § 362, 1. 13.—*ofereóde*, impersonal; there was a surviving of that, so there may be of this. 16.—The omitted line and a half reads:

þæt heó gearolice   ongieten hæfde
þæt heó eácen pæs:

See for Beadohild's misfortune the note on page 65, line 1. 20.—*Eormanric*. The Gothic king *Emanaricus*, the Alexander of the North, is mentioned in the Traveler's Song and in Beowulf. He was king of the Ostro-Goths, A.D. 375. The stories told of him are full of anachronisms and inconsistencies. 25.—*cyne-rices*, genitive of separation, § 317. 27.—*Heodening*, Heoden, is Hetele in Gudrun, Hedin in Snorri's Edda, Hithinus in Saxo. 30.—*Heorrenda* is celebrated in the German heroic poetry as *Horant*, in Snorri as *Hiarrandi*.

PAGE 70.—These rhymes are part of a poem of 87 verses in the Codex

NOTES. 93

Exoniensis. It is plainly a task poem to exhibit riming skill. The spelling obscures the sense, which needs all the light to be had. I have, therefore, used Grein's reformed orthography, and I add a Latin version by Ettmüller. Thorpe had pronounced it unintelligible. For the meter, see § 511.

    Hominum genus perit, pugnæ hasta lacerat,
        versutia procax pugnat, sagittam fraus præparat,
        fidejussionem cura mordet, audaciam senectus exscindit.
    Exilii tempus succrescit, iracundia jusjurandum cudit,
        criminum funes expanduntur, machinationes instructæ labuntur.
    Mœsta ira fodit, fovea retinaculum habet;
        ornatus albus polluitur, æstas calida frigescit.
    Populi prosperitas ruit, amicitia volvitur [evanescit],
        terræ vires inveterascunt, fervor frigescit.
    Mihi id Parca texuit et opus imposuit,
        ut foderem sepulcrum; neque hanc diram constitutionem
        evitare carne possum, quo ex tempore dies celer fugerit,
        arreptione necessaria me arripit [mors], ex quo nox venerit,
        quæ mihi patriam negat, et me hic habitatione privat.
    Si cadaver jacet, membra vermis comedit,
        verrucam non curat et cibum sumit,
        donec ossa tantum ex viro supersint,
        et ultimo nullum [os], nisi necessitatis virgula
        malum omen hic præbuerit, non erit fama tœdio affecta.
    Priusquam felix hoc cogitat, sæpissime se ipsum fatigat;
        gustat amarum crimen, non curat meliorem voluptatem,
        non recordatur hilaritatum gratias, hic sunt misericordiæ gaudia
        speranda in cœlorum regno. Eamus nunc sanctis similes
        criminibus liberati, a dedecoribus redempti,
        maculis puri, splendore cincti,
        ubi humanum genus debet coram creatore lætum
        verum Deum aspicere et in pace semper gaudere.

Note the use of adjectives as substantives: *fláh máh flited*, subtle hostile fighteth = hostile one, fiend; *bald ald ppited*, bold old severeth = old age cuts off the bold.

A BRIEF GRAMMAR

OF THE

ANGLO-SAXON LANGUAGE.

THE sections are numbered like the corresponding sections in the Author's Comparative Grammar of the Anglo-Saxon Language, so that the references in the notes of the Reader may answer for both when the topic is treated in both. The Comparative Grammar illustrates the forms of the Anglo-Saxon by those of the Sanskrit, Greek, Latin, Gothic, Old Saxon, Old Friesic, Old Norse, and Old High German.

INTRODUCTION.

1. During the fifth and sixth centuries, England was conquered and peopled by pagans (Saxons, Angles, Jutes, etc.) from the shores of the North Sea; the center of emigration was near the mouth of the Elbe. The conquerors spoke many dialects, but most of them were Low German. Missionaries were sent from Rome (A.D. 597) to convert them to Christianity. The Roman alphabetic writing was thus introduced, and, under the influence of learned native ecclesiastics, a single tongue gradually came into use as a literary language through the whole nation. The chief seat of learning down to the middle of the eighth century was among the Angles of Northumberland. The language was long called Englisc (English), but is now called Anglo-Saxon. Its Augustan age was the reign of Alfred the Great, king of the West Saxons (A.D. 871-901). It continued to be written till the colloquial dialects, through the influence of the Anglo-Norman, had diverged so far from it as to make it unintelligible to the people; then, under the cultivation of the Wycliffite translators of the Bible, and of Chaucer and his fellows, there grew out of these dialects a new classic language—the English.

2. The spelling in the manuscripts is irregular, but the Northumbrian is the only well-marked dialect of the Anglo-Saxon, as old as its classic period (10th century), which has yet been explored. The Gospels and some other works have been printed in it. The common Anglo-Saxon is sometimes called West-Saxon.

3. After the period of pure Anglo-Saxon, there was written an irregular dialect called Semi-Saxon. It has few strange words, but the inflections and syntax are broken up (12th century).

4. The former inhabitants of Britain were Celts, so unlike the invaders in race and speech, and so despised and hated, that they did not mix. There are in the Anglo-Saxon a handful of Celtic common names, and a good many geographical names: the relation of the Celtic language to the Anglo-Saxon is like that of the languages of the aborigines of America to our present English.

5. The Anglo-Saxon was shaped to literary use by men who wrote and spoke Latin, and thought it an ideal language; and a large part of the literature is translated or imitated from Latin authors. It is not to be doubted, therefore, that the Latin exercised a great influence on the Anglo-Saxon: if it did not lead to the introduction of wholly new forms, either of etymology or syntax, it led to the extended and uniform use of those forms which are like the Latin, and to the disuse of others, so as to draw the grammars near each other. There are a considerable number of words from the Latin, mostly connected with the Church; three or four through the Celts from the elder Romans.

6. There are many words in Anglo-Saxon more like the words of the same sense in Scandinavian than like any words which we find in the Germanic languages; but the remains of the early dialects are so scant that it is hard to tell how far such words were borrowed from or modified by the Scandinavians. Before A.D. 900 many Danes had settled in England. Danish kings afterward ruled it (A.D. 1013–1042). Their laws, however, are in Anglo-Saxon. The Danes were illiterate, and learned the Anglo-Saxon. Of course their pronunciation was peculiar, and they quickened and modified phonetic decay. It is probable that they affected the spoken dialects which have come up as English more than the written literary language which we call Anglo-Saxon.

7. The other languages sprung from the dialects of Low German tribes are Friesic, Old Saxon, and, later, Dutch (and Flemish), and Platt Deutsch. The talk in the harbors of Antwerp, Bremen, and Hamburg is said to be often mistaken by English sailors for corrupt English. These Low German languages are akin to the High German on one side, and to the Scandinavian on the other. These all, with the Mœso-Gothic, constitute the Teutonic class of languages. This stands parallel with the Lithuanic, the Slavonic, and the Celtic, and with the Italic, the Hellenic, the Iranic, and the Indic, all of which belong to the Indo-European family of languages. The parent speech of this family is lost, and has left no literary monuments. Its seat has been supposed to have been on the heights of Central Asia. The Sanskrit, an ancient language of India, takes its place at the head of the family. Theoretical roots and forms of inflection are given by grammarians as those of the Parent Speech, on the ground that they are such as might have produced the surviving roots and forms by known laws of change.

8. The following stem shows the order in which these classes branched, and their relative age and remoteness from each other. At the right is given the approximate date of the oldest literary remains. The languages earlier than these remains are made out like the Parent Speech; that is, roots and forms are taken for the language at each period, which will give the roots and forms of all the languages which branch from it, but not those peculiar to the other languages.

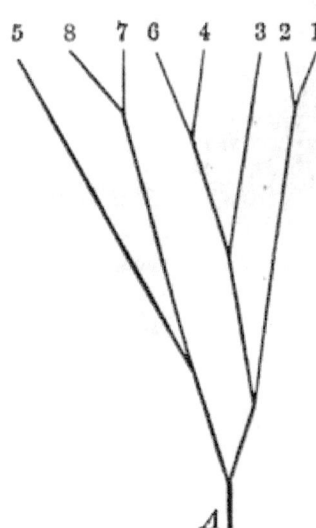

A. Indo-European. Parent Speech.
1. Indic. B.C. 1500. Sanskrit Vedas.
2. Iranic. B.C. 1000. Bactrian Avesta.
3. Hellenic. Before B.C. 800. Greek.
4. Italic. B.C. 200. Latin.
5. Teutonic. 4th Century. Mœso-Gothic Bible.
6. Celtic. 8th Century.
7. Slavonic. 9th Century. Bulgarian Bible.
8. Lithuanic. 16th Century.

9. The following stem shows the manner in which the languages of the Teutonic class branch after separating from the Slavonic. The Gothic (Mœso-Gothic) died without issue; the Low German is nearer akin to it than the High German is. The branches of the Scandinavian (Swedish, Danish, Norwegian) are not represented.

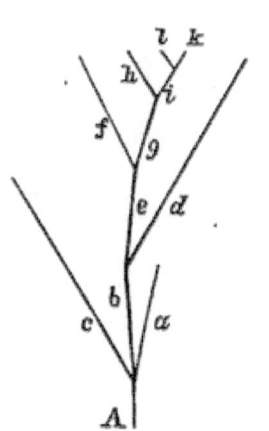

A. Teutonic. Theoretic.
a. Gothic. 4th Century.
b. Germanic. Theoretic.
c. Scandinavian. 13th Century.
d. High German. 8th Century.
e. Low German. Theoretic.
f. Friesic. 14th Century.
g. Saxon. Theoretic.
h. Anglo-Saxon. 8th Century.
i. Old Saxon. 9th Century.
k. Platt Deutsch. 14th Century.
l. Dutch. 13th Century.

PART I.

PHONOLOGY.

10. Alphabet.—The Anglo-Saxon alphabet has twenty-four letters. All but three are Roman characters: the variations from the common form are cacographic fancies. Þ þ (thorn), and Ƿ ƿ (wên), are runes. Ð ð (edh) is a crossed d, used for the older þ, oftenest in the middle and at the end of words.

Old Forms.		Simple Forms.		Roman.		Names.
A	a	A	a	A	a	ah
Æ	æ	Æ	æ	Æ	æ	ă
B	b	B	b	B	b	bay
C	c	C	c	C	c	cay
D	d	D	d	D	d	day
Ð	ð	Ð	ð	DH	dh	edh
E	e	E	e	E	e	ay
F	f	F	f	F	f	ef
G	ᵹ	G	g	G	g	gay
Þ ƕ	h	H	h	H	h	hah
I	i	I	i	I	i	ee
L	l	L	l	L	l	el
M	m	M	m	M	m	em
N	n	N	n	N	n	en
O	o	O	o	O	o	o
P	p	P	p	P	p	pay
R	r	R	r	R	r	er
S	s	S	s	S	s	es
T	t	T	t	T	t	tay
Þ þ		Þ	þ	TH	th	thorn
U	u	U	u	U	u	oo
Ƿ	ƿ	Ƿ	ƿ	VV vv (W) (w)		wên
X	x	X	x	X	x	ex
Y	ẏ	Y	y	Y	y	ypsilon

Some of the German editors use ä for æ, œ for ê, ü for e derived from i, ö for œ, œ for ê, j for i when a semi-vowel, and v for ƿ. Now and then k, q, v, z get into the manuscripts, mostly in foreign words, and uu or u for ƿ. The Semi-Saxon has a peculiar character for j (ȝ).

11. **Abbreviations.**—The most common are ᛡ = and, þ = þæt (*that*), ⁊ = oððe (*or*), and ¯ for an omitted m or n; as, þā = þam.

12. An **Accent** (´) is found in Anglo-Saxon manuscripts, but in none so regularly used as to make it an objective part of an Anglo-Saxon text. It is found oftenest over a long vowel; sometimes over a vowel of peculiar sound, not long; seldom, except over syllables having stress of voice. Sometimes it seems to mark nothing but stress. Most of the English editors represent it by an acute accent; the Germans generally print Anglo-Saxon with a circumflex over all single long vowels in the stem of words, and an acute over the diphthongs, as brôðer, freónd. In this book, to guide the studies of beginners, a circumflex is used over all long vowels and diphthongs, and the acute accent (´) over vowels only to denote stress.

13. **Punctuation.**—The Anglo-Saxons used one dot (.) at the end of each clause, or each hemistich of a poem, and sometimes three dots (:·) at the end of a sentence. Modern pointing is generally used in printed text.

14. **Sounds of Letters.**—*Vowels:*

a like *a* in *far*.	i like *i* in *dim*.
â " *a* " *fall*.	î " *ee* " *deem*.
æ " *a* " *glad*.	o " *o* " *wholly*.
ǽ " *a* " *dare* in New England.	ô " *o* " *holy*.
e " *e* " *let*.	u " *u* " *full*.
e in the breakings (not diphthongs) ea, eo, eâ, eô, very light.	û " *oo* " *fool*.
	y " *i* " *dim*, but with the lips thrust out and rounded. (French u.)
ê like *e* in *they*.	ŷ same sound prolonged.

Unaccented vowels are like accented in kind, but obscure.

The *consonants* have their common English sounds; but note

c like *k*, always.	i (=j) before a vowel, like *y*.
ch " *kh* in *work-house*.	s like *s* in *so*.
cp " *qu*.	t " *t* " *to*.
ð, like Engl. *th* in a similar word; *óder*, other, *dóð*, doth.	þ " *th* " *thin*.
	p " *w*.
g like *g* in *go*, always.	pl, pr, and final p nearly close the lips. (German w.)
h very distinct.	
hp like *wh* in New England.	x like *ks*.

PHONOLOGY.

15. Accent.—Rule 1. The primary accent is on the first syllable of every word : *bród'-er*, brother ; *uh'-cúd*, uncouth.

Exception 1. Proper prefixes in verbs and particles take no primary accent: such are *â, an, and, æt, be, bi, ed, for, ful, ge, geond, in, mis, ôd, of, ofer, on, or, tô, þurh, un, under, pid, pider, ymb, ymbe*: *an-gin'nan*, begin ; *æt-gad'ere*, together ; *on-geân'*, again. The syllable after the prefix takes the accent.

(*a.*) But derivatives from nouns, pronouns, or adjectives retain their accent : *and'-sparian* < *and'sparu*, answer ; *in'-peardlice* < *in'-peard*, adj., inward ; *ed'-nipian* < *ed'nipe*, renewed. Such are all verbs in *and-, ed-, or-*, found in Anglo-Saxon poetry ; many adverbs in *un-*, etc.

(*b.*) Many editors print as compounds adverbs+verbs, both of which retain their accent. Such are those with *æfter, bî, big, efen, eft, fore, ford, from, fram, hider, mid, nider, gegn, geân, gên, tô, up, ût, pel*.

Exception 2. The inseparable prefixes *â-, be- (bi-), for-, ge-*, are unaccented : *â-lŷs'-ing*, redemption ; *be-gang'*, course.

Rule 2. A secondary accent may fall on the tone syllable of the lighter part of a compound or on a suffix : *o'fer-cum'an*, overcome ; *heof'on-steor'-ra*, star of heaven ; *hŷr'end'e*, hearing.

EUPHONIC CHANGES.

27. Gémination is the doubling of a letter : when final or next to a consonant it is simplified or dissimilated, *mm* to *mb*, *nn* to *nd*, *ss* to *st*, *ii* to *ig*, *uu* to *up*: *dippan*, dip, makes *dip, dipte;* timbr for *timmr*, timber ; *spindl* for *spinnl*, spindle ; *lufast*, lovest, for *lufass, lufige* for *luftie*, love ; *bearupes* for *bearuues*, grove. Double *g* is written *cg*, double *f, bb*.

32. Umlaut is the assimilation of a vowel by the vowel of the following syllable.

	a-umlaut.	i-umlaut.	u-umlaut.
It changes	i, u,	a, u, ea, eo, â, ô, û, eâ, eô,	a, i,
to	e(eo), o.	e, y, y, y, ŵ, ê, ŷ, ŷ, ŷ.	(o)ea, eo.

a-umlaut : *helpan*, from root *hilp*, help ; *leofad*, root *lif*, live ; *boga*, from root *bug*, bow. The **i** which produces *i*-umlaut is often changed to **e** or dropped ; *man*, plur. *men*, from *meni* ; *fôt*, plur. *fêt*, feet, from *fêti*. *u*-umlaut : *hlid*, plur. *hleodu*, slopes.

33. Breaking is the change of one vowel to two by a consonant.

g, c, and **sc** may break a following *a* to *ea*, *o* to *eo*, *i* to *ie*, *â* to *eâ*, *ô* to *eô*. **l, r,** and **h** may break a preceding *a* to *ea*, *i* to *eo* (*io*), *ie* : *geaf*, gave ; *ceaster*, Latin *castrum*, camp ; *sceô*, shoe ; *sealm*, psalm ; *earm*, arm ; *hleahtor*, laughter ; *meolc*, milk.

41. Shifting is a weakening of a letter not produced by other letters : *a* to *æ*, *û* to *ê*, *eâ eô* to *ê*, etc. : *dæg* from *dag*, day.

PART II.

ETYMOLOGY.

NOUNS.

65. There are two classes of Declensions of Anglo-Saxon nouns:
(1.) **Strong**: those which have sprung from vowel stems.
(2.) **Weak**: that which has sprung from stems in **an**.

There are four declensions distinguished by the endings of the Genitive Singular:

Declension 1.	Declension 2.	Declension 3.	Declension 4.
es	e	a	an

66. SUMMARY OF CASE-ENDINGS.

	STRONG.							WEAK.		
	DECL. I.		DECL. II.		DECL. III.		DECL. IV.			
	Masc.	Neut.	Masc.	Neut.	Feminine.		Masc. Fem.		Masc.	Fem.	Neut.
Stem......	a	a	ia	ia	â	i	u		an	an	an
SINGULAR.—											
N. & V.....	–	–	e	e	u	–	u		a	e	e
Gen.	es	es	es	es	e	e	â		an	an	an
Dat.	e	e	e	e	e	e	â		an	an	an
Acc.	–	–	e	e	u, o	e, –	u		an	an	e
Inst.	ô	ô	â	ô	e	e	â		an	an	an
PLURAL.—											
N., A., & V.	âs	u	âs	u	â, e	e, â	u, o, â		an		
Gen.	â	â	â	â	â, enâ		â, enâ		enâ		
D. & Inst....	um	um	um	um	um		um		um		

A few masculines of Decl. 1st have some forms from **i**-stems or **u**-stems, §§ 86, 93.

67. **Gender.** General rules. For particulars, see §§ 268–270.

1. **Strong nouns.** All masculines are of the first or third declension; all feminines of the second or third; all neuters of the first.

2. *Abstract Nouns* have their gender governed by the terminations. In derivatives the feminine gender prevails.

3. *Compound Nouns* follow the gender of the last part.

4. MASCULINE are names of males; of the moon; of many weeds, flowers, winds; *man, guma,* man; *ꝑéland; móna,* moon; *mear,* horse; *þorn,* thorn; *blóstma,* blossom; *pind,* wind.

5. FEMININE are names of females; of the sun; of many trees, rivers, soft and low musical instruments: *cþén,* queen; *cú,* cow; *Ælf-þryde; sunnu, sunne,* sun; *âc,* oak; *Danubie,* Danube; *hpistle,* whistle; *hearpe,* harp.

6. NEUTER are names of wife, child; diminatives; many general names; and words made an object of thought: *pif*, wife; *bearn, cild*, child; *mægden*, maiden; *græs*, grass; *ofet*, fruit; *corn*, corn; *gold*, gold.

7. *Epicene Nouns* have one grammatical gender, but are used for both sexes. Such names of mammalia are masculine, except of a few little timid ones: *mús*, mouse (feminine); large and fierce birds are masculine; others feminine, especially singing birds: *nihtegale*, nightingale; large fishes are masculine, small feminine; insects are feminine.

68. **Cases alike.**—(1.) The nominative and vocative are always alike.

(2.) The nominative, accusative, and vocative are alike in all plurals, and in the singular of all neuters and strong masculines.

(3.) The genitive plural ends always in **â** or **enâ**.

(4.) The dative and instrumental plural end always in **um** (*on*).

DECLENSION I.

Stem in **a**. Genitive singular in **es**.

70.—I. Case-endings from stem **a**+relational suffixes. Nominative in —.

	MASCULINE.		NEUTER.
Stem.......	pulfa, *wolf*.		scipa, *ship*.
Theme.....	pulf.		scip.
SINGULAR.—			
Nominative..	pulf,	*a wolf*.	scip.
Genitive......	pulfes,	*of a wolf, wolf's*.	scipes.
Dative.......	pulfe,	*to or for a wolf*.	scipe.
Accusative....	pulf,	*a wolf*.	scip.
Vocative......	pulf,	*O, wolf*.	scip.
Instrumental..	pulfê,	*by or with a wolf*.	scipê.
PLURAL.—			
Nominative..	pulfás,	*wolves*.	scipu.
Genitive......	pulfá,	*of wolves*.	scipá.
Dative.......	pulfum,	*to or for wolves*.	scipum.
Accusative...	pulfás,	*wolves*.	scipu.
Vocative......	pulfás,	*O, wolves*.	scipu.
Instrumental..	pulfum,	*by or with wolves*.	scipum.

73. 2.—Long syllables drop plur. -*u*. 3.—*a* does not shift to *æ* in plur. of monosyllables in a single consonant. 4.—Umlaut of *i* to *eo* is rare. 5.—Gemination, see § 27. 6.—An unaccented short vowel before a single consonant is often dropped. 7, 8.—*g* and *h* interchange and drop. 9.—See § 27. 10.—Like *æg* decline *cealf, cild, lamb*.

STRONG NOUNS.—DECLENSION I.

	2. Long monosyllables.	3. Shifting.	4. U-umlaut.	5. Gemination.
Stem	porda, n. word.	daga, m. day.	fata, n. vat.	hlida, n. slope.	torra, m. tower.	spella, n. speech.
Theme	pord	dæg	fæt	hlið	tor	spel
Singular.						
N., A., & V.	pord	dæg	fæt	hlið	tor	spel
Gen.	pordes	dæges	fætes	hlides	torres	spelles
Dat.	porde	dæge	fæte	hlide	torre	spelle
Inst.	pordè	dægè	fætè	hlidè	torrè	spellè
Plural.						
N., A., & V.	pord	dagàs	fatu	hleodu (-i-)	torràs	spel
Gen.	pordà	dagà	fatà	hleodà (-i-)	torrà	spellà
D. & Inst.	pordum	dagum	fatum	hleodum (-i-)	torrum	spellum

	6. Syncope.		7. Stem in -ga.	8. Stem in -ha.
Stem	tungola, m. star.	tungola, n. star.	beâga, m. ring.	mearha, m. horse.	hóha, m. hough.
Theme	tungol	tungol	beâg	mearh	hóh
Singular.					
N., A., & V.	tung-ol, -ul, -el, -l		beá(g), h	mear(h), g, -	hóh, hó
Gen.	tung-oles, -ules, -eles, -les		beâges	meares	hós
Dat.	tung-ole, -ule, -ele, -le		beâge	meare	hó
Inst.	tung-olè, -ulè, -elè, -lè		beâgè	mearè	hó
Plural.					
N., A., & V.	m. tung-olàs, -ulàs, -elàs, -làs n. tung-olu, -ol, -ul, -el, -l		beâgàs	mearàs	hós
Gen.	tung-olà, -ulà, -elà, -là		beâgà	mearà	hóà
D. & I.	tung-olum, -ulum, -elum, -lum		beâgum	mearum	hóum

	9. Stem in -pa.		10. Stem +er.
Stem	bearpa, m., grove.	cneópa, n., knee.	æga, egg.
Theme	bearu	cneóp	æg, plur. æger
Singular.			
N., A., & V.	bear-u, -o	cneóp, cneó	æg
Gen.	bear-pes, -upes, -opes, -epes	cneó-pes, -s	æges
Dat.	bear-pe, -upe, -ope, -epe	cneó-pe, -	æge
Inst.	bear-pè, -upè, -opè, -epè	cneó-pè, -	ægè
Plural.			
N., A., & V.	bear-pàs, -upàs, -opàs, -epàs	cneó-pu, -p, -	æg-er-u, -ru
Gen.	bear-pà, -upà, -opà, -epà	cneó-pà, cneâ	æg-er-à, -rà
D. & I.	bear-pum, -upum, -opum, -epum	cneó-pum, -um, -m	æg-er-um, -rum

STRONG NOUNS.—DECLENSION I.

83.—II. Case-endings from stem **-ia** + relational suffixes.

84.—III. Case-endings from stem **-i** + relational suffixes.

Stem . hirdia, m.,	rîcia, n.,	byri, m.,	fôti, m.,	mani, m.,
shepherd.	*realm*.	*son*.	*foot*.	*man*.
Theme hird.	rîc.	byr	fôt	man

SINGULAR.—

Nom.	hirde	rîce	byre	fôt	man
Gen...	hirdes	rîces	byres	fôtes	mannes
Dat...	hirde	rîce	byre	fêt, fôte	men
Acc...	hirde	rîce	byre	fôt	man
Voc...	hirde	rîce	byre	fôt	man
Inst...	hirde	rîce	byre	fêt, fôte	men

PLURAL.—

Nom.	hirdas	rîcu	byre, -as	fêt, fôtas	men
Gen...	hirda	rîca	byra	fôta	manna
Dat...	hirdum	rîcum	byrum	fôtum	mannum
Acc...	hirdas	rîcu	byre, -as	fêt, fôtas	men
Voc...	hirdas	rîcu	byre, -as	fêt, fôtas	men
Inst...	hirdum	rîcum	byrum	fôtum	mannum

86. *Stem in* **i**. The plur. *-e* is found in names of peoples: *Dene*, Danes; *Rômâne*, Romans; *leôde*, men; and in *pine*, friend; *mere*, sea; and a few others. Umlaut, as in *fôt*, is found in *tôd*, tooth; so also in the feminines *bôc*, book; *brôc*, breeches; *gôs*, goose; *mûs*, mouse; *lûs*, louse; *cû*, cow, plur. gen. *cûnâ*; *burh*, gen. dat. *byrig*, borough; *turf*, turf. See § 90.

87. A few anomalous consonant stems which sometimes have genitive *-es* may be placed here.

Stems in -**nd** *and* -**r**.

SINGULAR.—   nd-stem.   r-stem.
Nom., *A.*, *& V.*.......... feônd.   brôđor (ur, er).
Gen. .... feôndes.   brôđor.
Dat. & Inst. .... feônde.   brêđer.

PLURAL.—

Nom., *A.*, *& V.*.......... feônd, -âs, fŷnd.   brôđor, brôđru (a).
Gen. .... feôndâ,   brôđrâ.
Dat. & Inst................ feôndum.   brôđrum.

Participial nouns in *-nd*, plur. *-nd*, *-ndâs*, are common. Like *brôđor* are fem. *môdor*, mother; *dôhtor*, daughter; *speostor*, sister. *Fæder* has undeclined forms, and also gen. *-es*, plur. *-âs*, *-â*, *-um*. *Neaht*, f., night, gen. *nihte*, *nihtes*, plur. *niht*. *Feld*, field; *ford*, ford; *sumor*, summer; *pinter*, winter, etc., have dat. *-â*.

DECLENSION II. (FEMININES).

Stem in **â** or **i**. Genitive singular in **e**.

88.—I. Case-endings from stem â+relational suffixes. | II.—Case-endings from stem **i**+relational suffixes.

Stem....	gifä, *gift*.	dǣdi, *deed*.
Theme...	gif.	dǣd.
SINGULAR.—		
Nominative..	gif*u*.	dǣd.
Genitive.....	gif*e*.	dǣd*e*.
Dative.......	gif*e*.	dǣd*e*.
Accusative...	gif*u*, gif*e*.	dǣd, dǣd*e*.
Vocative.....	gif*u*.	dǣd.
Instrumental..	gif*e*.	dǣd*e*.
PLURAL.—		
Nominative..	gif*á*, gif*e*.	dǣd*e*, dǣd*á*.
Genitive..	gif*á*, gif*ená*.	dǣd*á*.
Dative....	gif*um*.	dǣd*um*.
Accusative...	gif*á*, gif*e*.	dǣd*e*, dǣd*á*.
Vocative.....	gif*á*, gif*e*.	dǣd*e*, dǣd*á*.
Instrumental..	gif*um*.	dǣd*um*.

90. Stem.. 4. bôci, *book*. 5. mûsi, *mouse*. 6. ceasteri, *city*.
Theme bôc. mûs. ceaster, ceastr.

SINGULAR.—			
Nom. ...	bôc.	mûs.	ceaster.
Gen. ...	bêc.	mŷs.	ceastr*e*.
Dat. ...	bêc.	mŷs.	ceastr*e*.
Acc. ...	bôc	mûs.	ceaster. / ceastr*e*.
Voc. ...	bôc.	mûs.	ceaster.
Inst. ...	bêc.	mŷs.	ceastr*e*.
PLURAL.—			
Nom. ...	bêc.	mŷs.	ceastr*e* (*á*).
Gen. ...	bôc*á*.	mûs*á*.	ceastr*á*.
Dat. ...	bôc*um*.	mûs*um*.	ceastr*um*.
Acc. ...	bêc.	mŷs.	ceastr*e* (*á*).
Voc. ...	bêc.	mŷs.	ceastr*e* (*á*).
Inst. ...	bôc*um*.	mûs*um*.	ceastr*um*.

Feminines in -*ung* and a few others sometimes have dative -*á*.

92. *Head-cases in a Vowel.*—Genitive in **a.**

	1. sunu, *son.*	2. handu, *hand.*
Stem......	sun.	hand.
Theme....		
SINGULAR.—		
Nominative..	sun*u.*	hand.
Genitive.....	sun*á.*	hand*á.*
Dative.......	sun*á,* sun*u.*	hand*á,* hand.
Accusative...	sun*u.*	hand.
Vocative.....	sun*u.*	hand.
Instrumental.	sun*á.*	hand*á,* hand.
PLURAL.—		
Nominative..	sun*u* (*o*), sun*á.*	hand*á.*
Genitive.....	{ sun*á,* sun*en*á. }	hand*á.*
Dative.......	sun*um.*	hand*um.*
Accusative...	sun*u* (*o*), sun*á.*	hand*á.*
Vocative.....	sun*u* (*o*), sun*á.*	hand*á.*
Instrumental.	sun*um.*	hand*um.*

95. WEAK NOUNS.

Case-endings < stem **an** + relational suffixes.—Genitive in **an.**

(DECLENSION IV.)

	1. MASCULINES.	2. FEMININES.	3. NEUTERS.	CONTRACTS.
Stem.. {	hanan, *cock.*	tungan, *tongue.*	eágan, *eye.*	tâan, *toe.*
Theme	han.	tung.	eág.	tâ.
SINGULAR.—				
Nom....	han*a.*	tung*e.*	eág*e.*	tâ*e,* tâ.
Gen....	han*an.*	tung*an.*	eág*an.*	tâ*an,* tân.
Dat....	han*an.*	tung*an.*	eág*an.*	tâ*an,* tân.
Acc....	han*an.*	tung*an.*	eág*e.*	tâ*an,* tân.
Voc....	han*a.*	tung*e.*	eág*e.*	tâ*e,* tâ.
Inst....	han*an.*	tung*an.*	eág*an.*	tâ*an,* tân.
PLURAL.—				
Nom....	han*an.*	tung*an.*	eág*an.*	tâ*an,* tân.
Gen....	han*en*á.	tung*en*á.	eág*en*á.	tâ*en*á, tân*â.*
Dat....	han*um.*	tung*um.*	eág*um.*	tâ*um.*
Acc....	han*an.*	tung*an.*	eág*an.*	tâ*an,* tân.
Voc....	han*an.*	tung*an.*	eág*an.*	tâ*an,* tân.
Inst....	han*um.*	tung*um.*	eág*um.*	tâ*um.*

101. PROPER NAMES.

(1.) PERSONS.—*Names of women in* -u *or a consonant are strong, those in* -e *or* -a *are weak. Declension II., â-stem:* Begu, Freâparu; *i-stem:* Beadohild, Hygd, *and most others. Declension IV.:* Elene, Eve, Ada, Maria, *etc., from foreign names;* Dealhþeó(p), *dat.* Dealhþeón (§ 99).

Names of men in -u, -e, *or a consonant are strong, those in* -a *are weak. Declension III., u-stem:* Leófsunu? *Declension I., a-stem:* Ælfréd, Beópulf, Eádmund, Sigemund (*gen. also* Sigemunde<mund, *f. Rask*)? Déland, *and most other strong names;* syncopated: Ecgþeó(p), *gen.* Ecgþeópes, Ecgþeóes, *etc.;* Ongenþeó(p); Grendel, *gen.* Grendeles, Grendles, *etc.;* Hréðel; *ia-stem:* Ine, Hedde, Gíslhere, Dulfhere, Eádpine, Godpine, *and others from* -here *and* -pine; *umlaut not found:* Hereman, *dat.* Heremanne. *Declension IV.:* Ætla, Becca, *and many others.*

(*a.*) *Foreign names sometimes retain foreign declension, or are undeclined, but are generally declined as above; those in* -as, -es, -us *do not often increase in the genitive. Those from Latin* -us, *Greek* -ος, *of the second declension, sometimes drop their endings and take those of the Anglo-Saxon first:* Crist (<Christus), Cristes, Criste, *etc. In less familiar words* -us *oftenest stands in the nom. and gen., but Latin and Anglo-Saxon forms may mix throughout:* Petrus, *gen.* Petrus, Petruses, Petres, Petri, *dat.* Petro, Petre, *acc.* Petrus, Petrum; *so* -as *and* -es: Andreâs, *gen.* Andreâs, *dat.* Andreâ, *acc.* Andreâs, Andream; Héródés, Héródes, Héróde, Héród-em, -és, *or* -e.

(*b.*) *In Gothic these Latin and Greek names of the second declension are regularly given in the u-declension:* Paitrus, *gen.* Paitraus, *dat.* Paitrau, *acc.* Paitru (§ 93, *a*). *The Anglo-Saxon genitive* Petrus *may be a relic of the u-declension.*

(2.) PEOPLES.—*Plurals in* -âs *and* -e *are strong, in* -an *weak. Declension I., a-stem:* Brittâs, Scottâs, *etc.; ia-stem and i-stem:* Dene, *gen.* Den-â, -iâ, -igâ, -geâ (§ 85, *a*); Românû, *etc. Declension IV.:* Gotan, Seaxan, *etc.*

The singular is oftenest an adjective in -isc *regularly declined:* Egyptisc man, *Egyptian man;* Egyptisc ides, *Egyptian woman;* þâ Egyptiscan, *the Egyptians, etc. Sometimes* ân Brit, *a Briton.*

Often is found a collective with a genitive, or with an adjective, or compounded: Seaxnâ þeód; Filistêâ folc; Caldêâ cyn; Ebrêâ perâs; Sodomisc cyn; Rôm-pare (§ 86); Nord-men (§ 84, 3), *etc. Foreign names are treated as are names of persons.*

(3.) COUNTRIES.—*A few feminine names are found:* Engel, *England;* Bryten, *Britannia. Oftenest is found the people's name in the genitive with* land, rîce, êðel, *etc., or in an oblique case with a preposition:* Englâ land; Sodomâ rîce; on Eàst-Englum; of Seaxum; on Egyptum. *Foreign names are treated as are names of persons.*

(4.) CITIES.—*Names found alone are regularly declined according to gender and endings:* Rôm, *f.* Rôme; Babylon, *n.* Babylones; Sodoma, *m.* Sodoman. *Oftenest they are prefixed undeclined to* burg, ceaster, pîc, dûn, hâm, *etc.:* Lunden-pîc, Rôma-burg, *etc.; or the folk's name in the genitive followed by* burg, ceaster, *etc., is used:* Caldêâ burg. *Foreign names treated as names of persons.*

IV. ADJECTIVES.

INDEFINITE AND DEFINITE DECLENSIONS.

103. An adjective in Anglo-Saxon has one set of strong and one of weak endings for each gender. The latter are used when the adjective is preceded by the definite article or some word like it. Hence there are two declensions, the indefinite and the definite.

104.—I. *The Indefinite Declension.*

Case-endings < stem **a**, **â**, or **i** + relational suffixes.

	MASCULINE.	FEMININE.	NEUTER.
Stem...	blinda, blind.	blindâ, blindi, blind.	blinda, blind.
Theme.	blind.	blind.	blind.
SINGULAR.—			
Nom.	blind	blind(*u*) (*o*) (*e*)	blind
Gen.	blind*es*	blind*re*	blind*es*
Dat.	blind*um*	blind*re*	blind*um*
Acc.	blind*ne*	blind*e*	blind
Voc.	blind	blind(*u*)	blind
Inst.	blind*ē*	blind*re*	blind*ē*
PLURAL.—			
Nom.	blind*e*	blind*e*	blind(*u*) (*o*) (*e*)
Gen.	blind*rā*	blind*rā*	blind*rā*
Dat.	blind*um*	blind*um*	blind*um*
Acc.	blind*e*	blind*e*	blind*u*
Voc.	blind*e*	blind*e*	blind*u*
Inst.	blind*um*	blind*um*	blind*um*

105.—II. *The Definite Declension.*

Case-endings < stem **an** + relational suffixes.

	MASCULINE.	FEMININE.	NEUTER.
Stem..	blindan, *blind*.	blindan,	blindan,
Theme	blind.	blind.	blind.
SINGULAR.—			
Nom....	se blind*a*.	seô blind*e*.	þæt blind*e*.
Gen.....	þæs blind*an*.	þêre blind*an*.	þæs blind*an*.
Dat.....	þam blind*an*.	þêre blind*an*.	þam blind*an*.
Acc.....	þone blind*an*.	þâ blind*an*.	þæt blind*e*.
Voc.....	se blind*a*.	seô blind*e*.	þæt blind*e*.
Inst.....	þŷ blind*an*.	þêre blind*an*.	þŷ blind*an*.
PLURAL.—			
Nom....		þâ blind*an*.	
Gen.....		þârâ blinde*na*.	
Dat.....		þâm blind*um*.	
Acc.....		þâ blind*an*.	
Voc.....		þâ blind*an*.	
Inst.....		þâm blind*um*.	

106.—*Theme ending Short (Root Shifting).*

Stem..	glada, *glad*.	gladâ, gladi.	glada.
Theme	glad > glæd.	glad > glæd.	glad > glæd.
SINGULAR.—			
Nom....	glæd.	glad*u*.	glæd.
Gen.....	glad*es*.	glæd*re*.	glad*es*.
Dat.....	glad*um*.	glæd*re*.	glad*um*.
Acc.....	glæd*ne*.	glad*e*.	glæd.
Voc.....	glæd.	glad*u*.	glæd.
Inst.....	glad*ê*.	glæd*re*.	glad*ê*.
PLURAL.—			
Nom....	glad*e*.	glad*e*.	glad*u*.
Gen.....	glæd*râ*.	glæd*râ*.	glæd*râ*.
Dat.....	glad*um*.	glad*um*.	glad*um*.
Acc.....	glad*e*.	glad*e*.	glad*u*.
Voc.....	glad*e*.	glad*e*.	glad*u*.
Inst.....	glad*um*.	glad*um*.	glad*um*.

In the Definite Declension it has √*glad* throughout, and agrees wholly with *blind*. The ending -*u* may change to -*o*, -*e*, —.

122. Comparison.

Comparison is a variation to denote degrees of quantity or quality. It belongs to adjectives and adverbs.

(*a.*) In Anglo-Saxon it is a variation of stem, and is a matter rather of derivation than inflection; but the common mode of treatment is convenient.

(*b.*) The suffixes of comparison were once less definite in meaning than now, and were used to form many numerals, pronouns, adverbs > prepositions, and substantives, in which compared correlative terms are implied: *either, other, over, under, first,* etc.

(*c.*) Anglo-Saxon adverbs are in brackets: (*spíde*).

123. ADJECTIVES are regularly compared by suffixing to the theme of the positive *-ir* > *-er* or *-ór* for the theme of the comparative, and *-ist* > *-est* or *-óst* for the theme of the superlative.

The *Comparative* has always weak endings and syncopated stem.

The *Superlative* has both weak and strong endings.

ADVERBS are compared like adjectives: the positive uses the ending *-e*, the comparative and superlative have none; *-ir* drops.

Strong, spíd, *strenuous*; spídra; spídóst.
Weak, se spída; se spídra; se spídósta.
Adverb, (spíde); (spídór); (spídóst).

124. i-umlaut may change a, â, ea, eâ, eo, ó, u, û,
                         to e, ê, y, e, ŷ, y, ê, y, ŷ.

lang, long; *lengra* (*leng*); *lengest*.
eald, ald, old; *yldra, eldra*; *yldest, eldest*.

128. HETEROCLITIC forms abound from themes in *-ir* and *-ór, -ist, -óst*: *sél*, good; *-ra, -la,* (*síl*); —*est, -óst; ríce*, rich; *rícest, rícóst; glæd*, glad; *glædra, gledra*, etc. (§ 125). Some have themes with and without double comparison: *læt*, late; *lætra; latóst, latemest; síd*, late; *sídra* (*síd, sidór*); *sid-ást, -est, -mest.*

129. DEFECTIVE are the following. Words in capitals are not found.

(1.) *Mixed Roots:*

	POSITIVE.	COMPARATIVE.	SUPERLATIVE.
good,	{ gód } (pel) { BAT }	{ betera, betra, § 124 { bættra, § 125 (bet)	betst, betóst, -ást (betst)
bad,	{ yfel } (yfele) { peor } { sâm- }	{ pyrsa, (pyrs), { § 123, *b* { sæmra, § 124	{ pyrst, pyrresta, { (pyrst),(pyrrest) sæmest

DEFECTIVE ADJECTIVES.—DECAY OF ENDINGS. 111

	Positive.	Comparative.	Superlative.
great, *much,*	{ micel } (micle) { fela } (fela) MÂ	mâra, (mâ)	mæ̂st, § 124; 123, *a*
little,	{ lytel (lyt) LÆS (Goth. *lasivs*)	læssa (læs), § 35, *B*	læs-âst, -est, -t

(2.) *From Adverbs of time and place* (compare §§ 126, 127):

ever, *ere, erst,*	â-, æ̂-	{ (æ̂r) > æ̂rra, (æ̂r-ôr, -ur)	æ̂r-est
after- *ward,*	{ af-, æf-=of, æfterpeard	(æf-ter) > æftera	{ æf-tem-est æfter-mest, § 127
else,	(elles)	(ellôr), elra	—
fore,	forepeard, (fore)	fyrra	{ for-ma > (fyrmest), fyrst, fruma, § 51
far,	feor, (fyr)	fyrre, (fyr)	fyrrest (eo > y)
forth,	forðpeard, (forð)	(furð-ôr, -ur)	{ (furð-um), forð-m-est
behind,	{ hinde(r)peard, (hindan)	(hinder)	{ hinduma, hinde-ma, § 126, *b*
inner,	innepeard, (in)	innera	inne-ma, (-m-est)
mid,	{ middepeard, (mid)	—	{ med-ema (-uma?) mid-m-est
north,	{ norðepeard, (norð)	(norð-ôr)	norð-m-est
nether,	{ niðepeard, (niðe)	{ nið-ra, (nið-ôr, -er (i > eo)	{ niðema, § 126 niðe-m-est (i > eo)
upper,	ûfepeard, (up)	{ ufera, (ufôr)	{ yf(e)-m-est, § 124
outer,	ûtepeard, (ût)	ûtra, (uttôr, ûtôr)	{ ûtema, ûtmest, ŷt-(e-)m-est, § 124

So *sûðemest, eâstemest, pestemest,* south-, east-, west-most.

DECAY OF ENDINGS.—(1), Declension: Layamon, strong, sing. masc. —, *-es, -en, -ne*; fem. —, *-re, -re, -e*; neut. —, *-es, -en,* —; plur. *-e, -re, -en, -e*; but *n, s, r* may drop. Weak, *-e, -en,* as in § 102.—Ormulum, strong, sing. —, plur. *-e.* Weak, *-e.*—Chaucer, monosyllables as in Orm., others undeclined.—Shakespeare, no declension.

(2), Comparison: Layamon, Ormulum, *-re, -est.*—Chaucer (= Modern English), *-er, -est.*

V. PRONOUNS (*Relational Names*, § 56).

130. PERSONAL PRONOUNS (*Relational Substantives*).

	SING.—1. *I.*	2. *thou.*	3. *he,*	*she,*	*it.*
N.	ic	þû	hê	heô	hit
G.	mîn	þîn	his	hire	his
D.	mê	þê	him	hire	him
A.	mec, mê	þec, þê	hine	hîe, hî, heô	hit
V.	——	þû	——	——	——
I.	mê	þê	him	hire	him

PLURAL.—

N.	wê	gê	hîe, hî, heô	hîe, hî, heô	heô, hîe, hî
G.	ûser, ûre	eôper	heorâ, hyrâ	heorâ, hyrâ	heorâ, hyrâ
D.	ûs	eôp	him	him	him
A.	ûsic, ûs	eôpic, eôp	hîe, hî, heô	hîe, hî, heô	heô, hîe, hî
V.	——	gê			
I.	ûs	eôp	him	him	him

DUAL.—

				SING. NOM.	GENITIVE.	PLUR. NOM.
N.	pit	git	*P. Sp.* …	i-s, i-ja, i-t	i-sja	aj-as
G.	uncer	incer	*Latin* …	i-s, ea, i-d	ejus	ii, cæ, ea
D.	unc	inc	*Gothic*..	i-s, si, i-ta	is, izôs, is	eis, ijôs, ija
A.	uncit, unc	incit, inc	*O. Sax.*..	hi, siu, i-t	is, ira, is	siâ, siû, siu
V.	——	git	*O. H. G.*	i-r, siu, i-z	sîn, irâ, is	sie, siô, siu
I.	unc	inc	*O. Norse*	hann, hon,—	{hans, hen-} {nar,—}	——

131. REFLEXIVES are supplied by the personal pronouns with *self* (self), or without it. *Self* has strong adjective endings like *blind* (§ 103); in the nominative singular also weak *selfa*.

132. POSSESSIVES are *mîn, þîn, sîn, ûser, ûre, eôper, uncer, incer*. They have strong adjective endings (§ 103). Those in *-er* are usually syncopated (§ 79). *Úser* has assimilation of *r > s* (§ 35, *B*).

SING.—

	Masculine.	Feminine.	Neuter.
N.	ûser	ûser	ûser
G.	(ûseres) ûsses	(ûserre) ûsse	(ûseres) ûsses
D.	(ûserum) ûssum	(ûserre) ûsse	(ûserum) ûssum
A.	ûserne	(ûsere) usse	ûser
V.	ûser	ûser	ûser
I.	(ûseré) ûssê	(ûserre) ûsse	(ûseré) ûssê

PLUR.—

	Masc. & Fem.	Neut.
N.	(ûsere) ûsse (a)	ûser
G.	(ûserrâ) ûssâ	
D.	(ûserum) ûssum	
A.	(ûsere) ûsse	ûser
V.	(ûsere) ûsse	ûser
I.	(ûserum) ûssum	

133. DEMONSTRATIVES.

Definite Article.

1. *that* and *the*. | 2. *this*.

Nom.	se	seó	þæt	þes	þeós	þis
Gen.	þæs	þǽre	þæs	þisses	þisse	þisses
Dat.	þam, þǽm	þǽre	þam, þǽm	þissum	þisse	þissum
Acc.	þone (a, æ)	þá	þæt	þisne	þás	þis
Voc.	se	seó	þæt	—	—	—
Inst.	þý	þǽre	þý, þé	þýs	þisse	þýs

Nom.	þá	þás
Gen.	þára, þǽra	þissá
Dat.	þám, þǽm	þissum
Acc.	þá	þás
Voc.	þá	—
Inst.	þám, þǽm	þissum

134. RELATIVES.—(1.) *se, seó, þæt,* who, which, that, is declined as when a demonstrative (§ 133). (2.) *þe* used in all the cases, both alone and in combination with *se, seó, þæt,* or a personal pronoun, is indeclinable. (3.) *spá,* so, used like English *as* and Old German *so* in place of a relative, is indeclinable.

135. INTERROGATIVES are *hpá*, who; *hpæder*, which of two; *hpylc, húlic,* of what kind. They have strong adjective endings: *hpæder* is syncopated (§ 84.)

SING.—	Masc.	Fem.	Neut.	
Nom.	hpá	——	hpæt	
Gen.	hpæs	——	hpæs	
Dat.	hpam	——	hpam	Plural wanting.
Acc.	hpone	——	hpæt	
Voc.	——	——	——	
Inst.	hpam	——	hpý	

136. INDEFINITES.

(1.) *The Indefinite Article* ÂN $<$ *án*, one.

SING.—	Masc.	Fem.	Neut.	PLUR.— M., F., N.
Nom. ...	ân	ân	ân	âne
Gen. ...	ânes	ânre	ânes	ânrá
Dat. ...	ânum	ânre	ânum	ânum
Acc. ...	ânne, ǽnne	âne	ân	âne
Voc. ...	ân	ân	ân	âne
Inst. ...	âné	ânre	âné	ânum

138. NUMERALS.

	Cardinals.	Ormulum.	Ordinals.	Symbols.
1.	án	án	forma (fruma, ǽresta) fyrsta, § 129	I.
2.	tpegen, tpá, tu <tpa	twá	óðer	II.
3.	þrí, þreó	þreo, þré	þridda	III.
4.	feóper	fowwerr	feóperða (feórða)	IV.
5.	fíf	fíf	fífta	V.
6.	six	sexe	sixta	VI.
7.	seofon (syfone)	se(o)fenn, (·ffne)	seofoða (-eða)	VII.
8.	eahta	ehhte	eahtoða (-eða)	VIII.
9.	nigon (-en)	niȝhenn	nigoða (-eða)	IX.
10.	týn, tén	téne, (tenn)	teóða	X.
11.	endleofan (ellefne)		endleofta (eo>u, y, e)	XI.
12.	tpelf	twellf	tpelfta	XII.
13.	þreótýne	þrittêne	þreôteóða	XIII.
14.	feópertýne		feóperteóða	XIV.
15.	fíftýne		fífteóða	XV.
16.	sixtýne	sextêne	sixteóða	XVI.
17.	seofontýne		seofonteóða	XVII.
18.	eahtatýne		eahtateóða	XVIII.
19.	nigontýne		nigonteóða	XIX.
20.	tpêntig	twenntiȝ	tpêntigóða	XX.
21.	án and tpêntig		án and tpêntigóða tpêntigóða and forma	XXI.
30.	þrítig, þrittig	þrittiȝ	þrítigóða	XXX.
40.	feópertig	fowwerrtiȝ	feópertigóða	XL.
50.	fíftig	fífftiȝ	fíftigóða	L.
60.	sixtig	sextiȝ	sixtigóða	LX.
70.	hundseofontig	seofenntiȝ	hundseofontigóða	LXX.
80.	hundeahtatig		hundeahtatigóða	LXXX.
90.	hundnigontig		hundnigontigóða	XC.
100.	hundteóntig hund	hunndredd	hundteóntigóða	C.
101.	hund and án		án and hundteóntigóða hundteóntigóða and forma	CI.

ETYMOLOGY OF CARDINALS. 115

Cardinals.	Ormulum.	Ordinals.	Symbols.
110. hundendleofantig		hundendleofantigôða	CX.
120. hundtpelftig		hundtpelftigôða	CXX.
130. hund and þrittig		hund and þrîtigôða	CXXX.
200. tpa hund		tpa hundteóntigôða	CC.
1000. þûsend	þûsennde	(not found.)	M.

(*a.*) The order of combined numbers is indicated by the examples. The substantive defined is oftenest placed next the largest of the numbers.

(*b.*) Combined numbers are sometimes connected by *eâc* (added to) or *and* governing a dative: *þridda eâc tpêntigum* = 23d; sometimes by the next greater ten and *pana, læs,* or *bûtan: ânes pana þrittig,* thirty less one; *tpâ læs XXX,* two less than thirty; *XX bûtan ân,* § 393.

(*c.*) For *hund-* from 70 to 120, see § 139, *e*; indefinites, § 136, 2.

(*d.*) The unaccented syllables often suffer precession, sometimes syncope, often cacography.

Declension.

141. Cardinals.—1, *ân*, is declined, § 136.

N., A., V. 2, tpegen tpâ tu<tpa   3, þrî (-ŷ, -ie) þreô þreô (-iâ, -iô)
Gen. . . . .   tpegrâ, tpegâ   þreôrâ
D., Inst..   tpâm>tpæm   þrîm (-ŷm)

Like *tpegen* decline *begen, bâ, bu,* both.

4–19.—Cardinals from *feóper* to *tpelf,* and from *þreô-týne* to *nigon-týne,* are used as indeclinable, but are also declined like *i*-stem nouns of the First Declension (*byre,* § 84), oftenest when used as substantives: nom. acc. voc. *feópere,* gen. *feóperâ,* dat. inst. *feóperum.* Such forms of *eahta* are not found. *Týne<teón,* umlaut, § 32, 2.

(*a.*) Those in -*týne* have also sometimes a neut. nom. and acc. in -*u*>-*o,* or -*a: fiftýn-u, -o, -a* (fifteen); *þreôteno* (=thirteen). (*ĝ*>*î*>*e.*)

(*b.*) They are quasi-adjectives like *Dene,* § 86.

20–120.—Forms in -*tig* are declined as singular neuter nouns: *þritig* (thirty), gen. *þritiges;* or, as adjectives, have plural gen. -*râ,* dat. -*um: þritigrâ, þritigum.*

100–1000.—*Hund,* n., is declined like *porð,* § 73; *hundred* and *þûsend,* like *scip,* § 70; pl. *þûsend-u, -o, -e, -a* (Psa. lxvii, 17), § 393.

142. ORDINALS have always the regular weak forms of the adjective, except *óder* (second), always strong. Indefinites, § 136, 2.

143. MULTIPLICATIVES are found in *-feald* (fold): *ânfeald*, simple: *tpîfeald*, two-fold; *púsend-mælum*, thousandfoldly.

144. DISTRIBUTIVES may be expressed by repeating cardinals, or by a dative: *seofon and seofon*, seven by seven; *bi tpâm*, by twos.

145. In answer to *how often*, numeral adverbs are used, or an ordinal or cardinal with *sîđ* (time): *æne*, once; *tpipa* (*tpiga*), twice; *prípa* (*príga*), thrice; *priddan síde*, the third time; *feôper sîdum*, four times.

146. For adverbs of division the cardinals are used, or ordinals with *dæl*: *on preó*, in three (parts); *seofedan dæl*, seventh part.

147. An ordinal before *healf* (half) numbers the whole of which the half is counted: *hê pæs pâ tpâ geár and pridde healf*, he was there two years and (the) third (year) half=2½ years. The whole numbers are usually understood: *hê rícsóde nigonteóde healf geár*, he reigned half the nineteenth year=18½ years. A similar idiom is used in German and Scandinavian.

148. *Sum*, agreeing with a numeral, is indefinite, as in English: *sume tîn geár*, some ten years, more or less; limited by the genitive of a cardinal it is a partitive of eminence: *eóde eahta sum*, he went one of eight=with seven attendants or companions.

VERB.

149. The notion signified by a verb root may be predicated of a subject or uttered as an interjection of command, or (2) it may be spoken of as a substantive fact or as descriptive of some person or thing. In the first case proper verb stems are formed, or auxiliaries used, to denote time, mode, and voice; and suffixes (personal endings) are used to indicate the person and number of the subject: thus is made up the verb proper or finite verb. In the second case a noun stem is formed, and declined in cases as a substantive or adjective.

150. TWO VOICES.—The *active* represents the subject as acting, the *passive* as affected by the action. The *active* has inflection endings for many forms, the *passive* only for a participle. Other passive forms help this participle with the auxiliary verbs *eom* (am), *beón, pesan, peordan*.

(n.) The *middle* voice represents the subject as affected by its own action. It is expressed in Anglo-Saxon by adding pronouns, and needs no paradigms.

151. SIX MODES.—The *indicative* states or asks about a fact, the *subjunctive* a possibility; the *imperative* commands or intreats; the *infinitives* (and gerunds) are substantives, the *participles* adjectives. Certain forms of possibility are expressed by auxiliary modal verbs with the infinitive. They need separate discussion, and are conveniently called a *potential* mode.

152. FIVE TENSES.—*Present, imper'fect, future, perfect, pluper'fect.* The present and imper'fect have tense stems; the future is expressed by the present, or by aid of *sceal* (shall) or *pille* (will); the perfect by aid of the present of *habban* (have) or, with some intransitives, *beón* (be), *pesan* or *peordan* (be); the pluper'fect by aid of the imper'fect of *habban, beón, pesan,* or *peordan.*

157. CONJUGATION.—Verbs are classified for conjugation by the stems of the imperfect tense.

Strong Verbs express tense by varying the root vowel; *weak verbs,* by composition. Strong verbs in the imperfect indicative singular first person have the root vowel *unchanged*, or changed by accent (*progression*), or *contraction* with old reduplication.

No change.	Progression.	Contraction.	Composition.
CONJUGATION I.	II., III., IV.	V.	VI.
a > (æ, ea)	â, eâ, ô	eô > ê	+ de > te

158. Further subdivision gives the following classes. The Roman numerals give Grimm's numbers. We arrange in alphabetical order of the stem vowels of the imperfect. For the vowels in ( ), see §§ 32, 33, 41.

STRONG.

Class.	Root Vowel.	Present.	Imperfect Sing.	Plur.	Passive Participle.
1, X., XI.	a	i (> e, eo)	a (> œ, ea)	â (> â, ê)	e, u > o
2, XII.	a	i (> e, eo)	a (> æ, ea)	u	u > o
3, VIII.	i	î	â	i	i
4, IX.	u	eó, ú	eâ	u	o
5, VII.	â	a (> ea)	ô	ô	a
6, I.-VI.	a > ea, â, eâ, æ, ê, ô	eô > ô	eô > ô	a > ea, â, eâ, æ, ê, ô

WEAK (§§ 160, 165, *d*).

| 7, | affix -ia > -ie > -e > — | + edo > de > te | | + ed > d > t |
| 8, | affix -ô > -û; -ia > -ige, -ie | + ôde | | + ôd |

The present has the same radical vowel throughout all the modes, except in the *indic. sing.* 2*d* and 3*d persons* of Conj. 1, 3, 4, 5. These, especially if syncopated, retain *i, y* in Conj. 1; and have by i-umlaut *ŷ* in Conj. 3, *e* in Conj. 4, *y, œ̂, ŷ,* or *ê* in Conj. 5.

The imperfect has one radical vowel throughout, except in the indic. sing. 1st and 3d persons of Conj. 1, 2, 3.

The passive participle retains the root vowel, or, in Conj. 1, 3, has it assimilated, *a* changing to *e, u,* or *o,* and *u* to *o.*

THE CONJUGATIONS.

INDICATIVE PRESENT.	IMPERFECT.	PART. PAST.	
1st. 2d. 3d.	SING. PLUR.		
I. ete, it(e)st, it(ed);	æt, æ̂ton;	eten,	eat.
sitte, sit(e)st, sit;	sæt, sæ̂ton;	ge-seten,	sit.
nime, nim(e)st, nim(e)d;	nam, nâmon;	numen,	take.
stele, stilst, stild;	stæl, stæ̂lon;	stolen,	steal.
spimme, spimst, spimd;	spam, spummon;	spummen,	swim.
peorde, pyrst, pyrd(ed);	peard, purdon;	porden,	become.
II. rise, risest (rist), rised (rîst);	râs, rison;	risen,	rise.
stige, stihst, stihd;	stâh, stigon;	stigen,	ascend.
III. sûpe, sŷpst, sŷpþ;	seâp, supon;	sopen,	sup.
leófe, lŷfst, lŷfd;	leáf, lufon;	lofen,	love.
ceóse, ceósest (cŷst), ceósed (cŷst);	ceás, curon;	coren,	choose.
IV. gale, gæl(e)st, gæl(e)d;	gôl, gôlon;	galen,	sing.
stande, standest, standed (stent);	stôd, stôdon;	standen,	stand.
sperie, sperest, spered;	spór, spóron;	sporen,	swear.
hebbe (<hafie), hef(e)st, hêf(e)d;	hóf, hófon;	hafen,	heave.
V. fealle, feal(le)st (fylst), feal(le)d (fyld, feld);	feól, feóllon;	feallen,	fall.
sâpe, sâpest (sæ̂pst), sâped (sæ̂pd);	seóp, seópon;	sâpen,	sow.
beâte, beâtest (bŷtst), beâted (bŷt);	beót, beóton;	beáten,	beat.
græte, græt(e)st, græt(ed);	grêt, grêton;	græten,	greet.
pêpe, pêp(e)st, pêp(e)d;	peóp, peópon;	pêpen,	weep.
rôpe, rôpest (rêpst), rôped (rêpd);	reóp, reópon;	rôpen,	row.
VI. nerie, nerest, nered;	ner(e)de, ner(e)don;	nered,	save.
lufige, lufâst, lufâd;	lufó-de, -don;	ge-lufôd,	love.
telle, telest, teled;	teal-de, -don;	teald,	tell.
sêce, sêcest, sêced;	sôh-te, -ton;	sûht,	seek.

164. FIRST CONJUGATION.

Active Voice.

niman, to take.

Pres. Infinitive.	Imperfect Sing., Plur.	Passive Participle.
ni**m**an;	**n**a**m**, **n**âmon;	**n**u**m**en.

INDICATIVE MODE.
Present (and Future) Tense.

SINGULAR.	PLURAL.
ic nime, *I take.*	pê nima*d*, *we take.*
þû nim*est*, *thou takest.*	gê nima*d*, *ye take.*
hê nime*d*, *he taketh.*	hî nima*d*, *they take.*

Plur. -ad, and other plurals, change to -e before a subject pronoun.

Imperfect.

Singular.	Plural.
ic nam, *I took.*	pê nâm*on*, *we took.*
þû nâm*e*, *thou tookest.*	gê nâm*on*, *ye took.*
hê nam, *he took.*	hî nâm*on*, *they took.*

Future.
I shall or *will take.*

ic sceal (pille) nim*an*.	pê sculo*n* (pilla*d*) nim*an*.
þû sceal*t* (pil*t*) nim*an*.	gê sculo*n* (pilla*d*) nim*an*.
hê sceal (pille) nim*an*.	hî sculo*n* (pilla*d*) nim*an*.

Perfect.

Transitive Form.	Intransitive Form.
Sing. *I have taken.*	*I have (am) come.*
ic hæbbe num*en*.	ic eom cum*en*.
þû hæfs*t* (haf*dst*) num*en*.	þû eart cum*en*.
hê hæf*d* (haf*dd*) num*en*.	hê is cum*en*.
Plur.	
pê habba*d* num*en*.	pê s*ind* (sindon) cum*ene*.
gê habba*d* num*en*.	gê s*ind* (sindon) cum*ene*.
hî habba*d* num*en*.	hî s*ind* (sindon) cum*ene*.

Pluper'fect.

Sing. *I had taken.*	*I had (was) come.*
ic hæf*de* num*en*.	ic pæs cum*en*.
þû hæf*dest* num*en*.	þû pêre cum*en*.
hê hæf*de* num*en*.	hê pæs cum*en*.
Plur.	
pê hæf*don* num*en*.	pê pêro*n* cum*ene*.
gê hæf*don* num*en*.	gê pêro*n* cum*ene*.
hî hæf*don* num*en*.	hî pêro*n* cum*ene*.

OTHER FORMS: *nam, nom*; *nâmon, -an* ($\acute{a} > \acute{o}$); *sceal, scel*; *scul-on, -un, -an*; *sceol-on, -un, -an*; *pille, pile, pilt* ($i > y$); *hæbbe, hebbe, habbe*; *haf-a, -u, -o*; *hafest*; *hæfed*; *hæbbad*; *eom, eam*; *is, ys*; *sind, sint, sindan* ($i > y$, *ie, eo*), *ear-on, -un*. For *eom* may be used *peorde* or *beóm*; for *pæs, peard* (§ 178). Imp. plur. *-an, -um, -un, -en, -e*, occur.

169. Subjunctive Mode.
Present Tense.

Singular.	Plural
ic nime, (*if*) *I take.*	pê nimen, (*if*) *we take.*
þû nime, (*if*) *thou take.*	gê nimen, (*if*) *ye take.*
hê nime, (*if*) *he take.*	hî nimen, (*if*) *they take.*

Imperfect.

ic nâme, (*if*) *I took.*	pê nâmen, (*if*) *we took.*
þû nâme, (*if*) *thou took.*	gê nâmen, (*if*) *ye took.*
hê nâme, (*if*) *he took.*	hî nâmen, (*if*) *they took.*

Future.
(*If*) *I shall (will) take.*

ic scyle (pille) niman.	pê scylen (pillen) niman.
þû scyle (pille) niman.	gê scylen (pillen) niman.
hê scyle (pille) niman.	hî scylen (pillen) niman.

Perfect

Transitive Form.	Intransitive Form.
Sing. (*If*) *I have taken.*	(*If*) *I have (be) come.*
ic hæbbe numen.	ic sî cumen.
þû hæbbe numen.	þû sî cumen.
hê hæbbe numen.	hê sî cumen.
Plur.	
pê hæbben numen.	pê sîn cumene.
gê hæbben numen.	gê sîn cumene.
hî hæbben numen.	hî sîn cumene.

Pluper'fect.

Sing. (*If*) *I had taken.*	(*If*) *I had (were) come.*
ic hæfde numen.	ic pære cumen.
þû hæfde numen.	þû pære cumen.
hê hæfde numen.	hê pære cumen.
Plur.	
pê hæfden numen.	pê pæren cumene.
gê hæfden numen.	gê pæren cumene.
hî hæfden numen.	hî pæren cumene.

Other Forms: *scyle, scyl-en, -on, -an, -e* (*y* > *i, u, eo*); *hæbben, habban, habbon*; *sî, sîn* (*i* > *ŷ, îe, eó, ig*); *pær-en, -an, -on* (*æ* > *ê*). For *sî* may be *beó, pese, peorde;* for *pære, purde.* Plur. *-ân, -an, -on, -e,* occur.

172. Imperative Mode.

Sing.	Plur.
2. nim, *take*.	nim*ad*, *take*.

173. Infinitive.	Gerund.
nim*an*, *to take*.	tô nim*anne*, *to take*.

Present Participle.	Past Participle.
nim*ende*, *taking*.	num*en*, *taken*.

174. Imperative Stem *nama*.

	Sanskrit.	Greek.		Gothic.	O. Saxon.	O. Norse.	O. H. G.
Sing.	náma	νέμε,	*Latin* eme	nim	nim	nem	nim
Plur.	náma-ta	νέμε-τε,	*Latin* emi-te	nimi-þ	nima-d	nemi-ð	nema-t

Plural -tata > ta > t (§ 38) > d (shifting, § 41, a). O. F. = A. Sax.

175. Noun Forms.

1. Infinitive *nam + ana*; 2. Gerund. *nam + ana + ja*.

1. *Dative* ...	$\begin{cases} \text{nám-anâj-a} \\ (\S 79, a) \end{cases}$	$\begin{cases} \text{νέμ-ειν} < \text{-εναι} \\ (\S 70, a) \end{cases}$	nim-*an*	nim-*an*	nem-*a*	nem-*an*
2. (§ 120),	nám-anija, *Latin* em-endo, O. *Saxon* nim-annia > -anna.					nem-*enne*
3. *Pr. Part.*	náma-nt	$\begin{cases} \text{νέμο-ντ-ος} \\ \text{Lat. eme-nt-is} \end{cases}$	nima-*nd(a)-s*	nima-*nd*	nema-*nd-i*	nema-*nt-i*
4. *P. Part.* (Strong.)	$\begin{cases} \text{bhug-ná} \\ (\text{beat}) \end{cases}$	$\begin{cases} \text{τέκ-νο-ν (born)} \\ \text{do-nu-m (gift)} \end{cases}$	numa-*n-s*	numa-*n*	numi-*nn*	$\begin{cases} \text{ga-nom-} \\ \text{an-ér} \end{cases}$
5. *P. Part.* (Weak.)	$\begin{cases} \text{na(m)-tá} \end{cases}$	$\begin{cases} \text{νεμ-η-τό-ς} \\ \text{em(p)-tu-s} \end{cases}$	nasi-þ(a)s	(gi-)neri-*d*	tal-d-*r*	ga-neri-*t*

(*a*.) The dative case ending is gone in Teutonic infinitives. § 38.

(*b*.) Gerund -*enne* > -*ende* (§ 445, 2, *nn* > *nd*, § 27, 5), so in O. N.; M. H. Ger.; Friesic, O. Sax., and O. H. Ger. have a genitive *nim-annias*, -*an-nas* (-*es*); *nem-ennes*; and M. H. German has gen. *nem-endes*.

(*c*.) To these stems of the participles are added suffixes contained in the case endings. §§ 104–106.

(*d*.) The Greek verbals in -τός are not counted participles (Hadley, 261, *c*). Only weak verbs have -*da*, -*da*, in Teutonic. Few verbs have the participle in -*na* in Sanskrit; only relics are found in Greek and Latin, but all the strong verbs use it in Teutonic.

(*e*.) Weak stems in -*ia* and -*ô* have *i*, *e*, *ig* or *ige*, before -*an*, -*anne*, -*end*. § 165, *d*.

176. Periphrastic Conditional Forms.
Potential Mode.

Modal verbs *magan, cunnan, môtan, durran, pillan, sculan, pítan* > *utan*,
may,   can,   must,   dare,   will,   shall,   let us.

PERIPHRASTIC CONDITIONAL FORMS.

Present Tense.

Sing. Indicative Forms.	Subjunctive Forms.
mæg, can, mót, dear \\ meaht, canst, móst, dearst \\ mæg, can, mót, dear \\ Plur. \\ mágon, cunnon, móton, durron } niman.	mǽge, cunne, móte, durre \\ mǽge, cunne, móte, durre \\ mǽge, cunne, móte, durre \\ \\ mǽgen, cunnen, móten, durren, utan } niman.

Imperfect Tense, Indicative Forms.

Sing.
meahte, cúde, móste, dorste, polde, sc(e)olde
meahtest, cúdest, móstest, dorstest, poldest, sc(e)oldest
meahte, cúde, móste, dorste, polde, sc(e)olde
Plur.
meahton, cúdon, móston, dorston, poldon, sc(e)oldon
} niman.

Imperfect Tense, Subjunctive Forms.

Sing. meahte, cúde, móste, dorste, polde, sc(e)olde
Plur. meahten, cúden, mósten, dorsten, polden, sc(e)olden
} niman.

Gerundial Form.

I am to take = I must *or* ought to take *or* be taken.

Sing.	Plur.
ic eom \\ þú eart \\ hê is } tó nimanne.	pê sind \\ gê sind \\ hî sind } tó nimanne.

177. Other Periphrastic Forms.

1. *eom* (am) + present participle.

Present............ eom, eart, is; sind nimende.
Imperfect............ pæs, pǽre, pæs; pǽron nimende.
Future .... beóm, bist, but; beód nimende.
  sceal pesan nimende.
Infinitive Future... beón nimende.

2. *dón* (do) + infinitive, § 406, a.

Other Forms: meaht, meahte, etc. (ea>i); mág-on, -um, -un, -an (á>ǽ); meahtes; meaht-on, -um, -an, -en, -e (§§ 166, 170); can, con; const; cunn-on, -un, -an; cudes; cud-on, -an, -en; mót-on, -um, -un, -an, -en; mót-en, -an, -e; móst-es; móst-um, -on, -an; durre (u>y); durr-on, -an; dorst-on, -en; poldes; pold-on, -um, -un, -an, -e; sc(e)oldes; sc(e)old-on, -un, -an, -en, -e. Forms of *eom*, *peorde*, and *beóm* interchange (§ 178).

178. Passive Voice.
Indicative Mode.

Present and Perfect, *I am taken* or *have been taken.*

Singular.	Plural.
ic eom* (peorde) numen.	pê sind(on) (peordad) numene.
þû eart (peordest) numen.	gê sind(on) (peordad) numene.
hê is (peorded) numen.	hî sind(on) (peordad) numene.

Past and Pluperfect, *I was taken* or *had been taken.*

ic pǽs (peard) numen.	pê pǽron (purdon) numene.
þû pǽre (purde) numen.	gê pǽron (purdon) numene.
hê pǽs (peard) numen.	hî pǽron (purdon) numene.

Future.
1. *I shall be taken.*

ic beô(m)* numen.	pê beôd numene.
þû bist numen.	gê beôd numene.
hê bid numen.	hî beôd numene.

2. *I shall* or *will be taken.*

ic sceal (pille) beôn numen.	pê sculon (pillad) beôn numene.
þû scealt (pilt) beôn numen.	gê sculon (pillad) beôn numene.
hê sceal (pille) beôn numen.	hî sculon (pillad) beôn numene.

Perfect, *I have been taken.*

ic eom geporden numen.	*pê sind(on) gepordene numene.*
þû eart geporden numen.	*gê sind(on) gepordene numene.*
hê is geporden numen.	*hî sind(on) gepordene numene.*

Pluperfect, *I had been taken.*

ic pǽs geporden numen.	*pê pǽron gepordene numene.*
þû pǽre geporden numen.	*gê pǽron gepordene numene.*
hê pǽs geporden numen.	*hi pǽron gepordene numene.*

179. Subjunctive Mode.
Present.
(*If*) *I be taken.*

Sing.	Plur.
ic (þû, hê) beô numen.	pê (gê, hî) beôn numene.

---

* The forms of *peorde*, *eom*, and *beóm* interchange.

Past.

(If) I were taken.

SING.
ic (þû, hê) pǣre numen.

PLUR.
pê (gê, hî) pǣren numene.

180. IMPERATIVE MODE.

SING. *Be thou taken.*
pes þû numen.

PLUR. *Be ye taken.*
pesað gê numene.

181. INFINITIVE.
beôn numen, *to be taken.*

PARTICIPLE.
numen, *taken.*

---

182. PERIPHRASTIC CONDITIONAL (§ 176).
POTENTIAL MODE.
Present Tense.

SING. Indicative Forms.
mæg (&c.)
meaht (&c.)
mæg (&c.) } beôn numen(e).
PLUR.
mágon (&c.)

Subjunctive Forms.
mǣge (&c.)
mǣge (&c.)
mǣge (&c.) } beôn numen(e).
mǣgen (&c.)

Imperfect.

SING.
meahte (&c.)
meahtest (&c.)
meahte (&c.) } beôn numen(e).
PLUR.
meahton (&c.)

meahte (&c.)
meahte (&c.)
meahte (&c.) } beôn numen(e).
meahten (&c.)

For *beón* (infinitive) is found *pesan* or *peordan.* The forms interchange of *beó, sî, pese, peorde;* of *pǣre, purde;* of *pes, beó, peorit. Bist, bid* ($i > y$); *beó, beód* ($eó < ió$). Ælfric's grammar has indic. pres. *eom,* imperf. *pæs,* fut. *beó,* perf. *pæs fulfremedlîce* (completely), pluperf. *pæs gefyrn* (formerly); subjunctive for a wish, pres. *beó gyt* (yet), imperf. *pǣre,* pluperf. *pǣre fulfremedlîce;* for a condition, pres. *eom nu* (now), imperf. *pæs,* fut. *beó gyt* (yet); imperative *sî;* infinitive *beón.*

183. WEAK VERBS.—(Conjugation VI.)
Active Voice.

Pres. Infinitive.	Imperf. Indicative.	Passive Participle.
ner*ian*, *save;*	ner*ede;*	ner*ed.*
hŷr*an*, *hear;*	hŷr*de;*	hŷr*ed.*
luf*ian*, *love;*	lufóde;	(*ge-*)lufód.

Indicative Mode.
Present (and Future) Tense (§ 165, *d*).
I save, hear, love.

Singular.	Plural.
ic ner*ie*, hŷr*e*, luf*ige.*	pê ner*iad*, hŷr*ad*, luf*iad.*
þû ner*est*, hŷr*est*, luf*ást.*	gê ner*iad*, hŷr*ad*, luf*iad.*
hê ner*ed*, hŷr*ed*, luf*áđ.*	hî ner*iad*, hŷr*ad*, luf*iad.*

Imperfect (§§ 160, 166, 168).
I saved, heard, loved.

ic ner*ede*, hŷr*de*, lufóde.	pê ner*edon*, hŷr*don*, lufódon.
þû ner*edest*, hŷr*dest*, lufódest.	gê ner*edon*, hŷr*don*, lufódon.
hê ner*ede*, hŷr*de*, lufóde.	hî ner*edon*, hŷr*don*, lufódon.

Future (§ 167).
I shall (will) save, hear, love.

ic sceal (pille)	} ner*ian*, hŷr*an*, luf*ian.*	pê sculon (pill*ađ*)	} ner*ian*, hŷr*an*, luf*ian.*
þû scealt (pil*t*)		gê sculon (pill*ađ*)	
hê sceal (pille)		hî sculon (pill*ađ*)	

Perfect (§ 168).

Transitive.	Intransitive.
I have saved, heard, loved.	*I have (am) returned.*

Sing.			
ic hæbbe	} ner*ed*, hŷr*ed*, lufód.	ic eom	} gecyrr*ed.*
þû hæfst, hafást		þû eart	
hê hæfđ, hafáđ		hê is	

Plur.			
pê habb*ađ*	} ner*ed*, hŷr*ed*, lufód.	pê sind (sindon)	} gecyrr*ede.*
gê habb*ađ*		gê sind (sindon)	
hî habb*ađ*		hî sind (sindon)	

Ia, iga, igea, ga interchange, and *ie, ige, ge:* ô to á, a, u, e. For variations of auxiliaries and endings, see corresponding tenses of strong verbs.

CONJUGATION OF WEAK VERBS.

Pluper'fect (§ 168).

TRANSITIVE.	INTRANSITIVE.
I had saved, heard, loved.	*I had (was) returned.*

SING.
ic hæfde }
þû hæf*dest* } ner*ed*, hŷr*ed*, lufód.
hê hæf*de* }

ic pǽs }
þû pǽre } gecyrr*ed*.
hê pǽs }

PLUR.
pê hæf*don* }
gê hæf*don* } ner*ed*, hŷr*ed*, lufód.
hî hæf*don* }

pê pǽron }
gê pǽron } gecyrr*ede*.
hî pǽron }

184. SUBJUNCTIVE MODE.

Present (§ 170).
(If) I save, hear, love.

SINGULAR.	PLURAL.

ic }
þû } ner*ie*, hŷre, luf*ige*.
hê }

pê }
gê } ner*ien*, hŷren, luf*igen*.
hî }

Imperfect (§ 171).
(If) I saved, heard, loved.

ic }
þû } ner*ede*, hŷr*de*, lufóde.
hê }

pê }
gê } ner*eden*, hŷr*den*, lufóden.
hî }

Future (§ 167).
(If) I shall (will) save, hear, love.

ic scyle (pille) }
þû scyle (pille) } ner*ian*, hŷr*an*, luf*ian*.
hê scyle (pille) }

pê scylen (pillen) }
gê scylen (pillen) } ner*ian*, hŷr-
hî scylen (pillen) } *an*, luf*ian*.

Perfect (§ 168).

TRANSITIVE.	INTRANSITIVE.
(If I) have saved, &c.	*(If I) have (be) returned.*

SING. hæbbe } ner*ed*, hŷr*ed*,
PLUR. hæbb*en* } lufód.

sî }
sîn } gecyrr*ed(e)*.

Pluper'fect (§ 168).

(If I) had saved, &c.	*(If I) had (were) returned.*

SING. hæfde } ner*ed*, hŷr*ed*,
PLUR. hæf*den* } lufód.

pǽre }
pǽren } gecyrr*ed(e)*.

185. IMPERATIVE MODE (§ 174).
Save, hear, love.

SING.
2. ner*e*, hŷr, luf*a*.

PLUR.
ner*iad*, hŷr*ad*, luf*iad*.

186. INFINITIVE MODE (§ 175).
To save, hear, love.

Present. ner*ian* > ner*igan*, ner*igean*, ner*gan*; hŷr*an*; luf*ian* >
luf*igan*, luf*igean*.
Gerund. tô ner*ianne*, hŷr*anne*, luf*ianne*.

PARTICIPLES.
Saving, hearing, loving.

Present. ner*iende*, hŷr*ende*, luf*igende*.
saved. heard. loved.
Past.... ner*ed*, hŷr*ed*, (*ge-*)luf*ód*.

187. The special periphrastic forms and the whole passive voice of weak verbs are conjugated with the same auxiliaries as those of strong verbs (§§ 176–182).

---

188. PRESENTS (*Weak*).

(*a*.) Like *nerian* inflect stems in *-ia* from short roots: *derian*, hurt; *helian*, cover; *hegian*, hedge; *scerian*, apportion; *spyrian*, speer; *sylian*, soil; *þunian*, thunder, etc.

(*b*.) But many stems in *-ia* from short roots have compensative gemination of their last consonant where it preceded *i*— (throughout the present, except in the indicative singular second and third, and the imperative singular); *ci* > *cc*, *di* > *dd*, *fi* > *bb*, *gi* > *cg*, *li* > *ll*, etc.; indicative *lecge* (< *legie*), lay, *legest*, *leged*; *lecgad* (< *legiad*); subjunctive *lecge*, *lecgen*; imperative *lege*, *lecgad*; infinitive *lecgan*; part. pres. *lecgende*; part. past *leged*. So *reccan*, reach; *hreddan*, rescue; *habban*, have; *sellan*, give; *tellan*, tell; *fremman*, frame; *clynnan*, clang; *dippan*, dip; *cnyssan*, knock; *settan*, set, etc.

(*c*.) Like *hŷran* inflect stems in *-ia* > *-e* > — from long roots: *dŵlan*, deal; *dēman*, deem; *belǽpan*, leave; *mǽnan*, mean; *sprengan*, spring; *styrman*, storm; *cennan*, bring forth; *cyssan*, kiss, etc. Infinitives in *-ean* occur: *séc-ean*, § 175, *e*.

(d.) Like *lufian* inflect stems showing *-ŏ* in the imperfect: *árian*, honor; *beorhtian*, shine; *cleopian*, call; *hopian*, hope. Past participles have *ŏ, ă, e*; *gegearp-ŏd, -ăd, -ed*, prepared.

189. SYNCOPATED IMPERFECTS (*Weak*).

(*a.*) Stem *-e < -ia* is syncopated after long roots: *cīg-an*, call, *cīg-de*; *dǣl-on*, deal, *dǣl-de*; *dēm-an*, deem, *dēm-de*; *drēf-an*, trouble, *drēf-de*; *fēd-an*, feed; *hēd-an*, heed; *hȳr-an*, hear; *lǣd-an*, lead; *be-lǣf-an*, leave; *mǣn-an*, mean; *nȳd-an*, urge; *rēd-an*, read; *spēd-an*, speed; *spreng-an*, spring, *spreng-de*; *bærn-an*, burn, *bærn-de*; *styrm-an*, storm; so *sep-de* and *sep-te*, showed.

(*b.*) ASSIMILATION.—After a surd, *-d* becomes surd (*-t*). (Surds *p, t, c (x), ss, h*, not *f* or *s* alone, §§ 17, 30): *rǣp-an*, bind, *rǣp-te*; *bēt-an*, better, *bēt-te*; *grēt-an*, greet, *grēt-te*; *mēt-an*, meet, *mēt-te*; *drenc-an*, drench, *drenc-te*; *lȳx-an*, shine, *lȳx-te*; but *lȳs-an*, release, *lȳs-de*; *fȳs-an*, haste, *fȳs-de*; *rǣs-an*, rush, *rǣs-de*.

(*c.*) DISSIMILATION.—The mute *c* becomes continuous (*h*) before *-t*: *tǣc-an*, teach, *tǣh-te*; *ēc-an*, eke, *ēh-te* and *ēc-te*, 36, 3.

(*d.*) UMLAUT LOST.—Themes in *ecg*; *ecc, ell*; *enc, eng*; *ēc*; *ycg*, *ync*, i-umlaut for *acg*; *acc, all*; *anc, ang*; *ōc*; *ucg, unc*, may retain *a* (> *æ*; *ea*; *o*); *ō*; *u > o* in syncopated imperfects (§§ 209–211): *lecgan*, lay, *lægde*; *reccan*, rule, *reahte*; *cpellan*, kill, *cpealde*; *þencan*, think, *þohte*; *brengan*, bring, *brohte*; *rēcan*, reck, *rōhte*; *bycgan*, buy, *bohte*; *þyncan*, seem, *þohte*.

(*e.*) GEMINATION is simplified, and *mn > m* (Rule 13, page 10): *cenn-an*, beget, *cen-de*; *clypp-an*, clip, *clip-te*; *cyss-an*, kiss, *cys-te*; *dypp-an*, dip, *dyp-te*; *ēht-an*, pursue, *ēhte*; *fyll-an*, fill, *fyl-de*; *gyrd-an*, gird, *gyrde*; *hredd-an*, rescue, *hredde*; *hyrd-an*, harden, *hyrde*; *hyrt-an*, hearten, *hyrte*; *hæft-an*, bind, *hæfte*; *lecg-an*, lay, *leg-de*; *merr-an*, mar, *mer-de*; *mynt-an*, purpose, *mynte*; *nemn-an*, name, *nem-de*; *rest-an*, rest, *reste*; *riht-an*, right, *rihte*; *scild-an*, guard, *scilde*; *send-an*, send, *sende*; *spill-an*, spill, *spil-de*; *sett-an*, set, *sette*; *still-an*, spring, *stil-de*; *stylt-an*, stand astonished, *stylte*; *pemm-an*, spoil, *pem-de*.

(*f.*) ECTHLIPSIS occurs (*g*): *cēgan*, call, *cēgde, cēde*. See § 209.

190. PAST PARTICIPLES are syncopated like imperfects in verbs having lost umlaut, often in other verbs having a surd root (§ 189, *b*), less often in other verbs: *sellan*, give, *sealde, seald*; *ge-sēc-an*, seek, *ge-sōh-te, gesōht*; *sett-an*, set, *sette, seted* and *set*; *send-an*, send, *sende, sended* and *send*; *heán*, raise, *hedd*, raised.

ILLUSTRATIONS OF UMLAUT AND ASSIMILATION.

191. Presents.—*Illustrations of Umlaut.*

Conjugation	(I.)	(I.)	(I.)	(III.)	(III.)
	drep*an*, strike.	cum*an*, come.	beorg*an*, guard.	scûf*an*, shove.	creôp*an*, creep.
Sing.— 1.	drepe	cume	beorge	scûfe	creôpe
2.	{ drip(*e*)st { drep*est*	{ cym(*e*)st { cum*est*	{ byrh*st* { beorg*est*(*y*)	{ scŷf(*e*)st { scûf*est*	{ crŷp(*e*)st { creôp*est*
3.	{ drip(*e*)*d* { drep*ed*	{ cym(*e*)*d* { cum*ed*	{ byrh*d* { beorg*ed*(*y*)	{ scŷf(*e*)*d* (*t*) { scûf*ied*	{ crŷp(*e*)*d* { creôp*ed*
Plur.—	drep*ad*	cum*ad*	beorg*ad*	scûf*ad*	creôp*ad*

Conjugation	(IV.)	(IV.)	(V.)	(V.)	(V.)
	far*an*, fare.	bac*an*, bake.	feall*an*, fall.	lâc*an*, leap.	grôp*an*, grow.
Sing.— 1.	fare	bace	fealle	lâce	grôpe
2.	{ fær(*e*)st { far*est*	{ becst { bac*est*	{ felst { feall*est*	{ lêcst { lâc*est*	{ grêpst { grôp*est*
3.	{ fær(*e*)*d* { far*ed*	{ bec*d* { bac*ed*	{ fel*d* { feall*ed*	{ lêc(*e*)*d* { lâc*ed*	{ grêp*d* { grôp*ed*
Plur.—	far*ad*	bac*ad*	feall*ad*	lâc*ad*	grôp*ad*

192. *Illustrations of Assimilation.*

Conjugation	(I.)	(I.)	(I.)	(I.)	(I.)
	et*an*, eat.	tred*an*, tread.	bind*an*, bind.	cpeđ*an*, quoth.	les*an*, collect.
Sing.— 1.	ete	trede	binde	cpeđe	lese
2.	{ it(*e*)st { et*est*	{ tri(de)st { tred*est*	{ bin(t)st { bind*est*	{ cpist { cpeđ*est*	{ list { les*est*
3.	{ it*ed*, it { et*ed*	{ trit { tred*ed*(*i*)	{ bint { bind*ed*	{ cpiđ { cpeđ*ed*	{ list { les*ed*
Plur.—	et*ad*	tred*ad*	bind*ad*	cpeđ*ad*	les*ad*

Conjugation	(I.)	(III.)	(IV.) sleán<	(III.) fleôn<	(I.)
	berst*an*, burst.	leôg*an*, lie.	sleah*an*, slay.	fleoh*an*, flee.	licg*an*, lie.
Sing.— 1.	berste	leôge	sleâ	fleô	licge
2.	{ birst { berst*est*	{ lŷhst { leôg*est*	{ slehst (*y*) { sleng*est*	} flŷhst	{ ligst { licg*est*
3.	{ birst(*ed*) { berst*ed*	{ lŷh*d* { leôg*ed*	{ sleh*d* (*y*) { sleng*ed*	} flŷh*d*	{ li(g)*d* { li(c)ge*d*
Plur.—	berst*ad*	leog*ad*	sleâ*d*	fleô*d*	licg*ad*

	cpedan,	sleahan>	seahan>	ceósan,
	quoth.	sleán, slay.	seón, see.	choose.
Sing.—	cpæð	slóh (g)	seah	ceás
	cpæde	slóge	sǽge, sápe	cure
	cpæð	slóh (g)	seah	ceás
Plur.—	cpǽdon	slógon	sǽgon, sápon	curon
Part.—	cpeden	slægen	sepen	coren.

212. Preteritive Presents.—First Conjugation.—√a.

Indicative Sing.

Pres. .... (§§ 199, 200). ⎰mæg, meah-t (i); mágon (ǽ)(u); mǽg-e, -en; ——; mag-an (u); ——;
Imperf. .... meah-te (i), meah-ton (i); -te, -ten; am strong, (may), <have grown.

Pres. (§ 199). be-neah, ——; be-nugon; benug-e, -en; ——; benugan?; ——;
Imperf. .... be-noh-te, -ton (§ 211); -te, -ten; hold and use <have come to.

Pres. (§ 201). an(o), ——; unnon; unne, -en; ——; unn-an; (ge)unn-en;
Imperf. .... ú-de, -don (Goth. þ irregular), § 37; -de, -den; favor <have given.

Pres. (§ 201). can (o), canst (o); cunnon; cunne, -en; ——; cunn-an; ——;
Imperf. .... cú-de, -don (Goth. kunþa), § 37; -de, -den; know <have got. cúðe.

Pres. (§ 201). ge-man (o), -manst; -munon; -e, -en; gemun, -ad; gemun-an; ——;
Imperf. .... ge-munde, -don; -de, -den; remember <have called to mind.

Pres. (§ 203). sc(e)al (sceal), sc(e)alt; scul-on (eo); ⎰scul-e, en⎱ ——; sculan; ——;
                                                       ⎱(eo, y, i);⎰
Imperf. .... sc(e)ol-de (io), -don; -de, -den; shall <ought <have got in debt.

Pres. (§ 204). d(e)ar, d(e)arst: durr-on; -e, -en (y); ——; durran; ——;
Imperf. .... dors-te, -ton (Goth. daurs-ta); -te, -ten; dare <have fought.

Pres. (§ 204). þ(e)arf, þ(e)arf-t; þurf-on; þurf-e, -en(y); ——; þurf-an; ——;
Imperf. .... þorf-te, -ton; -te, -ten; need <have worked (opus est).

Second Conjugation (§ 205).—√i; ígan, not found, pitan, § 205.

Pres. ... áh, áhst; ágon; ág-e, -en; ——; ágan, -ne; ágende;
Imperf.. áh-te, -ton; -te, -ten; own <have earned or taken.
    náh = (ne + áh), &c., not own.

Pres. ... pát, pást (ǽ); piton; pit-e, -en; pit-e, -ad; pitan(y)-ne; piten, -de;
Imperf.. pis-te (y), -ton; ⎰pis-se, -son,⎱ ⎰-te, -se,⎱ know <have seen.
                          ⎱§§ 36, 3; 35,⎰ ⎱-ten, -sen;⎰
                          ⎱ B, pestan; ⎰
Pres. ... nát (= ne + pát), nyton (e); nyt-e, -en; ——; nitan (y); nyten, -de;
Imperf.. nyste, nysse; nyston (&c.); not know.

Third Conjugation (§ 206).—√u; dúgan not found.

Pres. ... deáh (g), ——; dugon; dug-e, -en; ——; dugan; dugende;
Imperf.. doh-te, -ton (§ 211); -te, -ten; is fit <has grown.

IRREGULAR VERBS. 131

FOURTH CONJUGATION (§ 207). — √ â ; *matan* not found.

Indicative Sing.
	1st & 3d.	2d.	Plur.	Subj.	Imp.	Infin.	Part.
Pres.	*môt*,	*môst* ;	*môton* ;	*môt-e, -en* ;	——— ;	*môtan* ;	——— ;
Imperf.	*môs-te,*	*-ton* (§ 36, 3) ;		*-te, -ten* ;	is meet<has met.		

Grimm takes *beô*, be, for a præteritive present from a *búan*, to dwell, of the Fifth Conjugation.

From an imperfect subjunctive of the Second Conjugation (Goth. *viljau*< √ *vıl*, inflected like *nemjau*, § 171) arise

| Pres. | *pille, pilt* ; | *pillad*(y) ; | *pill-e, -en* ; | *-e, -ad* ; | *pill-an* ; | *-ende,* |
| Imperf. | *pol-de, -don* (Goth. *vılda*) ; | *-de, -den* ; | will<have wished. | | | |

| Pres. | *nelle, nelt* ; | *nellad*(y,i) ; | *-e, -en* ; | *-e, -ad* ; | *-an* ; | *-ende;* |
| Imperf. | *nol-de, -don*, &c. | | | *ne + pille*, will not. | | |

pi > *po*, assimilation (§ 35, 2, *a*) ; *i* > *e*, a-umlaut ; *pi* > *y*, §§ 32, 23 ; *ll* > *l*.

213.—II. VERBS WITHOUT CONNECTING VOWEL (Relics of Sanskrit 2d Class, § 158) :

(1.) The common forms of the substantive verb are from three roots: √ *as*, √ *bhu*, √ *vas*.

(*a*.)—
	Sanskrit.	Greek.	Latin.	Gothic.	O. Saxon.	Anglo-Saxon.	O. Norse.
Stem,	as, s	εσ	es, s	is, s	is, s	is, ir, s ;	er
SING.—1.	ás-mi	εἰ-μί>ἐσ-μι	*s-u-m	i-m<is-m	———	eo-m	ea-m	e-m<er-m
2.	ás-(s)i	ἐσ-σί, εἶ	es-	is-	———	———	ear-t	er-t
3.	ás-ti	ἐσ-τί	est-t	is-t	is-t	is-	———	er-
PLUR.—1.	*s-más	ἐσ-μέν	*s-u-mus	———	*s-ind	*s-ind(on)	ear-on	er-u-m
2.	*s-thá	ἐσ-τέ	es-tis	———	*s-ind	*s-ind(on)	ear-on	er-u-ð
3.	*s-ánti	ἔ-άσι, εἰσί	*s-unt	*s-ind	*s-ind(un)	*s-ind(on)	ear-on	er-u

As > *s*, compensation, gravitation (§§ 37, 38) ; *as* > *is*, precession (§ 38) ; *ys* < *is*, bad spelling ; *s* > *r*, shifting (§ 41, 3, *b*) ; *irm* > (*eorm*) > *eom, arm* > (*earm*) *eam*, breaking (§ 33) ; second person *-s* and *-t* (§ 165) ; *nt* > *nd*, shifting (§ 19), *nt* is often found. Seond-on, -un (ie, y), u-umlaut? (§ 32) ; *-on* in *earon* (O. Norse *er-u-m*) (§ 166, *a*) ; in *sind-on*, a double plural through conformation (§ 40) ; *aron, caron*, are rare in West Saxon.

The subjunctive (Sansk. *s-jâ-m, Greek ἰ*-iŋ-v, Lat. *s-iê-m* > *sîm*, Goth. *s-ija-u*, O. H. Ger., O. Sax., Ang.-Sax. *s-î*, O. Norse *s-ê*) is inflected like the imperfect given in § 171. Anglo-Saxon has also *sî* > *sig* (dissimilated gemination, § 27) > *sie, seó* (a peculiar progression, § 25) > *sŷ* (bad spelling) ; so plur. *sin, sien, seón, sŷn*. The subjunctive often has the force of an imperative, and is given as the imperative in Ælfric's grammar.

(*b*.) √ *bhu*, be. Sansk. *bhav-ámi*, Greek φύ-ω, Lat. *fu-i*, correspond in form to Goth. *báu-an*, Ang.-Sax. *bû-an*, dwell. From the same root are found forms without a connecting vowel in Ang.-Sax., O. Sax., O. H. Ger. In O. Sax. are only *biu-m, bi-st* ; in O. H. Ger. *pi-m, pi-s, —*, plur. *pi-rumes, pi-rut, pi-run* (*r* < *s* < √ *as*). Ang.-Sax. has *beó-(m)* (*iô*), *bi-st* (*y*), *bi-d* (*y*), plur. *beód* (*iô*), and a present subjunctive, imperative, and infinitive, with the

132   IRREGULAR VERBS.

common endings; $eó > ŷ > y > i$, umlaut, precession, and shifting (§§ 32, 38, 41).

(c.) √ *vas* > *vis* (ablaut) is inflected in the First Conjugation, §§ 199, 197, but the present indicative forms are so rare that they are not given in the grammars.

PARADIGMS FOR PRACTICAL USE.

PRESENT:

SING.	Indicative.	Subjunctive.	Imperative.	Infinitive.	Participle.
ic	eom, beó(m);	sî, beó, pese;			
þû	eart, bist;	sî, beó, pese;	beó, pes;		
hê	is, bid;	sî, beó, pese;		beón,	
PLUR.—				or	pesende.
pê	sind(on), beód;	sîn, beón, pesen;		pesan;	
gê	sind(on), beód;	sîn, beón, pesen;	beód, pesad;		
hî	sind(on), beód;	sîn, beón, pesen;			

IMPERFECT:

SING.—				
ic pæs;	pære;			
þû pære;	pære;			
hê pæs;	pære;			ge-pesen.
PLUR.—				
pê, gê, hî pæron;	pæren;			

The negative *ne* often unites with forms beginning with a vowel or *p*: *neom* = *ne* + *eom*; *nis*; *næs* = *ne* + *pæs*, p. p. *næsrende* < *ne pærende*, etc.

(2.) √ *dha*, place: Sansk. *da-dhâ-mi*, Greek τί-θη-μι, Goth. —, O. Sax. *dó-n*, O. H. Ger. *tuo-n*, do. Anglo-Saxon imperfect from reduplicated theme *dad*; *a* > *æ* (ablaut, § 199) > *y* > *i*, irregular weakening. § 168.

	Indicative Sing.	Plur.	Subj.	Impernt.	Infin.	Participle.
Pres. ...	dó, dé-st, dé-d;	dó-d;	dó, -n;	dó, -d;	dó-n;	do-nde.
Imperf.	did-e (y), -est, -e;	-on (æ);	-e (æ), n;			dó-n, dé-n.

(3.) √ *ga*, go: Sansk. *g'i-gâ-mi*, Greek βί-βη-μι, Goth. *gaggan*, O. Sax. *gâ-n*, O. H. Ger. *gê-n*. Imperfect from √ *i* (Sansk. *é'-mi*, Greek εἶ-μι, Lat. *i-re*, go, § 158, a) > Goth. *i-ddja*, weak form strengthened.

Pres. ... gâ, gæ-st, gæ-d; gâd; gâ, -n; gâ, -d; gâ-n;
Imperf. eó-de, -dest, -de; -don (§ 37); ge-gâ-n.

From the same root are the nasalized forms *gangan*, imperf. *geóng*, *gêng*, *giêng* (§ 208, b); *geongan* (§ 201); and *gengan*, imperf. *gengde*.

214. REDUPLICATE PRESENTS (Relics of Sanskrit 3d Class, § 158): *gangan* < √ *ga* > *ga-gâ-mi*, go (§ 213); so *hangan*, *standan*, § 216).

215. STEMS IN -*ia* of strong verbs (Relics of Sanskrit 4th Class, § 158): *fricge*, inquire, etc. (§ 199); *sperie*, swear, etc. (§ 207, d).

PART III.

SYNTAX.

271. **Syntax** is the doctrine of grammatical *combinations of words*. It treats of the use of the etymological forms in discourse—their agreement, government, and arrangement.

SIMPLE COMBINATIONS.

272. There are four simple combinations: the *predic′ative, attrib′utive, objective,* and *adverbial.*

273.—I. **Predicative**
= *nominative substantive + agreeing verb;*
= *nominative substantive + agreeing predicate noun;*
= *nominative substantive + predicate adverb.*

gold glisnád, gold glistens; *gold is beorht,* gold is bright; *Ælfréd þæs cyning,* Alfred was king; *ic com hér,* I am here.

(*a.*) This is a combination between a **subject**, of which something is said (= *gold, Ælfréd, ic*), and a **predicate**, which is said of the subject (= *glisnád, beorht, cyning, hér*).

(*b.*) **Copula.**—The sign of predication is the stem-ending of a notional verb (= *á* in *glisnád*), or is a relational verb (*is, þæs, com*). The substantive verb, when so used, is called the *copula*—a good name for any sign of predication. **Copulative** verbs take a predicate noun.

(*c.*) *Quasi-predicative* is the relation between the implied subject and predicate in a *quasi-clause.* § 278, *d.*

274.—II. **Attributive** = *agreeing noun + substantive;*
= *genitive substantive + substantive.*

gód cyning, good king; *Ælfréd æðeling,* Alfred the prince; *Englá land,* land of the Angles.

(*a.*) This combination expresses the relation of **subject + attribute** as taken for granted. The leading substantive is called the **subject**, that to which the attribute belongs (*cyning, Ælfréd, land*); an **attributive** is the agreeing adjective (*gód*), or genit. substantive (*Englá*); an **appositive** is the agreeing substantive (*æðeling*).

(*b.*) The sign of this relation is the agreeing case-endings, or the attributive genitive ending, or a preposition (§ 277, 2).

K

275.—III. **Objective** = *verb + governed noun.*
= *adjective + governed noun.*

ic huntige heortâs, I hunt harts; *hê sylð him hors,* he sells him a horse; *gilpes þû gyrnest,* thou wishest fame; *þære fæhðe hê gefeah,* he rejoiced at the vengeance; *hî macað hine (tó) cyninge,* they make him king; *hpî segst þû mê gôdne,* why callest thou me good? *beóð gemindige Loðes pîfes,* remember Lot's wife.

(*a.*) This combination expresses the relation of an *act* or *quality* to its *completing notional object*.

Objective verbs or adjectives are those which need such object (*huntige,* etc.).
Subjective need no such object (*ic slæpe,* I sleep).
Transitive verbs have a suffering object (*huntige, syld, macað,* etc.).
Intransitive have no suffering object (*gyrnest, gefeah*).

The completing object may be
suffering (=*direct*), an accusative merely affected (*heortâs, hors, hine, mê*);
dative (=*indirect*=*personal*), a receiver to or for whom is the act (*him*);
genitive, suggesting or exciting the act (*gilpes, fæhðe, pîfes*);
factitive, a product or result in fact or thought (*cyninge, gôdne*).

(*b.*) The sign of relation is the case-ending or a preposition.

(*c.*) Many Anglo-Saxon verbs require an object, when the English by which we translate them do not. Many objects conceived as *exciting* in Anglo-Saxon are conceived as *suffering* in English; many as merely adverbial.

(*d.*) The factitive object often has a quasi-predicative relation to the suffering object, agreeing with it like a predicate noun (*mê + gôdne*). Such clauses are nearly equivalent to two (why sayest thou that I am good?).

276.—IV. **Adverbial** = *verb + adverb* or *adverbial phrase.*
= *adjective + adverb* or *adverbial phrase.*
= *adverb + adverb* or *adverbial phrase.*

ic gâ ût, I go out; *ic singe ælcê dæg,* I sing each day; *þê sprecað gepemmodlîce,* we speak corruptly; *hê com mid þâ fæmman,* he came with the woman; *mid sorgum libban,* to live having cares; *hpî fandige gê mîn,* why tempt ye me? *miclê mâ man is sceâpe betera,* man is much (more) better than a sheep.

(*a.*) This combination is between an *act* or *quality* and its *unessential relations*. The most common relations are place (*ût*), time (*ælcê dæg*), manner (*gepemmodlîce*), co-existence (*mid fæmman, mid sorgum*), cause (*hpî*), intensity (*miclê, mâ, sceâpe*).

(*b.*) The sign is an adverbial ending, case-ending, or preposition.

(*c.*) The *adverbial* combination is given by Becker as a subdivision of the *objective,* but the linguistic sense of the Indo-European races uniformly recognizes the adverb as a separate part of speech.

277. Equivalents of the Noun and Adverb in the combinations:

(1.) For a SUBSTANTIVE may be used a *substantive noun or pronoun*, an *adjective* or any of its equivalents, an *infinitive*, a *clause*, any *word* or *phrase* viewed merely as a thing.

(2.) For an ADJECTIVE may be used an *adjective noun or pronoun*, an *article* (attributively), a *participle*, a *genitive substantive*, an *adverb*, a *preposition with its case*, a *relative clause*.

(3.) For an ADVERB may be used an *oblique case* of a noun with or without a preposition, a *phrase*, a *clause*.

SENTENCES.

278. A **Sentence** is a thought in words. It may be
declarative, an assertion, *indicative, subjunctive,* or *potential;*
interrogative, a question, *indicative, subjunctive,* or *potential;*
imperative, a command, exhortation, entreaty; a species of
exclamatory, an expanded interjection. §§ 149–151.

(*a.*) A clause is *one finite verb* with its subject, objects, and all their attributives and adjuncts. Its *essential part* is its predicative combination. The (*grammatical*) subject of the predicative combination, its attributives and adjuncts, make up the *logical* subject of the clause; the *grammatical* predicate and its objects with their attributives and adjuncts make up the *logical* predicate.

(*b.*) A subordinate clause enters into grammatical combination with some *word* in another (principal) clause; co-ordinate clauses are coupled as wholes.

(*c.*) The sign of relation between clauses is a relative or conjunction.

(*d.*) **Quasi-clauses.** — (1) *Infinitives, participles,* and *factitive* objects mark quasi-predicative combinations, and each has its quasi-clause. (2) *Interjections* and *vocatives* are exclamatory quasi-clauses.

279. A **Sentence** is *simple, complex,* or *compound.*

280. A **simple** sentence is *one independent* clause.

I. A predicative combination.

Verb for predicate: *fisceras fisciad,* fishers *fish.*
Adjective: *God is gôd,* God is *good.*
Genitive: *tôl Cæsares is,* tribute is *Cæsar's.*
Substantive: *Cædmon pæs leôdpyrhta,* Cædmon was a *poet.*
Adverb: *pê sind hêr,* we are *here.*
Adverbial: *God is in heofenum,* God is *in heaven.*
Subject indefinite: (*hit*) *snipd,* it snows; *mê þyrst,* me it thirsteth.

II. Clause with attributive combination.

Adjective attribute: *gód gold glisnád*, good gold glistens.
Genitive: *folces stemn is Godes stemn*, folk's voice is God's voice.
Appositive: *pé cildra sind ungelærede*, we *children* are untaught.

III. Clause with objective combination.

Direct object: *Cædmon þorhte leóðsangás*, Cædmon made *poems*.
Dative: *læn mé þrí hláfás*, give me three loaves.
Genitive: *þæt pif áhlóh drihtnes*, the woman laughed at *the lord*.
Factitive: *Simónem hé nemde Petrum*, Simon he named *Peter*.

IV. Clause with adverbial combination.

Place: *ic gá út*, I go *out*.
Time: *ic gá út on dægréd*, I go out *at dawn*.
Manner: *se cyning scrýt mé pel*, the king clothes me *well*.
Co-existence: *mid sorgum ic libbe*, I live *with cares*.
Cause: *hé hás is for cylde*, he is hoarse *from cold*; *se cnapa þýpað oxan mid gadisené*, the boy drives oxen *with an iron goad*.

281.—V. Abridged complex sentence. Clause containing a quasi-clause. § 278, *d*.

Infinitive: *tǽc ús sprecan*, teach us *to speak*.
Factitive: *hpí segst þú mé gódne*, why callest thou *me* (to be) *good?*
Participle (adjectival): *ic hæbbe sumne cnapan, þýpendne oxan*, I have a boy, (*driving*) *who drives oxen*; (adverbial, gerund), *Boetius gebæd singende*, Boethius prayed *singing*; (absolute), *þínre durá beloccnre, bide þinne fæder*, *thy door having been locked*, pray thy father.

282.—VI. Abridged compound sentence (§ 284). Verbs>verb.

Compound subject: *hé and seó síngað*, he and she sing.
Compound predicate: *hé is gód and pís*, he is *good and wise*; *seó lufáð hine and mé*, she loves *him and me*.

283. A **complex** sentence is one *principal* clause with its *subordinate* clause or clauses. § 278, *b*. The subordinate may be a

Substantive: (subject), *is sægd þæt hé com*, *that he came* is said; (object), *ic pát þæt hé com*, I wot *that he came*; (appositive), *ic com tó þam, þæt hé pære gefulpód*, I came for this, *that he might be baptized*.
Adjective: *stæf-cræft is seó cæg, þe þará bóca andgit unlýcd*, grammar is the key, *that unlocks the sense of the books*.
Adverb: (place), *hpider þú gǽst, ic gá*, I go *whither thou goest*; (time), *ic gá hpænne þú gǽst*, I go *when thou goest*; (manner), *þú sprǽce spá spá án stunt píf*, thou spakest *as a stupid woman speaks*; (intensity),

beóð gleápe spá nædran, be wise *as serpents*; *leófre is hlehhan þonne grǽtan*, it is better to laugh *than cry*; (cause = efficient, motive, means, argument, condition [protasis to an apodosis], concession, purpose) *hit þunráð forþam God pilt*, it thunders *because God wills*; *paciað, forþam þe gê nyton þone dæg*, watch, *because ye know not the day*; *Onsend Higeláce, gif mec hild nime*, (protasis) *if me battle take*, (apodosis) send to Higelac, etc. Co-existence is usually in an abridged participial clause (§ 281).

284. **A compound** sentence is a number of *co-ordinate* clauses. § 278, *b*.

Copulative: *ic gâ ût and ic geocie oxan*, I go out *and* I yoke oxen.

Adversative: *fýr is gôd þegn, ac is frécne freá*, fire is a good servant, *but* is a bad master; *ne nom hê má, þeáh hê monige geseah*, he took no more, *though* he saw many.

Disjunctive: *ic singe oððe ic rǽde*, I sing *or* I read.

Causal: *forþý gê ne gehýrað, forþam þe gê ne synd of Gode*, therefore ye do not hear, (*for this that*) because ye are not of God.

---

482. PRINCIPAL RULES OF SYNTAX.
Substantives.
Agreement.

I. A **predicate** noun denoting the same person or thing as its **subject**, agrees with it in *case*, § 286.

II. An **appositive** agrees in *case* with its **subject**, § 287.

Nominative Case.

III. The **subject** of a *finite* verb is put in the **nominative**, § 288.

Vocative Case.

IV. A **compellative** is put in the **vocative**, § 289.

Accusative Case.
Objective Combinations.

V. The **direct object** of a *verb* is put in the **accusative**, § 290.

VI. **Impersonals** of *appetite* or *passion* govern an **accusative** of the person suffering, § 290, *c*.

VII. Some verbs of **asking** and **teaching** may have **two accusatives**, one of a *person*, and the other of a *thing*, § 292.

Quasi-predicative Combinations.

VIII. The **subject** of an *infinitive* is put in the **accusative**, § 293.

IX. Some verbs of **making, naming,** and **regarding** may have **two accusatives of** the *same person* or thing, § 294.

Adverbial Combinations.

X. The **accusative** is used to express **extent** of time and space after verbs, § 295.

XI. The **accusative** is used with **prepositions**, § 295, *c*.

DATIVE AND INSTRUMENTAL CASES.
Objective Combinations.

XII. An object of **influence** or **interest** is put in the **dative**, § 297.

XIII. Verbs of **granting, refusing,** and **thanking** may take a **dative** and genitive, § 297, *d*.

XIV. Words of **nearness** and **likeness** govern the **dative**, § 299.

XV. The **instrumental** or **dative** may denote an object of **mastery**, § 300.

XVI. Some words of separation may take an object **from which** in the **dative** or **instrumental**, § 301.

Adverbial Combinations.

XVII. The **instrumental** or **dative** may denote **instrument, means, manner,** or **cause**, § 302.

XVII. The **instrumental** or **dative** may denote **price**, § 302, *c*.

XVIII. The **instrumental** or **dative** may denote **measure of difference**, § 302, *d*.

XIX. The **instrumental** or **dative** may denote an object **sworn by**, § 302, *e*.

XX. The **comparative** degree may govern a **dative**, § 303.

XXI. The **dative** may denote **time when** or **place where**, § 304.

XXII. A **substantive** and **participle** in the **dative** may make an adverbial clause of **time, cause,** or **co-existence**, § 304, *d*.

XXIII. The **dative** with a **preposition** may denote an object of influence or interest, association, mastery, or separation; or an instrumental, ablative, or locative adverbial relation, § 305. **Instrumental**, §§ 306–308.

The dative, with or without *of*, is sometimes used for the genitive.

Genitive.
Attributive Combinations.

XXIV. An attributive genitive may denote the **possessor** or **author** of its *subject*, § 310.

XXV. An attributive genitive may denote the **subject** or **object** of a *verbal*, § 311.

XXVI. An attributive genitive may denote the **whole** of which its subject is part, § 312.

XXVII. An attributive genitive may denote a **characteristic** of its *subject*, § 313.

Predicative Combinations.

XXVIII. A **predicate** substantive may be put in the **genitive** to denote a **possessor** or **characteristic** of the subject, or the **whole** of which it is part, § 314.

Objective Combinations.

XXIX. The genitive may denote an **exciting** object, § 315.

XXX. Verbs of **asking, accusing, reminding**, may take an accusative and genitive, § 315, *a*.

XXXI. Verbs of **granting, refusing**, and **thanking** may take a dative and genitive, § 315, *b*.

XXXII. The **genitive** may denote an object affected **in part**, § 316.

XXXIII. The genitive may denote an **object of separation**, § 317.

XXXIV. The **genitive** may denote an **object of supremacy** or use, § 318.

XXXV. The **genitive** or **instrumental** may denote the **material** of which any thing is made or full, § 319.

XXXVI. The **genitive** in combination with *adjectives* may denote **measure**, § 320.

XXXVII. The **genitive** in combination with *adjectives* may denote the **part** or **relation** in which the quality is conceived, § 321.

Adverbial Combinations.

XXXVIII. The **genitive** may denote **by what way**, § 322.

XXXIX. The **genitive** may denote **time when**, § 323.

XL. The **genitive** may denote **means, cause**, or **manner**, §§ 324, 325.

XLI. The genitive with a preposition is sometimes used to denote instrumental, ablative, or locative adverbial relations, § 326.

Prepositions.

XLII. A **preposition** governs a **substantive**, and shows its **relation** to some other word in the clause, § 327.

Adjectives.

XLIII. An **adjective** agrees with its **substantive** in *gender, number,* and *case,* § 361.

XLIV. The **weak forms** are used after the **definite article, demonstratives,** and **possessives**; and often in attributive *vocatives, instrumentals,* and *genitives.* **Comparative** forms are all weak, § 362.

Pronouns.

XLV. A **substantive pronoun** agrees with its **antecedent** in *gender, number,* and *person,* § 365.

Adverbs.

XLVI. **Adverbs** modify *verbs, adjectives,* and other *adverbs,* § 395.

Verbs.

Agreement.

XLVII. A **finite verb** agrees with its **subject** in *number* and *person,* § 401.

Voices.

XLVIII. The **active** voice is used to make the *agent* the *subject* of predication, § 408.

XLIX. The **passive** voice is used to make the direct *object* of the action the *subject* of predication, § 409.

Tenses.

L. **Principal** tenses depend on principal tenses, **historical** on historical, § 419.

Modes.

LI. The **indicative** is used in *assertions, questions,* and *assumptions* to express **simple predication,** § 420.

LII. The **subjunctive** is used to express **mere possibility, doubt,** or **wish,** § 421.

LIII. The **subjunctive** may be used by **attraction** in clauses subordinate to a subjunctive, § 422.

PRINCIPAL RULES OF SYNTAX. 141

LIV. The subjunctive may be used in a **substantive** clause expressing something *said, asked, thought, wished,* or *done,* § 423.

LV. The subjunctive may be used in **indefinite adjective** clauses, § 427.

LVI. The subjunctive may be used in **indefinite adverbial** clauses of place, § 428.

LVII. The subjunctive may be used in adverbial clauses of future or *indefinite time,* § 429.

LVIII. The subjunctive may be used in clauses of **comparison** expressing that which is *imagined* or *indefinite,* or descriptive of a *force.*

LIX. The subjunctive is used in a **protasis** when proposed as possible, the *imperfect* when assumed as *unreal,* § 431.

LX. The subjunctive may be used in a **concessive** clause, § 432.

LXI. The subjunctive is used in clauses expressing **purpose,** § 433.

LXII. The subjunctive may express a **result,** § 434.

LXIII. The **potential** expresses **power,** liberty, permission, necessity, or duty, § 435.

LXIV. The **imperative** is used in **commands,** § 444.

XLV. The infinitive is construed as a **neuter noun,** § 446.

XLVI. The **gerund** after the **copula** expresses what *must, may,* or *should* be done, § 451.

LXVII. The **gerund** is sometimes used to describe or define a **noun,** § 452.

LXVIII. The **gerund** may be used as a **final object** to express an act on the first object, § 453.

LXIX. The **gerund** is used to denote the **purpose** of motion, § 454.

LXX. The **gerund** with an **adjective** may express an act for which any thing is *ready,* or in respect to which any thing is *pleasant, unpleasant, easy, worthy,* § 454.

LXXI. A **participle** agrees with its **substantive** in *gender, number,* and *case,* § 456.

LXXII. A **participle** may govern **the case** of its verb, § 456.

INTERJECTIONS.

LXXIII. The **interjection** has the syntax of a **clause,** § 461.

CONJUNCTIONS.

LXXIV. **Co-ordinate** conjunctions connect **sentences** or **like parts** of a sentence, § 462.

LXXV. A **subordinate conjunction** connects a **subordinate clause** and the **word** with which it combines, § 467.

PART IV.

PROSODY.

496. Prosody treats of the *rhythm* of Poetry.

497. Rhythm is an orderly succession of beats of sound.

This beat is called an *ictus* or **arsis**, and the syllable on which it falls is also called the *arsis*. The alternate remission of voice, and the syllables so uttered, are called the **thesis**.

498. Feet are the elementary combinations of syllables in verse.

(*a*.) Feet are named from the order and make of their arsis and thesis. A monosyllabic *arsis* + a monosyllabic *thesis* is a *trochee*; + a dissyllabic *thesis* is a *dactyle*, etc.

Stress. In Anglo-Saxon these depend on the *accented* syllables, which are determined by the stress they would, if the passage were prose, receive to distinguish them from other syllables of the same word, or from other words in the sentence.

Accent is therefore verbal, syntactical, or rhetorical. An unemphatic dissyllable may count as two unaccented syllables, like the second part of a compound. Secondary accents may take the arsis.

1. A **tonic** is a single accented syllable + a pause.
2. A **trochee** is an accented + an unaccented syllable.
3. A **dactyle** is an accented + two unaccented syllables.
4. A **pæon** is an accented + three unaccented syllables.
5. A **pyrrhic** is two unaccented syllables; a **spondee** is two accented; an **iambus** is an unaccented + an accented; an **anapæst** is two unaccented + an accented; a **tribrach** is three unaccented; a single unaccented syllable is called an **atonic**; and unaccented syllables preliminary to the normal feet of a line are called an **anacrusis** (striking up) or *base*.

(*b*.) **Time.** The time from each ictus to the next is the same in any section. It is not always filled up with sound. More time is given to an accented than an unaccented syllable.

(*c*.) **Pitch.** The English and most other Indo-Europeans raise the pitch with the verbal accent; the Scots lower it. With the rhetorical accent the pitch varies every way.

(*d*.) **Expression.** Feet of two syllables are most conversational; those of three are more ornate; those of one syllable are emphatic, like a *thud* or the blows of a hammer. The trochee, dactyle, and pæon, in which the accented syllable precedes, have more ease, grace, and vivacity. Those feet in which the accented syllable comes last have more decision, emphasis, and strength (Crosby, § 695). The Anglo-Saxon meters are trochaic and dactylic; the English oftener iambic and anapæstic.

499. A verse is an elementary division of a poem.

It has a twofold nature; it is a series of feet, and also a series of words.

(a.) As a series of feet, it is a sing-song of regular ups and downs, such as children sometimes give in repeating rhymes.

As a series of words, each word and pause would be the same as if it were prose, as persons who do not catch the meter often read poetry.

The cantilation never is the same as the prose utterance; lines in which it should be would be prosaic.

The art of versification consists in so arranging the prose speech in the ideal framework of the line that the reader may adjust one to the other without obscuring either, and with continual happy variety.

(b.) The manner of adapting the *arsis* and *thesis* to the prose pronunciation is different in different languages. In Sanskrit, and classical Greek and Latin, the *arsis* was laid on syllables having a *long sound*, and variety was found in the play of the prose accent. In other languages, including modern Greek and Latin, the *arsis* is made to fall on *accented* syllables, and free play is given to long and short vowel sounds, and combinations of consonants. The Sanskrit and Greek varied farther from prose speech in the recitation of poetry than modern habits and ears allow. The Hindoos still repeat Sanskrit poetry in recitative.

500. Verses are named from the prevailing foot *trochaic, dactylic, iambic,* and *anapæstic,* etc.

Verses are named from the number of feet. A **monometer** is a verse of one foot; a **dimeter** of two; a **trimeter** of three; a **tetrameter** of four; a **pentameter** of five; a **hexameter** of six; a **heptameter** of seven; an **octometer** of eight.

(a.) A verse is *catalectic* when it wants a syllable, *acatalectic* when complete, *hypercatalectic* when redundant.

501. **Cæsura.**—Anglo-Saxon verses are made in two *sections* or **hemistichs.** The pause between these sections is called the **cæsura.** A *foot cæsura* is made by the cutting of a *foot* by the end of a *word.*

(a.) **Expression.** The character of versification depends much on the management of the cæsuras. When the weight of a verse precedes the cæsura, the movement has more vivacity; when it follows, more gravity.

502. **Rime.**—Rime is the rhythmical repetition of letters.

Nations who unite arsis and prose accent need to mark off their verses plainly. They do it by rime. Other nations shun rime.

1. When the riming letters begin their words, it is called **alliteration.**
2. When the accented vowels and following letters are alike, it is called **perfect rime** (= rhyme).
3. When only the consonants are alike, it is called **half rime.**
4. When the accented syllable is final, the rime is *single*; when one unaccented syllable follows, the rime is double; when two, it is *triple.*

(a.) **Line-rime** is between two words in the same section. **Final-rime** between the last words of two sections or verses.

503. **Alliteration** is the recurrence of the same initial sound in the first accented syllables of words.

1. **Consonants.**—The first initial consonant of alliterating syllables must be the same, the other consonants of a combination need not be;

Beôpulf : breme :: blǽd (B., 18) ; *Caines : cynne :: epealm* (107) ; *Cristenrâ :: Cyriacus* (El., 1069) ; *cûde :: cnıht* (B., 372) ; *funden :: frófre* (7) ; *frǽtpum : flet* (2054) ; *geong : geardum :: God* (13) ; *geôgode :: gleâpôst* (C., 221, 1) ; *grimma : gǽst* (B., 102) ; *heofenum : hlǽste* (52) ; *hǽledâ : hryre :: hpate* (2052) ; *hnitan :: hringum* (Rid., 87, 4) : *sôðlice :: speotolan* (B., 141) ; *scearp : scyld :: scâd* (288) ; *scriðende :: sceapum* (Trav., 135) ; *Scottâ :: scip* (Chr., 938) ; *þeód :: þrym* (B., 2) ; *pên : plenco :: prǽc* (338).

2. **Vowels.**—A perfect vowel alliteration demands different vowels : *isig : ûtfûs :: ǽdelınges* (B., 33) ;—sometimes the same vowels repeat: *eorlâ : cordan :: côper* (B., 248).

(*a.*) **sc, sp,** or **st** seldom alliterate without repeating the whole combination; but: *scyppend :: scrifen* (B., 106) ; *spere : sprengde :: sprang* (By., 137); *strǽlâ : storm :: strengum* (B., 3117).

(*b.*) Words in **ia-, iô-, iu-, Hie-,** alliterate with those in **g-**. They are mostly foreign proper names. See §§ 28, 34.

Iacobes :: gôde (Psa., lxxxvi, 1, and often) ; *Iafed : gumrincum* (C., 1552) ; *Iordane :: grêne* (C., 1921) ; *Iôbes :: God* (Met., 26, 47) ; *gôda : geâsne :: Iudas* (El., 924) ; *Iudêâ :: God* (El., 209) ; *gleâp : Gode :: Iuliana* (Jul., 131, and often) ; *gomen : geardum :: iu* (B., 2459), so frequently *iu=geô, giὀ* (formerly) and its compounds ; *Hierusolme :: God* (Ps. C., 50, 134) ; *gongad : gegnunga :: Hierusalem* (Gûth., 785) ; written *gold : Gerusalem :: Iudêâ* (C., 260, 11).

(*c.*) It is said that *þ* may alliterate with *s* by Dietrich (Haupt Zeit., x, 323, 362). No sure examples found. C., 287, 23, is a defective line.

504. A perfect Anglo-Saxon verse has three alliterating syllables, two in the first section, the other in the second.

Frum'|sceaft' | *Fir'|â`* ‖ *Feor'|ran`* | *rec'|can`* (B., 91).
the origin of men from far relate.

(*a.*) The repeated letter is called the *rıme-letter*; the one in the second couplet the *chief-letter*, the others the *sub-letters.* The **F** of *feorran* in the line above is the *chief-letter*; the **F** in *frumsceaft* and *firâ* the *sub-letters.*

(*b.*) One of the *sub-letters* is often wanting.

(*c.*) Four or more rime-letters are sometimes found.

Leânes . . Leôhte . . ‖ . . Lête . . Lange (C., 258).

In pairs : *þæt' he* | *God'e* | *pol'd,e`* ‖ *geong'|ra`* | *peorð'|an`*,
that he to God would a vassal be (C., 277), where *g* and *p* both rime, and so often.

505. The Anglo-Saxons used line-rime and final-rime as an occasional grace of verse. See § 511.

506. Verse in which alliteration is essential, and other rime ornamental, is the prevailing form in Anglo-Saxon, Icelandic, Old Saxon. Specimens are found in Old High

German. Alliteration in these languages even ran into prose, and is one of the causes of the thoroughness with which the shifting of the initial consonants has affected the whole speech, § 41, B.

507. Verse with final rime, and with alliteration as an occasional grace, is the common form in English and the modern Germanic and Romanic languages. It is common in the Low-Latin verses of the Anglo-Saxon poets, and it is by many supposed to have spread from the Celtic.

COMMON NARRATIVE VERSE.

508. Beda says of rhythm: "It is a modulated composition of words, not according to the laws of meter, but adapted in the number of its syllables to the judgment of the ear, as are the verses of our vulgar poets. * * * Yet, for the most part, you may find, by a sort of chance, some rule in rhythm; but this is not from an artificial government of the syllables. It arises because the sound and the modulation lead to it. The vulgar poets effect this rustically, the skillful attain it by their skill."—Béd., 1, 57. These remarks on the native poets are doubtless applicable to their Anglo-Saxon verses as well as their Latin; and whatever general rules we may find running through these poems, we may expect to find many exceptional lines, which belong in their places only because they can be recited with a cadence somewhat like the verses around them.

509. The common narrative verse has four feet in each section.

A. 1. An arsis *falls* on every prose accent, § 15, and the last syllable of every section. But note contractions below, 7.

2. At least one arsis on a primary accent, or two on other syllables follow the chief alliterating letter, § 504.

3. An arsis *should* fall on the former of two unaccented syllables after an accented long (the vowel long or followed by two consonants), and on the latter after an accented short.

scyld'|um' bi|scer'e|de', ‖ scynd'|an' ge|ner'e|de' (Rime Song, 84).

4. An arsis *should not* fall on an unaccented proper prefix (â-, be-, ge-, etc., § 15), or proclitic monosyllables (be, se, þe, etc.), or short endings of dissyllabic particles (nefne, odde, þonne, etc.), or short tense-endings between two accented shorts in the same section.

5. An arsis *may* fall on a long, on a short between two accents (after a long frequent, after a short, less so), on the former of two unaccented shorts.

grorn' | torn' | græf'|ed', ‖ græft' | ræft' hæf'|ed' (Rime Song, 66).
spylc'e | gi' | gant' | ás' ‖ þâ' pid | God'e | punn' | on' (B., 113).
nip'|e' | niht'-|peard' ‖ nyd'|e' | sceol'|de' (C., 185, 1).
pord' purd'|i' | an'. ‖ Veól' | him' on | inn' | an' (C., 353).
burh' | tim'|bre' | de' (C., 2846). Rare with short penult of trisyllable.

B. 6. The thesis is mute or monosyllabic; but syncope, elision, synizesis, or synalœpha is often needed to reduce two syllables.

7. An anacrusis may introduce any section. It is of one syllable, rarely two, sometimes apparently three, with the same contractions as the thesis.

Lêt'on | þ(â) of er | fif'el | pæg' ‖ fâm'|i'ge | scrid'|an' (El., 237).
puld'or'|-cyn'ing es' | pord' ‖ ge)peot'an | þâ' þâ | pit'(i)gan | prý'(An.,802).
spic'ód,(e) ymb' þá | sáp'|le' ‖ þe) hir'e | âr' þâ | sien'(e) on|lâh' (C., 607).

Synizesis of -*anne*, -*lic*, -*scipe*, *þenden*, and the like. Synalœpha of *ge-*, *þe*, and the like.

 sorh' *is* | *mê*' *lô* | *secg*'|*anne*' ‖ *on*' | *sef*'*an* | *mîn*'|*um*' (B., 473).
 præłlic'*ne* | *pund*'*or*|-*madú*'|*um*' ‖ (B., 2174).
 fyrd'|-*sear*'*o* | *fús*' | *lícu*' ‖ (B., 232).
 eaht'|ô'don | eorl'|-scipe' ‖ (B., 3174).
 þes'*an* | *þend*'*en ic* | *þeald*'|*e*' ‖ (B., 1859).
 þegn'*âs* | *synd*'*on ge*|-*þþær*'|*e*' ‖ (B., 1230).
 þâr'*â þe* | *pid*' *spâ* | *mic*'|*lum*' ‖ (C., 2095).
 þæt næfre)G*rend*'|*el*' *spâ* | *fel*'|*a*' ‖ *gry*'|*râ*' *ge*|*frem*'*e* | *de*' (B., 591).

So we find *hpædere* (B., 573), dissyllabic; *hine* (B., 688), *ofer* (B., 1273), monosyllabic; and many anomalous slurs in the thesis or anacrusis.

8. The order of the feet is free, varying with the sense. In later poetry, as more particles are used, the fuller thesis grows more common.

9. The Anglo-Saxons like to end a sentence at the cæsura. So Chaucer and his French masters stop at the end of the first line of a rhyming couplet. So Milton says that "true musical delight" is to be found in having the sense "variously drawn out from one verse into another."

10. The two alliterating feet in the first section, and the corresponding pair in the second section, are chief feet. Some read all the rest as thesis.

510. Irregular sections are found with three feet, or two.

1. Sections with contracted words where the full form would complete the four feet.

 heân hûses=*heâ*'|*han*' | *hú*'|*ses*' (B., 116)
 deâdpic seûn=*deâd*'|*pic*' | *seo*'|*han*' (B., 1275).

2. Sections with three feet and a thesis:

  prym' | (*ge*)|-*frun*'|*on*' (B., 2).
  lif' | *eâc*' | (*ge*)|*sceóp*' (B., 97).

Heyne finds in Beowulf feet of this kind with *â-*, *æt-*, *be-*, *for-*, *ge-*, *of-*, *on-*, *to-*, *þurh-*. Similar sections with proclitic particles are found: *men*' | (*ne*)|*cunn*'|*on*' (B., 50); (*be*)|*ýd*'|*lâf*'|*e*' (B., 566); *Lêt*' | (*se*),*heard*'|*a*' (B., 2977); (*þe*)|*him*' | *þæt*' | *pif*' (C., 707).

3. Sections with Proper Names. Foreign Names are irregular:

  Sem' | *and*' | *Cham*' | (C., 1551), and so often.

4. Sections with two feet and a thesis:

  man' | (*ge*)'|*þeón*' (B., 25). *Loth*' | (*on*)' *fôn*' (C., 1938).

511. Rhyme is found occasionally in most Anglo-Saxon poems. A few contain rhyming passages of some length. One has been found which is plainly a Task Poem to display riming skill. All sorts of rimes are crowded together in it. It has eighty-seven verses.

LINE-RIME.

 Half-rime: *sâr*' | *and*' | *sor*'|*ge*'; ‖ *súsl*' | *þrôp*'.*ed*'|*on*',
  pain and sorrow; sulphur suffered they (C., 75).

LONG NARRATIVE VERSE.   147

Perfect-rime:
  Single: *fláh'* | *máh'* | *flít'*|*ed'*, ‖ *flán'* | *mán'* | *hpít'*|*ed'*,   [62].
           foul   fiend fighteth,   darts the devil whetteth (Rime-song,
           gâst'|*á'* | *peard'*|*um'*. ‖ *Hæfd'*|*on'* | *gleâm'* and | *dreâm'*,
                                They had   light and   joy (C.,
  Double: *frôd'*|*ne'* and | *gôd'*|*ne'* ‖ *fæd'er* | *Un'*|*pên'*|*es'*,   [12].
           wise   and   good   father of Unwen (Trav., 114).
  Triple: *fer'*|*ed*|*e'* and | *ner'e*|*de'*. ‖ *Fíf'*|*tên'*|*a'* | *stód'*—,
           (God) led   and   saved (C., 1397).

FINAL-RIME.
  Half-rime: *spâ'* | *líf'* | *spâ'* | *deâd'*, ‖ *spâ'* him | *leôf'*|*re'* | *bid'*.
           either life   or   death, as to him liefer   be (Ex.,
           37, 20; Crist., 596, and a riming passage).

Perfect-rime:
  Single: *nê'* | *forst'*|*es'* | *fnæst'*, ‖ *nê'* | *fŷr'*|*es'* *blæst'*,
           no   frost's   rage,   nor   fire's blast,
  Double: *ne*) *hægl'*|*es'* | *hryr'*|*e'*, ‖ *ne*) *hrím'*|*es'* | *dryr'*|*e'*,
           nor hail's   fall,   nor rime's   descent (Phœnix, 15,
           16; Ex., 198, 25, where see more).
  Triple: *hlûd'*|*e'* | *hlyn'e*|*de'*; ‖ *hleôd'*|*or'* | *dyn'e*|*de'*,
  (The harp) loud   sounded;   the sound   dinned (Rime-song, 28).

LONG NARRATIVE VERSE.

512. The common narrative verse is varied by occasional passages in longer verses. The alliteration and general structure of the long verse is the same as of the common; but the length of the section is six feet. Feet are oftenest added between the two alliterating syllables of the first section, and before the alliterating syllable of the second section.

  Spâ' | *cpæd'* | *snott'*|*or* on | *môd'*|*e'*, ‖
  ge) *sæt'* | *him'* | *sund'*|*or'* *æt* | *rún'*|*e'*. ‖
  Til' bid | *se'þe his* | *treôp'*|*e'* *ge*|*heald'*|*cd'*: ‖
  ne) *sceal'* | *næf're his* | *torn'* *tô* | *ryc'e*|*ne'*
  beorn' | *of his* | *breôst'*|*um'* *â*|*cŷd'*|*an'*,
  nemd'e hê | *ær' þâ* | *bót'*|*e'* | *cunn'*|*e'*,
  eorl' | *mid'* | *eln'*|*ê'* *ge*|*fremm'*|*an'*:
  pel' bid | *þam' þe him* | *âr'*|*e'* | *séc'*|*ed'*,
  frôf'|*re'* *tô* | *Fæd'*|*er'* on | *heof on*|*um'*,
  þær' | *ús'* | *eal' seô* | *fæst'nung* | *stond'*|*ed'* (Wanderer, 111+).

(*a*.) Sometimes a section of four feet is coupled with one of six:
  ge) *pinn'*|*es'* | *pid'* | *heor'â* | *pald'*|*end'* ‖ *pít'*|*e'* | *þol'*|*iad'* (C., 323).

(*b*.) Four or more alliterative letters are found oftener than in common verse. Three seldom fail. A secondary weak alliteration is sometimes found in one of the sections.

(c.) This verse is rather a variety of the Common Narrative than another kind.

513. The Common Narrative is the regular Old Germanic verse. Rules 1, 2, 3, 4, 6, 7, of § 509, are rules of that verse. In the 5th the Anglo-Saxon uses greater freedom. It also corresponds with the Old Norse *fornyrdalag*. In it Old English alliterating poems are written.

> In' a | som'er | ses'|on' ‖ whan) soft' | was' the | sonn'|e'
> I) shop'e | me' in | shroud'|es' ‖ as) I' a | shep'e | wer'|e'
> In) hab'ite | as' an | her'e|mite' ‖ un)hol'|y' of | work'|es'
> Went' | wyd'e | in' þis | world' ‖ wond'|res' tō | her'|e'.
> Ac) on' a | May' | morn'yng|e' ‖ on) Mal'|uern'e | hull'|es'
> Me' by| fel' a | fer'|ly' ‖ of) fair'|y' me | thouʒt'|e'.

Piers the Plowman, 1–6.

(a.) The *anacrusis* has a tendency to unite with the following accented syllable, and start an *iambic* or *anapæstic* movement. The change of inflection endings for prepositions and auxiliaries has also favored the same movement. In Old English it often runs through the verses. See Final perfect-rime, § 511.

Alliterative Prose.

514. Some of the Anglo-Saxon prose has a striking rhythm, and frequent alliteration, though not divided by it into verses. Some of the Homilies of Ælfric are so written (St. Cûðbert). Parts of the Chronicle have mixed line-rime and alliteration.

515. Verses with the same general form as the Anglo-Saxon continued to be written in English to the middle of the fifteenth century. Alliteration is still found as an ornament of our poetry, and the old dactylic cadence runs through all racy Anglo-Saxon English style.

So they went | up to the | Mountains | to be|hold the | gardens and | orchards,
The | vineyards and | fountains of | water; | where | also they | drank and | washed themselves,
And did | freely | eat of the | vineyards. | Now there | were on the | tops of those | Mountains,
Shepherds feeding their flocks; and they stood by the highway side.
The pilgrims therefore went to them, and leaning upon their staffs,
As is common with weary pilgrims, when they stand to talk with any by the way,
They asked, Whose Delectable Mountains are these?
And whose be the sheep, that feed upon them?—BUNYAN, *Pilgrim's Progress*.

VOCABULARY.

The letters have the following order: a, æ, b, c, d, ð, e, f, g, h, i, l, m, n, o, p, r, s, t, þ, u, p, x, y. A figure after a verb denotes its conjugation as given in the author's Grammar: (1) meaning a verb having ablaut from a root in -a-; (2) one in -i-; (3) one in -u-; (4) one in -a>ó; (5) having a contracted imperfect in -é-, -eó-; (6) having a compound imperfect in -de>-te. < or > is placed between two expressions, one of which is derived from the other, the angle pointing to the derived one; § denotes a section in the Grammar.

á, adv., aye, always, ever.
abbud, es, m., abbot.
abbudisse, an, f., abbess.
Abel, es, m., Abel.
ábeódan (3), bid.
ábítan (1), bite.
ábregdan (1), brandish.
ábúgan (3), bow.
ac, conj., but.
Acca, n, m., Acca.
ácennan (6), bear, produce.
áceorfan (1), carve, cut.
ácsian (6), ask.
ácpedan (1), speak.
ácpelan (1), die.
ácýðan (6), show.
Adam, es, m., Adam.
ádíligian (6), destroy.
ádl, e, f., sickness.
ádræfan (6), drive.
ádreógan (3), support.
ádrífan (2), drive.
ádýdan (6), kill.
áð, es, m., oath.
áfandian (6), find.
áfæstnian (6), fasten.
áfédan (6), feed.
áfellan (6, § 209), fell.
áflýman (6), drive.
áfyrran (6), remove.
ágalan (4), sing.
ágan (§ 212), own, have; ágan út, to make out.
ágeldan (1), pay.
ágen, adj., own.
ágifan (1, § 199), give.
áhebban (4), elevate.
áhsian (6), ask.
áhte<ágan.
áhýdan (6), hide.
áhurdan (6), harden.
áþilian (6), profane.
ald, adj., old.
aldor, es, n., life.
álecgan (6), lay, put.
áleófan (3), belie.
Aler, es, m., Aller.
áliecgan<æc.
áliegan (1), fail.
Alleluia, n, m., Hallelujah.
alpalda, adj., almighty.
alpealda, n, m., almighty.
álýfan (6), permit.
álýsan (6), ransom.
ámánsumian (6), excommunicate.
ámyrran (6), obstruct.
an, prep., on.
án, num., art., one, au, a, alone.
ancor, es, m., anchor.
and, conj., aud.

anda, n, m., rage, spite.
andettan (6), confess.
andgit, es, n., understanding.
andrysno (§ 88, g.), f., ceremony.
andsparian (6), answer.
andspar-u, -e, f., answer.
andsperian (6), answer.
andpeard, adj., present.
andpeardnes, se, f., presence.
andplita, n, m., countenance.
andpyrdan (6), answer.
ánfeald, adj., simple.
anfón (5, § 224), comprehend.
angel, es, m., hook.
Angelcyn, nes, n., race of Angles.
Angelþeód, e, f., nation of Angles.
Angle, plur. m. (§ 86), Angles.
ángyld, es, n., restitution.
ánhýdig, adj., constant.
Anláf, es, m., Anlaf.
ánlic, adj., peerless.
ánlipig, adj., individual.
ánmódlíce, adv., with one accord.
ánrǽd, adj., constant.
ansýn, e, f., face.
ántíd, e, f., same time.
ánunga, adv., wholly.
anpeald, es, m., power.
apostol, es, m., apostle.
apostolic, adj., apostolic.
ár, e, f., honor, favor.
ár, e, f., oar.
áræran (5), rear.
arcebisceop, es, m., archbishop.
árfæstnes, se, f., piety.
árian (6), honor.
árísan (2), arise.
Armorica, n, m.
ársmið, es, m., coppersmith.
árstæf, es, m., blessing.
árpurde, adj., venerable.
árpurðlíc, adj., venerable.
ásá<æsc.
ásceran (1), shear.
ásendan (6), scud.
ásettan (6), fasten up, throw down.
ásingan (1), sing.
ásleán (6, § 207), strike.
ásmeágan (6), contrive.
áspendan (6), expend.
ástellan (6), establish.
ástígan (2), go up, go upon.
ástreccan (6), stretch.
áspámian (6), smoulder.
átión (3), draw away.

áter-tán, es, m., poison twig.
atol, adj., direful.
ápreótan (3), become irksome.
ápýstrian (ý>í), (6), be darkened.
Augustín-us, es (§ 101), Augustine.
áuht, es, n., aught.
ápacan (4), spring.
ápeccan (6), awake.
ápeorpan (1), throw.
ápéste, adj., deserted.
ápiht, es, n., aught.
ápritan (2), write.
ápyrdan (6), injure.
áxian (6), ask.

æcer, es, m., acre.
ǽdre, adv., quickly.
Æðelbald, es, m.
Æðelberht (er=ir=ri), es, m.
ǽðelbyrn, adj., noble born.
ǽðele, adj., noble.
ǽðeling, es, m., noble, prince.
Æðelinga íge, Athelney.
Æðelfrið, es, m.
Æðelheard, es, m.
ǽðellíce, adv., nobly.
Æðelréd, es, m.
Æðelréding, es, m., son of Æthelred.
Æðelstán, es, m.
Æðelpulf, es, m.
Æðelpulfing, es, m., son of Æthelwulf.
Æðerêd, es, m.
Æðulfing=Æðelpulfing.
ǽfæst, adj., orthodox.
ǽfæstnes, se, f., religion.
ǽfen, nes, n., evening.
ǽfen-leóð, es, n., evening song.
ǽfen-ræst, e, f., evening rest.
ǽfen-tíd, e, f., eventide.
ǽfent=ǽfæst.
ǽfnan (6), accomplish.
ǽfre, adv., ever, always.
æfter, prep., after.
æftera, adj., second, next.
æfterfyligan (6), follow.
ǽg, es, plur. -eru, n., egg.
ǽgðer ... and, ǽgðer ge ... ge, both ... and.
ǽgðer, pron., either, each.
ǽghpæðer, pron., either, each.
ǽghpǽr, adv., every where.
ǽghpelc (e=i=y), pron., every.
ǽghpider, adv., in every direction.
ǽgpeard, e, f., wardenship of the sea.

L

VOCABULARY.

æht, e, f., possession, power.
æht-e, an, f.=æht.
æl, es, m., eel.
æle, pron., each, all.
ælcor, adv., otherwise.
ælde (§ 86), plur. m., men.
ælepûta, n, m., eel pout.
Ælfréd, es, m.
ælfremede, adj., foreign.
Ælfpryd, e, f., Ælfthryth.
Ælfpeard, es, m., Ælfweard.
Ælle, es, m.
ælmihtig, adj., all mighty.
ælpig=ânlîpig.
æmtig, adj., empty.
ænge, adj., narrow.
ænig, pron., any.
ænlic, adj., peerless.
ænlîce, adv., elegantly.
ænnecân.
ær, prep. adv., before, early.
ærdæg, es, m., dawn.
æren, adj., brazen.
ærend-raca, n, m., messenger.
ærest, adj., adv., first, erst.
ærmergen (e=o), es, m., dawn.
ærra, adj. comp., former.
ærþon, conj., before.
æsc, es, m., ash, spear, ship.
Æsc, es, m.
Æscpine, e, m., Æscwine.
æt, prep., at, to.
æt, es, e, m. and f., food, eating.
æt, ætoncetan.
ætberan (1), bear to.
ætberstan (1), escape.
ætcôpan (6), show.
ætforan, prep., before.
ætgædere, adv., together.
ætgeafa, n, m., food giver.
Ætla, n, m., Attila.
ætsomne, adv., together.
ætþesan (1), assist.
ætpindan (1), fly out.
ætþpan=ætcôpan.
æpelm, es, m., fountain.
æpfæst, adj.=æfæst.
æx, e, f., ax.

bâdcbîdan.
balapumcbealu.
bald, adj., stout.
bâmcbegen.
bân, es, n., bone.
bana, n, m., murderer.
bâr, es, m., boar.
barncbeornan.
bât, es, m., boat.
bæcere, e, m., baker.
bædcbiddan.
bædan (6), demand.
bæd, es, n., bath.
bælc, es, m., canopy.
bæl-egsa, n, m., prodigy of fire.
bærncbegen.
bærcberan.
bærnan (6), burn.
bærnet, es, n., burning.
be, prep., by.
Beadohild, e, f.
beado-leĩma, n, m., slaughter-flame, sword.
beadu-lâc, es, n., slaughter-play, battle.
beâg, beâh, es, m., ring, bracelet, diadem.

beâg-hroden, adj., adorned with a diadem.
bealcettan (6), utter.
beal-u, -apes, n., evil.
beâm, -es, m., beam, pillar.
beân, e, f., bean.
beard, es, m., beard.
bearm, es, m., bosom, lap.
bearn, es, n., child, son.
be-arncbe-irnan.
beâtan (5), beat.
beæftan, prep., behind.
bebeôdan (3), order.
bebod, es, n., command.
bebûgan (3), circle, extend.
bebyrgan (6), bury.
bêccbôc.
beceorian (6), murmur at.
becuman (1), come.
Léda, n, m.
bed, des, n., bed.
bedrîfan (2), drive.
beeôdecbegân.
befeallan (5), fall.
be-fôn, -féng, -fangen (5), hold.
beforan, prep., before.
befrînan (1), ask.
befyllan (6), fell, throw down.
be-gân, -côde, -gân (5), exercise.
begangan (5), practise.
begeondan, prep., beyond.
begeôtan (3), pour over.
begen, bâ, bu (§ 141), both.
beginnan (i=y), (1), begin.
begîtan (1), get.
begrînian (6), snare.
begyrdan (6), gird.
behâit, es, n., promise.
behealdan (5), hold, behold.
behéfe, adj., becoming.
behôfian (6), need.
be-irnan (1), occur.
belîfan (2), leave.
belimpan (1), pertain, belong, conduce.
belle, an, f., hell.
bén, e, f., prayers.
beniman (1), deprive.
beod, es, m., table.
beôn (§ 213), be.
beôdan (3), offer, bode.
beorg, es, m., mountain.
beorht, adj., bright.
beorhte, adv., brightly.
Beorhtric, es, m.
beorn, es, m., hero.
beornan (1), burn.
Beornpulf, es, m., Beornwulf.
beôr-þegu, e, f., beer-drinking, convivial.
Beôpulf, es, m., Beowulf.
beran (1), bear.
berîdan (2), beset.
bescîran (2), shear.
bescncan (6), sink.
bescôn (1, § 197), look.
bestelan (1), steal.
bespîcan (2), trick, catch.
bespingan (1), whip.
bet, adv., better.
betæcan (a>æ) (4), take.
betra, betst (§ 129), adj., better, best.
betpeoh, prep., among.
betpeônan, adverb, between times.
betpeônum, prep., among.

betpux, prep., among.
betýnan (6), close.
bepurfan (1, § 212), need.
bepeotian (6), care for.
bepindan (1), grasp.
bî, prep., by.
bîdan (2), bide.
biddan (1), ask.
bedrorencb.drôsan (2), bereft.
bîfian (6), tremble.
bîg=bî.
bîgang (a>o), es, m., course, worship.
bîgengere, es, m., cultivator.
bîgleofa, n, m., food.
bihrôsan (3), ruin.
bil, les, n., bil, sword.
bilepit, adj., gentle.
bilepitnes, se, f., gentleness.
bindan (1), bind.
binnan, prep., within.
biô=beô, biod=beôd.
birhtu, e, f., brightness.
bisceup, es, m., bishop.
bisceopdôm, es, m., bishopric.
bisceopstôl, es, m., bishop's seat.
bisceopsunu, a, m., bishop's son.
bismor, es, n., contempt.
bismerpord, es, n., abusive word.
bistandan (4), stand by.
bîspel, les, n., fable.
bîtan (2), bite.
biter, adj., bitter.
bîpaunecbîpâpan (5), blow.
blâpan (5), blow.
blæc, adj., black.
blendian (6), blind.
blîcan (2), shine.
blîðe, adj., blithe.
blîð-heort, adj., blithe-hearted.
blîð-môd, adj., blithe-minded.
blis, se, f., bliss.
blissigan (6), rejoice.
blôd, es, n., blood.
blonden-feax, es, n., gray head.
blôstma, n, m., flower.
bôc, bêc, f., book.
bôcere, s, m., book-man, scholar.
Bôclæden, adj., Roman.
bôclic, adj., scholarly.
bodian (6), preach.
bodung, e, f., preaching.
bôg, es, m., leg.
bolca, n, m., gangway.
bold-agend, adj., householder.
bolster, es, m., bolster.
bord, es, n., shield.
bord-hreôða, n, m., shield.
burg-sorg, e, f., borrow-sorrow.
bôsm, es, f., bosom.
bôt, e, f., expiation.
botm, es, m., bottom.
brâd, adj., broad.
brædan (6), spread.
brædan (6), roast.
breahtm, es, m., noise.
brecan (1), break.
bredan (1), braid.
brengan, brohte (6), bring.
breôst, es, n., breast.
brid, des, m., young bird.
bridel-þþang, es, m., bridle-thong.

VOCABULARY. 151

brim, es, u., tide, sea.
brim-clif, es, n., sea-cliff.
brod, es, n., broth.
bróŏor, bréder (§ 87), brother.
bróga, n, m., terror.
bront, adj., high.
brúcan (3), use, feel, have.
brún, adj., brown.
Brutus (§ 101), m.
brycgian (6), bridge.
brýd, e, f., bride.
bryhtm, es, m., glance.
Brytene, f., Britannia.
Brytenland, es, n., Britain.
Brytenpealda, n, m., sovereign of Britain.
brytta, n, m., distributor.
Bryttas, plur. m., *cúthe,* Britons.
Bryttisc, adj., British.
Brytpealdas, plur. n., British.
bu < *begen.*
bufon, adv., above.
búan (3), inhabit.
búgan (3), turn.
búgian (6), inhabit.
búa-e, -, f., goblet.
búr, es, n., chamber, bower.
burg, burh, e, f., city.
burgpare, plur. m., citizens.
burh-hlid, es, n., slope from a citadel.
bútan (on), prep., without.
bútan (on), conj., unless.
butere, an, f., butter.
butergepeor, es, n., butter-churning.
buterie, es, m., bottle.
bycgan (6), buy.
bydel, es, m., preacher.
bylígu, plur. f., bellows.
bým-e, -an, f., trumpet.
byrgan (6), taste.
byrgan (6), bury.
byrgels, es, m., sepulcher.
byrig < *burg.*
Byrin-us, es, m.
byrnan (6), burn.
byrn-e, -, f., coat of mail.
byrn-piga, n, m., mailed warrior.
bysen, e, f., example.
bysgian (6), occupy, busy.

Cain, es, m.
calend, es, m., month.
can < *cunnan.*
Cantpare, plur. m. (§ 86), people of Kent.
Cantparebyrig, e, f., Canterbury.
capitol-mæss-e, an, f., first mass.
carcern, es, n., prison.
Carl, es, m., Charles.
carleás, adj., careless.
Caron, es, m., Charon.
cáscre, s, m., cæsar, emperor.
Caton, es, m., Cato.
Cædmon, es, m.
ceác, es, m., cup.
Ceadda, n, m.; Ceadding, es, m., son of Ceadda.
Ceadpalla, n, m.
cealdian (6), grow cold.
ceáp, es, m., price, goods.
ceáp-eádig, adj., rich.

ceás < *ceósan.*
ceaster, e, f., city.
ceaster-gepar-e, an, f., citizen.
ceasterpare, plur. m. (§ 86), citizen.
Ceáplin, es, m.; Ceáplining, es, m., son of Ceawlin.
Céft, ind. m.
cempa, n, m., soldier.
Cénbryht, es, m.; Cénbryhting, es, m., son of Cenbryht.
céne, adj., bold.
Cénferd, es, m.; Cénferding, es, m., son of Cenferth.
Cénfús, es, m.; Cénfúsing, son of Cenfus.
Cent, ind. f., Kent.
Centland, es, n., Kent.
Centpine, s, m.
cénpealh, es, m.
ceól, es, m., keel, ship.
Ceólpulf, es, m.; Ceólpulfing, es, m., son of Ceolwolf.
ceorl, es, m., man, husband, layman, farmer, freeman.
ceósan (3), choose.
cépeman, nes, m., merchant.
Cerber-us, -es (§ 101), m., Cerberus.
Cerdic, es, m.
cer, res, m., turn, time.
cése, s, m., cheese.
cíd, es, m., growth, shoot.
cíld, es, plur. *cild* and *cildru* (§ 82), n., child.
cíldhád, es, m., childhood.
cínbán, es, n., chin-bone.
cínberg, e, f., chin-cover.
Cippanhám, mes, m.
ciric-e, an, f., church.
cláâ, es, m., cloth, clothes.
Claudi-us, -es (§ 101), m., Claudius.
clǽne, adj., clean, pure.
cleófa, n, m., cellar.
clom, mes, me, m., f., chain, clamp.
cluistor, es, n., cloister.
clypian (6), call, cry.
clyppan (6), embrace, accept.
cnapa, n, m., boy, youth.
cníht, es, m., boy, youth.
Cnut, es, m.
cnyl, les, m., bell-stroke.
cnyssan (6), knock, beat.
coc, es, m., cook.
cólian (6), cool.
Colman, nes, m.
Columba, n, m.
com, cóm < *cuman.*
cométa, n, m., comet.
con = *can* < *cunnan.*
Corfes-geat, es, n., Corfgate.
corn, es, n., corn, grain.
crabba, n, m., crab.
cræft, es, m., craft, trade, skill.
cræftig, adj., crafty, skillful.
Crécas, plur. m., Greeks.
créda, n, m., creed.
cringan (1), cringe, fall.
crismlýsing, e, f., loosing of the fillet bound round the head at baptism, crism-loosing.
Críst, es, m., Christ.
Cristen, adj., Christian.
crystendóm, es, m., christendom.

cúd, adj., known.
Cúda, n, m.
cúthe < *cunnan.*
Cúdgils, es, m.; Cúdgilsing, es, m., son of Cuthgils.
Cúding, es, m., son of Cutha.
cúdlíc, adj., certain.
cúdlíce, adv., clearly, openly, courteously.
Cúdred, es, m.
culter, es, n., coulter.
cuman (1, § 200), come.
cumbol, es, n., signal.
cunnan, pres. *can,* imp. *cúde* (§ 212), know, am able.
cunnian (6), experience.
cpealm, es, n., death.
cpeccan (6), shake.
cpedan (1), say.
cpén, e, f., woman, wife, queen.
cpic, adj., alive.
cpide, s, m., sentence, saying.
cpiman > *cuman* (1), come.
cpybl-ráf, adj., ravenous.
cydde < *cydde* < *cydan.*
cyd, de, f., home.
cydan (6), announce.
cýle, s, m., cold.
cyme, s, m., coming.
cymlíce, adv., comely.
cyn, nes, n., kin, kind.
cyne-bearn, es, n., prince.
cyne-bót, e, f., king's blood-money.
cyne-cyn, es, n., royal race.
Cynegils, es, m.; Cynegilsing, es, m., son of Cynegils.
Cyneheard, es, m.
cyne-helm, es, m., crown.
cyne-ríce, s, n., kingdom.
Cynepulf, es, m., Cynewolf.
cyning, es, m., king.
Cynric, es, m.; Cynricing, es, m., son of Cynric.
cýpan (6), sell.
cýpeniht, es, m., youth for sale.
cýpman, nes, m., merchant.
cyric-e, -an and *-ean,* church.
cyrlisc, adj., *cyrlisc man* = *ceorl.*
cyrran (6), turn.
cýs-gerun, es, n., curd.
cyst, es, m., choice, best.

dafenian (6), become.
dǽd, e, f., deed.
dæg, es, m., day.
dægderlíc, adj., present.
dæghpamlíce, adv., daily.
dægred, es, n., dawn.
dægrédlíc, adj., matin.
dægsceald, es, m., day-shield.
dǽl, es, m., share, part.
dǽlan (6), deal, divide.
deád, adj., dead.
deád, es, m., death.
dear < *durran.*
deáppig-federe, adj., dewy-feathered.
Déda, n, m.
dégol, es, n., secret.
Dene, plur. m., Danes.
Denise, adj., Danish.
deófol, es, m., devil.
deófolgild (*i=y), es, n.,* idol, idolatry.

VOCABULARY.

deóp, adj., deep.
deópe, adv., deeply.
deóplíce, adv., deeply.
deór, es, n., beast.
Deór, es, m.
deorc, adj., dark.
deóre, adj., precious, dear.
deorfan (1), work.
Deorpent-e, -n, f., Derwent.
deórpyrde, adj., precious.
Dére, plur. m., inhabitants of Deira. Latin *de ira* means *from wrath*.
díet<dón.
díc, es, m., ditch, dike.
Diocletían-us, -es (§ 101), m., Diocletian.
dógor, es, m., day.
dógor-rím, es, n., number of days.
dóhtor (§ 87, 100), f., daughter.
dóm, es, m., doom, judgment, law, choice, power, honor.
domne, s, m., Lord.
dón, dést, déd, imp. *dyde, díde*, pp. *dón* (§ 212), do, make.
Dorceceaster, e, f., Dorchester.
Dorsǽte, plur. m., people of Dorsetshire.
dorst<durran.
draca, n, m., dragon.
dreám, es, m., harmony, joy.
dreccan (6), afflict.
drenc, es, m., drink.
dreógan (3), suffer, practise.
dreórig-hleor, adj., dreary-faced.
drífan (2), drive.
drihten (v>i), es, m., Lord.
driht-guma, n, m., nobleman.
driht-néás, plur. m., slain in battle.
drincan (1), drink.
drohtnían (6), live.
dryhten (v>i), es, m., Lord.
dryht-guma, n, m., nobleman.
dugud, e, f., mankind, man, company.
durran, dear, imp. *dorste* (§ 212), dare.
duru, e, f., door.
dynt, es, m., blow, dint.
dýre, adj., dear.
dýrne, adj., secret.
dyrstíg, adj., daring.
dyrstígnes, se, f., boldness.
dysig, adj., foolish.
dysígnes, se, f., foolishness.

ð, see *þ*.

eá, interj. with *lá*, ah! oh!
eá, f. (§ 100), river.
eác, adv. conj., also.
eácen, adj., august.
Eádberh, es, m.
Eádgár, es, m., Edgar.
eádig, adj., blessed.
eádiglíc, adj., blessed.
eádígnes, se, blessedness.
eádmódlíce, adv., humbly.
Eádmund, es, m., Edmund.
Eádréd, es, m.
Eádríc, es, m.
Eádwíg, es, m.
Eádpine, s, m., Edwin.
eáðe, adj., easy.

eáðmédu, plur. n., humility.
eág-e, -an, n., eye.
eahta, num., eight.
eahtoda, num., eighth.
eal, pron., all.
eálá, interj., ah! oh!
eáland, es, n., island.
eald, adj., old.
eald-gesegen, e, f., old saying.
eald-gestreón, es, n., old treasure.
ealdían (6), grow old.
ealdor - biscop, es, m., chief priest.
ealdor-dóm, es, m., first rank.
ealdor-man, nes, m., nobleman, senator.
ealdorscipe, s, m., first rank.
eald-riht, es, n., old custom.
Eald Seaxe, plur. m., Old Saxons.
eald-spel, les, n., old discourse.
Ealhstán, es, m.
eallunge, adv., altogether.
ealspá, adv., just as.
ealu, pes, n. (§ 81), ale.
eal-pihte, plur. f., all things.
eam=eom, am.
Eárcenbriht, es, m.
eard, es, m., earth.
eard-geard, es, m., land.
eardían (6), dwell.
eár-e, -an, n., ear.
earfoð, es, n., toil.
earfóðlíc, adj., toilsome.
earm, es, m., arm.
earm, adj., poor.
earmlíce, adv., wretchedly.
eást, adv., east.
eásta, n, m., east.
eástan, adv., from the east.
East-Angle (-Engle), plur. m., East-Angles.
Eást - Dene, plur. m., East-Danes.
Eástran, plur. f., Easter.
Eást-Seaxe, plur. m., East-Saxons.
éce, adj., eternal.
écean, écere<éce.
ecg, e, f., edge.
Ecgbriht, es, m.; *Ecgbrihting, es*, m., son of Ecgbriht.
Ecgburht, es, m.=*Ecgbriht*.
Ecgpeóp, es, m.
edor, es, m., hedge, fence.
éð, adv., easier.
Edandún, e, f.
éðel, es, m., home, country.
éðelpeard, es, m., landlord.
efne, adv., even so; interj., well.
efstan, (6), hasten.
eft, adv., after, again.
ege, s, m., fear.
egsían (6), be fearful.
ehta, num., eight.
éhtan (6), pursue.
ele, s, m., oil.
Eleutheri-us, es (§ 101), m.
ellen, es, m. n., might, heroism.
Ellendún, e, f.
ellenpeorc, es, n., mighty work.
ellenpódnes, se, f., fervor.
elles, adv., otherwise.
ende, s, m., end.

ende-byrdnes, se, f., order.
ende-dæg, es, n., last day.
ende-leán, es, n., retribution.
ende-sǽta, n, m., shore-guard.
endleofan, num., eleven.
engel, es, m., angel.
Englá-land, es, n., England.
Engle, plur. m., Angles.
Englisc, adj., English.
ent, es, m., giant.
eode, róde<gán, go.
eodor, es, m., prince.
eodorcan (6), ruminate.
eofor-líc, es, n., boar's figure.
Eóforpíc, es, n., York.
Eóforpíc - ceaster, e, f., York town.
eom (§ 213), am.
eord-búende, plur. m., dwellers on earth.
eord-e, -an, f., earth.
eord-mægen, es, n., might of earth.
eord-tílð, e, f., agriculture.
eord-peal, les, m., earth wall.
eóred, es, n., troop.
eorl, es, m., nobleman, earl, man.
eorlíc, adj., manly.
eorlscipe, s, m., nobility, manliness.
Eormanríc, es, m.
eornostlíce, adv., earnestly.
eoten, es, m., giant.
eotenísc, adj., made by giants.
eóp, eópíc, pron. plur., you.
eóper, pron. poss., your.
erceháð, es, m., archiepiscopacy.
erían (6), plough.
esne, s, m., servant, man.
etan (1), eat.
Eurídíc-e, -an, f., Eurydice.

fácen, es, n., fraud, crime.
fáge, es, n., plaice.
fáh, *fág*, adj., blent, stained.
fáh-mon, nes, m., foeman.
fáh, *fág*, adj., hostile.
fámíg-heals, adj., foamy-necked.
fand<findan.
fárð<fáh.
faran (4), go.
Faraón, es, m., Pharaoh.
faród, es, m., stream, flood.
fæc, es, n., space, time.
fæder, es (irreg., §§ 87, 100), m., father.
fǽge, adj., damned, deathlike.
fægenían (6), fawn.
fægen, adj., glad.
fæger, adj., fair.
fǽhð, e, f., feud.
fær, es, n., ship.
fǽr-bryne, s, m., fearful blaze.
fǽr-grípe, s, m., sudden gripe.
fǽrlíce, adv., suddenly.
færnes, se, f., transit, travel.
fæst, adj., fast, firm.
fǽstan (6), fast.
fæste, adv., fast, firmly.
fæsten, es, n., fasting.
fæsten, es, n., fastness.
fæsthafol, adj., tenacious.
fæsthýdíg, adj., constant.
fæstlíc, adj., firm.

VOCABULARY. 153

fæstlice, adj., firmly.
fæstnung, e, f., stability.
fæstræd, adj., constant.
fæt, es, n., vessel.
fætels, es, m., pouch.
feallan (5), fall.
fā-sceaft, adj., deserted.
feax, n., hair.
Februari-us, -es (§ 101), m., February.
fēdan (5), feed.
fēde, es, n., power to walk.
fefer-ādl, e, f., fever.
fēhst < fōn.
fel, les, n., leather.
fela, ind., many, much.
fela-hrōr, adj., very strenuous.
fela-meahtig, adj., very mighty.
feld, es, m., field.
feld-hūs, es, n., tent.
feolgan (1), enter.
Félix, es, m. (§ 101).
fen, nes, n., fen.
fēng < fōn.
feoh, feōh, feōs, n., flock, wealth.
feohtan (1), fight.
feōnd, es, m., enemy, fiend.
feōnd-grāp, e, f., foe's gripe.
feōnd-scipe, s, m., hostility.
feor, adj., far.
feor, adv., far.
feor-būend, adj., far-dwelling.
feor-cund, adj., foreign.
feorð-a, -e, -a, num., fourth.
feorh, feores, m. n., life.
feormian (5), entertain.
feorran, adv., from far.
feorrancund, adj., from far.
feor-peg, es, m., far away.
feóper, num., four.
feōpertig, num., forty.
feōpertyne, num., fourteen.
fēran (5), go.
fēr-clam, mes, m., sudden peril.
ferd, es, m. n., mind.
ferhð, es, m. n., mind, life.
ferian (6), bear.
fers, es, n., verse.
fetel-hilt, es, n., belted hilt.
fetor, e, f., fetter.
fīf, num., five.
fīfel-cyn, nes, n., race of fifels, sea-monsters.
fīfta, num., fifth.
fīftēna, num., fifteen.
fīftig, num., fifty.
findan (1), find.
finger, es, m., finger.
firās, plur. m., men.
fisc, es, m., fish.
fiscere, s, m., fisher.
fiscian (6), fish.
flā, n, f., dart.
flāh, adj., hostile.
flān-hred, adj., equipped with darts.
flax-e, -an, f., flask.
flǣsc, es, n., flesh.
flǣsc-mete, s, plur. -mettas, m., meat.
fleāh < flēogan or flēon.
fleōgan (3), fly.
flēohan, flēon (?), flee.
flet, tes, n., hall.
flītan (2), strive, fight.
flōc, es, n., flounder.

flōd, es, m., flood.
flota, n, m., ship.
flōpan (5), flow.
fōdor, es, n., fodder.
folc, es, n., folk.
folc-cpēn, e, f., people's queen.
folc-gefeoht, es, n., great battle.
folclic, adj., common.
folc-leāsung, e, f., false report.
folc-scaru, e, f., shire.
folc-stede, s, m., public place.
fold-būend, e, plur. m., inhabitants.
fold-e, -an, f., earth, land.
fold-pela, n, m., wealth.
folgian (6), follow.
fōn, fēng (6), catch, take.
for, prep., for, before.
foran, adv., aforetime.
for-bærnan (6), burn.
for-beōdan (3), forbid.
for-beran (1), bear, forbear.
for-brecan (1), break.
for-bȳgean (6), depreciate, neglect.
for-dōn (irreg., 6), undo, destroy.
forð, adv., forth, afterward; brengan, utter; fēran, die; gān, succeed; trōn, conduct.
forð-fōr, e, f., departure.
forð-heald, adj., stooping.
forð-sīð, es, m., death.
forð-peg, es, m., departure.
fore, adv., for him.
fore, prep., before.
fore-lēcen, es, n., prodigy.
fore-gangan (5), precede.
fore-gengea, n, m., forerunner.
fore-mǣre, adj., renowned.
fore-sprecen, adj., aforesaid.
foreþeard, adj., early.
for-gifan (1), give, forgive.
for-gildan (1>, ie, y, e), give, pay.
for-gyrdan (6), gird.
for-gytol, adj., forgetful.
for-hæfednes, se, f., abstinence.
for-helan (1), conceal.
for-hergian (6), harry.
for-hogian (6), despise.
for-hōhnes, se, f., contempt.
forhtful, adj., timid.
for-hpon, adv., why.
for-lǣtan (5), leave, neglect, permit, lose.
for-leōsan (3), destroy, lose.
for-lidenes, se, f., wreck.
forma, num., first.
for-niman (1), take away.
for - scrīfan (2), proscribe, doom.
for-scōn (1), despise.
for-slēan (1), break.
for-spannan (5), seduce.
forst, es, m., frost.
for-standan (4), withstand.
for-speigan (1), devour.
for-þam, -pan, -þrm, -þon, -þȳ, because, for, therefore, wherefore.
for-pel, adv., very.
for-purdan (1), perish.
for-precan (1), drive.
for-pyrcan (6), obstruct.
fōt, es (§ 84), m., foot.
fracod, adj., mean.

fram, prep., from.
Francan, plur. m. (§ 101), Franks.
Franc-land, es, n., France.
frætpan (6), adorn.
frætpe, plur. f., ornaments.
freā, n, m., lord.
freca, n, m., wolf (hero).
frēcne, adv., boldly.
frecnes, se, f., danger.
fremde, adj., foreign, strange.
fremian (6), aid, profit, exercise, perpetrate.
fremman (6) = fremian.
fremsumnes, se, f., kindness.
Franciscan, plur. m., French.
freō, adj., free.
freōlic, adj., free, noble.
freōlice, adv., freely, nobly.
freōn (6), love.
freōnd, es, m., friend.
freōndscipe, s, m., friendship.
freōsan (3), freeze.
freum < freō.
frið, es, m. n., peace, protection.
frigman, nes, m., freeman.
Frig, e, f., goddess of love.
frignan (1), ask.
frōd, adj., wise.
frōfor, e, f., solace, aid.
from = fram, prep.
fruma, n, m., beginning, maker, king.
frum-cyn, es, n., stock.
frum - sceaft, e, f., creation, birth.
frymð, es, e, m. f., beginning.
frȳnd = freōnd.
frȳsan = Frȳsan, adj., Frisian(?).
Frȳsisc, adj., Friesic.
fugol, es, m., bird.
fugelere, s, m., fowler.
fuhton < feohtan.
ful, les, n., goblet.
ful, adj., full.
ful-fremman (6), perform.
fulgon < felgan.
fullice, adv., fully.
fulluht = fulpiht.
ful-neāh, adv., nearly, almost.
fultum, es, m., he'p.
fultumian (6), help.
fulpiht, es, m., baptism.
funden < findan.
furdon, adv., just, moreover.
furdor (o > u), adv., further.
furdra, adj., greater.
fūs, adj., prompt, ready.
fūslic, adj., ready
fyl, les, m., slaughter.
fyligean, fylgean (6), follow.
fyllan (6), fill.
fylstan (6), aid.
fȳr, es, n., fire.
fyr, adv., far.
fyrd, e, f., army, expedition.
fyrd-getrum, es, n., battle array.
fyrd-hrægl, es, n., coat of mail.
fyrdian (6), make a campaign.
fyrd-searu, pes, n., equipment.
fyren, e, f., crime.
fȳren, adj., fiery.
fȳr-heard, adj., hardened with fire.
fyrhtan (6), conjure.

VOCABULARY.

fyrhto, e, f., fright.
fyrlen, adj., remote.
fȳr-leoht, es, n., firelight.
fyrmest, adj., first.
fyrn-gepin, nes, n., old fight.
fȳr-spearca, n, m., spark.
fyrst, es, m., time, due time.
fyrpit (i, e, y), es, n., curiosity.
fyrpet-georn, adj., inquisitive.
fȳsl, e, f., flat.

gaderian (6), gather.
gaderung, e, f., gathering.
gadīsen, es, n., gudiron.
gagol, es, n., tribute, rent.
gafol-gelda, n, m., rent-payer.
Gai-us, -es, m., Caius.
galdor, es, n., incantation.
Galpalās, plur. m., people of Gaul; France, § 101.
gamenian (6), game, pun.
gamol, adj., old.
gān (§ 208), imp. *cōde,* p. p. *ge-gān,* go.
gangan (5), go.
gang-dæg, es, m., Rogation day. Three days before Ascension were so called from processions.
gār, es, m., dart, spear.
Gār-Dene, plur. m., Danes of the Spear.
gār-secg, es, m., ocean.
gāst (ā > ǣ), es, m., ghost, spirit.
gærs, es, n., grass.
gæst, es, m., guest.
gæstliċ, adj., hospitable.
ge, conj., and; both .. and.
gē, see *þū,* ve.
gea, particle, yea.
geaf < gifan.
ge-āhnian (6), appropriate.
ge-āhsian (6), inquire out.
geald < gildan.
gealdor-cræft, es, m., incantation.
ge-andettan (6), confess.
ge-andpyrdan (6), answer.
geāp, adj., vast.
gēar, es, n., year.
geara, adv., carefully.
gearcian (6), prepare.
geard, es, m., yard, home.
gearu (o), wes, adj., ready.
gearoliċe, adv., clearly.
gearpian (6), prepare.
ge-ārpurdian (6), respect.
ge-āscian (6) = ge-āhsian.
geat, es, n., gate.
Geāt, es, m.
Geātās, plur. m., Goths.
geatoliċ, adj., ornate.
geat-peard, es, m., gate-keeper.
ge-ærnan (6), run to, reach.
ge-bannan (5), order.
ge-bæhan (5), attain.
ge-bǣru, e, f., action, means.
ge-bed, es, n., prayer.
ge-bēodan (3), bid.
ge-beorhliċ, adj., safe.
ge-beorscipe, s, m., beer-drinking.
ge-bētan (6), pay.
ge-began (i < y) (6), buy.
ge-bīdan (2), bide.
ge-biddan (1), pray.

ge-bīgan (i < y) (6), convert.
ge-bindan (1), bind.
ge-bīmung, e, f., example.
ge-blōdgian (6), bloody.
ge-bōcian (6), enroll, give.
ge-bohte < ge-byegan.
ge-bregdan (1), brandish.
ge-brengan (6), greet.
ge-bringan (1), bring.
ge-brōðor, irreg., § 87, brothers.
ge-brosnian (6), break.
ge-būan (6), frequent.
ge-būr, es, n., cottage.
ge-byre, s, m., occasion.
ge-bycgan (6), buy.
ge-cēlnes, se, f., refreshment.
ge-cēosan, -cēas, -curon, -coren (3), choose.
ge-cīdan (2), quarrel.
ge-ċīgan (6), call.
ge-cwordlǣcan (6), study.
ge-cringan (1), fall.
ge-cpedan (1), say.
ge-cpylman (6), kill.
ge-cȳdan (6), proclaim, make known.
ge-ċīgan (6), call.
ge-cynd, es, n., kind, nature.
ge-cyrran (6), turn.
ge-cyrredṇys, se, f., conversion.
ge-dafenian (6), become, fit.
ge-dǣlan (6), part.
ge-dēfe, adj., fit.
ge-dēman (6), judge, arrange.
ge-deorf, es, n., work.
ge-deorfan (1), work.
ge-dōn (6), do.
ge-dreccan (6) afflict.
ge-driht, e, f., throng.
ge-drȳme, adj., joyous.
ge-drymer, es, n., conjuration.
ge-dyrnan (6), conceal.
ge-earnian (6), earn, merit.
ge-fenlǣcan (6), imitate.
ge-endian (6), end.
ge-endung, e, f., death.
ge-eode < ge-gān.
ge-faran (4), depart, die.
ge-fægen, adj., glad.
ge-fæstnian (6), fasten.
ge-feohan, f. on (1), rejoice.
ge-feoht, es, n., fight.
ge-feohtan (1), fight.
ge-f-ōwle < ge-feohan.
ge-fēra, n, m., companion.
ge-fēran (6), go, reach, become.
ge-fērscipe, s, m., society.
ge-fexōd, adj., provided with head of hair.
ge-flit, es, n., contention.
ge-flitfulliċ, adj., contentious.
ge-flyman (6), rout.
ge-fōn, -fēng, -fangen (5), catch, take.
ge-fræteppian (6), adorn.
ge-frætpian (6), adorn.
ge-fremian (6), make, do.
ge-fremman (6), make, do.
ge-frēōn (6), free.
ge-frignan (1), ask, learn.
ge-frīnan (1), ask, hear of.
ge-fullian (6), baptize.
ge-fultumian (6), help.
ge-fylcan (6), collect.
ge-fyllan (6), fill, fulfill.
ge-fyrn, adv., formerly.
ge-fȳsan (6), hasten.

ge-gaderung, e, f., gathering.
ge-gān (see *gān*), go, travel, attain.
ge-gearpian (6), prepare.
ge-giengan, -glengde, -glencde (6), adorn.
gegnum, adv., in the way.
ge-grētan (6), greet.
ge-grīpan (2), gripe.
ge-gyrpan (6), prepare.
ge-hālgian (6), hallow.
ge-hātan (5), name, promise.
gehāt-land, es, n., promised land.
ge-hæftan (6), catch, bind.
ge-hēgan (6), afflict.
ge-hǣlan (6), heal, save.
ge-harp, adj., suitable.
ge-healdan (5), hold, keep, control.
ge-hēran (6), hear.
ge-herian (6), praise, laud.
ge-hērnes, se, f., hearing.
ge-hrēōtan (3), obtain.
ge-hnīġan (2), be humbled.
ge-hreōstan (3), load, adorn.
ge-hpā, pron., each, whoever.
ge-hpæder, pron., either.
ge-hpǣr, every where.
ge-hpelc (e, i, y), pron., each.
ge-hpyrfan (6), convert.
ge-hȳdan (6), hide, bury.
ge-hȳran (6), hear.
ge-ladian (6), invite.
ge-ladung, e, f., church.
ge-læccan (6), catch.
ge-lǣdan (6), lead, bring.
ge-læran (6), teach.
ge-læred, adj., learned.
ge-lǣstan (6), follow, stand by.
ge-lǣte, as > an, f., meeting.
ge-lēafa, n, m., belief.
ge-lēafful, adj., faithful.
ge-lēnan (6), endow.
ge-leornian (6), learn.
ge-liċ, adj., like.
ge-lica, n, m., like.
ge-liċe, adv., like.
ge-līcian (6), please.
ge-lēhtan (6), approach.
ge-limpan (1), happen.
ge-limpliċ, adj., convenient.
ge-lomp = gelamp < gelimpan.
gelustfullian (6), delight.
ge-lustfulliċe, adv., earnestly.
ge-lȳfan (6), believe, trust.
ge-lyffed, adj., infirm.
ge-man < gemunan.
ge-mǣran (6), celebrate.
ge-mǣre, s, n., boundary.
ge-mearcian (6), mark, plan.
ge-mēde, s, n., consent.
ge-met, es, n., manner.
ge-mētan (6), meet.
ge-metliċe, adv., moderately.
gemon < gemunan.
ge-mong, -mang, es, n., crowd; on *gemong* (§ 341), amongst.
ge-munan (irreg., § 212), pres. -*man,* -*mon,* -*munon,* imp. -*munde,* remember.
ge-mund-byrdan (6), protect.
ge-mynd, e, es. f. n., memory.
ge-myndig, adj., mindful.
ge-myngian (6), remember.
ge-myntan (6), intend.
ge-nam < geniman.

VOCABULARY. 155

ge-nǽgan (6), supply.
ge-nǽglan (6), nail.
ge-neádian (6), compel.
ge-neahhe, adv., enough.
ge-nemnan (6), name.
ge-nerian (6), save.
Genesis (§ 101), Genesis.
genge, adj., progressive.
ge-niman (1), take.
ge-nipian (6), renew.
ge-nýdan (6), press; *nearu-ned*, captivity.
geó, adv., of yore.
geocian (6), yoke.
geofu=gifu.
geogod, e, f., youth.
Geol, es, n., Yule, Christmas.
geómor, adj., sad.
geond, prep., through, beyond.
geond-styrian (6), move throughout.
geond-þencan (6), contemplate.
geong, adj., young.
geonglic, adj., youthful.
ge-openian (6), open.
georne, adv., carefully, cheerfully.
geornfulnes, se, f., desire.
geornlíce, adv., gladly, diligently.
gotan (5), pour.
ge-rád, adj., artful, skillful.
ge-rǽcan (6), reach.
ge-rǽdan (6), read.
ge-rǽde, s, n., trappings.
gerǽf, es, n., fate.
ge-réfa, n, m., reeve, sheriff.
ge-reccan (6), compute.
ge-record, es, n., speech.
ge-reordung, e, f., meal.
ge-resp, adj., established.
ge-rídan (2), overrun.
ge-rísan (2), suit, become.
ge-rísenlic, adj., fit.
ge-rísenlíce, adv., fitly.
Germanie, es, f., Germany.
ge-samnian (6), assemble.
ge-samnung, e, f., assembly.
ge-sápon<ge-seón.
ge-sǽd<ge-secgan.
ge-sǽlig, adj., happy.
ge-sǽlilíce, adv., happily.
ge-scád, es, n., difference.
ge-scarp-hpil, e, f., the hour of fate.
ge-sceaft, e, f., creature, fate.
ge-sceap, es, n., creation, fate.
ge-sceppan (5), create, shape.
ge-sceran (1), shear, sever.
ge-scý, es, n., covering for the feet.
ge-scyldan (6), shield.
ge-scyrpan (6), clothe, deck.
ge-sécan (6, § 209), seek.
ge-secgan (6, § 209), say, tell.
ge-sédan (6), manifest.
ge-sellan (6, § 209), pay, give.
ge-sénian (6), cross, bless.
ge-séon (1, § 199), *-seah, -sápon, -sǽgon, sepen, see*.
ge-set, es, n., seat.
ge-settan (6, §§ 188, 190), set down, set up, people.
ge-sid, des, m., comrade.
ge-sid-mǽgen, es, n., band of comrades.
ge-sígan (2), prostrate.

ge-sihd, e, f., sight.
ge-singan (1), sing.
ge-sittan (1), sit, settle on.
ge-sleán (1), slay, forge.
ge-spannan (5), fasten.
ge-spong, es, n., clasp.
ge-sprǽc-e, es, n., conversation.
ge-stadelian (6), establish.
ge-stáh<gestígan.
ge-standan, -stód (4), attack.
ge-steal, es, n., space.
ge-stéd-hors, es, n., stallion, steed.
ge-stígan (2), mount.
ge-stillan (6), cease.
ge-strangian (6), strengthen.
ge-streón, es, n., wealth.
ge-stýran (6), guide, stop.
ge-sund, adj., sound, safe.
ge-sundfullíce, adv., safely.
ge-sundrian (6), separate.
ge-swore, es, n., gloom.
ge-sweorcan (1), darken.
ge-swican (2), fail.
ge-sputelian (6), reveal.
ge-syllan (6), sell.
ge-synto, o (§ 88, *a*), success.
ge-tǽcan (6), show.
ge-tæl, es, n., series.
ge-temian (6), tame.
ge-teón, -teág, -teáh, -togen (3), draw, educate.
ge-timber, es, plur. *getimbro*, building.
ge-trúpian (6), trust.
ge-trýpe, adj., true.
ge-trymman (6), comfort.
ge-tpǽfan (6), distract.
ge-týan (6), instruct.
ge-týhtan (6), teach.
ge-þafian (6), permit.
ge-þafung, e, f., assent.
ge-þah<ge-þicgan.
ge-þeahl, e, f. n., counsel.
ge-þeahta, n, m., counselor.
ge-þeahtend, es, m., counselor.
ge-þencan (6, § 209), think.
ge-þeódan (6), join, devote.
ge-þeóde, s, n., speech.
ge-þeódnes, se, f., desire.
ge-þeófian (6), steal.
ge-þeón (3), grow.
ge-þicgan, -þeah, -þah (1), receive.
ge-þincd, es, n., dignity.
ge-þingan (1), grow.
ge-þingian (6), compound.
ge-þoht, es, m. n., thought.
ge-þolian (6), suffer.
ge-þristian (6), dare.
ge-þuht<ge-þyncan, þǽs ge-þuht, seemed.
ge-þpǽrian (6), accord.
ge-þpǽrnes, se, f., concord.
ge-þyld, e, f., patience.
ge-þyncan (6, § 211), seem.
ge-pádan (4), go.
ge-pǽde, s, n., clothes, weeds.
ge-pæterian (6), water.
ge-peald, e, es, f. n., power.
ge-pealdan (5), be strong.
ge-peaxan (5), grow.
ge-pefan (1), weave.
ge-pemmedlíce, adv., corruptly.
ge-pendan (6), turn.
ge-peorc, es, n., work.

ge-peordan (1, § 204), become, be made, happen.
ge-peordian (6), adorn.
ge-peorpan (1), pass away.
ge-pinan (i<i) (2), win.
ge-pilnian (6), wish.
ge-pinnan (1), fight.
ge-pin, nes, n., fighting.
ge-pislíce, adv., certainly.
ge-pita, n, m., witness.
ge-pitan (2), depart, go.
ge-pitenes, se, f., departure.
ge-pitnes, se, f., knowledge.
ge-pordan<ge-peordan, come to pass.
ge-porht<ge-pyrcan.
ge-prit, es, n., scripture, writing, letter.
ge-puna, n, m., custom.
ge-pundian (6), wound.
ge-punian (6), be wont.
ge-purdan=ge-peordan.
ge-pyldan (6), subdue.
ge-pyrcan(ean), -porhte (6, § 211), work, build, utter.
ge-pyrht, es, n., deed.
ge-pyrman (6), warm.
ge-ýcan (6), add.
ge-yppan (6), disclose.
ge-yrnan (y<i) (1), run to.
gid, des, n., song.
giet, adv., yet.
gif, conj., if.
gifen, geaf, gaf (1), give.
gifen, es, n., sea, flood.
gifernes, se, f., greediness.
gifre, adj., greedy.
gif-u, e, f., gift.
gigant, es, m., giant.
gilp, es, m. n., glory.
gilp-hlæden, adj., vaunt-laden.
gim, mes, m., gem.
gisel, es, m., hostage.
gist, es, m., guest.
git, adv., yet.
giu>geó, adv., of yore.
gladlíce, adv., gladly, cheerfully.
glæs, es, n., glass.
Glæstinga-burg,gen.dat.*-burge, -byrig*, f., Glastonbury.
gleáp, adj., clever.
Gledpeceaster, e, f., Gloucester.
gleáplic, adj., clever.
gleó-man, nes, m., glee-man.
gleópian (6), jest, sing.
glídan (2), glide.
gluto (Latin), glutton.
God, es, m., plur. *-as, -u*, m. n., God.
gód, adj., good.
godcund, adj., divine, godly.
godcundlíce, adv., divinely.
godcundnes, se, f., godliness.
Godmundingahám, es, m.
god-spel, les, n., Gospel, God's word.
god-spellian (6), preach.
gold, es, n., gold.
gold-fáh, adj., adorned with gold.
gold-finger, es, m., ring-finger.
gold-hroden, adj., adorned with gold.
gold-smid, es, m., goldsmith.
gombe, -an, f., tribute.
gongan=gangan, go, occur.

VOCABULARY.

Gordian-us, es (§ 101), m.
Gotan, plur. m., Goths.
grafan (4), dig, grave.
gram, adj., fiendish.
grama, n, m., devil.
grǽdig, adj., greedy.
græf, es, n., grave.
græft, es, e, m. f. n., sculpture.
græs, es, n., grass.
greát, adj., great.
Grecisc, adj., Grecian.
Gregori-us, es, e, um, m., Gregory.
Grendel, es, m.
gréne, adj., green.
grétan (6), greet, approach.
grim, adj., grim.
grið, es, n., peace.
grim-helm, es, m., masked helm.
grimman (1), fret, hasten.
grin, e, f., net.
grindel, es, m., clog.
gróf < grafan.
grorn, es, n., grief.
grópan (5), grow.
grund, es, m., ground.
grund-pyrgen, ne, f., wolf of the abyss.
gryre-sið, es, m., way of horror.
gúð, e, f., fight, war.
gúð-beorn, es, m., fighting man.
gúð-cræft, es, m., fighting force.
gúð-cyning, es, m., warrior-king.
gúð-fana, n, m., battle-flag.
gúð-fremmende, s, m., warriors.
gúð-sceáðe, s, n., war-weeds.
gúð-leoð, es, n., war-song.
gúð-mód, adj., battle-loving.
Gudrum, es, m.
gúð-searo, plur. n., equipment.
gúð-peard, es, m., general.
guma, n, m., man.
gyd = gid.
gyden, e, f., goddess.
gyddian (y < i) (6), say, sing.
gyfen < gifan.
gyld, es, n., tax.
gyldan (y < i) (1), pay.
gylt, es, m., guilt.
gyman (6), care, keep.
gym = gim.
gyrd, e, f., rod.
gyrla, n, m., clothes.
gystra, n, adj. *gystran*, adv., yesterday.
gyt = git, yet, again.

habban, hæfde (6), have.
hacod, es, m., pike.
há lian (6), consecrate.
hǽðre, adv., serenely.
hafela, n, m., head.
hafoc, es, m., hawk.
hál, adj., whole, hale.
hálettan (6), hail.
hálgian (6), sanctify.
hálig, adj., holy.
hálignes, se, f., holiness.
hál-pende, adj., sanctifying.
hám, es, dat. *hám, háme*, m., home.
Hámtónscír, e, f., Hampshire.
hand, a, f., hand.
hár, adj., hoar.

hara, n, m., hare.
Hardacnút, es, m.
Harold, es, m.
hás, adj., hoarse.
hát, adj., hot.
hátan, héht, hét, passive *hátte* (5), order, call.
hát-pende, adj., torrid.
habbe < habban.
hǽð, e, f., heath.
hǽðen, adj. and subs., heathen.
hǽðen-scipe, s, m., heathenism.
hæft-méce, s, m., hafted sword.
hægel, es, m., hail.
hæol-far-u, -e, f., hail-shower.
hǽl, e, f., hail, safety.
hǽleð, es, m., man, hero.
Hǽlend, es, m., Saviour.
hælfter, e, f., halter.
hǽlu (o) (§ 88, *g*), hail, safety.
hærfest, es, m., harvest.
hæring, es, m., herring.
hǽs, e, f., hest, order.
hǽt-u, -e, -o, f., heat.
hé, pron., he.
heado-lidend, es, m., sailor.
heado-spát, es, m., battle-sweat, blood shed in battle.
heado-pád, e, f., battle dress.
heáfod, es, m. n., head.
heáfod-burh, e, f., capital.
heáfod-man, nes, m., head-man.
heáh, heá, héh (§ 118), adj., high.
heáh, adv., high.
heáh-cyning, es, m., high king.
heáh-deór, es, n., tall deer.
heáh-fæst, adj., changeless.
heal, le, f., hall.
heal-ærn, es, n. (§ 229), hall.
healdan (5), hold.
healf, adj., half.
healf, e, f., half, part, side.
Healfdene, s, m.
heal-reced, es, n., hall.
heals, es, m., neck.
heán, adj., humble, poor.
Heánríc, es, m., Henry.
heard, adj., hard.
heardlíce, adv., stoutly.
hearg (h), *e*, plur. *á, ás*, f. m., shrine, idol.
hearm, es, m., harm, distress.
hearp-e, -an, f., harp.
hearpere, s, m., harper.
hearpian (6), harp.
hearpung, e, f., harping.
hearra, n, m., Lord.
hebban, hóf, hafen (4), heave, move.
hédern, es, n., pantry.
hefsian (6), grieve, distress.
hefon = heofon.
hege, s, m., hedge, inclosure.
héhstan < heáh.
héht < hátan.
hel, le, f., hell.
hel-dor, es, n., hell-gate.
helm, es, m., helmet, cover, protector.
Helmingás, plur. m., descendants of Helm.
hel-paran, -pare, m. pl., dwellers in Hades.
hengen, ne, f., stocks.
Hengest, es, m.
heó < hé.

Heodeningás, pl. m., descendants of Heoden.
heofon, es, m., heaven.
heofona, n, m., heaven.
heofon-beácen, nes, n., sign from heaven.
heofon-candel, e, f., heafen-candle, fiery column.
heofon-col, les, n., coal of heaven.
heofon-líc, adj., heavenly.
heofon-ríce, s, n., heaven's kingdom.
heofon-torht, adj., heavenly bright.
heofon-peard, es, m., heaven's guardian.
heold < healdan.
heolster-sceadu (o), *e*, f., lurking-holed darkness.
heolstor, es, n., lurking-place.
heonan, adv., hence.
heord, e, f., keeping.
heord-geneát, es, m., hearth-sharer.
heoro-grim, adj., fiercest (sword-grim).
heoro-pulf, es, m., warrior (sword-wolf).
Heorrenda, n, m.
heort (heorot), es, m., hart.
Heort (Heorot), es, n.
heort-e, an, f., heart.
hér, adv., here.
here, s, heriges, herges (§ 85), m., host.
here-cist, e, f., squadron.
here-fugol, es, m., army-bird.
here-gyld, es, n., army-tax.
herenes, se, f., praise.
here-reáf, es, n., spoil.
here-syéd, e, f., fortune of war.
here-toga, n, m., general, leader.
here-preát, es, m., squadron.
herges < here.
hergung, e, f., harrying.
herian (6), praise, laud.
herigendlíce, adv., so as to praise.
hét < hátan.
hí, hie < hé.
hid, e, f., hide (of land).
hider, adv., hither.
híg = híg.
híg, interj., ha!
híg, es, n., hay.
higdi-fæt, es, n., cunning bag.
hige, s, m., mind.
Hígeláe, es, m.
hild, e, f., battle.
Hild, e, f.
hilde-bil, les, n., battle-axe.
hilde-deór, adj., fierce.
hilde-pǽpen, nes, n., weapon.
hilt, es, m. n., hilt.
hind, e, f., hind.
hinder, adv., back.
hió = heó.
hí-réd, es, m., family.
hip, es, n., shape, look.
hip-cúð, adj., well known.
hládan (4), imbibe.
hláf, es, m., bread, loaf.
hláf-ǽta, n, m., domestic.
hláf-ord, es, m., lord.
hlæst, es, n., load.
hlǽp, es, m., tomb, cave.

VOCABULARY.

157

hleahtor, es, m., laughter.
hleápan (5), leap.
hleó, pes, m., cover, guardian.
hleór-ber-e, -an, f., visor.
hlifian (6), rise.
hlísa, n, m., fame.
hlúd, adj., loud.
hlutor, adj., loud, clear.
hlyn, nes, m., sound, music.
hlyt, es, m., lot.
hóciht, adj., hooked.
hof, es, n., house, court.
hogian (6), think.
hold, adj., kind, devoted.
holen, es, m., holly.
holm, es, m., billow, sea.
holm-clif, es, n., sea-cliff.
holmig, adj. *holmegum*, stormy.
homola, n, m., shaveling; i. e., fool, madman, or slave so punished for crime.
hond=hand.
hond-gemót, es, n., battle.
Honori-us, -es, m. (§ 101).
horn, es, m., horn.
horn-geáp, adj., broad between the pinnacles.
hors, es, n., horse.
Horsa, n, m.
hraðe, adv., soon, quickly.
hran, es, m., whale.
hrædlíce, adv., quickly.
hræde=hraðe.
hræfen, es, m., raven.
hrægl, es, n., clothes.
hreám, es, m., shouting.
hreáp, adj., raw.
hrefn=hræfen.
hrémig, adj., exulting.
hreó, hreóh, adj., rough.
hreópon<hrópan.
hreósan (3), rush.
hríð, e, f., snow-squall.
hrím, es, m., frost, rime.
hrinan (2), touch.
Hring - Dene, plur. m., Ring Danes.
hringed-stefna, n, m., the ring-prowed.
hring-mǽl, adj., ring-graced.
Hróðgár, es, m., Hrothgar.
hróf, es, m., roof.
hróf-sele, s, m., roofed hall.
hron-rád, e, f., whale-path, sea.
hrópan (5), cry.
Hrunting, es, m.
hruse, -an, f., earth.
hrýðig, adj., storm-beaten.
hrýman (6), shout.
hrystan (6), clink.
hú, adv., how.
húð, e, f., prey, spoil.
Humbr-e, -an, f., Humber.
Hunás, plur. m., Huns.
hund, es, m., hound.
hund, es, n., hundred.
hund-nigon-tig, es, n. num. (§§ 139, 141), ninety.
hundred, es, n., hundred.
hund-twelf-tig, es, n. num. (§§ 139, 141), twelve tens, 120.
hunig - spét, adj., sweet as honey.
hunta, n, m., hunter.
huntian (6), hunt.
huntoð, es, m., hunting.
huntung, e, f., hunting.

hús, es, n., house.
húsel, es, n., housel, eucharist.
hpá, pron. int., who.
hpanan, hpanon, adv., whence.
hpatung, e, f., divination.
hpæder, pron., whether, which.
hpæder, conj., whether.
hpæð-re, adv. conj., yet.
hpæl, es, m., whale.
hpænne, adv. conj., when.
hpær, adv. conj., where.
hpæt, adv. interj., what, why.
hpæt - hpega, -hpegu, pron., somewhat.
hpætlíce, adv., promptly.
hpearfian (6), move.
hpele=hpile.
hpeól, es, n., wheel.
hpeóp<hpópan.
hpeorfan (1), wander.
hpíl, e, f., time, while.
hpile, pron., of what kind, which, what, who, any one.
hpílum, hpilon, adv., sometimes, once.
hpistlung, e, f., whistling.
hpít, adj., white.
hpítan (6), sharpen.
Hpítern, es, n., Whitern.
hpon=hpam<hpá, somewhat, a little; *ná tó pæs hpon*, not to a little of that, not at all.
hpón=hpam?
hponan=hpanan.
hpópan (5), threaten.
hpurfe<hpeorfan
hpý, adv., why.
hpyle=hpile.
hvyrfian=hpyrfan (6), tread the earth.
hý=heó<hé.
hyegan, hogode (6, § 211), think, attend.
hýd, e, f., hide.
hyd, e, f., port.
hyge, s, m., mind.
Hygeláe, es, m.
hyge-leást, e, f., scurrility.
hyhtlíc, adj., delightful.
hýnd, e, f., humiliation.
hýran (6), hear.
hyrde, s, m., guard.
hýrsumian (6), obey.

ic, pron. I.
ídel, adj., idle, vain, void, empty, deserted.
ides, e, f., woman, queen.
Iropete, an, f., Judith.
irted<etan, eat.
íg, e, f., island.
íg-land, es, n., island.
Iotea, indec., Iley.
Il, indec., Iunn.
ilea, m. ilee, f. n., pron., same.
in, prep., in, into, on.
inbryrd?nes, se, f., inspiration, stimulation.
inca, n, m., complaint.
incund, adj., internal.
íne, s, m.
infær, es, n., entrance.
in-gang, es, m., entrance.
innan, adv. prep., within, in.
inne, adv., within.
intinca, n, m., sake, cause.
intó, prep., into.

ipeard, adj., inward, inmost.
Iotan, plur. m., Jutes.
íop=eóp, see *pú*.
íren, es, n., iron.
íren, adj., iron.
íren-bend, es, m., iron band.
irnan (1), run.
is, verb<*com.*
ísen, adj., iron.
ísene-smið, es, m., iron-smith.
ísig, adj., icy.
Israel, es, m., Israel.
itat<etan, eat.
Iuli-us, -es, -i (§ 101), m., Julius, July.
Ixion, es, m.

lá, interj., lo! oh!
lác, es, n., gift.
láð, adj., baneful, hostile.
láf, e, f., relic.
lag-u, -e, f., law.
lago-flód, es, m., flood of waters.
lagu-cræftig, adj., knowing the sea.
lagu-strǽt, e, f., sea-road.
láh<lihan.
lampreda, n, m., lamprey.
land, es, n., land.
land - búende, s, m., inhabitants.
land-fruma, n., m., prince.
land-gemyreu, plur. n., landmarks, bounds.
land-man, nes, n., inhabitant.
land-scipe, s, m., landskip.
land-sittende, s, m., landholder.
lang, adj., long.
lange, adv., long.
lang-sum, adj., long-drawn.
lár, e, f., lore, teaching, counsel, command.
láróp, es, m., teacher.
lást, es, m., footprint, track.
Laurenti-us, -es (§ 101), m.
Lavitá, plur. f., Lapithæ.
lǽdan (6), lead.
lǽfan (6), leave.
lǽgon<lícgan.
lǽne, adj., transitory.
lǽran (6), teach.
lǽresta<lǽsesta<lǽs.
lǽs, adv., less; *pý lǽs*, lest.
lǽssa, adj., § 129, less.
lǽs-u, -e, f. leasow, pasture.
lǽtan, léort, lét (6, § 208), let, order.
lǽped, adj., lay, lewd.
leáf, es, n., leaf.
leáf, e, f., leave, permission.
leáfnes-pord, es, n., leave.
leán, es, n., loan, pay.
leás, adj., destitute, devoid.
leás, adj., false, base.
leásung, e, f., lying.
lecgan (6), lay.
Leden, adj., Latin.
leðer-hosa, n, leather stocking.
Legaceaster, e, f., Chester.
lencten, es, m., spring.
Lencten-fæsten, es, n., Lent.
lenge, adj., belonging.
lengest<lang.
Leo, n, nis (Latin), m., § 101.
leód, e, f., people, men.

VOCABULARY.

leód, es, m., weregild, fine for killing a man.
leód, es, m., prince.
leód-gehyrgea, n, m., protector of the people.
leód-mægen, es, n., host.
leódon=leódum<leód.
leód-perá, pl. m., people.
leód-peród, es, n., host.
leód, es, n., lay, poem.
leód-cræft, es, m., poet's art.
leód-cræftig, adj., skilled in poetry.
leód-sang (a>o), es, m., song.
leóð-pyrht, e, f., poesy.
leóf, adj., dear; (a word of courtesy), my, sir.
leófséd, -ó te<lífían.
leógan (3), lie, falsify.
leóht, es, n., light.
leóht, adj., light.
leóht-mód, adj., light-minded.
leóma, n, m., light, splendor.
leomum<lim.
leornere, s, m., learner, scholar.
leornian (6), learn.
leornung, e, f., learning.
lét<létan.
letani-e, an, f., litany.
libban, lifde (6), live.
lic, es, n., body.
lic-etung, e, f., hypocrisy.
licgan (1), lie, wait.
lic-hama, -homa, n, m., body.
lícian (6), please.
lícumlic, adj., bodily.
lida, n, m., sailor.
liden<líðan.
lið<licgan.
lídan (5), sail.
líf, es, n., life.
lifer, e, f., liver.
lífían, leofole (6), live.
lig, es, m., flame.
liged<licgan.
lig-fýr, es, n., flame.
lig-ræc, es, m., lightning.
lim, es, n., limb.
lim, es, m., lime.
Lindesse, ind., Lindsey.
Lindisfarena-eá, f. (§ 101), Lindisfarne Island.
lind-hæbbende, pl. m., shieldbearers.
lioðo-bend, es, e, m. f., limbbonds, fetters.
Liofa, n, m.
lis, se, f., bliss, favor.
lixan (6), shine.
loc, ces, m., lock of hair.
loc, es, n., fold.
lókian (6), look.
lof, es, n., praise.
lof-sang, es, m., hymn.
lond-ryht, es, n., land title.
longad, es, m., longing.
longe, adv., long.
longsum, adj., lasting.
lopystr-e, -an, f., lobster.
losian (6), he lost, escape.
lúcan (3), lock, close.
Luci-us, -es (§ 101), m.
luf-e, -an, f., love.
lufian (6), love, favor.
luflíce, adv., dearly, for a high price.
luf-týme, adj., benevolent.

luf-u, -e, f., love.
Lunden, es, m., London.
lust, es, m., pleasure, desire.
lustlíce, adv., willingly.
lutian (6), lurk.
lyft, es, e, m. n. f., air.
lyre, s, m., loss.
lystan (6), impers., please.
lytel, adj., little.
lytig, adj., cunning.
lytling, es, m., little one.

má, indec., more.
má, adv., more.
maðelian (6), speak.
máððum, es, m., precious gift, gem.
máððum-, máððum-gifa, n, m., gem-giver.
magás<mæg.
mágon<mugan.
mag-u(o), -á, m., man.
mago-driht, e, f., crowd of youth.
mago-rinc, es, m., man.
máh, adj., base.
man, nes, men, m., man.
mán, es, n., crime.
man-cpealm, es, m., death.
man-cyn, nes, n., mankind.
mán-dæd, e, f., evil deed.
mangere, s, m., merchant.
manian (6), remind.
manig (i>e), adj., many.
manig-feald, adj., manifold.
man-slikt, e, f., manslaughter.
mán-spara, n, m., perjurer.
mára, máre, adj., greater, more.
Martin-us, -es (§ 101), m.
Marti-us, -es (-i, Latin), m., March.
max, es, n., net.
mæð, e, f., measure, age.
mæg<mugan.
mæg, es, plur. mægás, kinsman.
mæg, es, plur. mægás, kinsman.
mægð, e, f., tribe, family.
mægen, es, n., might, strength, multitude.
mægen-fultum, es, m., strong support.
mægen-ræs, es, m., strong assault.
mægen-pud-u, -á, m., strong wood, spear.
mæl, es, n., time, meal, token; *Cristes mæl,* cross.
Malcolm, es, m., Malcolm.
mær, e, f., glory.
mære, adj., clear, illustrious.
mæsling, es, n., brass.
mæsse-, -an, f., mass.
mæsse-preóst, es, m., priest.
mæst, es, m., mast.
mæst, adj., greatest, most.
mæst, adv., most.
máte, adj., weak.
mætton<metan.
mé, see ic, I, me.
meaht<mugan.
meare, e, f., mark, border.
Mearce, plur. m., Mercians, Mercia.
meare-stapa, n, m., treader of the marches.

meare-preát, es, m., border host, crossing the border.
meare-peard, es, m., watch of the border, wolf.
mearg, meares, m., horse.
med-micel (i<y), adj., not much, some.
medo-ærn, es, n., mead hall.
medo-ful, les, n., mead beaker.
méde, adj., worn, sick.
medel-pord, es, n., formal word.
mehte<meahte<mugan.
melcan (1), milk.
melda, n, m., informer.
Mellit-us, -es, m.
meltan (1), melt.
menig-u(o), -o, -e, f., crowd.
menniscc, es, n., man.
mennisenes, se, f., incarnation.
meodo-ræden, ne, f., treat of mead.
meodo-setl, es, n., mead seat.
meodu-heal, le, f., mead hall.
meole, e, f., milk.
meord, e, f., reward.
meotud, es, m. (of God), creator, fate.
Merantún, es, m., Merton.
mere, s, m., sea.
mere-liðende, s, m., sailor.
mere-spin, es, n., dolphin, porpoise.
mere-pif, es, n., woman of the sea.
met>mettum, adj., painted.
metan (1), mete, pass through.
métan (6), meet, find.
mete, s, pl. mettás, m., food, viands.
mete-þegen, es, m., table servants.
micel, adj., great, much.
miclum, adv., greatly.
mid, prep., with.
mid, adv., also.
mið, adj., mid, middle.
middan-eard, es, m., earth.
middan-eard-lic, adj., earthly.
middan-geard, es, m., earth.
mid-dæg, es, m., midday service.
Middel-Angle, plur. m., Middle Angles.
middel-finger, es, m., middle finger.
midde-niht, e, f., midnight.
miht, mihte<mugan.
miht, e, f., might, power.
mihtig, adj., mighty.
míl, e, f., mile.
mild-hórt, adj., merciful.
mil-pæd, es, m., mile path, long road.
milts, e, f., pity, mercy.
mín, pron., mine.
mis-dæd, e, f., misdeed.
mis-lic, adj., various.
mód, es, n., mind, spirit.
mód-gehygd, e, f., conjecture.
mód-gepone, es, m. n., wisdom, thought.
mód-hpæt, adj., spirited.
módig, adj., spirited.
mon<man.
móna, n, m., moon.
mon-cyn=man-cyn.

VOCABULARY. 159

mónad, móndes, m., month.
monig=manig.
monian=manian, exhort.
mór, es, m., moor, mountain.
mordor, es, n., murder.
mord-peorc, es, n., murder.
mór-fæsten, es, n., fastness in a moor.
morgen, es, m., morning.
morgen-gyf-u, -e, f., morning gift.
morgen-spéþ, es, m., morning sound.
mor ne<morgene.
mótan, móste (§ 212), may, must.
Móyses, m., Moses.
múð, es, m., mouth.
múgan, mæg, meahte, mihte (§ 212), may, can, be able.
Múl, es, m.
mund, e, f., hand.
mund-bora, n, m., protector.
mund-byrd, e, f., protection.
mund-gripe, s, m., gripe.
munt, es, m., mount.
munuc, es, m., monk.
munuc-hád, es, m., monk's condition.
murnan (6), mourn.
muscl-e, -an, f., muscle.
mycel=micel.
myne, s, m., minnow.
mynster, es, n., monastery.
myr-e, -an, f., mare.
myrgen, e, f., joy.

ná, adv., never, not.
nabban, næfde (6), have not.
naca, n, m., ship.
nador, conj., neither.
nalge=ne-dge.
næht, adv., not.
nalæs, adv., not at all.
nalles, adv., not at all.
nam<niman.
nama, n, m., name.
nán, adj. subs., no, none, nothing.
næs-u(o), e, f., nose.
nát=ne pát.
nát-hpyle, pron., I know not who, some one.
nædr-e, -an, f., adder.
næfne=nefne.
næfre, adv., never.
nænig, pron., no one, not any.
nænne=nán.
nære=ne pære.
næs=ne pæs.
næs, adv. conj., not.
ne, adv. conj., not, nor, neither.
né, adv. conj., nor.
neah, adv., enough.
neáh, adj. adv. prep., nigh.
neahl, e, f., night.
neá(h) - læcan, læhte (6), approach.
nearpe, adv., narrowly.
neát, es, n., cattle.
neá - peat, e, f. m., neighborhood.
néd, e, f., need, necessity.
nefne, conj. prep., unless, except.
néhstan<neáh.
nele<ne pille, § 212.

nellan<ne pillan (§ 212), will not.
nemde, conj. prep., unless, except.
nemnan (6), name.
neód, e, f., desire.
neód-líce, adv., eagerly.
neód-pearf, adj., needful.
neód-pearfie, adj., needful.
neodone, adv., beneath.
neom=ne eom, am not.
neósan (6), visit.
neósian (6), visit.
nergend, es, m., savior.
Nero, nes, m.
net, tes, n., net.
next<neáh.
nic=ne ic, not I.
ní-cend, adj., new born.
Nið-hád, es, m.
nid-sele, s, m.
nid-per, es, m., foe.
nigon, num., nine.
nigon-gylde, adv., nine-fold.
nigon-teóde, num., nineteenth.
niht, e, f., night.
niht-helm, es, m., night's veil.
niht-sang, es, m., night song.
niht - scú - a, - an, - pan, m., night's shade.
niht - peard, es, m., night's guard.
niman (1), take.
Ninna, n, m.
nípan (2), darken.
nís=ne is.
nípe, adj., new.
nó, adv., never, not.
nóht, f. n., nothing.
nóht=náht, not.
nolde<nellan.
noma=nama.
nón, e, f., noon, nones.
nord, adv., north.
nordan, adv., from the north.
Nordan-hymbre, pl. m., Northumbrians.
nordan-peard, adj., northward.
nord-dæl, es, m., north.
Nord - hymbre, pl. m., Northumbrians.
Nord-men, pl. m., Northmen.
nord-peg, es, m., way to the north.
Nord-pegás, pl. m., Norway.
Normandig, e, f., Normandy.
notian (6), use.
nú, adv. conj., now.
nýd, e, f., need, necessity.
nýd-gráp, e, f., resistless hand.
nýhstan<neáh.
nýmde=nemde.
nyt, adj., useful.
nytan=ne pitan, know not.
nýten, es, n., cattle.
nýtnes, se, f., use.
nytenys, se, f., ignorance, dulness.
nyt-peord, adj., useful.
nyt-pyrdnes, se, f., utility.

ó, adv., ever, any where.
óð, prep., even to.
óð pæt, óð pe, until, till this.
óð-pæt-pe, until.
odde, conj., or.
óder, pron., other, either.

óð-standan (4), stop.
óð-ýpan (6), appear.
of, prep., from, of.
of-á-lædan (6), bring from.
of-áxian (6), learn from.
of-cuman (1), come from.
ofen, es, m., oven.
ofer, prep., over, against, after, by.
ofer-brædan (6), spread over.
ofer-cuman (1), overcome.
ofer-eáca, n, m., surplus.
ofer-códe<ofer-gán, pass by.
ofer - gepeorc, es, n., upperwork.
ofer-holt, es, n., shield.
ofer-hroþs, es, m., voracity.
ofer-met, tes, n., excess, pride.
ofer-spiðan (6), overpower.
ofer-teldan (1), cover.
ofer-pintran (6), winter.
Offa, n, m.
of-lyst, adj., very eager.
of-on<of-unnan.
ófust, e, f., haste.
of-sleán (5), slay.
of-stician (6), stab, kill.
of-stingan (1), stab, kill.
oft, adv., often.
of-unnan, -úde, § 212, envy.
Olaf, es, m.
Olanig, e, f., Olney isle.
oleccan (6), soothe.
ombeht, es, m., servant.
on, prep., on, upon.
on-ælan (6), kindle.
on-bærnan (6), enkindle.
on-be-lædan (6), inflict.
on-bryrdnes, se, f., instigation, inspiration.
on-cerran (6), turn, change.
on-cunnan, -cúde, § 212, accuse.
on-drædan (5), dread, fear.
on-drysenlic, adj., fearful, reverend.
onettan (6), hasten.
on-findan (1), find.
on-fón, féng, fangen (5), receive, attain, take, find.
on-gangan (5), advance.
on-geán, prep., against.
ongeán, adv., again.
on-ginnan (1), begin.
on-gitan (í, ir, y) (1), perceive, know.
on-gitenes, se, f., knowledge.
on-hón, -héng (5), hang.
on-hyldan (6), rest, lay.
on-innan, adv., within.
on-lænan (6), loan, give.
on-líhan, -lag (2), give.
on-lúcan (3), unlock, open.
on-rídan (2), ride.
on-scúnian (6), shun.
on-secgan (6), sacrifice.
on-sendan (6), send.
on-seón, -seah, -ségon, etc. (1), see, look on.
on-slæpan (6), sleep.
on-spífan (2), sweep, swerve.
on-pacan (4), awake, is born.
on-pendan (6), change.
open, adj., open.
openlíce, adv., plainly.
ór, es, n., origin.
orene, s, pl. ða, sea-monster.
ord, es, n., beginning.

160 VOCABULARY.

ord-fruma, n, m., prince.
Ordgár, es, m.
ordian (6), aspire.
ór-eald, adj., very old.
oretta, n, m., warrior.
Orfeus (§ 101), m., Orpheus.
or-gylde, adj., without were-gild.
or-mǽte, adj., immense.
or-trýwe, adj., distrustful.
Osric, es, m.
ostre, -an, f., oyster.
Ospald, es, m., Oswald.
Ospio, m., Oswio.
oxa, n., m., ox.
oxan-hird, es, m., ox-herd.
Oxná-ford, es, m., Oxford.

pápa, n, m., pope.
pápan-hád, es, m., office of pope.
Parcas, pl. m., Parcæ, fates.
pater-noster, Latin, indec., m. n., our father, Lord's Prayer.
Paulin-us, es, m.
pællen, adj., purple.
pæl, les, m., purple cloth, pall.
Pedride, -an, f.
Pefenasæ, indec., Pevensey.
Pelagi-us, es, acc. -um, § 101.
Penda, n, m.
Peortanea, indec., Purteney.
Petr-us, -es, § 101, Peter.
Pihtás, pl. m., Picts.
Pihtisc, adj., Pictish.
pinepinel-e, -an, f., pinewin-cle.
plegian (6), play.
pliht, e, f., plight, danger.
pliht-líc, adj., dangerous.
prætig, adj., deceitful.
preóst, es, m., priest.
prim, e, f., prime, service for sunrise.
prófian (6), prove, regard.
Puclan-cyrc-e, -an, f., Puckle-church.
pund, es, n., pound.
pusa, n, m., purse.
Pyhtás, pl. m., Picts.

racent-e, -an, f., chain.
rád, e, f., raid.
rád<rídan.
rade, adv., quickly.
rand-piga, n, m., shielded war-rior.
rǽd, es, m., counsel.
rǽding-e, f., reading.
Rǽdpald, es, m.
rǽg-e, -an, f., roe.
ræst=rest.
reád, adj., red.
Reád, adj., Red.
reáf, es, n., robe, spoil.
reáf-lác, es, n., rapine.
récan, róhte (6), care.
reccan, reahte, rehte (6), reach, repeat.
reced, es, m. n., house, hall.
réde, adj., fearful, truculent.
rén, es, m., rain.
reóc, adj., fierce.
reogol-líc, adj., regular.
rest (e>x), e, f., rest.
restan (6), rest.
répet, es, n., voyage.

Rícard, es, m., Richard.
ríce, adj., rich, mighty.
ríce, s, n., kingdom.
ricene, adv., straightway.
ríclíce, adv., royally.
rídan (6), ride.
rídan (2), ride, oppress.
riht, adj., right, correct.
riht, es, n., right.
rihte, adv., rightly.
riht-líce, adv., rightly.
riht-ryne, s, m., right course.
ríman (6), count, reckon.
rínan (6), rain, wet.
rinc, es, m., man, hero.
rinnan (1), run.
rísian (6)=rísian.
Rudbeard, es, m., Robert.
ród, e, f., cross, rood.
róde-tácen, es, n., sign of the cross.
rodor, es, m., sky.
róf, adj., stout, illustrious.
rosian (6), prevail.
Róm, e, f., Rome.
Rómáná-burh, e, -byrig, f., § 101, Rome.
Rómáne, pl. m., Romans.
Rómánisc, adj., Roman.
Róme-burh, e, f., Rome.
rómigan (6), strive for, use.
rós-e, -an, f., rose.
rót, adj., gay.
rót-líce, adv., cheerfully.
rówan (6), sail, row.
rúm, adj., roomy, ample, vast.
rúm-heort, adj., great-heart-ed.
rún, e, f., secret, reflection.
rún-stæf, es, m., runic letter.
rycene=ricene.
ryht=riht.
ryne, s, m., course.

sál, es, m., rope, net.
sálum, 54, 19=sǽlum.
samod, adv., together, also.
sanct, adj., saint, holy.
sand, es, n., sand, shore.
sang, es, m., song.
sár, adj., sorry.
sárig, adj., sorry, sad.
Satan, es, m.
sáp(ol), e, f., soul.
sǽ, s, m. f., sea, lake.
sǽ-bát, es, m., sea-boat.
sæc, es, n., strife.
sǽ-coc, ces, m., cockle.
sǽd, p.p., sǽde, sǽnde<secgan.
sǽ-fæsten, es, n., fortress-sea.
sæl, es, n., hall.
sǽl, es, e, m. f., time; on sǽlum, happy, safe.
sǽ-líc, adj., maritime.
sǽlan (6), tie, bind.
sǽ-næs, ses, m., promontory.
sǽ-ríma, n, m., sea-shore.
sǽ-pud-u, -á, -es, m., ship.
scacan (4), fly, flow.
scand-líce, adv., slanderously.
scad, es, n., shade, darkness.
scær-u, -e, f., tonsure.
sceat, tes, m., seat, 1-20th of a shilling.
scead-u(o), -e, f., shade, dark-ness.
sceada, n, m., enemy.

sceaft, es, m., shaft, spear.
Sceaftes-burh, e, -byrig, f., Shaftesbury.
sceal<sculan.
sceam-u, -e, f., shame.
sceán<scínan.
scéap, es, n., sheep.
sceáp-hirde, s, m., shepherd.
scear, e, f., (plow)-share.
scearn, es, n., dung, litter.
sceat, tes, m., the seat of Mer-cia; 30,000=£120.
sceát, es, m., lap, region.
sceát<sceótan.
sceápere, s, m., spy.
sceápian (6), look at, observe.
sceáđan (6), scathe, harm.
Sceáfing, es, m., son of Seef.
sceán-e, -an, f., guard of a sword-hilt.
sceó, s, m., shoe.
sceóc<sceóc<scacan.
sceolon<sculan.
sceóp-gereorde, s, n., poetry.
sceóta, n, m., trout.
sceótan (3), shoot.
sceótend, es, m., shooter.
sceó-pyrhta, n, m., shoemaker.
sceppan, scóp, sceóp (4), shape, create, build, give (name).
Scíđía, n, f., Scythia.
scild (i<y), es, m., shield.
scilling, es, m., shilling.
scínan (2), shine.
scinom<scínum<scínan.
scip, es, n., ship.
scip-here, s, m., naval force.
scír, adj., bright.
scír, e, f., shire.
scír-man, nes, m., man of a shire.
scolde<sculan.
scóp, es, m., poet, singer.
scutian (6), shoot.
Scottás, pl. m., Scots.
Scottisc, adj., Scottish.
scríđan (2), go, travel.
scrífan (2), enjoin at confes-sion, shrive.
scród, es, n., clothing.
scrýdan (6), clothe.
scúfan (3), shove.
sculan, pres. sceal, sculon, sce-olon, scyle; imperf. sceolde, scolde, § 212, shall, will, ought, should, would.
scyld, e, f., guilt, debt.
scyld, es, m.=wild.
Scyld, es, m.
scyld-hreóđa, n, m., shield.
scyldig, adj., guilty, under pen-alty.
Scylding, es, m., descendant of Scyld.
scyld-piga, n, m., shielded war-rior.
scyndan (6), haste, flee.
scypen, e, f., stable.
scyppend, es, m., creator.
scyte-finger, es, m., shooting finger, forefinger.
se, seó, pæt (article) the; (de-monstrative) that; (relative) who, that.
scalm, es, m., psalm.

VOCABULARY. 161

sealt, es, n., salt.
sealtere, s, m., salter.
Scalpud-u, -á, m., Selwood.
seámere, s, m., tailor.
sear-u(o), -upes, -upe, n. f., armor, contrivance, art.
searo-fear-u(o),-upes,n., snares.
searo-hæbbend, es, m., one having arms.
Seax-burh, -burge, f.
Seaxan, pl. m.=Seaxe, Saxons.
sécan, sécan, sóhte (6), seek, approach.
seeg, es, m., man, hero.
secgan, sægde>sæde (6), say.
sefa, n, m., mind.
segel, es, m. n., sail.
segl-ród, e, f., sail-yard.
segen, es, m. n., sign.
sél, adj., good.
sel-cúd, adj., rare.
sebl-guma, n, m., house-man, man of low rank.
seldan (a>o), adv., seldom.
sele, s, m., hall, house.
sele-dreám, es, m., joy in hall.
sele-ful, les, n., hall goblet.
sele-rædend, es, m., hall watcher.
sele-pegn, es, m., hall servant.
self, pron., self.
self-pil, les, n., self-will.
sellan, sealde (6), give.
sel-lic, adj., sole, excellent.
semian (6), stay.
semningá, adv., suddenly.
sendan (6), send.
sénian (6), sign, cross, bless.
seó<se; seó<com.
seó, n, f., pupil (of the eye).
seóc, adj., sick.
seóðan (3), seethe, cook.
seofoða, num., seventh.
seofon (o, a), num., seven.
seofon-teóða, seventeenth.
seofon-tig, seventy.
seofon-týne, seventeen.
seolfor - smid, es, m., silversmith.
seomian=semian.
seón (1), see.
seono-ben, ne, f., wound of the sinews.
Sergi-us, -es, m.
setl, es, n., seat.
setl-gang, es, m., setting.
setl-rád, e, f., setting.
settan (6), set, put.
se-peáh, adv., nevertheless.
se-pe, whoever.
Sever-us, -es, m.
sí<eom.
sib, be, f., peace.
siccetung, e, f., sigh.
síd, adj., great.
síde, adv., far.
síd-e, -an, f., silk.
sídian, sídel for sídad (6), extend.
síd-fædmed, adj., great-bosomed.
siddan, adv. conj., afterward, after.
sígan (2), sink, go.
sige, s, m., victory.
sige-eddig, adj., blest with victory.

Sigebriht, es, m.
sige-cyning, es, m., victorious king.
sige-folc, es, n., victorious people.
sige-hréðig, adj., glorious with success.
Sigel-parðs, pl. m., Ethiopians.
Siperic, es, m.
sige-róf, adj., glorious with victory.
sige-sceorp, es, n., prize of victory.
sigor, es, m., triumph.
simle, adv., always.
sinc, es, n., treasure.
sinc-fæt, es, n., precious vessel, jewel.
sind, sindon, see eom, am.
sin-gal, adj., continual.
sin-gal-lic, adj., continual.
singan (1), sing.
sin-niht, e, f., unbroken night.
síð=seð.
sittan (1), sit.
six, num., six.
sixta, num., sixth.
sixtig, num., sixty.
six-týne, num., sixteen.
slæpan (5), sleep.
slæp-ern, es, n., dormitory.
sleán, slæd, imp. slóg, stóh, p.p. slægen (4), strike, slay.
slecge, s, m., sledge.
slege, s, m., blow.
sliт-heard, adj., terrible.
slitan (2), slit, tear.
smeágan (6), examine, reflect.
smid, es, m., smith.
smidd-e, -an, f., smithy.
smítan (2), smite.
smolte, adv., gently.
smylte, adj., gentle, pleasant.
snipan (6), snow.
snottor, adj., wise, sage.
snyttr-u(o), u(o), f., sagacity.
sód, adj., true, sure, just.
sóð, es, n., truth, justice.
sóð-fæstnes, se, f., truth.
sóð-li-ce, adv., verily, truly.
sóhte<sécan.
sól=sál.
solian (6), sólað for solað, soil.
Somersæte, pl. m., people of Somerset.
sonnod=samod.
sóna, adv., soon.
song, es, m., song.
song-craft, es, m., poet's art.
sorh, sorg, e, f., care.
sorgian (6), be anxious, be cumbered.
spearpa, n, m., sparrow.
spéd, e, f., speed, power.
spel, les, n., story, tale.
spellian (6), repeat.
spere, s, n., spear.
sprǽc, e, f., conversation, argument, discourse.
sprecan (1), speak.
spur-leðer, es, n., spur-leather.
spyrta, n, m., basket.
stæcung, e, f., stabbing.
stalian (6), steal.
stán, es, m., stone, rock.
standan, stód (4), stand, be, overhang, urge.

stán-hlid, es, n., stone slope.
stapul, es, m., post.
stæd, es, n., shore.
staf, es, m., letter, Scripture.
stær, es, n., history.
steáp, es, m., cup, mug.
steáp, adj., steep.
steare, adj., stiff, rough, severe.
stede, s, m., place.
steda, n, m., stud, steed.
stefn, es, m., prow.
stelan (1), steal.
stenc, es, m., stench.
steorra, n, m., star.
steort, es, m., tail.
stician (6), stick.
stíf, adj., stiff, firm.
stíd-frihd, adj., firm-minded.
stíd-lice, adv., severely.
stígan (2), mount.
stille, adj., still.
stille, adv., quietly.
stil-nes, se, f., stillness.
stód<standan.
stól, es, m., seat, throne.
stondan=standan.
storm, es, m., storm.
stóp, e, f., place.
strang, adj., strong.
strange, adv., strongly.
stræt, e, f., street, road.
stream, es, m., stream.
strenge, adj., strong.
strong=strang.
strong-lic, adj., firm, strong.
stunt, adj., dumb, stupid.
stýl-eeg, adj., steel-edged.
styria, n, m., sturgeon.
styrian (6), stir, play, sing.
styrman (6), storm.
súd, adv. and indec. adj.,south.
súða, n, m., south.
súdan, adv., to the south, from the south.
súdan-eástan, adv., indec. adj., lying to the southeast.
Súdan-hymbre, pl. m., Southumbrians.
súdan-peard, adj., lying to the south.
súd-healf, e, f., south half.
Súdrige, pl. m., men of Surrey.
súd-rima, n, f., south coast.
Súd - Seaxan, - Seaxe, pl. m., South Saxons.
súd-peg, es, m., south way.
sulh, es, m., plow.
sulh-scear, e, f., plowshare.
sum, pron., a certain one, some, a:—adv., with numerals, § 388.
sumer, es, m., summer.
sumur - hát, es, n., summer heat.
Sumor-sǽte, pl. m., people of Somersetshire.
sund, es, m., sea.
sundor, adv., apart.
sund-pud-u, -á, m., ship.
sunge<singan.
sunn-e, -an, f., sun.
sunne-beám, es, m., sunbeam.
sun-u, -á, m., son.
spá, adv. conj., so, as.
spác<spican.
spá-fela-spá, adv., so many as.

VOCABULARY.

spá-hpá-spá, pron., whosoever.
spá-hpæt-spá, pron., whatsoever.
spá-hpylce-spá, pron., whatsoever.
span-rád, e, f., swan road, sea.
spá-þeáh, adv., yet, however.
spæc, ces, m., taste.
spǽs, adj., kind, pleasant.
spǽsendu, pl. n., feast.
speart, adj., black, swart.
spefan (1), sleep.
spefel, es, m., sulphur.
spefen, es, n., sleep, dream.
spéd, es, m., sound.
spegel, es, n., sky, sun.
Spegen, es, m., Swain.
speging, e, f., sound.
spegle, adv., glaringly.
spéigan (6), sound.
spele=spile.
spelgere, s, m., glutton.
speltan (1), die.
spencan (6), afflict.
speng, es, m, blow.
speord, es, n., sword.
speostor, indec. f., sister.
speot, es, n., crowd.
speotol, adj., clear.
speotole, adv., clearly.
spéte, adj., sweet.
spét-nes, se, f., sweetness.
spilt, adj., strong.
spíte, adv., strongly, very; *spitóst*, most.
spidrian (6), vanish, cease.
spifan (2), sweep.
spift, adj., swift.
spiftere, s, m., slipper.
spile (*i, y, e*), pron., such, as.
spilce, adv., as if, moreover, as it were, as.
spin, es, n., swine, wild boar.
spingel, e, f., blow.
spinsung, e, f., melody.
sponcor, adj., weak, laming.
sputol=speotol.
spylce=spilce.
spynsian (6), sound (as music).
sý=sí, seó.
syddan=siddan.
sylf=self.
syllan=sellan.
syllt=sellte, wonderful.
symbel, es, n., feast, supper.
symle<sumble<symbel.
symle, adv., always.
syn, ne, f., sin.
synderlíce, adv., peculiarly, individually.
syndrig, adj., sundry.
syn-gryn, e, f., sin's evil.
synod, es, m., synod.
synt=sint<eom, am.
syrc-e, -an, f., sark, mail.

tácen, e, f., token.
tam, adj., tame.
tán, es, m., rod, lot.
Tantal-us, es, m.
Tátpine, s, m., Tatwin.
tǽcan, tǽhte (6), teach.
tela, adv., well.
tellan, tealde (6), tell, reckon.
temian (6), tame.
tempel, es, n., temple.

teóða, num., tenth; *teóde healf*, 9½, § 394.
teón, teáh, togen (3), draw, withdraw.
teón (6), make, fit out.
Teólfinga-ceaster, e, f., Southwell.
thearfe=þearfe.
thume-pord=þona-pord.
tíd, e, f., time, day, hour.
tíhd<teón, draw.
tíhting, e, f., exhortation.
til, adj., good, fit.
tílian (6), till, treat.
tíma, n, m., time.
timbran (6), build.
tin, es, n., tin.
tintreg-líc, adj., tormenting, infernal.
Títy-us, -es, m.
tó, prep., to, at, from, in, as, for.
tó, adv., too.
tó-, dis-, apart.
tó-brecan (1), break down, storm.
tód, es, pl. *tét, tóðas*, m., tooth.
tó-forun, prep., before.
tó-gædre, adv., together.
tó-geánes, prep., against.
tó-gelǽdan (6), bring to.
tó-genéðan (*é, ý*) (6), compel.
tó-geþ'ódan (6), unite.
tó-ge-ýcan, -ýhte (6), add.
torn, es, n., affliction.
tó-slítan (2), tear.
tó-þon, adv., so.
tó-peard, adj., coming.
tó-pearpan (1), cast aside, overthrow, destroy.
tó-pídre, prep., against.
tredan (1), trend, pass over.
trendel, es, m., disk.
Trenta, n, m., Trent.
treó, treóp, es, n., tree.
treóp, e, f., truth, pledge.
treóp-pyrhta, n, m., carpenter.
treppe-, -an, f., trap.
trimman (6), strengthen, are serried.
Tuda, n, m.
tún, es, m., town.
tunge, -an, f., tongue.
tún-geréfa, n, m., town officer.
tpá, num., two.
tpegen, num., twain, two.
tpelf, num., twelve.
tpelf-mónad, es, m., twelvemonth.
tpelfta, num., twelfth.
tpentig, num., twenty.
tpípa, num., twice.
tpý-bóte, adj., fined double.
týdran (6), produce.
týn, týne, num., ten.
týn-pintre, adj., ten-year-old.

þá, art., *<se*.
þá, adv. and conj., then, when.
þafian (6), like, assent to.
þáh<þihan.
þancian (6), thank.
þancung, e, f., thanks.
þanne, adv., conj., then, than, when, yet, but.
þanon, adv., thence.
þás<þes.

þáþá, adv., conj., when, since.
þænne=þanne.
þær, adv., conj., there, where, if.
þær-rihte, adv., straightway.
þær-tó, adv., besides.
þær-tó-eácan, adv., besides.
þær-pid, adv., therewith.
þæs<se.
þæs, adv., therefore, after, so; —*þæs þe*, because.
þæt<se.
þæt, conj., that, so that.
þætte, conj., that, so that, when.
þe, rel. pron., indecl., who, that, which; —with dem. or personal pron. making them relative, § 380+.
þe, conj., that, or, than.
þé<þú.
þeáh, adv., conj., though, yet.
þeáh-hpæðere, adv., conj., yet.
þeahte<þeccan.
þeahtere, s, m., counselor.
þearf, e, f., need, use.
þearf<þurfan.
þearfa, n, m., needy one.
þearle, adv., very much, hard.
þeáp, es, m., custom.
þeáp-líce, adv., mannerly.
þeccan, þeahte (6), cover.
þegen, es, m., thane, servant, soldier, knight.
þencan, þohte (6), think, ponder.
þenden, conj., while.
þengel, es, m., prince, lord.
þéniau (6), supply, attend.
þénung, e, f., use, supply.
þeód, e, f., people.
þeódan (6), serve.
þeód-cyning, es, m., people's king.
þeóden, es, m., lord.
þeóden-hold, adj., dear to the lord.
þeód-gestreón, es, people's treasure.
þeód-scipe, s, m., discipline.
þeóf, es, m., thief.
þeón, þeáh, þúgon (3), grow.
þeós<þes.
þeóstor, es, n., darkness.
þeóstr-u(o), -u(o), f., darkness.
þeóp, es, m., servant.
þeópa, n, m., servant.
þeópan (6), serve.
þeóp-dóm, es, m., service.
þeópian (6), serve.
þeópot, es, m., servitude.
þes, þeós, þis, pron., this, this one.
þicgean, þeah, þégon (1), take.
þider, adv., thither.
þíhan, þáh (2), grow.
þín, pron. adj., thine, thy.
þince<þyncan.
þing, es, n., thing.
þiossum<þes.
þis<þes.
þoden, es, m., whirlwind.
þohte<þencan.
þolian (6), suffer, lose, withstand.
þon<þam, adv., *núht þon læs*, not the less.

VOCABULARY. 163

þonc-word, es, n., thanks.
þonc<sc.
þonne=þanne.
þonon=þanon.
þonon-peard, adj., gone thence.
þrācia (Lat. indecl., § 101), Thrace.
þrag, e, f., time, state of things.
þræc-píg, es, m., fierce fight.
þræl, es, m., thrall, slave.
þreát, es, m., company, band.
þreó<þrí, num., three.
þridda, num., third.
þri-gylde, adv., threefold.
þriste, adj., bold.
þriste, adv., confidently.
þrittig, prittig, num., thirty.
þrittigoða, num., thirtieth.
þrópian (6), suffer.
þrópung, e, f., suffering.
þryð, e, f., strength, force.
þryð-pord, es, n., word of power.
þrym, mes, m., might, glory; —þrymmum, mightily.
þú, þé, gé, pron., thou, thee, ye.
þúf, es, m., standard.
þuhte<þyncan.
þúma, n, m., thumb; þúman nægl, es, m., thumb nail.
þunian (6), spread.
þunor, es, m., thunder; þunres dæg, Thursday.
þurfan, þearf, þorfte, irreg. (§ 212), need.
þurh, prep., through, by.
þurh-brúcan (3), enjoy.
þurh-fleógan (3), fly through.
þurh-stingan (1), stab through.
þurh-punian (6), continue.
þurstig, adj., thirsty.
þus, adv., thus.
þúsend, num., thousand.
þúsend-hípe, adj., of a thousand shapes.
þpang, es, m., thong.
þpitan (2), cut off.
þý, instr., <se; adv., þý lustlícor, the more cheerfully; þý læs, lest; for þý, therefore, because, since.
þýfð, e, f., theft.
þyhtig, adj. strong.
þylc, pron., the like, such.
þyle, s, m., orator, master of ceremonies.
þyncan, þuhte (6, § 211), seem.
þynne, adj., thin.
þyrel, þyrl, es, n., hole.
þyrel, adj., pierced.
þýs, þysses<þes.
þýpan=þeópan (6), drive.

údon<unnan.
úð-pita, n, m., philosopher.
ufan, adv., above.
uht-e, -an, time before light.
uht-sang, es, m., nocturn, hymn before light.
umbor, es, n., infant.
un-árímedlic, adj., uncounted.
un-bunden, adj., unbound.
unc<ic.
un-cdfscipe, s, m., inactivity.
un-clǽne, adj., unclean.
under, prep., under, among.

under-bæc, adv. prep., behind.
under-fón, -féng (5), undertake, accept.
undern, es, m., third hour, 9 o'clock.
undern-tíd, e, f., third hour.
under-standan (4), understand.
under-þeódan (6), addict, submit.
un-dyrne, adv., discovered.
un-eáðe, adv., hardly.
un-eáðelíce, adv., with difficulty.
un-foreseadpódlíc, adv., unexpectedly.
un-forht, adj., fearless.
un-gedered, adj., unharmed.
un-gefræglíce, adj., remarkably.
un-geláred, adj., untaught.
un-gelíc, adj., unlike.
un-gemetes, adv., immeasurably, very.
un-gemetlíc, adj., immeasurable.
un-gesǽld, e, f., misfortune.
un-gréne, adj., not green.
un-hǽl-u(o), -u(o), f., disaster.
un-heánlíce, adv., nobly.
un-hneáþ, adj., liberal.
un-læd, adj., poor.
unnan, an, úðe, irreg., § 212, grant.
un-nyt, adj., useless.
un-rǽd, es, m., bad counsel.
un-riht, adj., wrong.
un-rím, es, n., uncounted number.
un-scæddig, adj., innocent.
un-srennan (6), unfasten.
un-stille, adj., restless.
un-stilnes, se, f., disturbance.
un-synnig, adj., guiltless.
un-trum, adj., infirm.
un-trumnys, -trymnes, se, f., illness.
un-tyder, es, m., evil race.
un-pær, adj., unaware; on un-pær, unawares.
un-pealt, adj., steady.
up, adv., up.
up-ástignes, se, f., ascension.
up-líc, adj., heavenly.
up-rodor, es, m., heaven.
úre, pron. poss., our. See íc.
urnon<írnan.
ús, see íc.
út, adv., out.
út-ádrífan (2), drive out.
utan<putan<pitan, let us.
útan, adv., without.
úte, adv., out, without.
út-e-áde<út-gán, irreg., go out.
út-fús, adj., ready to go.
út-gang, es, m., departure.
uton=utan.
út-rǽsan (6), rush out.

pá, interj., woe, Oh.
pác, adj., weak, poor.
pacian (6), watch.
pacol-líce, adv., watchfully.
pacolre, comp. of pacol, very watchful.
pdfian (6), be astonished.
pagian (6), wag, be moved.
pá-lá-pá, interj., alas.

paldend, es, m., ruler, king.
palend<pealds.
pan<pinnan.
pand<pindan.
pang, es, m., plain.
párig, adj., soiled.
paróð, es, m., shore.
par-u, -e, f., wares, goods.
paru, pære, f., care.
pascan (4), wash.
pát<pítan.
pæcc-e, -an, f., watch.
pǽd, e, f., vestment, clothes.
pǽfels, es, m., robe.
pǽg, es, m., wave, ocean.
pǽg-holm, es, m., deep sea.
pǽl, es, n., slaughter, death.
pǽl-ceásig, adj., slaughter-choosing.
pǽl-fyll-u(o), -e, f., glut of slaughter.
pǽl-gár, es, m., death-bearing spear.
pǽl-gífre, adj., greedy for slaughter.
pǽl-hlenc-e, -an, f. (slaughter link), coat of mail.
pǽl-reóp, adj., cruel.
pǽl-sleaht, -sliht, es, m., slaughter.
pǽl-stóp, e, f., field of death.
pǽpen, es, n., weapon.
pǽre, pǽron<pesan.
pǽr-líce, adv., warily, carefully.
pǽrter, es, m., dweller.
pæs<pesan.
pæstm, es, e, m. f. n., fruit.
pæstm-bǽre, adj., fruitful.
pæter, es, n., water.
pæter-helm, es, m., (ice) water-helmet.
pæterian (6), water.
pæter-pyl, les, m., spring of water.
pé, pron. plur. of pú, we.
peá, n, m., woe.
peal, les, m., wall, mound, shore.
pealds, m. plur., (strangers) Welch, Britons.
pealdan (5), control, govern.
pealh-stód, es, m., interpreter.
pealh-peóp, -peón, m., Wealh-theow.
peallan (5), gush; spring up.
peal-steal, les, m., castle site.
peard, e, f., guard.
peard, es, m., watchman, warder.
peardian (6), inhabit.
peard<peordan.
pearm, adj., warm.
pearp<peorpan.
peaxan (4), wax, grow.
pecta, n. m., pecting, es, m., son of Wecta.
ped, es, n., pledge.
péddan (6), be mad.
peddian (6), pledge.
ped-bróðer, plur. -bróðru, § 87, pledged brother, Christian brother.
peder, es, n., weather, tempest.
peder-polcen, es, m. n., stormcloud.
pedmor, es, m., Wedmore.

VOCABULARY.

pefod, es, n., altar.
peg, es, m., way; on peg, away.
pegan (1), bear, march.
peg-ferend, es, m., wayfarer.
peg-nest, es, n., provision for a journey.
peí, interj., alas.
pel, adv., well.
péland, es, m., Weland.
pel-gehpǽr, adv., every where.
pel-hpyle, pron., each.
pelig, adj., rich.
pén, e, f., hope.
péna, n, m., hope.
pénan (6), ween, hope.
pendan (6), turn, go.
pent < pendan.
peofed = pefod.
peoh, peós, m., idol.
peóld < peallan.
peóp < pépan.
peore, es, n., work.
peord, adj., worth, esteemed.
peordan (eo, u, y); peard, purdon; purden (1), be, become.
peord-ful, adj., worshipful.
peord-georn, adj., eager for honor.
peordian (6), honor, worship, praise.
peord-mynd, es, n. f., honor.
peorpan (1), throw.
peoruld, e, f., world.
peoruld-hád, es, m., secular condition.
peóx < peaxan.
per, es, m., man.
pépan (5), weep, cry.
per-cyn, nes, n., mankind.
pered = perod.
périg, adj., weary.
per-leás, adj., unmarried.
perod, es, n., crowd, company, folks.
pesan; pæs, pǽron; ge-pesen (1), be.
pestan, adv., from the west.
péste, adj., waste.
pé ten, nes, m. n., waste.
pésten-gryre, s, m., horror of the desert.
pest-Seaxan (ea>e), -Seaxe, plur. m., West-Saxons.
pí-, es, n., dwelling, village, camp.
picce-cræft, es, m., witchcraft.
piccian (6), use witchcraft.
pic-freod-u, e, f., care of a village.
picg, es, n., horse.
pícian (6), dwell, stop.
pid, adj., wide.
píde, adv., widely, afar.
pido-bán, es, n., collar-bone.
pid, prep., against, towards, with, for.
pideriún (6), oppose.
pid-innan, adv., within.
pid-metenes, se, f.,comparison.
pid-sacan (4), renounce, forsake.
pid-standan (4), withstand.
pid-st nt < pid-standan.
pid-útan, adv., without.
pif, es, n., woman, wife.
pif-cýfd, de, f., visit to a woman.
pif-man, nes, m. f., woman.

píg, es, m., fight.
píga, n, m., fighter, warrior.
pig-bed, es, n., altar.
pigferd, es, m., Wigferth.
piht, e, f. n., wight, creature, whit.
piht, e, f., Wight.
pihtgils, es, m., Wihtgils.
piht-pare, plur. m., inhabitants of the Isle of Wight.
pi-lá, interj., alas.
pil-cuma, n, m., welcome one.
pild-deór, pildeór, es, n., wild beast.
pile < pillan.
pilfrid, es, m., Wilfrith.
pilla, n, m., wish, purpose.
pillao, pile, pille, polde, irreg., § 212, will, would.
pilhelm, es, m., William.
pilnian (5), wish.
pilsǽte, plur. m., people of Wiltshire.
pil-síd, es, m., chosen course.
piltún, es, m., Wilton.
pín, ea, n., wine.
pind, es, m., wind.
pindan (1), wind, twist.
pine, s,m., friend, beloved lord.
pine-mæg, es, m.,beloved kinsman.
pinnan (1), fight, strive.
pintanceaster, e, f., Winchester.
pinter, es, m. n., winter.
pinter-ceald, adj., cold as winter.
pinter-stund, e, f., winter hour.
pinter-tíd, e, f., winter time.
pía, n, m., leader.
pís-dóm, es, m., wisdom.
píse, -an, f., manner, way.
pi-fæst, adj., very wise.
pisian (6), direct, rule.
pis-lic, adj., wise.
pisson, piste < pitan.
pist, e, f., food, prey.
píta, n, m., wise man, senator, counsellor.
pitan; pát, piton; piste, piston, pisson, irreg., § 212, know, observe.
pitan (2), subj. piton, putan, utan, § 443, go, let us.
píte, s, n., punishment, penalty.
pítegung, e, f., prophecy.
pitig, adj., wise.
pítnian (6), punish.
pitódlíce, adv. conj., certainly, verily, but, for.
pitta, n, m.: pitting, es, m., son of Witta.
planc, adj., spirited, proud.
plítan (2), look.
plite, s, m., look, beauty.
plite-beorht, adj., beautiful.
plitig, adj., beautiful.
plone = plane.
póden, es, m., Woden.
pódening, es, m., son of Woden.
polcen, es, m. n., cloud.
polde, polden < pillan.
pom = pam, mes, m.n., spot,sin.
póma, n, m., noise.
pon, ponne (o<a), adj., dark.
pon-sǽlig, adj., unhappy.

pon-sceaft, e, f., misfortune.
póp, es, m., cry, whoop.
porc = peorc.
pord, es, n., word.
pord-hord, es, n., word-hoard.
porhte < pyrcan.
pórian (6), wander, go to waste.
porn, es, m., much, many.
porold-cræft, es, m., secular calling.
poruld = peoruld.
poruld-gesceaft, e, f., created world.
poruld-ping, es, n., thing of the world.
prád, adj., hostile, bad.
prád-líc, adj., severe.
præcca, n, m., wretch.
præc-fæc, es, n., time of misery.
præt, te, f., decoration, jewel.
precan (1), punish.
precaten-hill, adj., with a twisted hilt.
pridan (2), wreathe, bind.
pritlan (6), grow; prited for priáad for the rhyme.
prítan (2), write.
prixendlíce, adv., in turn.
puc-e, -an, f., week.
pud-u, á, m., wood, tree.
pudu-truop, es, n., tree of the forest.
pudup-e, -an, f., widow.
pudu-pésten, nes, m. n., uninhabited forest.
puldor, es, n., glory.
puldor-cyning, es, m., king of glory, God.
puldor-fæder, es, m., glorious father, God.
puldor-torht, adj., gloriously bright.
pulf, es, m., wolf.
pulf-heard, es, m., Wulfhard.
pultur, es, m., vulture.
punden-mǽl, adj., etched in curves, damaskeened.
punden-stefna, adj., having a curved prow.
pundon < piodan.
pundor, es, n., wonder.
pundor-líc, adj., wonderful.
pundrian (6), wonder, admire.
punian (6), dwell, frequent, remain.
punnon < pinnan.
punung, e, f., dwelling.
purde < peordan.
purdian = peordian.
purd-mynt = peord-mynd.
putan, utan, utan < pitan.
pylfen, adj., wolfish.
pylle, -an, f., spring.
pylm, es, m., flood, tide.
pyn, ne, f., joy, delight.
pyn-sum, adj., winsome.
pyrcan, pyrcean, porhte (6, § 211), work, make, do.
pyrd, e, f., fate.
pyrd, adj., worthy, guilty.
pyrde < peordan.
pyrhta, n, m., worker, maker.
pyrm, es, m., worm, serpent.
pyrm-fáh, adj., varicolored.
pyrm-líc, es, n., body of a serpent.

VOCABULARY. 165

pyrpan (6), turn, be refreshed.
pyss-a, -e, adj. comp., worse.
pyrt, e, f., herb, plant.
pyrt-gemang, e, f., spices, perfume.
pyrtgeorn, es, m., Wyrtgeorn.
pýscan (6), wish.

Ybernia, n, m., Ireland.
ýd, e, f., water.
ýdan (6), lay waste.
ýd-lád, e, f., watery way.
ýd-lida, n, m., ship.
yfel, adj., evil.
yfel, es, n., evil.

yfele, adv., evilly.
ylca=ilca.
yld, e, f., age.
ylde, plur. m., men.
yldest<eald.
ylding, e, f., delay.
yld-u(o), e, f., age, old age.
ylf, e, f., elf, lamia.
ylp, es, m., elephant.
ymb, prep., about, after, according to.
ymbe, prep., about, after, next.
ymb-eóde<-gán, go around.
ymb-settan (6), set around.

ymb-sittan (1), >*ymb-sittend, es*, m., neighbor.
ymb-spræce, adj., whereof people talk.
ymb-útan, adv. prep., about.
yppan (6), open, disclose.
yrpe, adj., detected.
yrdling, es, m., ploughman, farmer.
yrfe, s, n., inheritance.
yrfe-peard, es, m., inheritor.
irre, adj., wrathful.
ýtemest, adj., sup. <*út*, outmost, extreme.
ýttra, adj. comp. <*út*, outer.

APPENDIX TO VOCABULARY.

ádrincan (1), be quenched.
ágén, prep., towards.
áhafen<áhebban.
áhte, ought.
ald, age, 70, 3.
álède<áleegan, lay, remit.
áléh<álégan.
á-limpan (1), happen, come.
á-lýfan (6), be permitted.
á-myrran (6), spend.
Angel, es, m. n., Angeln.
ánsylde, adv., once.
anlicnes, se, f., likeness.
áróda, p. p. of *árian*.
á-settan (6), set on.
á-springan (1), rise.
á-styrian (6), stir.

æ, f., law.
æfæst, adj., pious.
æfter, prep., among.
æfter-genga, n, m., successor.
æ-gleáp, adj., learned in the law.
æl, e, f., awl.
ælc, any.
ær, es, n., bronze.
æt-eópan (6), appear.

be, prep., with, concerning.
beáh<bágan.
bedn-cool, des, m., husks.
be-clyppan (6), embrace.
be-eóte, beset.
be-fón (5), clothe.
be-gýman (6), take care.
be-healdan (5), take care.
behéfe, convenient.
beheonan, this side of.
bódan (3), demand.
beorgan (1), guard.
bεót, es, n., promise.
be-reáfian (6), strip.
bern, es, n., barn.
be-sceápian (6), look at.
be-seón (1), look around.
bétan (6), repair.
be-tæcan, -tæhte (6), assign.
be-pencan (6), bethink.
bi-hroren<bihreósan.
binna, n, m., bin.
bi-scerian (6), sever, free.

bi-perian (6), protect.
blác, bright, pale.
blác-mód=blid-mód.
blindnes, se, f., blindness.
blís, se, f., kindness.
blótan (5), sacrifice.
borgian (6), borrow.
brecan (1), urge.
búend, es, m., inhabitant.
bufan=bufon, above.
búgan (3), submit.
burh-hlid, es, n., mountain slopes.
burh-sittend, adj., dwelling in town.
burh-paru, e, f., city, citizens.
bútan, búton, if only, except, but.

canon, es, m., canon.
cearian (6), care.
cú, cý, f., § 86, cow.
cuma, n, m., stranger.
cpehte<peccan.
cyn, nes, n., *cynná*, gen. plur., courtesies, etiquette.
cýpan (6), keep.
cyrran (6), submit.
cyssan (6), kiss.

deór-frid, es, m., deer-park.
driht, e, f., throng, company.
dugude and geogode, old and young.
dydrung, e, f., illusion.

éac spilce, also.
éacen, adj., pregnant.
ealdor, es, m., chief.
caldor man, nes, m., governor.
eal-fela, adj., very many.
eallinga=eallunge.
ear, es, n., ear of corn.
carfod, e, f., tribulation.
ètel-peard, prince.
egesa, egsa, n, m., terror.
egeslic, adj., terrible.
ehtnes, se, f., persecution.
eln, e, f., ell.
eolet, es, m., bay.
eord-scræf, es, n., grave.

fandian (6), tempt, try.

fædm, es, m. f., expanse.
fæt, adj., fat.
feá, feápa, few.
feccan (6), fetch.
feor, prep., far from.
feorlen, adj., far.
ferd=fyrd.
ferh, es, m., swine.
findan (1), attend to.
floc-mælum, adv., in flocks.
flota, n, m., sailor, fleet.
folgad, es, m., service.
for-beódan (3), restrain.
ford-bær(u), o, e, f., creation.
forgitan (1), forget.
for-gýman (6), disobey.
for-nom<far-niman.
for-scrincan (1), wither.
for-spillan (6), waste.
for-peordan=for-purdan.
ful-fremed, perfect.
þá . . . furdum, as soon as.
fyr, farther.
fyrd-pic, -es, n., camp.
fyrhto (undeclined), fear.

galan (4), sing.
gear-dæg, es, m., day of yore.
geare, adv., well.
gearpe, adv., well.
ge-bædan (6), constrain.
ge-belgan (1), *gebealg hine*, was angry.
ge-blissian (6), bless, rejoice.
ge-brocian (6), break.
gebúr, es, m., door.
ge-byrian (6), belong.
ge-ceósan (3), decide.
ge-crong = gecrang < ge-cringan.
ge-dælan (6), allot.
ge-edenian (6), add.
ge-éðle, subdue.
ge-fýsed, stimulated, eager.
ge-gaderian (6), gather.
ge-gyrela, n, m., robe.
ge-herian (6), harry.
gehrpæde, adj., little.
ge-lyfed, adj., of advanced age.
ge-mét, p. p. of *gemétan*.
gemong, prep., among.
gene(á)h)-læcan (6), approach.

M

VOCABULARY.

ge-nípan (2), darken.
ge-nóh, enough.
ge-nýt, genýdan, compel.
geomore, adv., sadly.
ge-rǽdan (6), advise.
gesceaft, e, f., object, thing.
ge-seted, p. p., situated.
get=git.
ge-timbrian (6), build.
ge-þungen, p. p., great.
ge-unrét, p. p., unhappy.
ge-þenman (6), profane.
gepihnung, e, f., wish, effort.
gepræc<ręprecan (1), avenge.
gildan (1), pay.
gilp-cpide, s, m., boasting.
giõ=geõ.
gól<galan.
grama, n, m. (Lat. ira), wrath.
grin, e, f., snare, noose.
grund, es, n., abyss.
gum-cyn, nes, n., tribe.
gylden, adj., golden.
gýman (6), watch.

hátian (6), hate.
hægelian (6), hail.
heáh, adj., right (hand), deep (sea).
Hereda-land, es, n., Norway.
hinder-geáp, adj., sly.
hring, es, m., ring (on the hand).
hunger, es, m., hunger, famine.
hpá, any one.
hpæder þe, or.
hpæl, es, n., wheel, circuit.
hpeorfan (1), turn.

inælan (6), kindle.
inbindan (1), unbind.
ís, es, n., ice.

ladian (6), invite.
on láste, forsaken.
lǽce, s, m., physician.
lǽce-hús, es, n., doctor's house.
leahtor, es, m., reproach.
leáx, es, m., salmon.
leód-geld, es, n., wergild.
leorning-cniht, es, m., disciple.
leornung, e, f., school.
licgan (1), lie dead.
líhan, láh (2), lend.
lili-e, -an, f., lily.
linden, adj., linden.
list, es, m. f., art.
lybbend<lifian.

man, nes, m., one.
mánful, adj., sinful.
manigfealdlíce, adv., manifoldly.
manna, n, m., man.
mǽl, es, n., portion.
mǽnan (6), bemoan.
mǽnigo=menigo, multitude.
mæsse-reáf, es, n., mass-robe.
mæst-ráp, es, m., mast rope.
méd, e, f., meed.
medume, adj., small.
meldian (6), speak, utter, display.

merpd, e, f., mirth, delight.
mete, s, m., dinner.
metod=meotud.
Metten, e, f., Mettená, plur., Fates.
mid þý, when.
mild-heortnys, se, f., mercy.
mon=man.

nápiht, naught.
nǽdl, e, f., needle.
nægl, es, m., nail.
nebs-u, -e, f., nose.
neópol, adj., deep, profound.
nid, es, m., hostility.
nid-sele, s, m., hall beneath the sea.
nihtes, by night.
norðern, adj., northern.
æt nýhstan, at last.
nýten, es, n., beast.

óð-beran (1), bear away.
óðer, second.
of, prep., with.
ofer-prigan (2), dress.
of-lyst, adj., desirous.
of-teón, -teáh (3), draw off.
on, in; on án, together; on ford-peg, for departure.
on-gemong, prep., among.
on-géa=on-geán.
on-stellan, -stealde (6), establish.

pallium=pæl.
peneg, es, m., penny.
pluccian (6), pluck.

rá, n, m., roe-buck.
rand, es, m., shield.
rǽdan (6), read.
ræft, es, m., mold.
ræran (6), raise.
redfere, s, m., robber.
reliquiás (Latin), relics.
Reste-dæg, es, m., Sabbath.
rice, s, n., reign.
rihtpísnes, se, f., righteousness.
rípan, ráp (2), reap.
rýpan (6), ravage.

sacerd, es, m., priest.
sápan (5), sow (seed).
seacan (4), shake.
sceada, n, m., robber.
sceadenes, se, f., robbery, injury.
sceard, adj., p. p., mutilated.
scearp, adj., sharp, keen, wise.
sceat, tes, m., money.
se, whoever.
síð, es, m., adventure, departure, time, § 145.
síð-fæt, es, m., course.
siddan, as soon as.
snyttrum, adv., skillfully.
sóð-cpide, s, m., true word.
són, es, m., sound.
spéd, e, f., living, property.
spédig, adj., rich.
stacn, n, m. f., stake, pin.
styric, es, m., steer, calf.

sunna, n, m., son.
spá, which.
spícan (2), fail.
spimman (1), swim.
spincan (1), toil.
spýðre, comp. of spíð, right (hand).
syfernes, se, f., soberness.
syllan (6), sell.
syxtig-feald, adj., sixty-fold.

tǽlan (6), slander.
timbrian (6), build.
tó ricene, too quickly.
tó þel, so well.
torht, adj., bright.
tunec-e, -an, f., tunic.
tpá, twice, 31, 29.
tpelfta niht, Twelfth night, Epiphany.

þá, since.
þane=þone<se.
þanon, whence.
þæs þe, after.
þpæilíce, adv., fitly.
þrimilce, s, m., May, on þam mónde pripa on dæg meolcódon heord neát.
prot-e, -an, f., throat.
þrycean (6), oppress.
þýslic, such.

ultor, es, m., vulture.
un-dyrne, adv., unmistakably.
un-rihtpís, adj., unrighteous.

pax-georn, adj., voracious.
pæl-ceasega, n., slaughter-chooser, raven.
pǽr, e, f., promise, faith.
pederás, pl. m., Weder-Goths.
pel, very.
penge, s, n., cheek.
peordian (6), present.
peorod=perod.
pered, adj., sweet.
perian (6), wear, defend.
pið, opposite to.
pigend, es, m., warrior.
piht; mid pihte, by any means.
pilcuminan (6), welcome.
pilsumnes, se, f., devotion.
pin-sǽl, es, n., wine hall.
pis-e, -an, f., business, affair.
pitad=piton, know.
pléttu, n, m., nausea.
plíte-pam, mes, m., disfigurement of looks.
præce, s, m., exile.
præc-síð, es, m., exile.
precan (1), sing.
príxlan (6), exchange, sing.
pundrum, adv., wondrously.
purman=pyrmum?

ýdlád, e, f., voyage.
yldo, undeclined; age.
yldesta, n, m., prince.
ymb-hýdig, adj., anxious.
yrre, s, n., wrath.
ýst, e, f., storm.

THE END.

www.ingramcontent.com/pod-product-compliance
Lightning Source LLC
Chambersburg PA
CBHW020246170426
43202CB00008B/244